HUMBLED

HUMBLED

How California's Monterey Bay Escaped Industrial Ruin

Glenn Church
Kathryn McKenzie

Vista Verde Publishing
Royal Oaks, California
2020

Humbled: How California's Monterey Bay Escaped Industrial Ruin
by Glenn Church and Kathryn McKenzie

©2020 Glenn Church and Kathryn McKenzie
All rights reserved.

Published in the United States by Vista Verde Publishing
P. O. Box 176 Moss Landing, California 95039

www.vista-verde-publishing.com

ISBN: 978-1-7351092-0-6
E-ISBN: 978-1-7351092-1-3

Jacket art by Adobe Stock
Jacket and book design by Mara Reynolds

Printed in the U.S.A.
First Printing August 2020

Dedicated to our sons
Ross, Jackson, Hunter and Kristopher

Contents

IMAGES

x

ACKNOWLEDGEMENTS

As with many other large undertakings, this book would not have been possible without the encouragement and aid of a great many other people.

In particular, we were fortunate that several of the journalists of that time are still with us, and were eager to help after we approached them. We are indebted to Stanley Cloud, formerly of the *Monterey Peninsula Herald*, and Ray March, of the *Salinas Californian*, who even after all these years had amazing recall of the events that transpired around the Humble issue. They filled in backstories and gave us invaluable context about the people and the politics of the time through a long series of emails. They patiently walked us through their reporting and added details that they couldn't put into their original stories. We also must thank Eric Brazil, former reporter and editor at the *Californian*, for putting us in touch with Cloud and March.

We have retired Congressman Sam Farr to thank for getting the ball rolling on this in the first place, and for his guidance and help along the way, as well as commenting on an early manuscript.

We also were fortunate to be able to talk to others who were involved in working against Humble, including Bill Burleigh and Ruth Andresen, and their recollections gave us unique insight into their contributions in opposing the Humble project.

We also gained valuable assistance from the families of Supervisors Beauford T. "Andy" Anderson, Arthur Atteridge and Tom Hudson. In particular, Jim Anderson, Michael Atteridge and Tom Hudson the younger were generous with their time in answering our questions and allowing us to use treasured photos of their fathers.

Others who we depended on for their meticulous recall and attention to detail include Benicia historians Dr. Jim Lessenger and Reg Page, who spent an afternoon regaling us with tales of the Armory and taking us on a tour of the present-day Benicia Industrial Park.

Mark Silberstein, executive director of the Elkhorn Slough Foundation, provided maps and historical background on the slough and what had been planned for it prior to Humble. Joel Pablo, clerk for the Monterey County Board of Supervisors, gave us access to important historical documents that had been long buried. And patient resource librarians at Monterey Public Library, the Marina branch of Monterey County Free Libraries, and Steinbeck Library in Salinas aided us in many hours of perusing microfilm and finded other information.

We also are grateful for the people who took the time to read initial drafts and give us feedback, including Mary Arnold, Susan Gerbic, Margie Kay, Julie Reynolds Martínez, Keith McKenzie, Claudia Meléndez Salinas, Steve Andre, and Mark and Claire Osborn.

Also thanks to people we spoke with for understanding the historical context of these events and attitudes on the Central Coast towards the environment and business, including Hal and Dorothy Hyde.

Thanks also to the *Monterey Herald, Salinas Californian,* and the *Carmel Pine Cone* for allowing us to reprint historic photos and editorial cartoons.

And to our friends and family, thank you all for hanging in there with us.

INTRODUCTION

The Monterey Bay has been our home for our entire lives. Both of us grew up here during the 1960s and '70s, played on its beaches, and admired the seabirds and marine creatures at its edge. And both of us remember vividly the PG&E plant in Moss Landing, which was visible at even relatively minor elevations. The tall stacks of this industrial plant from 1965 on dominated bay views as it exhaled dark clouds of smoke into the air.

We also remember the thin line that appeared now and then, a yellow or brown horizontal brushstroke in the sky. As kids, we didn't think about it all that much, but as years passed, it disappeared, just as mysteriously as it showed up. Now we know that this was the mark of the area's inversion layer, trapping unburned hydrocarbons and other pollutants underneath. As air quality has improved, it has vanished.

Just think how thick this layer would have been, had a 50,000-barrel-a-day oil refinery actually been able to operate and grow here. Eventual expansion would likely have turned it into a 150,000 to 200,000-barrel-a-day oil refinery with associated industries for refinery byproducts such as asphalt, plastics, chemicals, lubricants and synthetic materials. The very real fear of the day was that once Humble Oil was operating, as one refinery opponent put it, an endless "parade of smokestacks" would arrive to destroy tourism, agriculture and the natural beauty of the Monterey Bay area.

In the 1950s, a thriving industrial park was the dream of county leaders throughout Monterey County, focusing on a Moss Landing master plan that proposed a massive complex that also included factories, residences and recreational activities. This plan would have reshaped not just North Monterey County but the entire bay, with oceangoing ships cruising down a dredged Elkhorn Slough and massive freighters and tankers unloading at Moss Landing. The Monterey Bay and Elkhorn Slough sanctuaries probably would never have happened. Tourism and agriculture would probably not have survived, at least as we know them now.

This book began from an offhand remark from our friend, retired Congressman Sam Farr, who said the Humble Oil refinery "would have changed everything" about the Monterey Bay region. That sparked the idea that a book to capture this period in Monterey Bay history was long overdue. And as we found during our research, the battle over this refinery was a critical turning point in the future of the bay—Moss Landing could have easily ended up as a major industrial area, but for the efforts of those who fought to preserve the beauty and unique qualities of the bay and surrounding area.

The Humble controversy was a watershed moment in the history of the Monterey Bay area. It is easy to conjecture about "what ifs" in many things in life, but Humble was more than a "what if." Humble had its permit. All it had to do was build. It did not. This is the story of how and why one of the world's largest corporations, an icon of American industry, eventually had enough and walked away. It was one of the first battles of the modern environmental age, a clash between the past ethos of industrialization at all costs and a burgeoning environmental movement. It is also a lesson in how people can make a difference and change their world.

You may notice that this narrative is centered, with few exceptions, around the public words and actions of white males. In the 1960s, women were expected to stay home and raise families, and people of color were related to the background. But we know that many women worked tirelessly behind the scenes, especially to oppose Humble, by writing letters, making phone calls and gathering petition signatures. No doubt people of all ethnicities were involved in unseen ways. Unfortunately, the public record reflects little of their efforts.

This book would have not been possible without the posthumous contribution of Glenn's father, former Monterey County Supervisor Warren Church, who died in September 2017 and left behind a room full of filing cabinets, containing everything from old newspapers to his personal notes on issues during his time as supervisor. Those records provided a first-hand account of Warren's thought processes and strategy as he tried to balance his constituents' desires, personal feelings and public responsibilities.

After we began going through Warren's papers after his death, we realized that we had a treasure trove of information that disclosed the complicated story of the Humble Oil project and how it was ultimately turned away, thanks to the combined efforts of ordinary citizens, mid-century influencers, and wily politicians who never gave in to corporate interests.

The story of how Humble Oil almost came to the Monterey Bay—and how it was defeated—is not just a retelling of history, but a cautionary tale for the future. The message of the refinery that almost was is that it remains crucial for us to be vigilant about our environment, to protect what we love, and to fight for what we believe.

Glenn Church and Kathryn McKenzie

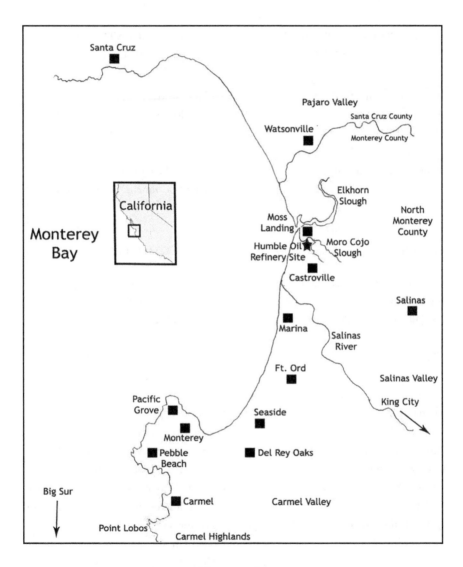

Map of the Monterey Bay region
Kathryn McKenzie and Glenn Church

CAST OF CHARACTERS

MONTEREY COUNTY BOARD OF SUPERVISORS

Warren Church, District 1
Arthur Atteridge, District 2
Harold Henry, District 3
Beauford T. "Andy" Anderson, District 4
Thomson Hudson, District 5

MONTEREY COUNTY STAFF AND ADVISOR

William Stoffers, county counsel
Edward Munson, sanitation director
Edward DeMars, planning director
Don Stewart, assessor
Emmet McMenamin, county clerk
William O'Connell, refinery consultant

HUMBLE OIL REPRESENTATIVES

D I Bolding, public relations spokesperson
Frank Church, engineer
J.K. Jamieson, president, Standard Oil of New Jersey
Charles Jones, president, Humble Oil
Jack Gardner, fuel products and general planning manager, Humble Oil
Michael Haider, chairman, Standard Oil of New Jersey
Paul Hamerly, attorney for Humble Oil
George Swisher, engineer
J. Prince Warner, vice-president, Humble Oil
R.A. Winslow, assistant general manager, Humble Oil

OTHER PLAYERS

Jack Bias, executive vice-president, Grower-Shipper Vegetable Association
Stanley Cloud, journalist, *Monterey Peninsula Herald*
E.F. Darley, professor, University of California, Riverside
Richard Harris, Superior Court judge
Phillip Leighton, professor emeritus of chemistry, Stanford University
John Maga, chief of California Health Bureau of Air Sanitation
Ray March, journalist, *Salinas Californian*
John Middleton, professor, University of California, Riverside
James Ritch, general manager Contra Costa Development Association
Matthew Walker, legal counsel, S.F. Bay Area Air Pollution Control District

OPPONENTs

Ansel Adams, photographer
Ruth Andresen, geologist/environmentalist
Gus Bauman, retired industrialist
Wayne Bowman, president Farm Bureau
William Burleigh, Six Cities Fund
Attorney
Robert Burton, Santa Cruz County
Supervisor
Peter Cailotto, planning commissioner
Harry Casey, publisher, *King City Rustler*
William Howard Church, professor, Naval
Postgraduate School
Ted Durien, managing editor, *Monterey
Peninsula Herald*
Keith Evans, planning commission chair
Fred Farr, state senator
George Faul, president, Monterey
Peninsula College
Col. Allen Griffin, publisher, *Monterey
Peninsula Herald*
Larry Hearne, agribusinessman
Charles Kramer, retired industrialist
A.G. Michaud, president, Del Monte
properties
Earl Moser, retired oil executive
Mits Nakishima, flower grower
Gunnar Norberg, Carmel City
Councilmember
Dave Williams, farm superintendent,
Bruce Church Inc.
Gordon Sinclair, editor, *Santa Cruz
Sentinel*

SUPPORTERS

Douglass Allmond, rancher
Don Barsotti, artichoke grower
Francis Cislini, publisher, *Salinas
Californian*
Chester Deaver, former Monterey County
Supervisor
Peter DiMarco, Castroville Chamber of
Commerce representative
George Hobbs, vice-president, Bud Antle
Inc.
Daniel Krishun, planning commissioner
Thomas Ludcke, community development
representative, PG&E
Vince Moore, executive Director, MCID
Charlotte Wilbur, planning commissioner
W.H. Wilbur, Agricultural Advisory
Committee member

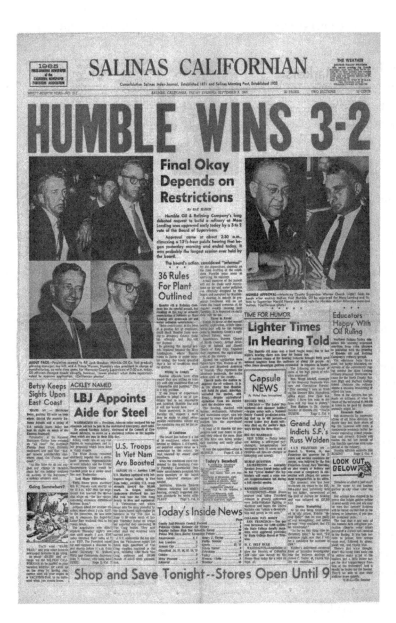

September 3, 1965 headline, courtesy of Salinas Californian.

1

HUMBLE WINS

September 2-3, 1965

"The death of beautiful Monterey County has begun."

Dr. and Mrs. Russell Pratt

The people who stumbled out of the Monterey County Board of Supervisors chambers just before 3 a.m. were too tired to cheer, or jeer, or express much emotion at all. In a way, it was not surprising—they had just come out of a marathon special meeting that dragged on with a few breaks for 17-plus hours, since 10 a.m. the previous day. It was the longest meeting in county history, and opponents and supporters alike were dead on their feet.

Or maybe they were in shock that the measure to approve an oil refinery on the edge of Monterey Bay had actually passed. Fears of widespread air and water pollution and the detrimental health consequences surely dragged some into gloom. Others dreaded the addition of a multi-smokestack monstrosity destined to blight the local landscape. For many, the blot of a refinery meant the slow demise of one of Monterey County's top industries: tourism. Some farmers of the fertile Salinas Valley, known as the Salad Bowl of the World, winced at the thought of forthcoming crop damage. And perhaps others were already grieving for a beautiful yet fragile bay ecosystem that now surely seemed doomed.

Joining in that early morning procession from the supervisors' chambers were supporters of Humble Oil's refinery project. They saw an opportunity for jobs and a larger tax base for schools, fire districts and other government services. Most of these people also feared the impact of pollution, but felt that controls could manage any possible damage. The people of North Monterey County, where the refinery was planned, represented a working-class community often orphaned from the prosperity of agriculture in the Salinas Valley or the tourist dollars pouring into the Monterey Peninsula.

"When the vote was over ... there were no cries of elation, no applause, no demonstrations of glee," reported the *Monterey Peninsula Herald* of Humble supporters, describing them as "drained of their energy by the rigors of combat." It was September 3, 1965, and Humble Oil and Refining Co. had won, despite the emotional objections of environmentalists, farmers, tourism boosters and those who simply objected to the foul sight of a 50,000-barrel-a-day refinery being established near the tiny fishing village of Moss Landing, halfway between Monterey and Santa Cruz. The bitter fight had been raging since February and was being closely watched, not just by county residents, but also by neighboring counties that had no voice in the matter.

"Death brings grief," said an open letter to the board of supervisors, submitted by Dr. and Mrs. Russell Pratt of Carmel. "This grief is ours to share today. The death of beautiful Monterey County has begun."

The stakes were as high as they get. Humble Oil had submitted its application seven months earlier to build a refinery at Moss Landing. The company was expanding rapidly as demand for petroleum products continued to grow in the United States. The postwar economic boom had continued, people were buying automobiles in ever-increasing numbers, and now it was expected that even teenagers would have their own wheels. And all those Ford Mustangs, Chevy Impalas and Cadillacs needed fuel.

Humble Oil, a powerful affiliate of Standard Oil of New Jersey, had cast its corporate eye on the West Coast market. In particular, it wanted California, which then had the fastest-growing market for gasoline in the country. Humble had started as a crude oil producer in Texas in the early 1900s, but then expanded into refining as well as oil delivery and transportation, a massive system that included more than 12,000 miles of pipeline, 19 ocean-going tankers, and numerous barges and tows. In addition, by the 1960s, it had retail outlets across the country under the names Humble, Esso and Enco. In a few years, Standard Oil of New Jersey, Humble and the other affiliates would merge and rebrand under the now familiar name of Exxon.

Adding a refinery in California would allow Humble to supply gas stations on the West Coast at a reduced cost. The company had done its homework, looking at various sites between Seattle to San Diego. Moss Landing emerged as its first choice—the site, already earmarked for industrial use and located near a deepwater port, seemed perfect.

Monterey County—which relied on agriculture and tourism as two pillars of its economy—was divided against itself. On the Monterey Peninsula, well-to-do residents of Carmel and Monterey took up the environmental banner against the project. In the Salinas Valley, farmers were split on the matter: some saw it as another step in the march of progress, while others feared the impact of air pollution on their crops. In Salinas and North Monterey County, support for the refinery was strong, as many residents looked to the jobs and economic benefits of a thriving industrial center in Moss Landing.

"Long-time students of county politics say they cannot remember an issue in the past which divided the county so completely and was so fraught with political, economic and sociological implications," wrote Stanley Cloud in the *Herald*, adding that unconventional alliances of Democrats and Republicans joined forces both for and against the Humble Oil project.

Emotions were running at a fever pitch in the supervisors' chambers on Thursday, September 2. At this point, there had already been a lengthy series of meetings regarding the project, culminating in this special meeting to vote on Humble's refinery permit.

Media from all over the Monterey Bay area and beyond were on hand. Reporters crammed in, jostling for a free table to write upon, television stations focused on a multitude of speakers, and local radio station KIDD ran on-air coverage from gavel to gavel as if it was a championship sporting event.

Board Chair Thomson J. Hudson of Monterey, supported by Beauford T. "Andy" Anderson of Seaside, at first proposed to hold the vote until another day, but three supervisors insisted on proceeding —Warren Church, whose district included the Humble project, Harold G. Henry of South Monterey County, and Arthur C. Atteridge of Salinas.

Hudson, the flamboyant, bowtie-wearing senior member of the board, had staked his opposition to the project early on. Hudson's dark good looks and charisma elevated him to the center of attention in any gathering. A pro-business Republican with a strong conservationist streak, he had developed a reputation promoting scenic views and abhorring billboards as the county's population grew, and industry drew nearer. He even proposed removing Highway 68 between Salinas and Monterey from the state highway system and incorporating it into the county road system so as to better preserve its beauty. In this epic meeting over Humble, Hudson was relentless as he tried to pull every trick that he could out of his political hat to halt the project. His district was the heart of the opposition, and they supported Hudson wholeheartedly.

Joining with Hudson in opposition to Humble was Anderson, a former mayor of Seaside, whose mild, balding appearance hinted little at his heroic past. Anderson was a man of enormous courage. As a Congressional Medal of Honor recipient in World War II at the Battle of Okinawa, Anderson risked his life to save the men under his command. Although his district split over the Humble issue, polls showed most of his constituents favored the refinery. But Anderson personally felt the project was wrong, and his determination never wavered. Even as a new supervisor who took office just months earlier, he courageously defied a majority of his constituents' wishes. Anderson's reasoning was out of the ordinary for his district too. Despite representing a largely urban, working class area that would benefit from more industry, Anderson was concerned that the refinery was "the first step" in changing the region from an agricultural region to an industrial one.

Representing South Monterey County was stout, bespectacled Harold Henry, a staunch conservative, who had thrown his lot into backing Humble early on when his district overwhelmingly supported it. In the last few weeks before this meeting, that support had cracked as many leaders in the agricultural community developed second thoughts over fears of pollution damage to their crops. Henry strongly backed expanding the county's tax base, and that appeared to guide him as agriculture grew increasingly divided. Although it was briefly thought that Henry might change his vote in the weeks leading up to the meeting, he stuck to his support.

From Salinas, the largest city in the county, was its former mayor, Arthur Atteridge. Towering over the other board members at 6'4", Atteridge was a serious, soft-spoken man with a friendly demeanor. Salinas had long sought to bring in industry to diversify its agricultural heritage, and with Humble's project just a few miles away to the north, the residents of Salinas envisioned a growing economic boom. Whether Atteridge personally favored the project or not, his constituents supported it overwhelmingly. While there was some talk that Atteridge's vote might also sway to a no in the weeks prior to the meeting, his allegiance to his constituents' wishes was never in doubt.

In the northernmost district sat newly elected Warren Church, the youngest member of the board, although already showing a touch of gray hair. Like the other supervisors, Church had publicly declared that he had made up his mind in May. Unlike the other four supervisors, Church refused to divulge his decision. This made Church the swing vote on a 2-2 deadlocked board. While his constituents expressed strong support for Humble's refinery, those people also held deep concerns about pollution. Church had run the year before in a six-man race where he pulled an upset victory over three-term incumbent Chester Deaver, one of the county's key architects in the plan to industrialize Moss Landing.

Church was the only candidate in that race who openly opposed the incorporation of North Monterey County, one of the divisive issues of the election. He also campaigned on the promise of kickstarting the county's parks program, seeing as Monterey County was one of the few counties in the state without a park system. Those conservationist positions seemed counter to supporting the industrial plans of Humble. As Ray March of the *Salinas Californian* reported in a pre-vote analysis of the supervisors' positions on Humble: "An oil refinery just does not match a park."

The board sat through three and a half hours of statements by refinery supporters, and then more than nine hours of public testimony with some breaks in between. "The lengthy parade of speakers opposing the refinery fermented audience charges that Chairman Hudson was trying to stall the hearing into a torpor," reported the *Watsonville Register-Pajaronian*, the town's newspaper. Although Watsonville was in Santa Cruz County, it was just a few miles north of Moss Landing, and residents there had been following the Humble hubbub closely, with hopes that the town would become a bedroom community for future refinery workers.

Hudson angrily denied that he was deliberately delaying the vote: "There's no intention on my part to do anything but give everybody a chance to be heard," he told the audience in the Salinas supervisors' chambers. Yet Hudson tried four times to continue the hearing to a future date, but he was overruled by a majority of the board at each attempt. Although tempers thinned to the breaking point for some, for others the length of the proceedings was simply too much. Some audience members collapsed into cat naps; several attendees fell asleep.

At one point, Atteridge, an avid baseball fan, kept an ear toward a radio at the press desk tuned to a doubleheader that the San Francisco Giants were playing. Periodically, Atteridge would lean over and inquire about the score. With the score tied in the second game of the doubleheader, Atteridge turned, scooped up the radio and disappeared into a back room behind the board chambers. He returned a few minutes later handing the radio back to its owner and announcing that the Giants were ahead. The doubleheader ended before the supervisors' meeting was half over.

At another point, a doctor rose to talk about air pollution, and glanced at William J. O'Connell, an expert on refinery pollution that the county had hired who was smoking a cigar. The doctor made a derogatory comment about the cigar and air pollution, but was quickly interrupted by Hudson, who usually smoked three cigars a meeting.

"Let's have no comments about cigars before this board," Hudson said.

A rancher from King City in South Monterey County, sitting through 15 hours of testimony, finally rose to talk and complained of saddle sores.

As the meeting progressed into the afternoon, it was easy to read most of the board members. Hudson and Anderson posed critical questions to Humble officials; Henry and Atteridge offered up more friendly inquiries. All the while, Church sat poker-faced, never revealing his inclinations and hardly asking a question. As evening approached, the board remained deadlocked at 2-2.

Comments by the public ranged from adamant arguments for or against the Humble project to personal recollections. The speakers included representatives from local business and agriculture in addition to concerned members of the public.

Humble officials tried to reassure the standing-room-only crowd that the refinery would be efficient and clean, and unlikely to cause either air or water pollution. Said Humble executive Jack Gardner of oil spills, "The record of oil industry and our company in particular is that such accidents are rare." Humble scientist Dr. George Swisher weighed in as well: "... a modern, well-controlled refinery can definitely be classed as a clean industry and would pose no threat to Monterey County."

"There's no need whatsoever to be scared about a refinery in Monterey County," stated Humble Vice President J. Prince Warner. Warner went on to call the conditions recommended by the county's Planning Commission as "more restrictive and more complete" than those at either Los Angeles or San Francisco "or in the entire United States."

"We feel strongly that agriculture and industry can live together in this valley," said Rod Ferguson, chair of the Committee for Planned Growth in Monterey County.

Tom Dunne, city manager of Salinas, stated, "assuming the plant will continue operating in such a manner as will avoid damage to the agriculture industry in the county ... the city council restates its unanimous support for the Humble Oil development."

Douglass Allmond, who ran a strong third in the primary of the 1964 supervisorial race where Church would later defeat Deaver in November, also expressed his support of Humble. Allmond pointed out that disagreeable industries had existed for a long time, including the "smelly sardine canneries in Monterey" and the old whaling station at Moss Landing. Challenging Hudson's many critical comments towards Humble, Allmond responded, "I don't remember any of the Salinas residents or those from North County trying to come and close down your canneries, Tom."

Speaking in favor of Humble was former Monterey County Supervisor Chester Deaver. Deaver had emerged as a strong advocate of Humble in North County, signing petitions and declaring that if he were still on the board, he would vote in favor of it. Deaver saw industry as the future of Monterey County.

"We're now talking about an industry (agriculture) that has reached its climax. In Monterey County, we have just about expanded agriculture to its limits. Most of the good usable land is now in agriculture production," Deaver declared. Deaver, who had also backed the development of the Firestone Tire and Rubber plant south of Salinas a few years earlier, said Humble would provide more taxes than Firestone and help draw more industry into Monterey County.

"You can't sit idly by and see opportunity pass you up," exclaimed Deaver.

Also in favor of Humble's project was Kenneth Davis, a vice president of Bechtel Corp. who touted himself as a Sierra Club member. "I'm here to just express the confidence ... that such a (clean) refinery can be built today." Unbeknown to many, Bechtel was a prominent background player in Humble's search and ultimate decision for a West Coast refinery.

Most Peninsula residents were much less confident that pollution could be avoided. Merchants and officials who wanted to promote the Monterey Peninsula as an ideal vacation destination did not want to see any more eyesores on the bay. It was bad enough that smokestacks at PG&E's Moss Landing power plant were there in plain view and at that very time being constructed to a height of 500 feet. Plans for the further expansion of the "Mighty Moss" were underway, including a nuclear power plant. Monterey, which was just starting to talk about how to turn disreputable Cannery Row into a tourist spot, did not want unsightly industry sprouting along the water's edge.

The threat of air pollution was what really galvanized ordinary citizens in the matter. Smog had become an enormous problem in California, particularly in the Los Angeles basin to the south and in the San Francisco Bay Area to the north. Due to the California highway system, residents were dependent

on their cars for transportation, and although fledgling air pollution control districts had been established in several regions around the state, there
was no way to control automobile emissions without the cooperation of car
manufacturers. Los Angeles, in particular, had some of the dirtiest air in the
world then, and activist groups like Stamp Out Smog were demanding that
something be done. Anyone who traveled to L.A. during this period was well
aware of the lung-burning, eye-watering effects of air pollution, and Monterey
County residents feared it as well.

However, the view on pollution was not unanimous by any stretch. The coun-
ty-hired pollution consultant, O'Connell, said, "I don't believe a 50,000-bar-
rel-a-day refinery will create a smog condition." Adding to the conflicting
testimony was John Maga, chief of the Air Sanitation Bureau for the State
Department of Public Health, who stressed that Monterey County did not have
an air pollution problem and there were no clear-cut trends to one developing.

Of the people who got up to speak at the meeting, it was obvious that
those in agriculture were particularly at odds over the Humble project. Some,
like George Hobbs of Bud Antle Inc., gave it a big thumb's up: "We sincerely
feel, as agriculture, that we can live with this industry in the Valley," he told
the county supervisors.

But others, like Dave Williams, farm superintendent for Bruce Church Inc.,
were adamantly against anything that could harm the county's $160 million
agriculture business. Williams, also chair of the group Individuals for Clean
Industry, cited statistics and reports regarding weather patterns in the Salinas
Valley, how inversion layers could trap pollutants above local farmland, and
the damage these contaminants could inflict on plant life. "The decision you
gentlemen make can have an effect on tens of thousands of acres, and millions
of dollars worth of crops," Williams testified.

The farming community had been relatively silent for months over the
Humble controversy. It was only in the last few weeks that organized opposition, including by the county Farm Bureau, which in itself was split, emerged
to question the wisdom of allowing industry that might negatively impact
agriculture. However, this opposition appeared to come too late to make any
significant difference.

Arnold Frew of King City, a member of the King City Citizens for Clear
Air Committee: "I don't believe there's a place in the world where you have
the agricultural growth, the agricultural wealth and production that we have
here. I am very skeptical about this type of industry."

The burgeoning flower industry in North Monterey County and Watsonville expressed considerable concern about Humble. Many of the growers, like Mits Nakishima, had left the San Francisco Bay area to escape the pollution damaging their crops and now feared the same issues here. Mits Nakishima appealed to the supervisors' sensibilities and to the flags of the United States and California hanging behind Hudson, as well as to a non-existent Monterey County flag.

In Castroville, near the proposed Humble site, agriculture's position was one of concern. Primarily an artichoke-growing region, most of the farmers opposed Humble, but there were exceptions. Don Barsotti, speaking for the California Vegetable and Artichoke Growers Association, expressed support. "We feel that we have more at stake than most of the people, and we whole-heartedly support the Humble application." A few years earlier, Humble, keeping its name and intent secret from Barsotti, purchased the land from him.

Monterey Peninsula residents like Charles Kramer, leader of the group Citizens for Clean Air, did their best to dissuade the board. "We are fighting to preserve one of the most beautiful and unique areas in the nation ... An oil refinery will endanger that environment."

"This (plan for a refinery) is called progress," said Salinas pediatrician Dr. Rex Whitworth. "This is avarice. This is greedy ... if life and death is emotional, then I'm emotional."

State Senator Fred Farr, a resident of Carmel, took his place speaking before the supervisors. Farr, had endured a nightmare year. In January, his wife passed away. Then, just a little over a week before the September 2 meeting, he had been vacationing in Colombia with his two daughters while visiting his son, Sam, who was working as a Peace Corps volunteer there. Farr's youngest daughter, Nancy, was thrown from a horse and died. Yet Farr, the statesman that he was, suppressed the pain and tragedy encompassing him and rose in defense of his constituents and the Monterey Bay that he loved to plead with the supervisors to deny Humble's permit.

"If there is a conflict in the testimony of the experts," Farr said, "I say why take a chance."

Altogether, 23 speakers spoke in favor of the refinery, while 28 spoke against. The speakers were not limited to the time limit of three minutes as is now the custom. Many also rose to speak repeated times to reiterate a favorite point, inject a new emphasis or counter an opposing viewpoint. Much if not all of the discussion was to no avail as it seemed the supervisors had already made up their minds. As one of Henry's constituents spoke against Humble,

Henry decided that he had heard enough. He spun around in his chair and began reading a newspaper.

As the meeting drew toward midnight, Hudson made repeated calls for breaks, which were rebutted by other supervisors, and caused further mumblings that he was stalling. That prompted Hudson to push the meeting on into the early morning hours.

"I suggested adjournment to the other supervisors, and they wanted to go ahead. Now they have to take the penalty," declared Hudson.

Hudson questioned the premise of state pollution official John Maga, that Humble would not add appreciably to air pollution. When Hudson stated that Humble's refinery would not help air quality, an "Aww" murmured through the crowd. Hudson angrily insisted, "I have the right to ask questions" and threatened to clear the chambers if further heckling continued.

The clock ticked past midnight, and groans and murmurs of "no" rose in the audience from the anti-Humble crowd as the board discussion began to turn favorably toward Humble. Hudson banged his gavel numerous times to bring order.

By the early morning hours, it was clear from the questions being asked that Church had thrown in his lot with the pro-Humble Henry and Atteridge. The discussion shifted to conditions with Anderson saying that he wanted more information before voting.

"Let's vote on the decision now. We can take the regulations later," Atteridge responded.

Church jumped on Atteridge's suggestion. He spoke that he was supporting Humble's application because the taxes would provide for needed services. He continued that the refinery would add less pollution and impose fewer burdens on county services than more labor-intensive industries. Church then moved to approve the Humble proposal with the conditions for the permit to be added at a later date.

Each of the supervisors then took their turn to explain their vote. Atteridge asserted that Humble would provide needed taxes for the Flood Control and Water Conservation District. Henry backed Atteridge and added that the district was a crucial water resource for agriculture. Anderson, expressing his opposition, emphasized that Monterey County now had "good, clean growth," and he did not want Humble to interfere with that. Then a sharp verbal squabble between Hudson and Henry arose as Hudson began speaking.

"It's a little bit hard for me, as the senior member of this board ... to see the silver dollar guiding the destiny of this county, and that's what it is. It's tampering with the soul of Monterey County. This application was dropped on us like a match ... and it went up like a fire. Humble came in saying, 'We want to put in an oil refinery at Moss Landing.' Out of that approach came one of the most bitter ... strongest controversies of opinion this county has seen in some time. It's rather tragic to allow something like that to come in. The board turned its back on agriculture. Some of my fellow supervisors from the agricultural belt seem to be lacking," said Hudson.

"Just a minute, Mr. Hudson," interjected Henry.

"Let me finish," responded Hudson.

"If you keep that up, you won't be able to finish," Henry bounced back.

"There is the integrity of this county, the soul of this county," Hudson continued, "It got its leadership from the soil. So our loyalty to agriculture just wasn't there when it needed it ... I kind of like to make some of my decisions on what would happen ... if we made a mistake here. It would be a pretty substantial one."

"Clerk, call the roll," requested Hudson.

So it was. The longest meeting ended with a 3-2 vote to grant a special permit to Humble.

As both shocked and elated residents were reading the headlines in the local newspapers a few hours later on September 3, there seemed to be no hope for those who opposed Humble.

Now only the setting of conditions stood in the way of Humble's permit. Humble had grudgingly gone along with the 36 conditions that the Planning Commission had recommended for the project, but Humble was banking on the thought that with a favorable majority on the Board of Supervisors, some of those conditions might be lessened. Humble officials were on record as saying they would comply with any conditions that were "reasonable and justified."

In an editorial, Ted Durien, managing editor of the *Herald*, castigated the supervisors who had cast "yes" votes: Atteridge, Henry and Church.

"Humble Oil, our new neighbor, had three supervisors in their pocket when the hearing started. They were still there when the vote was taken," said the *Herald*, long suspecting that Church was a pro-Humble vote.

"Don't get us wrong," the editorial continued. "We have nothing against this company, or heavy industry for that matter. We simply feel Monterey County is no place for an oil refinery, and all the refineries that will follow as night follows day."

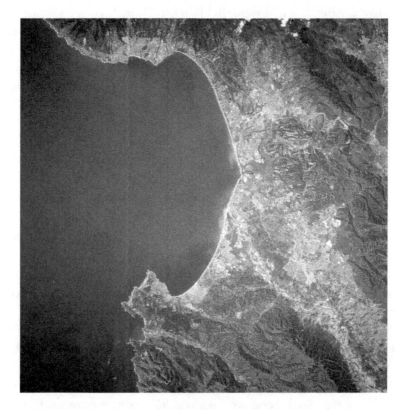

Aerial photo of Monterey Bay, NASA

Artist's rendering of the refinery project in Moss Landing, part of Humble's public relations kit.
Authors' collection

2

A NATURAL WONDER

*"It was such an isolated area at the time. Moss Landing
was nothing but a fishing port."*

Ruth Andresen

No one, not even the paleogeologists, are quite sure when the Monterey
Bay as we know it came into being. Its genesis is still being debated in
scientific circles. One theory is that over millennia, prehistoric rivers and
lakes emptied out on the coast, and then much of the seafloor shifted north
as tectonic plates did their sideways shuffle. In the last few million years, the
Santa Cruz Mountains reared up and the Salinas River wriggled this way and
that, changing its position in relation to the bay.

However it happened, there is a fact that cannot be denied: Monterey Bay
has a mind-bogglingly deep submarine canyon that is a rarity among submarine
canyons of the world. One end of it is just a few hundred meters from shore.
A topographical map shows the canyon as a huge blue crack in the bottom
of the bay, with one craggy finger pointed straight at Moss Landing. From
there, the canyon deepens as it snakes 95 miles into the Pacific, rivaling the
Grand Canyon in scale. A website for MBARI, the Monterey Bay Aquarium
Research Institute, waxes poetic: "If the water drained from Monterey Bay,
the newly revealed terrain would be stunning, with cliffs, gorges, valleys, and
spires matching the scenery found in some of our most beautiful national
parks." It is because the canyon end is so close to shore that a deepwater port
is possible at Moss Landing.

This geologic curiosity plays a vital role in the biology of the bay. Monterey Bay is famed for its extraordinary biodiversity—some 500 species of fish thrive there as well as more than 30 types of marine mammals, from sea otters to blue whales, as well as hundreds of bird species. The bay is situated where it receives great benefit from wind-driven upwelling, which pushes surface water out of the water and allows cold, nutrient-filled waters from below to rise to the top, and this encourages the growth of seaweed and phytoplankton. It may be that the depths of the canyon provide exceptional nutrients, either in quality or quantity, or both. In any case, the seaweed and phytoplankton happily grow, and for fish, the Monterey Bay is an underwater smorgasbord. These fish in turn become a feast for the other creatures that inhabit the bay and its environs.

At the center of Monterey Bay, where the deep submarine canyon jutes to the east, lies the Elkhorn Slough. Its shallow waters flow seven miles inside the coastline with fingers stretching into various channels and ponds, creating thousands of acres of tidal saltwater marshes. The slough is an important migratory respite for birds flying up and down the California coast. Altogether over 340 species of birds have been identified there. It is a home to a variety of mammals – deer, opossum, racoon, bobcats, mountain lions and skunks. In small pools, rare amphibians cling to existence. Oak woodlands lean over its waters as a stark contrast to two ecosystems. The slough is a remarkable scene of diversity and adaptation. Today saltwater primarily fills its waterways, but in ages past the waters have been brackish and fresh. It is a paradigm representing how nature evolves and always adjusts to survive to changing environs. At the edge of its waters stands the massive power plant owned in 1965 by PG&E (Pacific Gas and Electric).

Early explorers to Monterey Bay did not know why life was prolific here, only that it was. Almost as soon as they saw that biological wealth, they were looking for ways to exploit it. "No country is more abundant in fish and game of every description," wrote Captain Jean-Francois de la Pérouse in his journal in 1786 as he surveyed Monterey Bay. He marveled at the numbers of whales and birds he saw, and eyed sea otter fur as a potential revenue source—an early harbinger of the southern sea otter being hunted almost out of existence in the next hundred years.

There followed the bay's boom-and-bust cycles. Whaling, an enormously important industry from the 1700s into the 1800s, fell by the wayside during the American Civil War, as cheaper and more readily available kerosene came into vogue as lamp fuel. The sea otter saw its population mowed down to a few dozen individuals as its fur was harvested for fashionable hats and capes.

Monterey's famously aromatic sardine canneries were also responsible for polluting the bay in the first part of the 20th century, with fish offal casually dumped directly into the water, and the odiferous air swirling around the city as hundreds of thousands of tons of sardines were canned or otherwise processed for products ranging from fertilizer to salad oil. The canneries finally shut down when sardine fishing collapsed—the tiny silvery fish could no longer be found in the bay waters, and no one knew why. Now this is attributed to natural ocean oscillations that kept them in southern California.

The next potential ecological disaster involved birds of all types, hit hard by manmade chemicals that impacted their reproduction; DDT was particularly damaging to eggs, thinning the shells so that they cracked when birds sat on them. Their numbers began to decline.

Yet the remarkable bay, given the chance to recover, always did. It cleansed itself of cannery pollution by the end of the 1950s. A small raft of sea otters had drifted back into Monterey Bay a few decades before, and gained a tentative foothold. The furry creatures dined extravagantly on the sea urchins and abalone that had overpopulated bay waters in the otters' absence; this in turn allowed the bay's kelp forest to flourish, which biologists took note of in the early 1960s.

Now, though, it looked as though industry was once more going to lay its mark on the bay's ecosystems. By 1965, PG&E's twin 225-foot towers were hard at work, releasing plumes of smoke into the air, visible to people living on both sides of the bay. This was seen by many as a sign of progress, something to be celebrated rather than feared. PG&E's Moss Landing facility announced at the end of 1963 that it was expanding. Eventually, it would become the second largest power plant in the world. The company's goal was to be ready to support power needs for the entire West Coast, and in particular, the electronics industry that was just taking baby steps in the San Jose area.

But some people were beginning to take note of what havoc humans could wreak on the environment. *Silent Spring*, the 1962 book by biologist Rachel Carson, detailed the DDT crisis for birds, and brought forth other evidence that showed the devastation of manmade chemicals on the natural world. It stirred up a firestorm of controversy in the United States and throughout the world with its heartbreaking descriptions of what pesticides could do to wildlife. Carson also detailed cases of human pesticide poisoning, and the link between cancer and pesticides. She also accused the chemical industry of being less than truthful, and derided public officials who too often took industry claims at face value.

One of the people who read Carson's book was Salinas resident Ruth Andresen, who took Carson's warnings to heart.

It was a turning point for Andresen, who had earned a degree in geology at Stanford University and had worked as a geologist for the military during World War II. She turned her intellect in a different direction after reading *Silent Spring*. She had been staying home raising her family, but as her children grew older, she decided it was time to challenge herself again. She took an environmental studies class at Monterey Peninsula College. "And from there, I bounced to UC Santa Cruz," said Andresen, still feisty in her late 90s.

University of California, Santa Cruz, had just started holding classes, but even in its early days it focused on the brand-new field of environmental science. In fact, it was so new that despite the furor kicked up by *Silent Spring*, most people outside the campus were not at all aware of what effects synthetic chemicals could have on nature. "It had not been public knowledge. It was only (known) at the university level or in-house at industries," she said. Andresen began sharing what she learned—through activities with the Campfire Girls, and also to some of the groups that she was involved with.

Andresen realized that she could act as a conduit for this vital information about the environment, none of which was part of the curriculum in schools in the mid-1960s: "You were just not taught things like this ... either you were part of it and you had contact with an educational source, or else you were left out. It simply was not discussed enough. And it was not common knowledge at that point, except for Rachel Carson."

Andresen learned about the proposed Humble Oil refinery when articles began appearing in the local papers prior to the first Monterey County Planning Commission meetings on the matter. She worried about the environmental impact of such a plant, and decided to get involved.

And she had first-hand knowledge of what the oil business could do to the land. Growing up in Oklahoma, Andresen had seen oil spills and seeps near her home and had been oppressed by the sulfurous, acrid air around her. She feared what a refinery might inflict on the beautiful Monterey Bay.

"It was such an isolated area at that time," Andresen said. "Moss Landing was nothing but a fishing port. And so (Humble Oil officials) felt they were on safe territory, because it was pretty well ignored. So that they could move in there and nobody would pay any attention."

However, there were some locals who were paying attention to the growing industry at Moss Landing, including Andresen, who vividly recalls how things were changing. "That's when we had the big growth surge in Salinas, post-war. And people were coming here. There was a lot of building. And the whole place was booming. Santa Cruz started growing. And PG&E was the major power plant for the whole West Coast."

"So that meant they were reflecting the growth in two counties, plus San Jose development also. PG&E was the single major source of energy on the West Coast, which people did not realize."

The price of progress was becoming obvious—at least as it impacted residents' views of the bay. People were no doubt reassured by the fact that any air pollution that might be present in the Monterey Bay area was minor, compared to what people had to endure in Los Angeles, 300 miles south.

Air pollution had been a fact of life in Southern California since the 1940s, and by the '60s, was so severe that "smog alerts" were issued on particularly bad days, and people urged to stay indoors to avoid the throat-burning, eye-reddening effects. Smog could be so thick as to obscure drivers' vision and cause car accidents, and it was being blamed by doctors for fostering lung infections, asthma and even cancer.

Scientists determined that the L.A. Basin was a perfect smog-creating environment, due to its unique topography and climate. Long before the United States took over California, the area had been known by the Spanish as Bahia de Fumes, or Bay of Smoke. For much of the year, high-pressure systems lie on top of the basin, which is hemmed in on three sides with mountain ranges. This warm air keeps the lid on a cooler layer of air, which is unable to rise. Thus particles in the cooler air, as well as unwelcome soot or smoke, have nowhere else to go and are trapped near the ground rather than escaping into the upper atmosphere. The phenomenon is called a temperature inversion.

What made the problem particularly vexing in mid-century Los Angeles was the presence of millions of automobiles, which were producing a variety of noxious gases that included unburned hydrocarbon particles. Lightly regulated industries in the Southland also emitted toxic fumes, and it was this chemical soup wafting through the streets that was impacting residents' health and safety. In the 1950s, smog was even blamed for mental health issues, and an uptick in murders and suicides.

Air pollution was so critical a problem that it was designated as "a natural disaster" in Pasadena and people throughout Southern California demanded that action be taken to alleviate the scourge. An Anti-Smog Action Committee formed in the late 1950s, and later Stamp Out Smog, a group of wealthy housewives who took up the cause and became a major player in the 1960s anti-air pollution movement.

Activism to protect the environment was not necessarily new, but the tactics by which the battles were fought were changing. Citizens' groups staged provocative publicity stunts that newspapers and television stations were happy to cover, such as the one used in Northern California to call attention to a proposed PG&E nuclear power plant on the Sonoma County coast.

On Memorial Day 1963, organizers released 1,500 helium-filled balloons from Bodega Head, each representing radioactive isotopes. Their random flight dramatized to local dairy farmers how far airborne contamination from the PG&E site could drift, then enter their grass and make its way into cows' milk. Each had a note attached: "This balloon could represent a radioactive molecule of Strontium 90 or Iodine 131. Tell your local newspaper where you found this balloon." The balloons descended in San Rafael and Fairfield, and also drifted into the East Bay. Some were found in the Central Valley, more than 100 miles away.

And for the first time, lawsuits and other legal means were being used in environmental issues. Only a handful of cases had gone to court by the mid-1960s. But the writing was on the wall: Judges were siding with environmentalists.

One of the hardest-fought controversies was taking place in New York's Hudson River Valley even as Monterey County organizers skirmished with Humble Oil. The Scenic Hudson Decision is credited with launching the modern environmental movement, and for the first time, preservation of an area's beauty could be considered a good enough reason to halt industrial development.

It seems likely that lawyers for Humble's parent company, Standard Oil of New Jersey, would have known about the Scenic Hudson case and been following it closely. The Scenic Hudson Decision was argued on Oct. 8 with the decision announced on Dec. 29, 1965. The case concerned a proposed 2,000-watt hydroelectric power plant to be built by Consolidated Edison, which was granted the right to proceed by the Federal Power Commission. Completing the power plant would have meant carving out the side of the iconic Storm King Mountain, and the plant itself could be considered disruptive to an area of great beauty and historic significance.

The Second Circuit Court of Appeals set aside the Storm King license and stated that, "The Commission's renewed proceedings must include as a basic concern the preservation of natural beauty and national historic sites, keeping in mind that in our affluent society, the cost of a project is only one of several factors to be considered." The landmark case introduced new precedents in environmental law, including the right of citizens to participate in environmental disputes, and federal and state regulation of the environment.

There was already some federal environmental legislation in place, but mainly it focused on curbing air and water pollution, and not aesthetic appeal. The first, the Air Pollution Control Act, was enacted in 1955. But this and other subsequent legislation was largely toothless. The first vehicle emissions standards were put into place in 1965, but it was not until the Environmental Protection Agency was established in 1970 that clean air regulations for industry could be enforced, and automakers finally took measures to ensure that cars burned gasoline more efficiently through the addition of catalytic converters.

In Monterey County in 1965, with only 220,000 residents and fewer vehicles, locals could still draw deep breaths of clean, healthy air. Yet as eyes began to turn toward Moss Landing, to some, the fumes of industry seemed like signs of danger, and a harbinger of worse things to come.

A sea otter dines on crab in the waters off Moss Landing.
Photo by Ron Eby, U.S. Fish and Wildlife Service

3

THE GATHERING STORM

February 15 – April 10, 1965

"We can build a good, clean sweet-smelling refinery."

J. Prince Warner, vice president of manufacturing, Humble Oil Co.

For the United States, 1965 was a turbulent year. The great economic post-World War II boom was slowly winding down. The country's main adversary, the Soviet Union, had amassed a huge nuclear arsenal and engaged in an increasingly active foreign policy with surrogates to upend the Western ways of democracy and capitalism. The Soviets still led the way in the space race, and in March completed the first spacewalk. The United States, now deep in its Gemini program, always seemed to lag a step behind the USSR.

Martin Luther King Jr. joined with other civil rights activists against discrimination in the South and faced intensifying violence by diehard segregationists. Civil rights activists disappeared, turning up dead days later. Amid all this, President Lyndon Johnson, fresh off a massive landslide victory against Barry Goldwater, forced through the landmark Voting Rights Act and signed it in August. With his mandate, Johnson also began to escalate the Vietnam War by steadily increasing the number of American troops to Southeast Asia. As the year wore on, anti-war protests erupted across the nation.

It was a tumultuous year for the Monterey Bay area as well. The bracero program ended. A huge labor shortage left crops rotting in the fields. Salinas Valley Strawberries, the region's largest strawberry grower, had just 482 pickers and claimed it needed 2,000 more. More than 1,300 residents turned out to give a hand in the harvest. In Santa Cruz, the University of California opened a new campus. At Moss Landing, PG&E prepared to step up its "Mighty Moss" power plant expansion by building two new 500-foot-high smokestacks.

Attorney W.K. Stewart, Ira Sandperl and Joan Baez listen as the Monterey County Board of Supervisors conduct a use permit hearing for Baez's Institute for the Study of Nonviolence in 1965. Courtesy of the Monterey Herald

In Carmel Valley, folk singer and Carmel Valley resident Joan Baez brought the Vietnam War home to Monterey County with an anti-war message. Baez sought a permit for her Institute for the Study of Nonviolence. However, Baez's opposition to the Vietnam War, and her curriculum of Gandhi and Thoreau, was a bit too radical for much of the community. Robert Pia, attorney for some residents who appealed her permit to the Board of Supervisors, expressed the apprehensions of many who felt that "Baez' non-violence image would destroy the public image of Carmel Valley as, 'one of the finest residential, resort areas in the West.'"

In December, the Board of Supervisors approved Baez's school on a 3-2 vote, in which a heavily conflicted Tom Hudson motioned to approve the permit with conditions. Also favoring the permit was Warren Church, who claimed that the conditions might violate the First Amendment's guarantees of free assembly and speech. For Hudson and Church, it was an odd juxtaposition of two supervisors who earlier that year had sparred publicly on the Humble Oil refinery permit.

Board of Supervisors Chair Tom Hudson greets incoming supervisors Warren Church, center, and Beauford "Andy" Anderson, on the front of the January 4, 1965, Salinas Californian.
Courtesy of Salinas Californian

The Baez school was in Hudson's district. It had considerable opposition, but either because of support for it or because of constitutional issues, Hudson felt compelled to tread a middle ground. He sought some way to pacify the opponents of the school. Controversial issues in a county supervisor's district always make a supervisor vulnerable. It is an easy way to make political enemies. Being the senior member of the board, Hudson knew that all too well.

Church did not face those constraints. His constituents were not deeply concerned about the Baez matter as it was miles away in Carmel Valley, far from the rolling hills of North Monterey County. Church could afford to make principled statements about the Constitution and First Amendment rights.

Humble Oil was a different matter altogether. The Humble project was in Church's district. The will of his constituents was paramount. Whatever decision Church made would need delicate handling. In his first year as a supervisor, Church was particularly vulnerable. Even if he wanted to, he lacked the political capital to stand against a majority of his constituents.

For Hudson, Humble offered no conflicts. Although he took an even-handed approach in the beginning, Hudson quickly became a major nemesis for Humble. A moderate Republican with an ardent conservationist streak, Hudson could see the havoc that an oil refinery in the middle of the Monterey Bay communities would create. Without hesitation, Hudson pursued all efforts to stop Humble from building its refinery. He was so committed that he hounded the oil company for nearly the entire fifteen-month controversy, from the Board of Supervisors' chambers in Salinas to the annual meeting of Humble in Cleveland, Ohio.

February 15, 1965, was a fair day along the Monterey Bay. With the temperatures in the mid-60s and the winds light, it was not unusual for that time of year. The newspaper headlines that day must have intrigued many people as they announced a new industry coming to the region, but few could imagine the tempest that would soon erupt over the issue, one that would last well into the following year.

That morning, J. Prince Warner, vice president of manufacturing for Humble Oil, announced the purchase of a 444-acre site bordering Highway 1 and Moro Cojo Slough in Moss Landing. Humble planned a $50 million, 50,000-barrel refinery covering a bit over one-quarter of the property.

Humble officials hoped it would take less than a couple of months to get the permits finalized so that they could move forward. They were already targeting approval from the Planning Commission on March 30 and hoped to appear before the Board of Supervisors on April 5. That would allow engineering surveys and technical testing to commence, which Warner estimated "are expected to cost in excess of a million dollars" and would take a year to

complete. The project would need another year to design and still another
to complete construction. In addition, Humble had to get approval from the
Moss Landing Harbor District Commission, for a pipeline across the old
Salinas River channel that would then extend a half-mile out into Monterey
Bay in submarine pipes, where supertankers holding a million barrels of oil
could unload. The U.S. Army Corps of Engineers would also have to sign off
on the pipes. PG&E already had a submarine pipeline to channel fuel to its
power plant so this was not a new concept. As plans progressed, the length
of Humble's submarine pipeline grew to a mile long, with a breasting island
at the end of it.

With its deepwater port, the developing Moss Landing industrial center appeared welcoming to Humble representatives. Local representatives,
especially from Monterey County Industrial Development Inc., had assisted
and guided the site selection. Humble had studied the Moss Landing site for
a long time. While Humble was the largest producer of petroleum products
in the United States, the company did not have a large presence on the West
Coast. The Moss Landing site intended to seize that opportunity to expand
into new markets.

"Good refinery sites are hard to come by on the Pacific Coast," Warner
said, "We have looked from Puget Sound to San Diego, and we believe the
balance at Moss Landing will fit into our picture quite well."

R.A. Winslow, assistant general manager of Humble manufacturing, con-
curred at a meeting with the Watsonville Chamber of Commerce:

"Deep water inshore was a prime consideration. There are few ports in the
world where modern deep-draught tankers can be handled. San Francisco—
Richmond they have to be lightered."

Lightering is the process of transferring oil from a larger ship to a smaller
vessel for the purpose of offloading on shore. It was a common practice at the
refineries along the relatively shallow San Francisco Bay waters.

Three years earlier, Humble hired Bechtel Corp. to locate a suitable site
for its new refinery. Moss Landing was the No. 1 site between Vancouver and
San Diego. There were a lot of desirable features including the pre-existing
industrial zoning, the nearby rail lines and central location in the state, but it
was the deepwater port that really drove Humble to Moss Landing. Deepwater
meant larger tankers. Larger tankers drove transportation costs down. The
result was a cheaper refined product. Humble saw the advantage that would
give the company as it tried to crack the California market.

Humble had recently acquired the rights to Wilmington Field off the shores of Long Beach. Estimates placed the oil field at one billion barrels. Moss Landing was conveniently located just three hundred miles away so that Humble could fulfill its promise that it would use mainly oil derived from California. Humble estimated that three or four domestic tankers would arrive per month and one or two from the Middle East or elsewhere. All this might have been true with a 50,000-barrel-per-day refinery, but as the refinery expanded, more foreign oil and oil from Alaska would arrive in supertankers. The economic reasoning for a deepwater port for the supertankers didn't hold up when oil needs shipping only a few hundred miles from Southern California. Supertankers are far more economical when thousands of miles are involved.

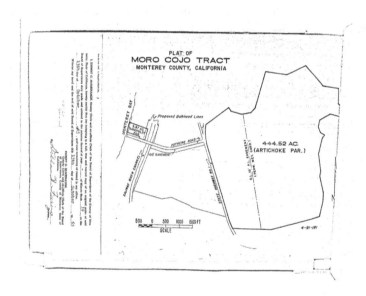

A plot map of the Moro Cojo tract, showing the land earmarked for the Humble Oil refinery. Office of the Clerk of the Board of Supervisors, County of Monterey

Two years earlier, Humble anonymously purchased the land for the refinery with the aid of a third party. Rumors intensified about the mysterious buyer when leases for the artichoke growers on the property were not renewed. Despite the initial secrecy, Humble promised to be a good neighbor. Officials were aware that there might be some opposition.

"We want everyone to know what we plan," explained Warner. "We want the cleanest refinery you can imagine ... an oil factory today is a much better neighbor than other types of industries."

Humble officials reassured the public that the air pollution from such a plant would not be noticeable. At a luncheon with the Monterey County Industrial Development directors, Jack Gardner, Humble's manager of fuel products and general planning, assured them that Humble would "bend over backwards" to fit into the community and "will meet every requirement regarding air and water pollution." MCID was the lead group promoting industrial development in the county.

The tax base would be large. Local jobs, at least for the construction, would be available. Monterey County Assessor Donald Stewart estimated that the Humble refinery would bring in $1 million in tax revenues. Humble's promise must have sounded too good to be true to some people. Still, to most of those who read that day's news, Humble promised a broad road to prosperity.

Tom Hudson, chair of the Board of Supervisors, sat down with Humble officials for breakfast prior to their announcement. Hudson's initial position was neutral.

"I have no position now regarding the plans," Hudson said, "but I, for one, must be convinced that the location of the plant in the county will be an asset without cost for our people."

Humble asserted that their new refineries were non-polluting, but Hudson "wanted absolute proof that a refinery can be built smog-free."

Humble promised that.

"We can build a good, clean sweet-smelling refinery," Warner emphasized at Humble's initial Monterey County Board of Supervisors' meeting, while claiming that air pollution instruments would not be able to detect anything originating from the refinery.

When pressed by Supervisors Andy Anderson and Harold Henry on wastewater, Humble had an answer for that too. Warner claimed the water used in the refining process was "neutralized." Warner referred to Humble's Baytown, Texas, refinery, claiming that the water leaving the refinery was cleaner than the water entering it from the Gulf of Mexico. As a bonus, Warner stated that the fishing was better where the wastewater discharged.

Humble had a promise for every concern, and a grandiose plan as well. The refinery would use only about one quarter of the site, "leaving plenty of room for expansion," said Gardner, who envisioned the refined products leaving the site by ship, rail, tank truck and possibly a pipeline.

The too-good-to-be-true claims of undetectable emissions, discharged wastewater in which fish thrived, and water that was cleaner than nature's own probably helped insert seeds of doubt in the minds of some. Humble appeared to be open and above board, promising benefits to the economy and the environment while being a good neighbor. However, these claims were dubious at best, coupled with the secretive way in which Humble acquired the Moss Landing site, suggested that the oil officials' words were more of a public relations ploy than reality.

While doubts were rising in the minds of Monterey Peninsula residents, and to a lesser extent in the rest of Monterey County, it was neighboring Santa Cruz County where the first opposition would gain public notice. Around March 10, the Santa Cruz County Planning Commission took the unusual step of sending a letter to the Monterey County Planning Commission expressing its "interest and concern" about pollution from the Humble refinery. The bitterness that would arise over the next few months in the Monterey Bay area played out in that contentious planning commission meeting. Commissioners had concerns about air pollution, oil spills and polluted beaches. On the other side were those who felt the future needed new business to continue the expansion of the post-war economy.

Although the vote was unanimous, Commissioner Bruce Woolpert's words represented the thoughts of many who felt this was the best use of land: "That area has a natural deep-water port. It was meant for heavy industry."

Commissioner Erle Byer warned of tankers blowing out their bunkers and dumping thousands of barrels of oil into the bay. Fellow Commissioner Elaine Reinelt warned of broken pipelines. "Nonsense," Woolpert stated, dismissing those fears without hesitation, "pipelines don't break."

"I'm on this commission to protect the interests of industry," Woolpert emphasized, "and its contributions to the economy of the county—and to heck with beauty."

The refinery's site was not even in Woolpert's county of Santa Cruz. Nevertheless, Woolpert and others from the pro-business, pro-job side saw a watershed coming. If Humble comes, so will more industry. If Humble is scared away, other industries would never come.

Humble would be the third industrial giant in Moss Landing, along with PG&E and Kaiser Refractories. The long-planned Moss Landing industrial center was starting to take shape. With Humble, the gates to development might finally be pried open permanently. In an editorial the day after Humble's announcement, the *Watsonville Register-Pajaronian* noted:

"What Humble thinks it may do at Moss Landing—and it's going to spend a cool million dollars just to study the site it's bought—is going to have some effect on the development of the harbor area, long designated as a proper site here for heavy industry. Industry begets industry; and if there ensues a Moss Landing triumvirate of PG&E, Kaiser and Humble, others will certainly follow."

The battle lines were drawn. Strong support was developing in Salinas. Although primarily an agricultural town, Salinas (also the largest city in Monterey County, and the county seat) was seeking to diversify and attract other industry. There had been many near misses: Hershey, Wrigley and Columbia Broadcasting Records all had considered Salinas-area locations, but did not follow through. The University of California set up its campus in Santa Cruz instead of Monterey County. There was one marked success—Salinas did secure a Firestone tire plant. Humble, as the *Salinas Californian* described it, was "a highly desirable type of industry."

The Salinas Chamber of Commerce, Alisal Chamber of Commerce and Castroville Chamber of Commerce announced their support for the Humble project in March. In April, the Marina and Seaside Chambers also expressed their support. Indeed, all the chambers of commerce in the county plus Watsonville came out in favor of the refinery by then, excepting Monterey Peninsula Chamber of Commerce, which took a neutral position.

Watsonville, already a bedroom community for most workers at Kaiser and PG&E, leaned strongly in favor of Humble as it saw itself housing refinery workers too. Others in Santa Cruz County, as the county Planning Commission indicated in the letter to its counterpart in Monterey County, were more apprehensive about the refinery.

Opposition from the Monterey Peninsula, primarily the Carmel, Pebble Beach and Carmel Valley areas was forming, but had yet to become the focal point of opposition. While many in the Salinas Valley were concerned about air pollution's effects on the crops, the concern represented a minority. As on the Peninsula, public opinion was still forming.

After the Salinas Chamber of Commerce announced its support, the atmosphere began to change. Stepping forward to express concerns with the way the matter was progressing was Jim Bardin of the Cattlemen's Association, also on the board of the Monterey County Air Pollution Advisory Committee that was beginning to peer into the Humble application. Bardin was one of the first in the agricultural community to warn that everyone needed to take a closer look at the Humble project.

"It upsets me that the (Salinas) Chamber of Commerce has already endorsed Humble when it knows even less than we do," declared Bardin.

Bardin also criticized the chamber as disrespectful for making its decision prior to a public report on a county fact-finding trip to Los Angeles, where oil refineries were inspected. The committee that traveled to Los Angeles earlier that week included Monterey County Planning Director Ed DeMars, Sanitation Director Ed Munson, four planning commissioners including Peter Cailotto, who would play a major role a few months later, and Supervisor Warren Church.

Front page of the February 15, 1965, Salinas Californian with the initial story about Humble Oil coming to Monterey County.
Courtesy of Salinas Californian

That report was helpful only in the sense that Monterey County officials discovered that they knew little about oil refineries or the laws to regulate them. DeMars said the trip was "very enlightening, if a bit confusing." He noted the need for expert advice. With the report in hand, the Air Pollution Advisory Committee Bardin sat on eventually recommended approval of the refinery, but also urged the adoption of Los Angeles County air pollution regulations.

Carmel resident Earl Moser, who would emerge as a prominent voice in opposition to Humble's plans, drew out in questioning at a public meeting that Monterey County's laws on air pollution did not address hydrocarbons. The problem was that Monterey County's air pollution laws were designed only for smoke and dust, not heavy industry.

John Maga, head of the air pollution division of the State Health Department, noted the gaping holes in the county's pollution laws. Maga and Munson called for a continuous inspection of air pollution. Maga also addressed the problem of odor, stating that it was harder to regulate.

"The oil companies say they can build a refinery that doesn't pollute the air," Maga said, "but that doesn't relate to odor when you live next door. They feel they aren't polluting the air if they meet requirements."

This did not sound like the "sweet-smelling" refinery that Warner originally promised, although Maga did admit that a Richfield refinery in Los Angeles was remarkably free of odor problems when he visited it.

Humble knew of the weak local ordinances that now worried county officials. The company's numerous comments about meeting local requirements appeared clearly aimed at Monterey County's lax or non-existent regulations as compared to those in San Francisco and Los Angeles.

"We assure you that our proposed refinery at Moss Landing ... will meet your local codes," Humble put forth in a statement read by Winslow prior to the recommendation to adopt Los Angeles County air pollution regulations.

Gardner and Winslow were both at the Air Pollution Advisory Committee's meeting when the recommendations came down to approve the refinery but to adopt Los Angeles air pollution controls. Prior to the recommendation to adopt Los Angeles regulations, Winslow tried to pacify the committee by saying that current regulations were adequate. Afterwards, neither man commented except to say the recommendation was too general, but Winslow agreed that Humble could meet Los Angeles County-style regulations that referred only to refineries.

This would be the first blip in Humble's plans. Undoubtedly, Humble saw Monterey County as a place with hardly any air pollution controls and little opposition. Now, Monterey County was thinking of adopting one of the nation's tougher pollution laws. Adopting these regulations was going to make Moss Landing less profitable, supertankers or not. Humble's goal of getting its proposal to the Board of Supervisors by April 5 for final approval was obviously not going to happen. The Planning Commission at the end of March was not even prepared to make a recommendation to the Board of Supervisors. However, it was prepared to receive the report from the subcommittee headed by Cailotto that traveled to Los Angeles.

One hundred people piled into the Planning Commission meeting on March 30. Humble attended in full force, with Warner and Winslow present. Also present was Humble's attorney in Salinas, Paul Hamerly of Noland and Hamerly. Humble's affiliate Esso sent senior engineer Frank Church, Richard Kilpert, another engineer, and Fred Ingram, an independent industrial hygiene expert, to handle the technical questions.

The recommendation to the Planning Commission that Monterey County adopt Los Angeles air pollution control regulations must not have been a huge surprise to Humble. The Air Pollution Advisory Committee had already made that recommendation. Next, Cailotto presented the findings which stipulated that Humble be approved "in principle" for a tentative one-year approval, but that Humble provide complete plans before pollution standards were set.

"Humble representatives have not yet defined the specific raw materials to be processed, the exact processing sequence that will be used, nor the complete slate of finished products that will be manufactured. This makes it difficult, if not impossible for the Planning Commission to initiate what they consider adequate controls to insure proper standards for air and water pollution," Cailotto said.

The claim that detailed regulations could not be determined without more information did not deter the subcommittee from proposing 18 conditions of its own. Besides adoption of the Los Angeles regulations, the subcommittee proposed limiting operations to three coking methods. Petroleum or pet coke is a high-carbon solid created from the oil refining process. The subcommittee's other proposals included hiring permanent county employees to monitor the plant, charging Humble for inspections, requiring compliance with standards of the Central Coast Regional Water Pollution Board, insuring against spills and leaks, guaranteeing immediate cleanup of marine spills and zoning distances between Humble's property and residential and commercial use.

Esso senior engineer Frank Church said Humble was "willing to accept a permit with appropriate sections of the Los Angeles code." However, those sections were only the air pollution controls. What was coming out of the subcommittee was more than that. Humble thought the only thing it needed to worry about was air pollution. However, it was the mid-1960s and zoning laws were just coming into effect across most of the country. Local communities were beginning to flex their political power on land use. Humble was not used to that.

The Humble men were stunned.

"It seemed extensive and too restrictive outside the field of air pollution," Winslow said as he left the meeting. "We don't understand it."

Humble came to Monterey County partially because the local regulations were undeveloped, but Humble also claimed those same regulations were more stringent than they actually were. Hamerly said the current regulations were more than enough to deal with air pollution concerns. He also warned that if the regulations were unreasonable, "Humble will take the refinery someplace else." That was a threat Humble would subtly infer several times in the months to come. At other times rumors would swirl that Humble was pulling out. Just as the rumors started to sound serious, Humble would crush them with a denial.

What really had Winslow shaking his head was not the non-air pollution conditions, but that Humble had to submit complete plans before conditions were to be set. It was going to cost $1 million and take a year to conduct engineering and other tests. Only then would Humble have its finalized plans. Humble was not going to sink this kind of money into its project without guarantees from the county on what to expect. Humble emphasized that it would comply with "any reasonable standards" for air and water pollution. It was a statement that its officials would repeat for months. "Reasonable" appears to have meant "few restrictions" to Humble.

The Planning Commission meeting also fired up old tensions in the county that had never subsided. Monterey County has long felt a divide between the Monterey Peninsula and Salinas that some have called "the lettuce curtain." People in one area tended to do business and socialize there, with a minimum of contact with the other area. Political and social organizations would have separate chapters in each place. Stemming from the early days of the county, this only grew worse over time, as the affluent Monterey Peninsula had an entirely different culture than working-class Salinas. The Humble controversy brought these old conflicts into sharper focus.

At the Planning Commission meeting, the *Salinas Californian* reported that the opposition came from the Monterey Peninsula, while Salinas was overwhelmingly in favor of Humble. In an editorial, the *Californian* summed up the resentment in Salinas:

"(Humble has) no real opposition to the granting of this permit—except for the Monterey Peninsula, whose citizens seem to oppose anything that they can't control."

That opposition was in the heart of Supervisor Hudson's district. In a *Californian* article, several Peninsula residents make their disdain for Humble perfectly clear. Gus Bauman of the Carmel Highlands Association declared that Humble would destroy Monterey County's greatest asset—unpolluted air and water. Throughout the Humble debate, residents and experts alike would claim Monterey County as one of the cleanest areas in the state in terms of air pollution.

Carmel City Councilman Gunnar Norberg said he preferred "more Carmels" and fewer refineries for Monterey County.

"I have never seen a refinery as beautiful as a cypress tree," stated C.W. Fisher of the Carmel Citizen's Committee.

William Howard Church, president of the Del Monte Properties Homeowner's Association at Pebble Beach and an instructor at the Naval Postgraduate School in Monterey, declared that "an excellent way to contaminate the air" was to allow refineries.

It was clear that Hudson's constituents did not want Humble to build. That allowed Hudson to stake his opposition whenever he felt comfortable. As a conservationist, opposing Humble was an easy position to assume. As a politician, it was a political necessity.

One point needs clarification, and it must have confused a few people during 1965. Throughout the Humble controversy, the surname Church appeared from four different and unrelated sources. Besides Supervisor Warren Church, Humble had a senior engineer named Frank Church. There is also William Howard Church, a professor at the Naval Postgraduate School in Monterey and president of the homeowners association in Pebble Beach, who would play a prominent role throughout the controversy. The press sometimes referred to him as William, other times as Howard and sometimes as William Howard—further adding to the confusion. In addition, one of the Salinas Valley's largest growers, Bruce Church Inc., would have representatives take a major role later in the year. There is no familial connection between any of these four Church families, and pure chance that a relatively uncommon surname appeared as significantly as it did.

As spring dawned in 1965, it became increasingly clear that a decision on Humble's proposal was not going to happen anytime soon. The Planning Commission set its May 11 meeting as a time for a decision. It hoped that another month would clarify the many questions that it had. Humble, on the other hand, must have been wondering why its proposal was generating so much controversy when Kaiser and PG&E had experienced so little opposition for their construction and proposed expansion.

U.S. highway maps were given away by Esso stations, one of several brand names used by Humble Oil.
Authors' collection

4

FROM HUMBLE BEGINNINGS

"Put a Tiger in Your Tank"

Humble slogan

Oil, a strange substance considered of little value for thousands of years, in the mid-1800s quite suddenly became the stuff that dreams—and incredible wealth—were made of.

It is called fossil fuel for good reason, since oil is formed from dead organisms that have been buried for millennia, and subjected to intense heat and pressure. The black goo had been observed seeping from the earth by a variety of humans through the ages, and some used it as an adhesive, or for building or waterproofing.

Natural asphalt derived from oil was used to construct the walls and towers of Babylon more than 4,000 years ago. Ancient Arabian scientists also found ways to distill it and use its byproducts. By 600 B.C., the Chinese were transporting oil through bamboo pipelines. But the knowledge of oil and its byproducts did not filter down to Western civilization. That would not be until the mid-19th century, when the idea of refining crude oil once again became vitally important.

Kerosene, derived from oil, was the wondrous fluid that made it possible to have reliable lamplight. In the days before electricity, lamps were a necessity for anyone who wanted to see much of anything after nightfall. At first, oil made from animal fat was widely used, but it was sputtering and inefficient. Then longer-lasting whale oil made its debut in the 1700s, but supplies were often haphazard, depending on the whalers' luck in hunting. Then the advent of the American Civil War put a huge dent in whale oil supplies and the search was on for a replacement. Kerosene would prove to be cheaper, more efficient and longer-lasting, and it was easier to ensure a steady supply to consumers.

But when the internal combustion engine was invented, oil truly became a commodity of necessity. The engines powered all kinds of machinery and vehicles to spark the Industrial Revolution, but it was the advent of the automobile that kicked oil production into high gear. Crude oil was refined to make fuel for cars in the form of gasoline and diesel, and a variety of other petroleum derivatives were needed to keep engines running smoothly.

The modern petroleum industry in the United States began with an oil strike in Pennsylvania in 1859. Hundreds of small oil producers and refineries sprang up in the area, only to be bought up or forced out of business by bigger producers. Especially infamous for his hardball business practices was John D. Rockefeller, founder of Standard Oil, which controlled 90 percent of U.S. petroleum refining capacity and pipelines by 1879.

In California, the first wells were drilled in the area of oil seeps, both in Northern and Southern California. The state's first gusher was in Pico Canyon, 35 miles north of Los Angeles, in 1876. It was the state's first commercial oil well. Soon to follow was California's first refinery in Newhall, which made kerosene and other products.

Oil companies popped up across the United States in the last years of the nineteenth and first years of the 20th century to accommodate the demand for petroleum products. Humble Oil, founded in 1911, was one of many, but it would soon become a force to be reckoned with. Its name has nothing to do with being modest—it was named after the company's origin point in Humble, Texas.

In reality, the company was the antithesis of its chosen name. It became a powerhouse, an overbearing behemoth in the petroleum industry for much of the 20th century as the largest domestic oil producer in the United States from the 1940s to the 1960s. Not only did Humble have oil fields, but also owned refineries and pipelines, and on the retail side, Humble gas stations provided its products to car-happy consumers.

Something a bit odd about the Humble brand was that the company, in a sense, was constantly competing against its parent company. In 1919, 50 percent of Humble was purchased by Standard Oil of New Jersey, giving Humble an infusion of cash while also allowing it to operate independently in many aspects. As the years went by, Standard Oil continued to buy into Humble, and by 1958, held 98 percent of Humble stock. Adding to the confusion were other brand names that Humble used, including Esso and Enco.

What's remembered best today about Esso and Humble is the classic advertising slogan "Put a Tiger in Your Tank." This, paired with an endearing cartoon tiger, began appearing in advertising for both brand names in 1959. The advertising campaign was so popular that gas stations even sold millions of fake tiger tails in the 1960s, which motorists would tie to their cars.

The multiple names and companies were all part of Standard Oil's strategy to dodge anti-trust laws in various states. Humble was a convenient front for its parent company since it appeared to operate as an independent entity. Humble could make inroads into states that were, for a variety of reasons, not friendly to Standard. Eventually, though, times changed—Standard Oil expanded and became a global colossus, and in 1972, consolidated all its operations under a single brand name, Exxon. It went on to merge with Mobil Oil and today is known as ExxonMobil, and remains one of the world's largest publicly traded oil and gas companies.

"Put a Tiger In Your Tank" was a famous Humble Oil ad slogan, accompanied by a cartoon tiger.
(Detail from back of Esso map)
Author's collection

At the time of the proposed refinery project in Moss Landing, though, Humble was still operating as a somewhat independent entity. Company officials were intent on expanding into the California market, and having refineries on the West Coast would enable Humble to deliver its products to Western consumers at less cost. In addition, exploration of Alaska's oil-rich lands signaled that West Coast refineries would be needed to handle that new source of petroleum, to refine it and get the products to where they were needed.

But as California residents were discovering, petroleum—whether on the refining end or in a car's gas tank—came with a significant environmental price tag.

All fossil fuels, when burned, emit harmful gases and particles. Leading oil companies were aware of this, because in 1946 they created a "Smoke and Fumes Committee" to fund scientific research of air pollution issues, according to documents published in 2016 by The Center for International Environmental Law. From 1957 on, Humble Oil knew of the rising level of carbon dioxide in the atmosphere and that it was likely to cause global warming. It has also been shown that oil companies knew there were harmful effects and chose to hide them from their customers.

Oil and gas production, processing and use release carbon dioxide and methane, as well as six major pollutants: carbon monoxide, nitrogen oxides, sulfur oxides, ozone, particulate matter and lead. There are also another 187 air toxins related to petroleum that today are regulated by the Environmental Protection Agency and states. All of these can be released at any point in oil's journey from beneath the earth to being burned in an engine.

In addition to many of these compounds being toxic on their own, some of their effects are enhanced by sunlight for a phenomenon called photochemical smog. This is produced when sunlight reacts with nitrogen oxides and volatile organic compounds (VOCs) in the atmosphere, with VOCs coming from gasoline, paint and other common sources. Sunlight triggers the formation of airborne particles and ground-level ozone, all of which combined to become the smog blanket that enveloped the Los Angeles basin in the mid-20th century.

Then as now, at least 75 percent of air pollution and smog is caused by emissions from gas-burning vehicles. Smog and air pollution has lessened with the addition of catalytic converters in American vehicles, starting in the 1970s. A much smaller percentage of air pollution is produced by industry, including refineries. Because crude oil must be heated in the separation and distillation process to create its many products, there is no avoiding the production of emissions, although some can be recaptured or "scrubbed" to reduce them.

Once crude oil arrives at a refinery, there are a variety of steps taken to turn it into useful products, which include physical separation, distillation and blending. In the first stage, oil is heated by a furnace as it enters a distillation tower. Over half of it vaporizes, and as the vapors rise in the column, various parts of it cool and condense to liquid, and are drawn off. For instance, a pamphlet from the Anacortes, Washington, refinery given to visitors in the 1960s explains that its distillation unit separated crude into five "fractions" which included gasoline, naphtha (used for high-octane gasoline), light gas oil and heavy gas oil (used in making turbine fuel and diesel fuel), and slurry oil. Then, as now, about half the crude oil that comes into a refinery becomes automotive gasoline.

Petroleum and its byproducts now are used in an astonishing array of products. When we think of petroleum, typically it's car products like gasoline and oil that come to mind. But plastics and synthetic rubber are also derived from petroleum, as are many types of waxes, greases and lubricating compounds. More than 6,000 products are made from petroleum and its byproducts, including propane, nail polish, fabric, dyes, crayons, heating oil, movie film, hair coloring, denture adhesives, fertilizers, flooring, perfume, insecticide, paraffin wax, asphalt, tar, petroleum jelly, soap and vitamin capsules, to name just a few.

One important step in the process is thermal cracking, which uses a catalyst and heat to create new, smaller molecules from larger ones, and enables more of the oil to be used as gasoline. Hydrocracking, using hydrogen and a catalyst, is another method for doing this. Carbon is also deposited on the catalyst during cracking and is called catalyst coke, and adds heat to the process when the coke burns off.

Petroleum coke is a byproduct of the refining process. As fuel is extracted from crude oil, solid carbon is left behind, called coke or petcoke. Coke can be used as a solid fuel for industry, or as a source of carbon for other uses. It is often used in electric power plants.

Thermal cracking, like any type of petroleum burning, produces air emissions. At the Richfield refinery in Long Beach in the 1960s, promoted as "The West's Most Modern Refinery," the plant's cracking unit would trap carbon monoxide in a waste heat boiler, which converted the dangerous gas to carbon dioxide. At Anacortes, hydrogen sulfide—the compound that smells like rotten eggs—was extracted during the cracking process and sent to a chemical plant for conversion to sulfuric acid. These are just two possible pollutants mentioned in the companies' literature, but it is unknown what other types of emissions may have escaped into the air around those refineries.

By the standards of the day, both the Long Beach and Anacortes plants appeared to be model industries. Anacortes, in fact, received an award for its care in avoiding water pollution, with a strict treatment program for all water used in the refinery process. Contaminants were removed and the water filtered and aerated before being returned to Padilla Bay.

However, it was a time before the formation of the EPA or any state imposing statewide pollution regulations. Regulations and monitoring had to be done on a city-by-city, or region-by-region basis. It was not until 1970 that the EPA was formed by executive order of President Richard M. Nixon, which marked a period of more intense scrutiny and study of what exactly oil refineries—and many other industries—were doing to the environment.

5

THE SWORDS ARE DRAWN

April 11—May 10, 1965

"Don't let them in. They will kill you."

Edwin Knight, former Governor of California

By mid-April, attorney Paul Hamerly's words at the Planning Commission meeting—that Humble Oil might look elsewhere if county restrictions were not reasonable—took on new relevance. Supervisor Tom Hudson announced at the end of the April 11 Board of Supervisors meeting that he had heard Humble was pulling out of Moss Landing and heading to Benicia. Hudson did not reveal his source, and Humble quickly denied it. Hudson did state that Humble was unhappy with the list of restrictions proposed by the Planning Commission's subcommittee.

"There are certain things in there that we don't entirely understand, and we hope to have them clarified at the next meeting," Hamerly confirmed while denying that Humble was pulling out.

"As far as I know, they are still expecting to come here," Hamerly stated as he once again tossed out the threat that Monterey County was not Humble's only choice. "Obviously they have some other alternatives that have been considered."

It was unlikely that the initial recommendation of the planning commission subcommittee was going to force Humble to surrender the site it had picked as the best on the West Coast. The proposals did not even carry the force of law. While Humble was certainly distressed by the recommendations, some that it had never experienced before (specifically the requirement that the company submit detailed plans before permit conditions were approved), it was way too early for Humble to leave Monterey County standing at the altar. More likely, Humble spread the rumor of pulling out in order to get more favorable conditions when the Planning Commission met in May. There remained robust support for the project. Letting the county know that it was feeling a bit snubbed by the unwelcoming conditions might get things back on track to the original, less rigorous conditions.

Humble's search for a West Coast facility was years in the making. That is evident in the purchase of the Moss Landing property two years earlier. While its consultants determined that Moss Landing was the best choice in the state, there were other suitors. And at least one of them was actively wooing Humble.

There were at least four sites on Humble's short list: Moss Landing, Benicia, Rodeo and Martinez. Oil refineries had been part of the landscape for decades in these bayside cities northeast of San Francisco. Refineries had been in Martinez, across the Suisun Bay from Benicia, since at least 1913. In neighboring Rodeo, a refinery had existed even earlier, since 1896. Richmond, on the same peninsula, had had one since 1901. Refineries were a well-established and accepted industry in the East Bay.

Of the alternate site choices, Benicia promised to be the most accommodating, because Benicia was facing a serious problem. In 1851, the Benicia Arsenal were established by the U.S. Army, two years after the Benicia Barracks were built. These were part of a large military reservation that was the Army's primary ordnance facility on the West Coast for more than 100 years. Notable Civil War generals, such as Ulysses Grant, Thomas Hooker and Edward Ord were stationed there prior to the war. (Coincidentally, Fort Ord in Monterey County, the former Army base there, was named for General Ord.)

The post's garrison ceased in 1898, but the Arsenal remained. It would remain a major weapons and ammunition center on the West Coast for the Army until its closure in 1964, which was part of a major reorganization of military bases during the Kennedy administration. The arsenal was the lifeblood of Benicia. With its closure, the city faced severe financial distress.

When the army announced the closure in 1961, Benicia immediately took action. Mayor James Lemos quickly pulled together a "Save the Arsenal" campaign. Lemos left with Governor Pat Brown to Washington, D.C. as they attempted to pressure officials to spare Benicia. It was to no avail.

Benicia was beginning to feel the pinch as the population began to decline. It did not have the money for new city vehicles. At times, it could not meet payroll. Even the bars and brothels began closing for a lack of business. Faced with this looming economic crisis, Lemos and city attorney James Bohn came up with a plan: turn the Benicia Arsenal into an industrial park. Benicia officials only had to look across the Suisun Bay to the smokestacks in Martinez and Richmond to see how that kept those cities alive.

Both men would leave a lasting legacy for Benicia. Lemos, who served for 35 years on the city council and as mayor, helped create modern Benicia. Bohn was a prominent and accomplished attorney who worked with the California legislature where he was involved in writing the first Uniform Building Code for the state, and also helped write the first legal codes for Guam and Alaska.

On a flight back from Washington after a failed negotiation with Bohn's high school classmate Secretary of Defense Robert McNamara, Lemos and Bohn devised an installment plan to buy the Arsenal from the General Services Administration. Benicia would then lease it to private entities that would pay the mortgage. It was complicated and required coordination from numerous agencies, including legislation from the state legislature. In addition, the GSA had never sold anything by installment.

This was called the Benicia Plan, which set the blueprint for military base closures and is still in use today. Coincidentally, the core parts of the Benicia Plan would later be used in the closure of Monterey County's Fort Ord. Turning the Benicia Arsenal into an industrial park was going to be a challenge. Multiple easements needed to be renegotiated. It seemed every entity surrounding the arsenal wanted a little piece of it. An even steeper challenge was that Benicia is a "city of the sixth class," which prohibited Benicia from incurring any debt. According to the state constitution, Benicia could not borrow money to began the conversion to an industrial park. Broke, and not able to borrow, equaled a disastrous situation.

Appraisals on the property came in low because of the specialized nature of many of the munition buildings that did not appear to have any civilian use and because only eleven of the arsenal's hundreds of buildings were useable without repairs. The value of the arsenal dropped to the bargain price of $4.5 million.

Seeking leasees for its new venture, Benicia sent approximately three hundred letters to development companies in North America, only Benicia

Industries, Bechtel Engineering and Cabot, Cabot and Lodge were interested. From those choices, Benicia wrangled a deal with Benicia Industries which fronted the money as an advance on future leases. The other two companies found involvement in Benicia too. Bechtel conducted extensive engineering studies, and Cabot emerged as a player in finding industry for the new industrial center. After repairs, the value of the arsenal was $33 million.

The deal seemed too good. The GSA suspected fraud and put investigators on it. No fraud was found. Benicia Councilman John "Jack" Cody also questioned the sale of a $33 million property to a private entity for $4.5 million. Cody sensed something was amiss with the lease and the obligations required by Benicia Industries in it. A complicated lawsuit followed where Cody suggested secret deals were cut. The GSA demanded that Benicia pay $10,000 a month for maintenance and security as the lawsuit delayed the sale. Once again, Benicia arranged for Benicia Industries to absorb those costs, subtracted from future rents and land sales.

The lawsuit fizzled. A judge ruled in favor of Benicia on Dec. 16, 1964. The deal was highly unusual, but legal. Once Benicia Industries took over, it started paying taxes. The Surplus Property Authority, which operated as the cover for the purchase of the arsenal, paid all the expenses for the city, including Bohn's attorney fees. As Dr. Jim Lessenger, historian for Benicia Historical Museum, wrote, "(Benicia) didn't pay a dime." The lease with Bechtel started in March 1965, just as Humble started to hit some bumps in Moss Landing.

Besides the engineering studies at Benicia, Bechtel had another role it was playing in this story. Bechtel had been involved in helping Humble Oil find refinery sites for its expansion on the West Coast. Now that Humble's refinery in Moss Landing was stirring dissatisfaction, and Bechtel had already identified Benicia as an alternative to Moss Landing, it would not be surprising if Bechtel nudged its oil client to consider a possible site in the north.

Benicia officials knew they were on the short list, but not as Humble's No. 1 choice for a refinery site. When word reached Benicia in early 1965 that Humble was encountering some difficulties in Monterey County, Lemos and Bohn contacted Humble about locating the new refinery at the site of the former Benicia Arsenal. Benicia offered everything that Moss Landing had except it lacked a deepwater port. As a bonus, the city had no air pollution restrictions at all, as the San Francisco Bay Area Air Pollution District did not cover Benicia at that time.

At the same board meeting where Hudson announced that Humble was moving to Benicia, Supervisor Warren Church, noting that the county lacked the expertise to deal with setting proper controls on a refinery, suggested that the county hire "a consultant on refineries." The board decided to put the suggestion off a week while it offered the services of a consultant if the Planning Commission desired it.

Once informed of the option, the Planning Commission jumped at the suggestion. A three-man committee of Supervisor Church, Planning Director Ed DeMars and Sanitation Director Ed Munson formed to hire an expert. Hudson moved that the expert look into the expansion of the new PG&E facility as well. PG&E was not fully committed to a nuclear power plant as it was also considering another fossil-fueled facility. The committee wasted no time. In less than a week, they hired William O'Connell, who had a background in air and water pollution. McConnell was charged with issuing a report prior to the May 11 Planning Commission meeting.

RESUME OF WILLIAM HOWARD CHURCH

Wm. Howard Church was born in Boise, Idaho, in 1911 and attended Whittier College, majoring in history and political science, with a minor in English. He received the B. A. degree in 1933.

In 1938, following five years of business experience, he was awarded a research and teaching fellowship at t he Graduate School of Public Administration, Univ. of Southern California. Included with his graduate experience was an internship in management research wi th Public Administration Service of Chicago. While at USC, he received a Calif. Secondary Credential in 1939 and the M. S. degree in public administration in 1941. His research was done under the direction of Professor John M. Pfiffner.

While on assignment with the U. S. Dept. of Justice, he was commissioned in the U. S. Navy and called to active duty in October 1942.

Detail from the resume of Professor William Howard Church, who spoke out against Humble as a co-founder of Citizens for Clean Air.
Calhoun: Institutional Archive of the Naval Postgraduate School

Monterey County had some resources for evaluating air quality. A few years earlier the county began limited monitoring of air pollutants. In 1958, the county acquired devices for measuring oxidant levels and particulate matter such as dust and soot. Oxidant levels were measured three times a day at the Health Department Laboratory in Salinas. In Monterey, samples were collected once a day. In King City, samples were collected once a week. For particulate matter, equipment in Salinas and Monterey collected samples every two hours. The results revealed air quality as described by officials as "excellent."

Back on the Monterey Peninsula, the city of Carmel's Planning Commission stepped into the fray. The commissioners urged the denial of Humble's permit, "unless positive proof can be presented that there will be no air or water pollution."

Illustration by artist Eldon Dedini, a nationally-known Monterey Peninsula resident, which appeared on a Citizens for Clean Air memo.
Authors' collection

At the same time, a powerful citizens' group formed on the Monterey Peninsula. Citizens for Clean Air announced their opposition to any industry that caused air pollution. The two co-chairs of Citizens for Clean Air were men with a history of working for industry. Earl Moser of Carmel was a retired oil company executive who spoke Humble's language and had the background to

challenge their claims. The other chair was Charles Kramer, a retired manufacturer. Their relentless work confronted Humble at every move it made in
the coming months to gain approval for the refinery.

William Howard Church, a professor at the Naval Postgraduate School,
was the third leader of this group that would hound Humble to the last of
its attempts. The three men, who all resided in Supervisor Hudson's district,
formed the nucleus of community opposition to Humble. They also assembled
a powerful coalition of a dozen groups ranging from the Sierra Club to the
Motel Owners Association of Monterey.

Professor Church stated during a press conference that the purpose of
the group was not simply to oppose Humble "but to oppose it as opening
the door to further industries of this type." These efforts against air pollution
would eventually lead to the creation of an air pollution control district, first
in Monterey County and later in the entire Monterey Bay area. Interestingly,
Professor Church admitted that Humble might not cause a damaging amount
of smog, but other industries that arrive afterwards would create significant
damage. The suggestion that Humble might be safe, also made by others, would
work against opponents of Humble in the short run.

Professor Church continued in his statement by blasting Humble as a
threat to agriculture, the environment, infrastructure and the health of children in North Monterey County. He said Citizens for Clean Air was willing
to work with chambers of commerce and other groups to bring in industries
that would not pollute. It bears mentioning that at this point, there was no
significant discussion that Moss Landing should not continue with its industrial
zoning in what was then described as the Moss Landing Area Development
Plan. The question was what industries were appropriate there—a question
that no one in the county bothered to raise when that plan was adopted less
than ten years earlier.

Professor Church also noted what would become a controversial detail
throughout the Humble affair. Church claimed that the Monterey Bay and
Salinas Valley had an inversion layer similar to that of the Los Angeles basin.
In an inversion, temperature and altitude contribute to create atmospheric
layers. Warmer air traps cooler air below it. It holds smog close to the ground
and prevents it from rising and dispersing. It is a common occurrence along
the California coast and easily visible when the ground-hugging fog commonly
seen along the Monterey Bay rolls in.

A week after Professor Church spoke at the press conference, 400 people
squeezed into Pacific Grove Junior High to hear an "impartial panel" of experts,

an event organized by Citizens for Clean Air. Of course, declaring that the panel was "impartial" was a doubtful proposition, seeing as it was put together by a group that unilaterally opposed any air pollution.

A surprising development was Supervisor Hudson opening the event. As chair of the Board of Supervisors, the final arbiter in this matter, Hudson might have been expected to hold his cards close to his vest. Now, early in the game, Hudson showed his colors as a Humble opponent. As a conservationist, he was not likely to cast a favorable eye on Humble anyway. However, with overwhelming support from the people in his district, Hudson did not need to fear a political backlash if he began to speak out.

Hudson always gravitated to the limelight, and the forum was an opportunity for Hudson to burnish his environmental credentials and grab some press attention without political repercussions. Although he would remain a bit behind the scenes until the matter came before the entire Board of Supervisors, it is likely that Hudson was organizing and working diligently with the leaders of Citizens for Clean Air from the beginning.

The panel's speakers were impressive. Included were A.J. Haagen-Smit, a professor at the California Institute of Technology and a member of President Johnson's Scientific Advisory Committee on Air Pollution, and S. Smith Griswold, director of the Los Angeles Air Pollution Control District. Also present was E.F. Darley of the University of California, Riverside, an expert on smog's effects on plants, and George Haltiner, professor and chair of the Department of Meteorology at the Naval Postgraduate School in Monterey.

None of the speakers that night believed that controls could limit pollution—a direct challenge to Humble's statements that it would not contribute to this problem. It was also a clear discrediting of Humble representative J. Prince Warner's comments in February that the refinery's emissions would not be detectable. Humble, perhaps realizing the outlandishness of that earlier statement and the growing sophistication of the opposition, had stopped making the claim of a "sweet-smelling" refinery.

The crowd at the junior high school must have exceeded the expectations of Citizens for Clean Air. They prepared cards asking for volunteers for distribution to the attendees, but they only had 300 cards and quickly ran out. The crowd, nearly unanimously opposed to Humble, further confirmed that the event was meant to energize the opposition than to operate as an "impartial" forum. It succeeded brilliantly.

Griswold, the director of the Los Angeles Air Pollution District, was particularly critical of the refinery industry. In the 17 years of the district's existence, millions of dollars had been spent, Griswold said, and, "Refineries are still not what we consider to be an outstanding industry from an air pollution standpoint ... No controls are 100% effective."

Darley said that crop damage from air pollution was evident in 26 states and would impact Salinas Valley agriculture, as he showed slides of smog-blighted lettuce. Darley called Monterey and Santa Cruz counties the "last remaining principle air shed in California without plant damage having been done by air pollutants."

Weeks later, C.R. Thompson of the Air Pollution Research Center at the University of California, Riverside, presented a report to the Council of California Growers that substantiated Darley's conclusions and surely stirred interest with Salinas Valley growers. Thompson stated that agricultural damage from smog existed in 28 California counties. The worst was in Los Angeles and Riverside counties; the least impacted: Monterey County. Thompson said that even indirect damage to crops had cost hundreds of millions of dollars, mainly to leafy vegetables—the primary crops of the Salinas Valley. Thompson also noted the damage to the flower industry in San Francisco. That was a concern that flower growers, especially in the Watsonville area, had already expressed. Some had moved from San Francisco to the Monterey Bay area for that exact reason.

Haltiner pointed to the Salinas Valley having a Los Angeles-like inversion layer at 1,000 feet, and the nearby mountains that helped create it. While Humble would admit that an inversion existed, it disputed that the inversion was the same as in Los Angeles, where thick, widespread smog was especially prevalent in the 1960s. Humble was not alone in that assertion.

Albert Vierra, a refinery supporter, submitted a letter later in the year to the supervisors that he had received from the national Weather Bureau Regional Office in San Francisco. Regional meteorologist L.W. Snellman confirmed to Vierra that the inversion at Monterey Bay was indeed different than the one in Los Angeles. Snellman said the inversions would be less frequent and occur at a higher elevation, and the higher elevation would result in a less dense concentration of pollutants. Snellman also pointed out that because of the topographical features of the long Salinas Valley and strong offshore winds, there would be less stagnation of the atmosphere than what exists in the Los Angeles Basin. Overall, Snellman concluded that the Monterey Bay area was "less susceptible to smog" than Los Angeles. However, the inversion debate would remain one of the hot topics throughout the Humble affair.

Haagen-Smit warned that in ten years the Monterey Bay area could look like Los Angeles if more industry arrived. Both Haagen-Smit and Griswold said that now was the time to either legislate heavy industry out, or to create strong enough controls to contain the pollution, although the two experts disagreed on how effective those controls might be.

Around the same time, the Pacific Grove Chamber of Commerce allowed Humble to present its side. At this forum, Humble representatives included Dr. George Swisher, who held a Ph.D. in chemical engineering, who again laid out that there would not be any noxious smells from the plant.

"Hydrogen sulfide smell (like rotten eggs) is a thing of the past for refineries," Swisher said, noting that the oil was never exposed to the air, so noxious fumes would not develop.

Pacific Grove resident and former president of the Audubon Society Elgin Hurlbert addressed Swisher intently on the safety of the refinery.

"The Monterey Peninsula is a division point for many forms of natural life. Some animal species do not exist north of here and others never go south of here. All it would take is one good spill and you've had it," Hurlbert explained.

Swisher admitted that accidents could happen. Asked by another member of the public if Humble could forego the submarine pipeline, which some feared might cause a spill, Swisher demurred that it would not be possible because the pipeline for unloading ships in the bay was the reason Moss Landing was at the top of Humble's list of choices.

Towards Salinas, some people grew increasingly agitated with the opposition from the Monterey Peninsula. "I would like to know what the people of Carmel and Pebble Beach have against industry," asked William Bartell of Alisal, who noted that the Monterey Peninsula was also the source of opposition against the now established Firestone tire plant in Salinas.

The divide was spreading in another direction as well. The *Santa Cruz Sentinel* placed itself firmly on the side of the Monterey Peninsula residents and the *Monterey Peninsula Herald* editors who wrote, "the *Herald*'s own interests, of course, lie in preserving the beauty and God-given future of the Peninsula at whatever costs in dirty smokestacks and polluted air and water."

The *Sentinel* added, "If there are any doubts, we prefer clean air."

The divide was not between just Monterey and Salinas, but Santa Cruz and a much more pro-Humble Watsonville, just inside the Santa Cruz County line and only ten miles from Moss Landing. The neighborhoods between Salinas and Watsonville would feel the positive economic effects of Humble. That meant jobs and more infrastructure to support it, from housing developments to shopping centers. It also meant on the Monterey County side that new taxes would pay for schools, roads, sheriff's deputies and other quality-of-life requirements. The refinery opponents from the Monterey Peninsula and Santa Cruz were not going to be the beneficiaries of those jobs, and they instead feared a refinery would chase away tourists and those jobs in recreation and hospitality forever lost.

Santa Cruz County realized that it had no say and no benefit, but that if something was to go awry, like an increase in smog, then it would suffer as much as anywhere else. That prompted the Planning Commission in the city of Santa Cruz to contact officials in Monterey County about forming an air pollution control district.

With growing questioning, Humble officials grew uneasy, and pumped up their public relations blitz on the Monterey Peninsula. Humble sent Swisher to the editors of the *Herald* in hopes of dimming the steady doubts drumming from its editorial pages. It seems that by now Humble realized that keeping the current lax county regulations on pollution was unrealistic. Instead, the company was trying to stay ahead of the calls for the strictest controls. Swisher said that Humble envisaged regulations like those in Los Angeles for Monterey County. He added that the Los Angeles regulations were the toughest anywhere. As Humble must have seen it, the advantages of a deepwater port still offset those tougher restrictions. Swisher explained that the ships would anchor a mile offshore, and then transfer oil to the refinery, where 88% of it would become gasoline with the rest transformed into jet fuel, high-quality diesel oil, heavy fuel and coke.

The *Californian* also hit back at the opponents. An editorial attacked Citizens for Clean Air for trying to discredit Humble and insinuate that the oil company was against clean air.

"Humble believes in clean air, too," declared the *Californian*. "It is a little strange that this astute committee (Citizens for Clean Air) and its even more astute advisors have chosen to ignore the marvels of modern technology, which Humble will use in the treatment, clean up and control of all emissions to the air and water."

The *Californian* charged that Citizens for Clean Air based their opposition solely on aesthetics and ignored the economic bonus of a large tax base and new jobs: "Industry has made tremendous strides in solving the problems of pollution. Humble is in the forefront in this research and progress." The *Californian* continued in urging the Planning Commission and Board of Supervisors to approve the Humble permit and "ignore the wind that blows from the Peninsula."

There was no doubt now. Monterey County was being torn apart in a bitter struggle among its residents. There was clearly a geographic tone to the argument, but, even worse, the two sides could not agree on what they were arguing about. One side saw it simply as an economic issue; the other side saw it as a pollution problem. Just outside the ring stood Santa Cruz County, trying to get in a few licks of its own. The temperatures were rising as summer approached, but the fever of partisans for and against Humble was even hotter, and it was going to get even worse.

As the day for the Planning Commission showdown approached, State Senator Fred Farr noted that Monterey County was one of the few counties in the state with relatively clean air. He urged the commissioners to thoroughly investigate and "satisfy" themselves that detrimental air pollution will not result.

"I know you will protect the best long-range interests of our county," Farr said.

Also weighing in was former California Governor Edwin Knight who happened to be in Monterey visiting his old Stanford chum Allen Griffin, publisher of the *Monterey Peninsula Herald*. Knight was considering challenging Governor Pat Brown in 1966. On Humble, Knight was far less diplomatic than Farr.

"Don't let them in," Knight emphasized. "They will kill you."

6

FACE-OFF AT THE PLANNING

COMMISSION

May 11, 1965

"We have many experts and even the experts are confused ...
I'm confused, you're confused ..."

Fred Naber, Carmel resident

On May 11, packed to capacity with 200 people, the Planning Commission deliberated at the Salinas City Council chambers with its new expert on pollution, William O'Connell. People lined the walls and lingered outside the building known as the Rotunda. As the meeting began, petitions signed by 998 people in favor of the Humble Oil proposal were submitted. Letters and petitions against the project totaled 433. The majority, 380, came from the Monterey Peninsula.

Humble brought forth its team to testify again on the safety and cleanliness of the refinery. Up first was attorney Paul Hamerly, who drew laughter at his contention that during the recent forum in Pacific Grove "none of the experts indicated that an oil industry is bad industry from the point of air pollution."

Hamerly pointed to a refinery operating just 14 miles from Waikiki Beach in Hawaii as an example of how a refinery and tourism could coexist.

"Humble is extremely anxious that we have adequate controls," stated Hamerly, concluding that "dirty industry breeds dirty industry."

Humble's experts admitted to the inversion layer, but strongly disagreed that the Salinas Valley was like the Los Angeles basin. Esso engineer Frank Church argued that the winds came from the southwest and the changing weather fronts would not allow smog to accumulate above the Monterey Bay's communities.

The Salinas City Council Rotunda, where people packed in to hear the Planning Commission deliberate on the Humble Oil refinery project. The building is still in use today.
Kathryn McKenzie

When O'Connell spoke, his testimony avoided the stronger statements prevalent to each side. "I believe a clean, as the word is used, refinery can be developed," asserted O'Connell. "No one can make the statement, however, that emissions won't come out, but they can be controlled so there will be no damage to crops, health or visibility." O'Connell, questioned by Earl Moser of the Citizens for Clean Air, asserted, "There is no reason, with adequate air resource management, Monterey County should ever face what happened in Los Angeles."

For those who had seen or read the statements from the experts at the Citizens for Clean Air panel a week earlier and then listened to this evening's testimony, too much information was breeding a new problem.

When Fred Naber of Carmel spoke, he pointed to all the experts and information, saying, "We have many experts and even the experts are confused ... I'm confused, you're confused ..."

Later in O'Connell's statement, he added to the growing call for an air pollution control district, stating the need for "a broad air pollution control regulation even without industry." O'Connell further urged the commission to not move in haste but deliberately. Members of the Planning Commission agreed.

"It is not possible to make a decision until a more complete report is in. I feel this should be continued," urged Commissioner Dr. E.P. Marcucci of Carmel Valley.

"The tool hasn't been forged yet that can allow us to come to a decision tonight," agreed Commissioner Peter Henderson of Salinas.

Just before midnight, on the motion of Commissioner Peter Cailotto, the planners set July 28 to develop a set of regulations and make its decision on Humble. While the delay set Humble's deadline back even further, overall the meeting was a welcome sign to the oil giant. A head count of the nine commissioners found four in favor of Humble with the rest uncommitted. The *Santa Cruz Sentinel* reported that the consensus among observers was that the Humble permit was "in the bag." The only thing holding up approval was a thorough report from O'Connell.

Humble representative R.A. Winslow offered the help of the company's air and water pollution experts. Winslow supported the delay if it was used "constructively."

"We were favorably impressed with the meeting," Winslow said.

Although Winslow hoped the regulations could be drafted sooner than the end of July, Humble officials had to be feeling good. After being badgered and questioned by Peninsula residents for the last couple of months, it seemed that things were now back on schedule with a few added regulations.

At the meeting, Commissioner Dan Krishun of Castroville spoke strongly for Humble. Krishun claimed Castroville had the highest tax rate in the county and that Humble would help ease that. He firmly stated that he was ready to vote for approval of Humble once the restrictions were finalized. However,

Krishun was aware of the concerns that Humble's opponents raised. Krishun was troubled that the refinery could foul the environment and wanted to limit "the specific number of air and water pollution units" that any future industry was going to produce. He also proposed setting up an industrial committee to limit and control those industries. Krishun made it clear that those who supported Humble were just as anxious about its impact as the opponents. Unlike Kramer, who was on the Monterey Peninsula, Krishun was right next door to the Humble project. Krishun wanted to know how much pollution "Monterey County can stand" before more industries started popping up.

Krishun's position was significant. He was the first prominent supporter of Humble to raise serious concerns about the detrimental effects of the oil refinery. In an issue that was beginning to severely polarize the county, Krishun was trying to find a balance between the economic benefits of Humble and deleterious effects of pollution. It was a balance that few were willing to try, but an effort that would bear important consequences when the Board of Supervisors took up the matter later in the year.

Other commissioners joined in, including Planning Commission Chair Keith Evans, who declared Krishun's idea had a "great deal of merit." Salinas Commissioner Perry Henderson, who also appeared to support Humble, stressed the need to "control and limit." However, while Krishun, Evans and Henderson stood behind the idea that pollution was controllable, Commissioner E.P. Marcucci was skeptical.

"How are you going to do it? Where are you going to draw the line?" queried Marcucci.

Krishun's concerns reflected the growing opinion in North Monterey County that while industry was needed in the Moss Landing area, people wanted it to be as clean as possible. When it came to pollution concerns, the two sides were not far apart. In terms of solutions, it was a different story. Humble was now triggering an emotional, almost knee-jerk reaction among those for or against it. The initial demand of many opponents that a Humble permit required strict regulatory controls had evolved to rejecting Humble's proposal entirely. Ironically, it was some Humble supporters who were now advocating strict controls.

While Humble talked a good game about pollution with its brand-new, non-polluting refineries, and publicly expressed bafflement at some of the regulatory controls proposed, the company was not stepping up to address those proper controls. Evans expressed that frustration: "I personally am disappointed in the lack of information from Humble regarding control."

To understand North Monterey County's support and concerns for Humble takes a grasp of its geography and people. Castroville borders Moss Landing, and Humble refinery's site was in the middle of the two communities. Krishun's appeal for the economic benefits that Humble would bring was already generating a lot of support in North County, which was not as affluent as the Monterey Peninsula. Excepting artichokes grown in Castroville, a slice of the Pajaro Valley and a few berry growers in the hills of Prunedale, it didn't have the large produce growers that dominated the Salinas Valley. Instead, the agriculture that existed were small, family-owned farms and dairies.

Old dairy buildings along Elkhorn Slough.
Kathryn McKenzie

At that time, North Monterey County had working-class communities and almost no zoning laws. Most of North Monterey County was without a building code until an interim ordinance was passed in 1963. The first permanent code for that part of the county was implemented at this time in May of 1965. Prior to that, anyone could build any home they desired on a 10,000-square-foot lot. North Monterey County clearly had a rural look about it. It was common to find abandoned vehicles in the front yard, poultry in the back yard and a side business in the garage. Many of the roads were unnamed and others unpaved. Cattle guards, those metal grids that discourage cows from wandering, could even be found on some of the county roads. North County became a magnet for those seeking affordable housing. Mobile homes dotted the area's canyons. The surge in growth put pressure on the limited infrastructure of roads and schools.

Castroville was the closest thing the area had to a city, but it was unincorporated and remains so to this day. Pajaro, at the county's edge next to Watsonville in Santa Cruz County, was smaller but similar to Castroville. It was also long neglected by the rest of Monterey County. In neighboring Prunedale, the closest thing to a community center was the Prunedale Grange. Situated nearby were Glenn's General Store, Jim Crane's barber shop and Deaton's Feed Store. It was all that Prunedale needed for that time. While the communities of North Monterey County were not destitute by any means, life was not always easy. Pollution was not a major concern. Putting food on the table and paying the bills was far more pertinent. Krishun channeled the hopes of those who saw the benefits that a larger tax base and jobs would bring.

The limited county budgets and programs left North County wanting for government services. The planned industrial center in Moss Landing and Humble in particular promised an influx of cash and a burst of prosperity for the community. It was not surprising that the opposition from Humble on the Monterey Peninsula was rubbing some North County folks the wrong way. In the minds of many, Carmel and Pebble Beach residents did not think about North County unless they were driving through it. Why did they think it was their business now to tell North County how to run its community?

Many of Krishun's fellow commissioners looked at Humble favorably as well. Charlotte Wilbur doubted if the commission had the legal right to turn down the project if Humble met all the conditions required. Mansfield and Cailotto gave favorable, if somewhat uncommitted nods too. In a welcoming sign to Humble, the commissioners from the Monterey Peninsula appeared open to supporting the refinery.

On the same day the Planning Commission kicked the decision to July, the Planning Commission for the city of Monterey responded favorably to Santa Cruz's request for an air pollution control district. It was one of the many steps that year that would eventually establish area-wide air pollution controls.

The Santa Cruz City Council also met and sent another letter to Monterey County officials, urging the adoption of air pollution control standards. This was at least the third request from three different government bodies in Santa Cruz County expressing the need for some air pollution control mechanism.

Another event happened the same day in Carmel. The city announced the hiring of a new city attorney. They chose 31-year-old William "Bill" Burleigh. Burleigh, in his new role, would play a significant part in combatting Humble later in the year.

7

A PARADE OF SMOKESTACKS

May 17 – June 4, 1965

*"One oil refinery can't make much difference. But one begets
a second, and a third is the symbol of heavy industry."*

C.D. Wheelock, Carmel resident

In mid-May, a week after the Planning Commission delayed its decision to July, one of the leaders of Citizens for Clean Air took its case straight to the stockholders of Standard Oil of New Jersey, Humble Oil's parent corporation. Standard Oil hosted its 83rd annual stockholders' meeting in San Francisco. Addressing the convention of 2,000 stockholders was Charles Kramer of Pebble Beach, who stressed that the people of Monterey County were "violently opposed to this refinery" in Moss Landing. It appears from Kramer's contact with Jersey Standard, as the company was referred to in shorthand, that he was able to deliver his speech at the meeting because he was a Standard Oil stockholder.

"Regardless of the outcome of this matter, control restrictions and regulations are now being drawn. If these regulations are not sufficiently strong, Humble or someone else will lead the parade of smokestacks that will finally blight an area that the state and nation can ill afford to have despoiled," asserted Kramer.

"If, on the other hand, your great corporation with its fine scientists, technicians and executives would cooperate with us to see that these regulations are such that no one, either now or in the future, could blight this beautiful area you will indeed have performed a great public service."

It was enough to get Michael Haider, chair and Chief Executive Officer of Standard Oil of New Jersey, to respond that "we are not interested in destroying one of the most beautiful areas of this country ... whether or not a refinery is permitted is a question for local citizens to decide. The only thing we can do is assure the local citizens that if a refinery is built it will not cause a smog situation or pollute the air or water as many people fear." Haider went on to claim that new refineries in Jamaica, Norway and Wales proved that pollution is a "very minor matter." Kramer refuted those words, stating that there was not any pollution damage yet because the Jamaica refinery was only recently constructed.

Kramer did not ask for Humble to pull its permit. That approach was in line with many in the opposition, which was somewhat divided between those who wanted no oil refinery at all, and those who wanted controls strict enough that pollution would not be a concern. Of course, Humble had promised all along that it would abide by any pollution regulations imposed by Monterey County.

At the Standard Oil stockholders' meeting, Kramer traveled to San Francisco with A.G. Michaud, president of Del Monte Properties, then the name of the company operating the Pebble Beach resorts. They had a brief discussion with Carl Reistle, chair of Humble Oil and Charles Johnson, the oil company's president. Both men agreed the meeting was too short to accomplish anything, but it was the first of an unknown number of encounters between Humble officials and Humble opponents. At their meeting, Kramer and Michaud pressed Humble to support the idea of an air pollution control district. Clearly, they were aware that Humble might not be stoppable so they needed to create the proper controls.

"We want to seek the assistance of Standard Oil of New Jersey in formation of a multi-county air pollution control district with rigid controls over air pollution and the ability to enforce those controls," said Kramer.

The request went nowhere. However, whether it was the meeting with Reistle and Johnson or encounters with stockholders or other Standard Oil officials, the meeting appears to have been a watershed moment for how Citizens for Clean Air and other opponents would move forward. The belief that

Humble's activities could be controlled declined, and support for an outright rejection of the permit grew.

Kramer said that legal opinion obtained by the opponents confirmed that if Humble built its refinery, "It would be politically and legally impossible to prohibit other dirty industry from coming in."

Monterey Mayor Minnie Coyle with Charles Kramer in a 1965 Monterey Peninsula Herald photo.
Courtesy of the Monterey Herald

The questionable legal advice to which Kramer referred lacked legs to stand on. The Board of Supervisors had direct control over land use issues. They could put a moratorium on future oil refineries, establish pollution controls that dirty industries could not meet, and shrink or even do away with the rest of the industrial zoning. Humble had spread disinformation about its "sweet-smelling" refinery, but the opponents were not immune to some fear tactics or exaggerations themselves.

There was widespread acceptance from all sides that the Monterey Bay area was something special and deserved all due protection. Rachel Carson's book *Silent Spring* had only been published a few years earlier in 1962. The environmental movement was stirring to life. The people of the Monterey Bay were at its forefront. Unwittingly, Humble had become a catalyst for the environmental movement in the region and one of the first local uprisings of the national environmental movement now taking shape. Whether or not a refinery was built, the controversy had unleashed a new awareness, a juggernaut for conservation that could never again be denied. For the first time since industrial zoning came to Moss Landing, people were beginning to question its appropriateness.

"One oil refinery can't make much difference. But one begets a second, and a third is the symbol of heavy industry generally, of more cars, more people, more dust, more gas, more smoke, in short of the upward creeping, stinking concentration of smog," wrote C.D. Wheelock of Carmel in a letter to the editor. "The basic concern here is the zoning of great areas around Moss Landing for heavy industry and a deepwater port."

The strong support that existed after World War II for an industrial park in Moss Landing was losing its appeal. PG&E and Kaiser Refractories crept in, but a foreboding feeling was growing. Those who felt that Humble would destroy the environment on its own were very few. When Humble officials said it would not do that, they were correct. This was especially so for a 50,000-barrel refinery, quite small by industry standards. What else would come? More refineries? Other heavy industries belching smoke and fumes? Monterey County finally had entered a debate on the appropriateness of industrialization in one of its most environmentally sensitive areas.

The Monterey Bay area had already undergone significant change since the arrival of Europeans. One of the obvious changes was the damming and channeling of the Salinas River in the 19th century. Eventually, human activity irreversibly changed the river's course so that it emptied next to the community of Marina instead of its historical path a mile north of the Elkhorn Slough. The steady flow of freshwater into the slough and along the eastern slopes of the dunes was gone. Now the only freshwater entering the slough came from runoff on the canyons fronting the slough's watershed. The diversion of the Salinas River had a profound effect on the Elkhorn Slough and the uniquely mixed fresh and saltwater environment that existed there. The Salinas River, known for one of the country's largest subsurface flows as described in Anne Fisher's classic *The Salinas: Upside Down River*, helped maintain a freshwater barrier between the Pacific Ocean and inland shallow freshwater aquifers. This never was a problem until agriculture and urban development began extensive pumping. As the water level dropped, saltwater intrusion was inevitable. The first signs of saltwater intrusion began in 1946, just as the idea of turning Moss Landing into an industrial center began to germinate. Humble had plans to use a massive amount of freshwater for its refinery. This was a huge future problem, but an issue not emphasized as strongly as pollution in the refinery debate.

Residents whose homes bordered the slough, like Nita Wells of Hudson Landing Road, would bitterly complain of the saltwater that relentlessly claimed a few feet of her property every year. She feared the loss of her well as her house's foundation buckled and vegetation slowly died from the encroaching saltwater marsh. Wells, a conservative Republican, was hardly an environmentalist, but she noted that what had been done in the name of industry would eventually make her home uninhabitable.

Humble's opponents were primarily from the well-to-do enclaves of Pebble Beach, Carmel, Carmel Valley and Carmel Highlands. These were people of influence, not just in Monterey County, but across the nation. They had wealth. They had contacts. This allowed the opponents an ability to generate influence far in excess of the minority view point they represented in Monterey County. If the opposition had not been some of the most influential and wealthy people in the country, it may have sputtered and died. Although the opponents may not have been in the majority, they did have enormous political power. They demanded to be heard. However, there is little doubt from polls, letters to the editor, public gatherings, petitions, unofficial surveys and newspaper interviews of people on the street, that a clear majority of Monterey County supported Humble. That set the stage for a political conflict perhaps never seen before, but certainly not since.

On their return from San Francisco, Kramer and Michaud with Col. Allen Griffin, president of the *Monterey Peninsula Herald*, and Gordon Sinclair, managing editor of the *Santa Cruz Sentinel*, announced that they were forming another group. This group did not specifically address Humble but advocated for the formation of a regional air pollution control district. The presence of Col. Griffin, as everyone called him, was significant. Griffin was a highly influential and respected member of the community who founded the *Monterey Peninsula Herald* in 1922. A decorated war hero who served and was wounded in both World Wars, he held every military decoration of valor except for the Congressional Medal of Honor. At the time he started the *Herald*, the Peninsula was known as a money-losing area for newspapers. In a few years, Griffin began running the paper in the black. Despite being a lifelong Republican, Griffin was tabbed by Democratic President Harry Truman three times to serve international economic agencies for the federal government. Griffin also was known for his efforts at the preservation of old buildings and environmental conservation. Joining forces with Michaud and Sinclair on the district formation lent weight to the endeavor.

Michaud announced that he would present the need for an air pollution control district to the Monterey County Board of Supervisors "now, and not after Humble or any other concern has started." Michaud declared that Sinclair would make a similar presentation to the Santa Cruz County Board of Supervisors with a third presentation to the San Benito County Board of Supervisors at a later date sought to consolidate the proposal in the tri-county area. The suggestion of a multi-county air pollution agency now sat firmly under public consideration.

The city of Monterey's Planning Commission then stepped back into the fray, urging that the county not issue a permit for Humble until an air pollution control district existed. Michaud had appeared at the city's planning commission meeting where he again argued for an air pollution control district so that "rigid standards" would be in place when an industry applied for a permit. Michaud noted that codified pollution standards for all industry were preferable over citizen outrage for each permit application. Days later, Monterey's call for an air pollution control district gained more support by a unanimous vote from the Peninsula Area Planning Commission, which comprised the various planning commissions of the Monterey Peninsula.

Michaud's next appearance was at the Board of Supervisors where, as chair of the Committee to Form an Air Pollution Control District, he urged the supervisors to pressure the state legislature to adopt legislation allowing such a district. Michaud argued that current state law prevented the supervisors from forming a district unless pollution exists to an "unfortunate degree."

"Unfortunately, the present air pollution control act does not authorize preventive measures ... thus, the horse must have fled the barn before the legislature allows you to lock the door," continued Michaud, " ... our area, in the opinion of our finest meteorologists, possesses the only clean air shed between Canada and Mexico."

The PG&E smoke stacks at "Mighty Moss" were raised to their current 500-foot height in 1965.
Kathryn McKenzie

Humble's attorney Paul Hamerly stated that Humble was not against an air pollution control district because the company realized that some of the most "stringent anti-pollution regulations in the country" were going to be placed on the refinery. In response, the Board of Supervisors passed the matter to county counsel for legal review and for a closer look by the county's Air Pollution Control Advisory Committee and Health Department. The growing debate over an air pollution district then caught the attention of State Senator Fred Farr of Carmel, who announced that he would try to incorporate the changes into a bill before the legislature and attempt to fast-track the changes into law.

While the Monterey Peninsula was organizing resistance to Humble's plans, the Castroville Chamber of Commerce lined up in support of its potential new neighbor with a petition drive. The chamber claimed it could gather at least 1,000 signatures quite easily. As with other supporters of the project, the petition expressed confidence that "the county will impose whatever controls are required to insure that there will be no air pollution problems arising from this refinery."

Citizens for Clean Air responded by submitting a petition of 5,000 signatures against Humble's permit. Their petition claimed the exact opposite position of the Castroville Chamber of Commerce. The anti-Humble petition stated that approval of the refinery would bring uncontrollable air and water pollution. Citizens for Clean Air, whether organizing at the local level or confronting Humble Oil at a stockholders meeting, stepped up their efforts. They moved to contact Laurance Rockefeller, chair of the White House Conference on Natural Beauty, and Interior Secretary Steward Udall. (A twist of irony here was that Rockefeller, a major conservationist, was the grandson of Standard Oil co-founder John D. Rockefeller.)

However, the decisive battle over Humble rested in Monterey County. As the *Santa Cruz Sentinel* expressed it, the debate over Humble's project was an "oil refinery war." It involved both sides claiming the support of public opinion. Just as competing experts faced off in public, so now there were competing petitions. These efforts attempted to influence the coming Monterey County Planning Commission meeting and, ultimately, the Board of Supervisors.

Although months away from a vote, by the end of May the members of the Board of Supervisors appeared to have made up their minds ahead of a still undecided Planning Commission. Supervisor Tom Hudson, who represented Pebble Beach, Carmel, Carmel Valley and areas south, was dead-set against Humble. Supervisor Andy Anderson, who represented the rest of the Peninsula including Monterey and Seaside, had a more divided constituency, but his vote was against Humble as well. In the rich agricultural lands of South Monterey County, there was no organized opposition yet, and Supervisor Harold Henry announced his support for Humble. Supervisor Arthur Atteridge of Salinas, a stronghold of pro-Humble supporters, also backed Humble. That left the supervisors divided at 2-2.

North Monterey County Supervisor Warren Church, in whose district Humble was to build, also announced that he had made up his mind. Mysteriously, Church refused to reveal what that decision was. He would keep that decision to himself right up to the vote. His silence fueled considerable speculation.

8

A PLAN FOR PROSPERITY

*"Moss Landing has much better facilities ... for industrial
expansion and would leave the Peninsula free to develop its
recreational facilities."*

Major General (Ret.) Robert McClure, Pebble Beach resident

As increasing opposition to the Humble Oil refinery grew, many old-time
politicos in the county could not have been more surprised. What was
happening in 1965 was a world apart from just a decade earlier in 1956, when
the Board of Supervisors, after years of considerable study, put together what
was a widely praised development plan for Moss Landing and the surrounding
communities. These observers, including many staffers in county departments
who helped write the development plan, were blindsided by the opposition,
as was Humble.

Since the 1930s, industry had been encouraged around the bay. The booming sardine industry on Monterey's Cannery Row eventually expanded to the
other major port in the county—Moss Landing. Directly to the west of the
PG&E power plant were canneries and sardine reduction plants, for grinding
fish waste into fertilizer, on a small strip of land known as "The Island." By
1944, Monterey and Moss Landing were processing 70,000 tons of sardines a
year. Unfortunately, just as Moss Landing was beginning its sardine boom, the
sardines stopped cooperating. They disappeared from Monterey Bay, ruining
the viability of not only the canneries in Monterey, but more recently built

plants in Moss Landing. Sardines became just another story in the boom and bust cycle that had marked Moss Landing its entire existence.

When industrialist Henry Kaiser located his plant there during World War II, hope again stirred for Moss Landing. During World War II, Kaiser Refractories made munitions for the war effort from processed dolomite at its quarry north of Salinas at Natividad. The quarry was established in 1942 and played a critical role in the development of a planned industrial complex for Moss Landing. After the war, the plant made bricks, and it employed a steady workforce. In December 1944, wartime legislation declared the dredging of Moss Landing Harbor as urgent for "the interest of increasing the fish catch in the area (Monterey Bay)." In 1946, the U.S. Army Corp of Engineers dredged and widened the Moss Landing harbor, allowing saltwater to flow freely into Elkhorn Slough which had become increasingly brackish after the Salinas River altered its course decades earlier. Pacific Gas & Electric, one of California's major electric companies, arrived in 1947 to construct a power plant that would eventually become the second largest fossil fuel power plant in the world. For the 1970s, PG&E planned a nuclear power plant for the area, maybe even three. Next came Standard Oil of California in the 1950s, developing a tank farm to store and distribute petroleum products. Texaco followed with more tanks of its own. Even the fishing industry made a comeback because the all-weather port enticed fleets from as far away as Alaska. Sport fishing "party boats" increasingly visited Moss Landing as well. The remaining canneries even found a bit of new life with new products like mackerel in tomato sauce and pickled squid. Slowly, Moss Landing's future began to brighten with industry as its major enterprise.

By the 1950s, the Moss Landing Harbor Commission asked the county for a master plan for the development of Moss Landing. On September 18, 1956, the Monterey County Board of Supervisors approved a massive area development plan that placed Moss Landing as the center of a new industrial economy to supplement tourism and agriculture. With areas zoned for indus-trial, recreational, residential and commercial development, the plan promised something for everyone. It encompassed 60 square miles from Watsonville to Castroville and from the Pacific Ocean to Highway 101. The current Highway 1 was to be turned into a frontage road with its bridge removed. A relocated Highway 1 would run to the east, crossing over the slough approximately 1½ miles to the east of the old Highway 1 bridge, and then merge into Castroville. The new bridge would be a 60-foot high span so ocean-going ships could navigate deep into the slough.

To the east of the slough, a new major road would replace much of winding Elkhorn Road. It would serve the industrial areas planned along the railroad tracks that extended from Moss Landing to Castroville. To the west, a new scenic road would hug the coast all the way to the Salinas River. Past the planned industry along the slough banks, as the slough winds towards Pajaro, were plans for recreational and urban development with residential zoning to the east. To the northwest, a large recreational lagoon fed by a channel from Moss Landing harbor and another from the mouth of the Pajaro River would extend inland about one mile at Zmudowski Beach. Another industrial zone was planned for the Pajaro area.

In this photo, taken as part of an EPA project in 1972, the PG&E plant looms over fishing boats in Moss Landing Harbor.
Environmental Protection Agency

The Planning Commission assured the county that the master plan was the result of a long process, "not hastily drawn," with ample community input and widespread support. The report stated:

"At the public hearings held by the commission no opposition was expressed indicating the results of a careful program of explaining and informing all interested groups, organizations, or individuals who are interested to the extent of taking the necessary time and effort to study the plan."

Calling for the "great potential" of the Moss Landing area to be realized, the report explained how it broadened its area to go much beyond Moss Landing.

"As the study progressed, it became increasingly evident that the study area should be enlarged to encompass a broader area; that to prepare a comprehensive, long term general plant the impact of industrialization upon the surrounding area should be considered, analyzed and fit into the pattern of future overall development."

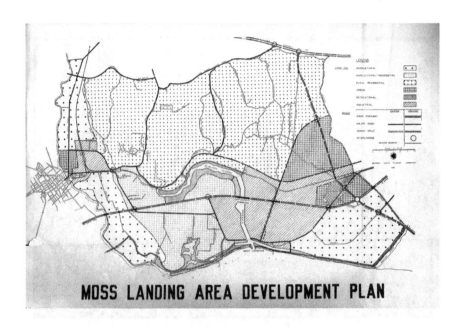

MOSS LANDING AREA DEVELOPMENT PLAN

This 1956 map shows Monterey County's plan to create a major industrial area in North Monterey County with Moss Landing as a focal point.
Elkhorn Slough Foundation

The 1956 master plan was three years in the making. That a development of this proportion and length of study would not receive a single voice of opposition to its basic premise is astounding. Some even called for its immediate adoption. The universal acceptance speaks to the prevailing attitude then that industrial development was a good thing. Other than those who suggested minor detail changes, the only opposition to any part of the plan was the moving of Highway 1 to the east. They were mainly concerned about the removal of the current low-level bridge over the slough.

At the forefront of the new plan were Monterey Peninsula representatives. One of the leading proponents was retired Major General Robert McClure of Del Monte Properties. Also strongly backing the Peninsula supporters and others throughout the county was North Monterey County Supervisor Chester Deaver, who was elected in 1952. In the 1964 election, Deaver's campaign literature focused on his major role in creating a plan for industrial growth at Moss Landing, including the altering of Highway 1 along the Elkhorn Slough and the future high-level bridge span over the slough.

"From a standpoint of forward thinking, Moss Landing has much better facilities than Monterey Bay for industrial expansion," McClure said, "and would leave the Peninsula free to develop its recreational facilities."

With Monterey Harbor designated as a place for recreational boating and swimming, the plan was for the Harbor Commission to acquire title to Elkhorn Slough, secure federal funding and reclaim thousands of acres for industrial development. Ships would enter the harbor and the slough, with convenient access to the railroad and highway.

"I'm positive this development will would benefit the whole county," said McClure.

This expansion was also pushed because the Moss Landing Harbor Commission was cash-strapped. It had debts and was not paying them. In 1946, the state granted the Harbor Commission the tidelands area in trust for 10 years. Those areas were to be developed and opened to the public within that period or revert to the state. In 1949, the commission faced litigation from the San Francisco Bridge Company for nearly $15,000 in unpaid bills for dredging. A five-year extension was negotiated, further spurring the development plan. By 1954, the commission was asking both the county and the primary industry association in the county, Monterey County Industrial Development Inc., for money to pay its bills. The county, under Supervisor Deaver's motion, granted a $10,000 loan to the district. A week later, it was found that state law forbids loans to harbor districts, so the commission continued scrounging for money.

As if that was not bad enough, the five members of the Harbor Commission began to squabble among themselves. Two directors, Roland Roberts and Paul Rubis, resigned at the end of 1955. Roberts and Rubis accused the other three board members of "non-cooperation" and "improper conduct of meetings," according to Robert Blohm, chair of the commission. Further adding to the intrigue was that Blohm had faced off against Deaver in 1952 in a losing bid for the supervisorial seat. Some of the problems among the commissioners arose over a disputed hiring of a public relations firm. Rubis and Roberts signed the contract with another director, Daniel Rhoades, but then Rhoades asked to have his name removed. The bickering continued until Rubis asked for support from the board, but Blohm, Rhoades and a third director, Joseph Kirby, pushed back, charging Rubis of trying to make them "yes men." Kirby, Rhoades and Blohm then resigned in an effort to get a new board appointed by the governor that would work better together.

"I'm tired of this wrangling and I want no more," said Blohm, but he was back on the board by the following year. Amidst this chaos, it is also surprising that one of Monterey County's largest and most ambitious developments had such widespread support.

Desperate for funds for its current bills and future development that included a deepwater port, the Harbor District expanded from Moss Landing and Castroville to include all of supervisorial districts 1 and 2, thereby tripling its tax base. The scheme proposed to the voters was eventual lower property taxes as the industrial and commercial activities of the Harbor District grew. At the forefront of this drive was Myron "Doc" Etienne. Etienne would eventually join with Paul Hamerly and Harry Noland, the Salinas law firm that handled Humble Oil's application for a refinery permit. Etienne had a colorful life himself as a founder of the Monterey Jazz Festival and part owner of the laboratory that was formerly the haunt of Ed Ricketts, John Steinbeck's great friend and model for "Doc" Ricketts in the author's novels. Etienne, a long-time activist with the California Rodeo in Salinas, is in the ProRodeo Hall of Fame.

With a larger district, Etienne and his allies argued that a deepwater port could flourish with ocean-going ships navigating straight up the Elkhorn Slough. Up to six ocean-going ships could be moored at Moss Landing with a harbor for small boats, the proponents argued. Grandiose proposals were presented, including discussion of development on up to 48,000 acres of the Monterey County countryside. Etienne reported what experts had considered for years—that Moss Landing had the potential of being a better harbor than the one in Los Angeles.

However, in less than ten years, universal support for the Moss Landing Area Development Plan would fracture, with the ironic plot twist that the Monterey Peninsula would lead the charge to oppose Humble, claiming it was an inappropriate place for an oil refinery. The truth was that it was the Monterey Peninsula that felt Moss Landing was the place to sequester all the dirty and stinky businesses like canneries and factories. In 1956, the Monterey Peninsula saw Moss Landing as a key linchpin in its own plan to become a recreational and tourist haven. By 1965, the coming industrial complex that the Monterey Peninsula helped create was abhorred as an unimaginable, out-of-control Frankenstein's monster.

9

WHITE KNIGHTS OF THE

DUCHY

June 3 – 28, 1965

"These white knights, known as the Citizens for Clean Air,
have adopted a battle plan of misrepresentation and delay."

The Salinas Californian

While efforts to create an air pollution control district slowly gathered steam and support, acrimony between the pro and anti-Humble advocates also gained momentum. The *Salinas Californian* lamented that when the July 28 Planning Commission meeting took place, more than five months would have passed since Humble first expressed its desire to build a refinery. The *Californian* editors claimed this was long enough, and expressed concerns the Planning Commission might delay a decision yet again. The *Californian's* ire was broad and damning. The editorial board blamed the Planning Commission for doing little in the first months to address its proclaimed lack of information about Humble's project.

The *Californian* had another beef too. William O'Connell, the county's hired expert on refineries, charged $250 a day, but the county had a budget of only

$1,000 for his services. The *Californian* called it a "farcical misunderstanding" between the Planning Commission and the Board of Supervisors that left O'Connell fewer than four days to prepare a report on the refinery and suggestions for adequate controls. However, the newspaper reserved its harshest words for the Monterey Peninsula and Citizens for Clean Air.

"Postponement and further postponement is the key to the petition-waving campaign against the oil company being conducted by the white knights of the duchy known as the Monterey Peninsula," fumed the *Californian*. "These white knights, known as the Citizens for Clean Air, have adopted a battle plan of misrepresentation and delay."

The *Californian* then accused the advocates of the air pollution control district as utilizing that idea for another delaying tactic against Humble. Anti-Humble proponents were demanding that a district be formed before Humble received its permit. While not opposing the idea of such a district, the *Californian* emphasized that months or years could pass before an air pollution control district was operational, and Humble would not be willing to wait that long.

O'Connell issued preliminary conclusions shortly after the *Californian*'s editorial, stating that he intended to suggest changes to the county's pollution laws and to the conditions in the permit for Humble. Those recommendations would primarily be about air pollution as water pollution was best handled by state agencies. O'Connell would not make a recommendation about granting a permit to Humble, but would focus solely on the regulations needed in a permit. He added that the initial conditions suggested by the Planning Commission subcommittee in March were included in his report. The regulations in his report were a mix of those currently in existence in both the Los Angeles and San Francisco areas. One of his key recommendations included the option of pulling the permit if Humble failed to meet the county's conditions.

Director of Sanitation Ed Munson asserted, "They (restrictions) will set levels of intolerance beyond which they (Humble) cannot go."

Humble officials seemed relatively unconcerned about the restrictions proposed by O'Connell. Jack Gardner and George Swisher, two of Humble's prominent engineers regularly making the rounds to drum up support for the project, constantly assured listeners that Humble could comply with any "reasonable" regulations.

"Reasonable," as Swisher said, "does not mean reasonably clean or reasonably dirty. It means complying with regulations that protect plant life, the population, and would preclude smog and objectionable odor."

Gardner and Swisher spoke a good game, even asserting that any odors at the refinery would be no more significant than what one smells when fueling a car at a gas station.

Humble had good reason not to be worried about whatever O'Connell proposed. O'Connell was a known factor in the oil industry. Rumors persisted that he was on Humble's payroll, but it was Standard Oil of California that O'Connell worked for as a consultant, as well as for the California State Senate on water pollution. Munson maintained that it was impossible to find a consultant of O'Connell's caliber that had not been retained by a major oil company.

The rumors did not deter Supervisor Tom Hudson, who had already expressed his opposition to Humble. "I'm thoroughly satisfied that O'Connell is in a good position to give excellent service," Hudson said.

O'Connell knew the oil industry, what its problems were and what was feasible. He was not likely to propose anything radical, although his proposals could be as strict as those currently in use in Los Angeles. However, the oil industry was already complying with those regulations.

What did concern Humble, which Gardner and Swisher unhesitatingly pointed out, was that until Monterey County adopted its own air pollution standards, Humble could not design its refinery. Tentative plans existed, but as Gardner said, "Definitive plans will have to wait a firm decision on the special permit." Ultimately, the demand for detailed refinery plans by the Planning Commission subcommittee fell to the wayside. While Humble prevailed in squelching that request, it was O'Connell's recommendations for pollution controls which helped alleviate that need.

Later in June, as O'Connell's budget ran dry, the Board of Supervisors reluctantly decided to grant another $1,000 for his expertise. Supervisors Arthur Atteridge and Warren Church hesitated to increase the budget for this, but eventually agreed to another $1,000 and no more. That secured O'Connell for the duration of the Planning Commission's review.

As the controversy dragged on, opponents found a new avenue to attack Humble. They sought to hurt Humble in the pocketbook by refusing to sign up for the company's credit cards. Slightly less than a year into the future, this tactic would go further when credit card holders of Humble's parent company, Standard Oil of New Jersey and its various companies, began cutting up their credit cards and mailing them in. Opponents also spread word of Standard Oil of New Jersey's fines for polluting waters on the East Coast and that the refineries there were not as pleasant-smelling as the one Humble claimed it could build in Moss Landing.

To circumvent criticism that opposition to Humble rested solely in the Monterey Peninsula, Charles Kramer formed a new anti-Humble organization named Salinas Valley Citizens for Clean Industry. With an ad in the *Californian*, Kramer raised questions about crop damage, a smog-prone Salinas Valley, health concerns, the failure of restrictions to control smog in Los Angeles and the concern that the arrival of Humble's refinery will entice more polluting industries to Moss Landing. Kramer asked for volunteers and signatures for the anti-Humble petition.

A recent photo of the Chevron Richmond refinery, which in 1965 was visited by the Monterey County supervisors on a fact-finding tour.
Courtesy of Audiohifi under Creative Commons license

Kramer and Humble's Jack Gardner and George Swisher faced off during this time at the Monterey Peninsula Junior Chamber of Commerce. Again, Humble representatives maintained that the oil company's operations would exceed any "reasonable standards for air and water cleanliness." Swisher, of Humble's manufacturing division, also emphasized that Humble has "no smoke but also cleans up its other elements."

"We certainly don't want to have to explain to the Board of Directors why a $50 million investment has been shut down," Swisher said regarding the pending regulation that Humble be closed it if violated conditions.

Kramer hit back that it was about more than Humble, because "anyone who thinks only in terms about one refinery at Moss Landing is not thinking clearly."

A couple of days later, that was the point from Matthew Walker, legal counsel for the San Francisco Bay Area Air Pollution Control District. Speaking to the area's members of the League of California Cities at the Outrigger Restaurant in Monterey, Walker predicted, "it is certain that other industries will follow. If you decide they will come in, you will have an industrial complex."

However, Walker embraced the notion that pollution from the refinery was controllable. Contrary to the expert opinion offered by a representative of the Los Angeles Air Pollution Control District, Walker said that there had been success in the last ten years controlling contaminants in the San Francisco Bay area. "I live within less of a mile of one large refinery. That refinery has been brought under control," said Walker.

He also expressed that Humble's choice of the Moss Landing property was an excellent selection: "There is a site there that is probably ideal for a refinery." Walker urged that people pressure the Board of Supervisors to impose controls. The proper ones, he said, would allow residents to live as close as 1,500 feet to the refinery. Walker did warn that efforts to combat pollution in the San Francisco Bay area were "dreadfully expensive" and Monterey County should not expect it to be "easy." Walker stressed that the real issue with Humble "is in the province of planning—not air pollution control."

In another development, the fear that "dirty industry breeds dirty industry," became a bit more real with the announcement that Standard Oil of California intended to begin oil exploration in the Monterey Bay. "It appears to me that Standard Oil of California is aware of the possibility that a refinery will be available in this area," warned Kramer. Gus Bauman, another major figure in Citizens for Clean Air, took that concern a step further, suggesting that now was the time to zone out all dirty industries: fat rendering; hog raising; junk yards; acid, explosive and fertilizer manufacturing; slaughterhouses; and oil refineries. Different versions of that proposal would occasionally pop up with only incremental success over the years.

With the Planning Commission meeting weeks away, both sides tried to chip away at each other's position. A whirlwind of activity sent almost daily news stories to the media. The Vietnam War, the space race and struggle for civil rights took a back seat in local newspapers' pages as Humble was on the minds of everyone in the Monterey Bay area, especially those in Monterey County. The debate ping-ponged from one argument to another and the newspapers filled up with letters to the editors. Some letter writers claimed they fled Southern California to get away from the smog and did not want it to happen here. Others spoke of the economic benefits the area would receive. In another case, an independent petroleum geologist from King City, who once lived near ten refineries in Los Angeles, stated that he never witnessed smog unless it blew over from the cars creating it. If there were any newspaper readers still sitting on the fence on the Humble matter, they must have been overwhelmed and confused by the conflicting information being bandied about.

At one of the earlier Planning Commission meetings, a discussion arose about visiting the San Francisco Bay area refineries. Finally, in mid-June, four members of the Planning Commission, Keith Evans, Daniel Krishun, Perry Henderson and Leon Stutzman, with four county employees—Assessor Don Stewart, Planning Director Ed DeMars, Deputy Counsel Roy Anderson and Sanitation Director Ed Munson, plus pollution consultant O'Connell—visited the refineries to find an almost surreal scene amid the trip.

The nine visited a massive 1,100-acre Chevron refinery first built in 1896 but which had been rebuilt under modern regulations. In the center of the refinery site sat a 160-acre recreation area that included a bowling alley, yachting, archery and three outdoor swimming pools. The group expressed surprise at the country club-like setting at the refinery.

"When we went through, people were sunbathing," DeMars said, adding that "It was quite clean."

In Pacific Grove, the City Council called for the formation of an air pollution control district for all of Monterey Bay. As with some of the other bodies that injected their opinion, the council asked Monterey County to withhold granting a permit to Humble until the strong new regulations were in place.

At the Salinas City Council, a different story played out. Vince Moore, executive director of Monterey County Industrial Development, recounted a trip to Oahu where he witnessed a new oil refinery in operation not far from Waikiki Beach in Honolulu.

"Agricultural fields came right up to the property," said Moore. "Their appearance is the same as I saw in the rest of the islands. I talked to one or two of the agriculturists. They found no fault with the plant ... This plant is a very fine, clean operating plant. I sniffed around and could find no odor."

Moore was not the only resident in the Monterey Bay area to find the Honolulu refineries perfectly acceptable. Erle Byer of Watsonville wrote of visiting the same refinery: "Our group enjoyed a Coke and explanation of the plant in the well-landscaped patio adjoining the offices and the crews' change rooms. For all practical purposes we could have been in the gardens of the Hawaiian Village or Chin Ho's Shangra La."

Monterey County Industrial Development also presented a progress report which counted that since 1951, 28 new industries had arrived in Monterey County with a payroll of $21 million. These industries added $700,000 to the tax base. The report also noted that all the benefits these industries created paled in comparison to what Humble offered. By itself, Humble promised to add $1 million to the county tax base. Around this time, Moore and Monterey County Industrial Development announced a petition drive in support of the refinery.

"A small group of people from one section of the Monterey Peninsula are at it again in an attempt to block industrial growth in Monterey County," Moore explained in a letter to Monterey County Industrial Development members. "Through misleading advertisements, write-ups and statements taken out of context, this group has caused much confusion and misunderstanding."

To the north, the Santa Cruz County Board of Supervisors heard an appeal from *Santa Cruz Sentinel* editor Gordon Sinclair, representing the Committee to Form an Air Pollution Control District, who urged supervisors to act in the growing call for a district for the tri-county area. Sinclair said this was not directed at Humble, but "to establish effective safeguards for clean air in the Monterey Bay area" for the future. The Santa Cruz supervisors expressed concern that the Monterey Bay area could become a "a pocket of smog" similar to Los Angeles. The supervisors voted in favor of the request.

Back on the Monterey Peninsula, the Monterey Chamber of Commerce called a special meeting to take up the Humble and air pollution control district debate. Humble attorney Hamerly and, once again, Citizens for Clean Air's Kramer, who seemed to be everywhere, faced off again before the chamber. Neither man presented anything new as directors raised pointed questions regarding the tourist industry. While Hamerly denied that pollution would reach the Monterey Peninsula, he agreed that if it did, the result would be disastrous for tourism.

Gordon Reid, one of the chamber's directors and a former petroleum distributor turned restaurateur, stressed that "if you have been around the refinery business at all, you know they attract satellite industries ... We are almost entirely dependent on the visitor industry," Reid continued. "If people have to come into an area, polluted either by eyesores or polluted air or dirty beaches, they will go back."

Kramer emphasized that smaller industries would be less polluting and bring more jobs which made them more desirable than Humble. However, director Wright Fisher pushed back as he claimed that more jobs meant more cars to cause pollution. Another director, Art Siever, noted that Fresno and Stockton had air pollution but no refineries or heavy industries with smokestacks.

The Monterey chamber appeared split on Humble and mulled the issue for a week before deciding on a 9-3 vote to recommend a tri-county air pollution control district in a resolution that made no mention of Humble Oil. Despite not mentioning Humble, Fisher stated that the chamber was asking the county not to grant a permit until an air pollution control district was in place. The three directors voting against the resolution included Reid. All three said the resolution was too weak.

"(The resolution might) kill the stink, but that's all," said Reid. "We are not a depressed area like Alabama. We don't need this sort of charity. We should tell them to take their refinery somewhere else. We want something that fits into our atmosphere."

With support for an air pollution control district growing in acceptance even among Humble supporters, A.G. Michaud of the Committee to Form an Air Pollution Control District appeared before the Monterey County Board of Supervisors again. All the proposed district needed was the blessing of Monterey County for it to be official. Michaud called for "Monterey County to take the lead" and create either a tri-county district or for Monterey County to create one by itself. While Michaud professed either option as desirable, his preference rested with the tri-county option.

Sanitation Director Munson responded that staff did not have a problem with either option, but that it was desirable for Monterey County to form a district by itself. Munson noted that several Monterey County cities, including Salinas, King City and Seaside, developed their own air pollution ordinances in recent years. Carmel and Pacific Grove, two hotbeds of anti-Humble and pro-air pollution control district support, failed to do so. A Monterey County district would establish air pollution standards for all cities in the county whether they had regulations or not.

Supervisors Henry and Atteridge wanted discussion of a district separate from the Humble controversy, with Henry even suggesting that further discussion should come after Humble was resolved. Atteridge noted that studies needed to be conducted on automobile pollution and future population growth from the entire Monterey Bay region spreading pollution into the county's environs. Supervisor Church followed Munson's lead, declaring his support for a district solely under the control of Monterey County. Eventually, the Board of Supervisors decided to kick it down the road for the second time, to July 15, as they directed the county's Air Pollution Advisory Committee to review it.

10

A Tale of Two Newspapers

June 22 – July 20, 1965

"It's news to Salinas Valley residents, but the people on the Monterey Peninsula apparently are being led to believe that that clean gray stuff that rolls in over the valley from the ocean is smog."

The Salinas Californian

As the Fourth of July weekend approached in the summer of 1965, so emerged a new controversy in the Humble Oil affair. This uproar arose over an aerial photograph of Salinas which showed a layer of cloudy haze over the city. The photograph came from Citizens for Clean Air, which had distributed the image around the time of the Monterey Chamber of Commerce meeting a week earlier. The *Monterey Peninsula Herald* ran the photograph on June 22 with the caption: "A Smoggy View of the Salinas Valley." The photograph looked at Salinas from the north as the camera peered toward King City. The layer appeared to hover a few thousand feet above the valley floor.

For those who live in Salinas or most of the Monterey Bay area, grayish matter lingering in the atmosphere is nothing new. It is fog, and in this area of California, especially in the summertime, fog is as omnipresent as the Pacific Ocean. It keeps temperatures low in the summer at the coast while inland areas heat up. However, Citizens for Clean Air claimed that the gray vapor hanging over Salinas in its photograph was not fog, but smog, the dreaded miasma that blanketed the Los Angeles basin and other areas. The group felt this provided strong evidence that Monterey County already was experiencing a smog problem, and Humble's refinery was only going to make it worse.

The *Salinas Californian*, never missing an opportunity to get another dig at the expense of its competitor on the Monterey Peninsula—or its Humble-opposing subscribers—took issue with the photograph. What the *Herald* called smog, the *Californian* called fog.

"It's news to Salinas Valley residents," the *Californian* wrote, "but the people on the Monterey Peninsula apparently are being led to believe that that clean gray stuff that rolls in over the valley from the ocean is smog."

"That's right. Smog. Not fog. They ran a picture in the *Monterey Herald* on June 22 on Page Five to prove it. This picture, after considerable travail from *Californian* engravers, is reproduced on the right from the *Herald*. *Californian* effort to produce a glossy copy were to no avail."

The *Californian* tried more than once to get a copy of the photograph and to find out who the photographer was. What time of day was the photograph taken? Who paid for it? What was the shutter speed? Were filters used? All those questions and a few others were never answered. The *Californian* reported that the *Herald* promised to send a copy to them. When it didn't show, the *Herald* claimed the photograph could not be found. The photograph credit line listed Carmel photographer Al Weber. Weber denied it. The *Herald* said Carmel resident Margaret Smith, an active member of Citizens for Clean Air, provided the photograph and credited Weber.

When the *Californian* contacted Smith, she refused to turn it over or sell a copy to the *Californian*, referring to "a little experimenting" that she and her cohorts were conducting. According to the *Californian*, Smith also declined to provide the name of the photographer. The *Californian* then began to refer to the subterfuge of Citizens of Clean Air as the "Not so Clean Committee on Air."

As the *Californian* mused that the photograph was part of the *Herald*'s campaign to "delay and kill" the Humble project, the newspaper also quoted Salinas Chamber of Commerce president Donald Grothe, who called the use of the photo by Humble opponents as "bordering on the ridiculousness." He then asserted that "'thinking' people" should be able to discern the difference between fog and "non-existent smog." Grothe referred to county Sanitation Director Ed Munson as stating that a smog condition had never existed in Salinas.

*The controversial aerial photo of the Salinas Valley sent to newspapers by Citizens for Clean Air,
which showed an inversion layer that the Monterey Peninsula Herald termed "smog" and the Salinas
Californian called "fog."*
Authors' collection

Sensing that it had caught Humble's opponents in a "blatant falsehood"
about smog, the *Californian*'s editors broadened their attacks in an attempt
to discredit the anti-Humble forces. They noted that the cities at the center
of the opposition—Monterey, Pacific Grove and Carmel—all opted out of
the county's first air pollution regulations in 1960, hardly a badge of honor
for the environmentalism most of the residents were now pushing. Next, the
Californian then called out the anti-Humble supporters for fueling the rumor
that the county's consultant, William O'Connell, was an employee of Humble.
He was not. Lastly, the *Californian* noted that the group seeking a multi-county
air pollution control district was almost entirely composed of people from the
clean air committee seeking to halt Humble. These people, in their anti-Humble
hats, protested loudly against the oil company, but when they put on their
anti-pollution hats, they claimed the need for anti-pollution laws had nothing
to do with Humble. The *Californian* was not buying the specious argument.

Yet the *Californian*'s editors were not without their own misrepresentation of facts, whether intentional or not. The *Californian* referred to the hotly contested industrial project of the 1950s, Firestone Tire and Rubber, and how that led to the establishment of industrial zoning at Moss Landing as the proper place for such development. The Moss Landing Area Development Plan, years in the making, was presented in 1956. Firestone came later. Discussions about Moss Landing as suitable for industry had been going on long before then, even during World War II. However, the *Californian* was correct that not a single person now opposing Humble came forth to oppose the zoning that allowed Humble. Indeed, no one in the county came forward at that time to oppose the industrialization of Moss Landing.

Another turn in the story of the photograph came in a July 20 newspaper ad in the *Californian* by the Salinas Valley farming giant Bruce Church Inc., one of the first agribusinesses to oppose Humble. Its firm opposition was critical in slowly eroding agriculture's initial support for the refinery. In the ad, the grower claimed ownership of the photo. They claimed the photo was taken on January 17, 1963 at 3 p.m. The intent of the photo was not to show smog or fog, but to display the inversion layer that hung over the Salinas Valley. Although the ad does not specifically clarify if it is smog or fog, it implies that it is fog. The controversial photograph remained prominent throughout the Humble debate, including its submittal to the Board of Supervisors during the September 2 meeting for a permit—even then, the photo was presented as evidence of smog.

From the beginning, Bruce Church Inc. called for the county to be selective in choosing industries so as not to damage agriculture. The company went on to express concerns over nitrogen oxides which can cause crop damage and lack an economical means for emission control. The company also noted that the Salinas Valley was the last major agricultural region in the state not affected by pollution. While current pollution levels were not at a level to cause damage, lettuce, spinach and celery would be most vulnerable if pollutants increased. Bruce Church Inc. further stated that the air pollution controls in place in Los Angeles County were incompatible with agriculture. Los Angeles' standards were one of the models considered for future Monterey County air pollution controls. While Bruce Church Inc. was not the sole voice crying of danger in the air, it was one of the most prominent. The company's representative, Dave Williams, spoke at forums wherever he could and to whomever would listen.

Los Angeles, once a rich agricultural county, saw the near total collapse of its agricultural industry in the decades leading up to the 1960s. While the city's explosive growth rapidly turned farmland into residential neighborhoods, it was not solely real estate dollars causing the land to be bought up. In the 1940s, pollution-vulnerable crops such as lettuce, spinach, beets, celery and endives were growing discolored and unsaleable. Onions, carrots and turnips fared better, but the food basket that Los Angeles once was would never again be. Studies by Dr. John Middleton of the University of California, Riverside Citrus Experiment Station confirmed that it was air pollution causing the damage, strangling the crops' ability to absorb water and nutrients. Middleton would arrive in Monterey County in July 1965 to spread his warnings that what happened in Los Angeles could happen in Monterey County.

In the book *Smogtown*, authors Chip Jacobs and William J. Kelly detailed the dramatic changes to Los Angeles agriculture in a short time span:

"Around D-Day, farmers in the area grew 47,800 acres of vegetables; by the time of John Kennedy's assassination in 1963, three-quarters of that acreage had no crops on it. Many growers ... eventually gave up, while others tried rearing resistant goods or moving to unspoiled fields to the north or south. ... In less than twenty years, smog would eradicate ten types of vegetables present in L.A. during WWII. The spectrum of locally grown cut flowers—gladiolus, chrysanthemums—withered with them."

After the *Californian*'s editorial questioning the independence of the Monterey Bay Area Pollution Control District Committee from the Citizens for Clean Air group, the newspaper followed up with a more complete story focusing solely on the two groups' similar membership. As mentioned above, the anti-pollution group was loaded with anti-Humble activists. Besides A.G. Michaud, the group included Charles Kramer, chair of Citizens for Clean Air; Carmel City Councilman Gunnar Norberg and Santa Cruz County Supervisor Robert Burton, who supported delaying the Humble application. In addition, representatives of the primary anti-Humble newspapers also sat on the committee: Allen Griffin and Gordon Sinclair. The committee rounded out with three residents of Monterey, a councilman, an attorney and a doctor, who were identified as not favoring Humble's project. When it was pointed out to Michaud that members like Kramer had somewhat conflicting roles, Michaud responded that some members had dual positions that were "In no way negative—to the desires of Humble to construct a refinery."

Amidst this consortium of Humble opponents, Francis Cislini, publisher of the *Californian*, was invited to join. Cislini, perhaps sensing that he was included as window dressing, declined to take part in the committee until the Humble application was settled. However, the *Californian* expressed support for an air pollution control district if it was not a "tool of a small, ill-informed group of reactionaries."

As efforts to form an air pollution control district continued, the committee behind it also invited Humble to partake in its creation. Monterey attorney Thomas Moore, a member of the committee, wrote a formal invitation to Humble which suggested that the committee's intent had been misunderstood "as an attempt to block the application of your company before the planning commission of Monterey County. This has never been our purpose."

Moore's letter led to a response from R.A. Winslow, assistant general manager of planning and manufacturing for Humble Oil. While the reporters covering the Humble story, primarily Stanley Cloud and Ray March, wrote balanced and fair stories, others at the newspapers wrote the headlines and sometimes tried to redirect the narrative to a different conclusion than the one the journalists expressed in the body of the story. Winslow's response was an excellent example.

"Humble Oil Declines Bid to Join Anti-smog Drive," rang the story's headline in the *Herald*.

"Humble Oil Willing to Aid in Pollution District Formation," blared The *Californian*'s version of the same letter from Winslow.

While the two articles were similar in nature, the editors of the two newspapers took selective bits from their respective articles to bolster their editorial bias. The *Herald*'s headline focused on Winslow's "no permit, no help" comment in his letter. The *Californian*'s headline reflected that once Humble's permit was secured, then Humble was willing to meet with the air pollution district committee on how its officials could be of assistance.

By emphasizing their editorial positions in their headlines, both newspapers either tried to shape their readers' thoughts on a complicated issue or pandered to the cemented positions of a majority of their readers. In fact, as the writers of both articles reported, Humble's position was not a clear no or yes. It was more of a public relations effort to look good while doing little. Winslow's letter included the oft-used word "reasonable." Humble always expressed its openness to "reasonable" controls, but each time a new condition was suggested, Humble stepped back in surprise at the restrictive nature.

In another instance, a subcommittee of the Monterey County Agricultural Advisory Committee took testimony from Dr. Ellis Darley of the Air Pollution Control Center of the University of California, Riverside. Darley had spoken earlier in May at the first Citizens for Clean Air forum. The advisory committee's goal was to present recommendations to the Board of Supervisors. Darley, to no surprise, was not in favor of Humble's project.

On the front page of the July 1 *Monterey Peninsula Herald*, an approximately 60-point headline read, "Smog Danger to Plants Told to County Growers" with the sub-headline "Refinery Effects Weighed." Of course, Humble's project was prominently discussed as a future pollution source. But on page three of the *Salinas Californian*, an article on the very same event read, "Air Pollution Caused Without Industry" with the sub-headline "Agriculture, Population Also Contribute," The two articles were, in fact, written about the same speech. Although in this case the headlines were not strikingly different, the placement of the stories and connotation of the headlines sought to emphasize specific parts of the articles content so as to appeal to the readership of each newspaper. That is not an uncommon policy for any newspaper, except that the amount of coverage and intensity of the Humble debate seemed to amplify this tendency. The *Herald* trumpeted the damaging information about Humble prominently; the *Californian* stuck the story deeper into the paper and created a headline that there were other sources of pollution than industry like Humble.

Most stories in the two main Monterey County newspapers were not slanted by headlines or story placement, but it was not an unusual occurrence to see, especially as the issue began to boil toward a conclusion before the Board of Supervisors. Whether it was the *Herald*, the *Californian* or the two Santa Cruz County newspapers, the *Santa Cruz Sentinel* or *Watsonville Register-Pajaronian*, the reporters covering the Humble story presented even-keeled stories. However, the sometimes-questionable editorial decisions on how to present these stories reflected the intensity of the debate and the new political fissures forming within Monterey County and the entire Monterey Bay area.

The bitter and partisan editorial battles between the *Californian* and *Herald* contrasted significantly with the *Register-Pajaronian*. The Watsonville paper was strongly pro-Humble initially, but as the debate raged, its position weakened to a more neutral stance. By the end, the *Register-Pajaronian* was more aligned with the anti-Humble forces than the pro-Humble groups.

One last observation on the media coverage deserves consideration. Allen Griffin of the *Herald* and Gordon Sinclair of the *Sentinel* sat on the group that sought to establish an air pollution control district. The group claimed to not be anti-Humble, but it was loaded with anti-Humble advocates. That made the presence of Griffin and Sinclair a highly unusual situation. Generally, journalists and editors are supposed to not involve themselves in controversial political issues as it taints the appearance of fair-mindedness. In fact, the only newspaper whose editors followed that journalistic tradition were those of the *Register-Pajaronian*.

In Darley's talk before the Agricultural Advisory Committee, he said that the Monterey Bay area would eventually have smog even without refineries and other industrial plants, although he noted that smog devices on cars could reduce that by 50 percent. A single refinery, controlled to Los Angeles standards, could cause as much pollution as 40,500 cars would generate, in Darley's estimation. As significant as the equivalent of tens of thousands of new cars on the road could be, Darley admitted that a single oil refinery would not substantially alter air quality in the Monterey Bay area.

Darley's talk also confirmed what both pro and anti-Humble forces had been saying from the beginning. Humble's refinery by itself, especially at a 50,000-barrel-a-day production, was not going to ruin the region's air. Indeed, it would be hardly noticeable in that regard. However, Darley insisted, it would expedite the day when air pollution would become a major factor. With an estimated population of 220,000 for Monterey County in 1965, Darley stated that the population would need to grow to 500,000 before significant air quality problems developed. The Humble refinery would add the equivalent of 20,000 people, but that was at its initial size of 50,000-barrels-a-day.

Speaking with Darley at the advisory committee meeting on July 1 was Edward Schuck, who worked at the same air pollution center as Darley, and Victor Osterlii from the University of California Agricultural Extension in Davis. The other two agreed with Schuck in what should have been some welcome news for Humble. In Los Angeles, pollution effects from oil refineries "are no longer a major contributor (to smog)," said Schuck. The real problem, he said, was automobiles.

Darley told the audience that the first signs of air pollution damage would appear in crops, shown in his slides of plants with brown leaves, denuded stalks and stunted growth. While the fear of pollution damaging crops concerned many in agriculture, Darley noted that ag had as much responsibility as industry in dealing with the problem. In particular, Darley mentioned agricultural burning and crop production as sources of air pollution. A new county-wide ordinance regulating air pollution took effect the day of Darley's talk, but it did not apply to agriculture.

"Agriculture should not be given a blanket exemption," expressed Darley. "All segments have to realize their responsibility to the community."

After the testimony by Darley and the other experts, the three-member subcommittee of the Agricultural Advisory Committee gave strong indications that it wanted pollution controls. The subcommittee appeared to support the suggestions made in May by Planning Commissioner Daniel Krishun to allot a certain amount of pollution units to industry and require that industry be located on large tracts of land.

"As I see it, we need some radical changes to live side by side," said William Wilbur, who chaired the subcommittee. "We have a right to be choosey."

The comments by Darley raised more doubts about the credence of the Citizens for Clean Air photograph since Darley, just as Bruce Church Inc. had done, admitted that pollution was not significant at that time. It was a recurrent theme as various other speakers through the Humble debate agreed that the Monterey Bay area had some of the cleanest air in the state. If those statements were true, then it could not be air pollution hanging over the Salinas Valley in the photograph.

With Darley's comments and Bruce Church Inc.'s admission that the photograph was about the inversion layer, it was clear that Citizens for Clean Air were sometimes playing fast and loose with the facts. The white knights of the duchy were not quite so pure after all.

11

A TRIBUTE TO TOURISM

"We shall always remember our visit to Monterey as one of the most agreeable episodes of our lives."

President Rutherford B. Hayes

While everyone feared air pollution, it was most worrisome for those in agriculture who foresaw an end to their way of life if a massive industrial complex formed in Moss Landing. Visions of dying and unsaleable crops danced in the minds of a growing number of Salinas Valley farmers. Humble Oil by itself was not the problem—it was what would follow Humble that heightened the anxiety.

On the Monterey Peninsula, pollution was also a concern, but more pressing than the dread of pollution was aesthetics. The Monterey Peninsula depended on tourism and many tourists came from the north. The primary routes for car travelers from the San Francisco Bay Area were either Highway 1 from Santa Cruz or Highway 156 via Highway 101 to the east. It just so happened that those highways converged about one mile south of Humble Oil's proposed site.

The factories of a 3,800-acre industrial complex spitting smoke into the bay's air would be directed at the line of sight of tourists, who were coming to the Peninsula to escape the urban and industrial development of the Bay Area. Smokestacks and dirty industry would not be a welcoming image to invite people to the playgrounds of the Monterey Peninsula, Carmel Valley, or pristine Big Sur. Monterey County was beautiful, and it traded on that quality. The beauty that begat tourism was being threatened.

There is little disagreement about the visual splendor of the Monterey Bay area. Early tourists began coming to enjoy the ocean vistas and the mild climate of the region in the late 1800s, after Southern Pacific began running trains to the Monterey Peninsula, where visitors would stay at the luxurious Hotel Del Monte and take horse-and-buggy excursions to Pebble Beach.

Hotel del Monte, near Monterey California.

The Hotel Del Monte, built as a destination for train passengers to the Monterey Peninsula, is considered the world's first luxury resort.
Collection of DeGolyer Library, Southern Methodist University

Rutherford B. Hayes was the first sitting president of the United States to visit the area, and he wrote about the hotel and its environs, "We shall always remember our visit to Monterey as one of the most agreeable episodes of our lives. We shall never forget that lovely hotel among the trees and flowers—and the climate: It was the perfect summer's day on the verge of winter."

The Hotel Del Monte was the start of large-scale tourism in the Monterey Bay area, as well as marking the Peninsula as a luxury destination, a label that persists to this day. Pebble Beach continues to draw the rich and famous to its golf courses and restaurants, and Carmel is filled with tycoons' vacation homes. Big Sur is the darling of Instagram users, who long to have dramatic cliffside weddings there.

Tourism, though, has not been a constant in the area's history, and has been pushed and pulled by industry throughout the decades. The overwhelming stench of the Monterey sardine canneries during the 1930s and '40s certainly didn't encourage visitors to come and play by the beach. Having a huge oil refinery, the kind that Humble Oil was proposing for Moss Landing, would also do little to enhance the local environment. Yet that was the type of industry that the movers and shakers of the Monterey Peninsula found acceptable in the 1950s.

Up until the late 19th century, Monterey had been known mainly for its historic adobes and its place in early California lore, when railroad magnate Charles Crocker formed a plan to make the town a sought-after destination that was conveniently reachable by rail. The Hotel Del Monte is considered to be the first true resort complex in the world, with an extensive garden, polo grounds, and later on, in 1897, the opening of an adjacent golf course that is still in use today. It was a clever strategy by California's "Big Four" railroad magnates, who opened the hotel in conjunction with Southern Pacific Railroad's property division, the Pacific Improvement Co. The hotel became the beginning and ending point for 17-Mile Drive, which gave people the opportunity for excursions to the coast. Today, 17-Mile Drive survives as the main road throughout the wealthy enclave of Pebble Beach.

The hotel burned down in 1887, was rebuilt, and destroyed again by fire in 1924. It was constructed again for the third time, opening in 1926. During World War II, the grand old hotel was requisitioned by the U.S. Navy and now headquarters the Naval Postgraduate School. Nevertheless, Hotel Del Monte marked the start of something big for Monterey County. As tourists flocked here in the early days, they discovered the local beaches, the beauty of wild places like Point Lobos, and the charm of the old Carmel Mission, burial place of the father of the California mission system, Father Junipero Serra.

In the early 20th century, developers in Carmel began selling small lots as places to build vacation cottages, and there was a similar effort in nearby Pacific Grove, where the Methodists established a summer retreat for church members. In 1934, Highway 1 was constructed along the Pacific coastline, with the section running through Big Sur and the Carmel Highlands providing breathtaking views for car travelers. Highway 1 would become in itself a popular tourist trek, and Big Sur residents responded by building restaurants and lodges to serve visitors and inspire them with views from rugged cliffs on the continent's edge.

Tourism kicked into high gear during the 1940s and '50s, when Fort Ord and other Monterey County military bases were bustling, and soldiers found time to see the sights on the Peninsula before shipping off to war.

The Santa Cruz Beach Boardwalk has been a major tourist attraction since it was first built in 1907.
This photo is dated 1972.
Environmental Protection Agency

By the 1960s, tourism was without a doubt a vital part of the economy in the Monterey Bay area. Local chambers of commerce had worked hard to promote the beauty of the area, boosted by glamorous photo spreads in *Life*, *Sunset*, and other glossy magazines. Movie stars and singers spent well-publicized honeymoons in Pebble Beach and Carmel, inspiring regular folks to do likewise. Other celebrities escaped the confines of Hollywood and found refuge along the Central Coast, a few becoming beloved figures in their communities for their good works, as Bing Crosby did with his Clambake charity golf tournament, the forerunner of today's AT&T Pro Am. Convention organizers found Monterey and Pacific Grove to be delightful destinations for industry gatherings, close to golf, fine dining and other attractions.

Visitor spending in 1966 alone produced an estimated $50 million for Monterey Peninsula hotels, motels, restaurants and other businesses. Today, close to $3 billion is injected into the Monterey County economy through visitor spending.

The tourist dollar was also important for communities on the other side of the bay in Santa Cruz County. Santa Cruz, too, had been enticing visitors to its beaches since the 19th century, where public bath houses capitalized on the craze of saltwater bathing for health. A saltwater "plunge," a deep indoor pool, at the Santa Cruz Beach Boardwalk was a popular attraction in its early days after the amusement park was built in 1907. Known as the "Coney Island of the West" in its heyday, the Boardwalk still thrills millions of people each year with its vintage wooden roller coaster, a selection of other more modern rides, and an enormous video arcade with games both antique and modern.

In the 1960s, a national movement to revitalize downtown areas led to a considerable amount of change in Old Monterey. Some of the homes and buildings from the past were razed and a new plaza was created near Fisherman's Wharf. Other historic buildings were preserved to create a "Path of History" that helped visitors trace the city's beginnings from the Spanish and Mexican eras.

The Monterey canneries, most of which shut down in the mid-20th century, had undergone their own form of urban renewal when a series of fires broke out along the long-neglected, derelict buildings. But eyes of civic leaders turned toward this waterfront area as a potential tourist attraction, sparked in part by John Steinbeck's 1945 novel *Cannery Row*. Fisherman's Wharf had already transformed itself into a fine dining district with numerous seafood restaurants, as a way to bring commerce back after fishing declined. It seemed natural in the go-go 1960s to make over adjacent Cannery Row into a place that would also bring in tourist dollars.

This new emphasis on tourism spurred Peninsula leaders to direct attention for industrial development to a new place. There, just 20 miles to the north in the little fishing village of Moss Landing, sat a couple of industrial giants already in place, a deepwater port and lots of waterways. It seemed a perfect place to put undesirable industry, except that the builders of Monterey tourism failed to comprehend the vision of a "parade of smokestacks," lying directly across the bay at Moss Landing within full view of the Monterey waterfront. Protecting the aesthetic appeal of the bay views as a precious resource, and one necessary to promoting tourism, was a concept that was only gradually taking hold.

The need to develop tourism even further in the area—and to preserve this pillar of the local economy—would set Peninsula businesspeople, civic leaders and many others solidly against the Humble Oil project.

12

PRELUDE TO BATTLE

July 9 – 21, 1965

*"The installation of an oil refinery (at the mouth of the
Salinas Valley) would be tantamount to a dead cat in your
air conditioning system."*

David Scott, Humble opponent

Early July found new concerns for the residents of Monterey County, starting with the fear of oil drilling in the Monterey Bay. PG&E began to move forward with plans to establish one or more nuclear power plants at Moss Landing. As significant as this was, it still took a back seat to the rapidly changing circumstances of the ever-growing Humble controversy.

These latest twists included the probable closure of Humble's close ally, Monterey County Industrial Development Corp., by an angry Board of Supervisors; a secretive pollster conducting telephone surveys to gauge the public's attitude toward Humble; fishing groups concerned about water quality; a forum involving a national expert on pollution damage to agriculture; more competing petition drives; reconsideration by farmers on the favorability of a refinery; and Monterey County's draft of possible conditions for review by the Planning Commission. This whirl of activity came just as the Planning

Commission prepared to render its decision on Humble's project at the end of the month.

With the previous month's news that Standard Oil of California was investigating oil deposits in Monterey Bay, city councils in Seaside and Pacific Grove passed resolutions calling for the Board of Supervisors not to grant permits for oil drilling in the bay's tidewaters. Although no permits had been submitted for any such endeavor, residents who opposed an oil refinery were on edge with the possibility of further encroachments by industry.

At the Monterey County Industrial Development Corp. installment dinner on July 10 at the Mark Thomas Inn in Monterey, PG&E community development representative Thomas Ludcke called Humble "a most desirable neighbor." The two industrial giants, PG&E and Humble, had plenty of reasons to stroke each other's back. Both had expansion visions and PG&E was a potential customer for Humble's fuels, at least in the short run.

"After 1970, PG&E's plans call for the use of atomic-fueled steam plants in most, if not all major installations," Ludcke said.

Included in these plans were power plants for south Moss Landing, directly across Highway 1 from the proposed Humble refinery. Ludcke stated that PG&E had plans for three power plants in total for the Moss Landing area by 1980, confirmed these facilities would be nuclear powered, and promised that the plants would provide more than 700 new jobs.

The fears of many Humble opponents—that a Humble refinery would open the floodgates to development on the remaining vacant parcels of the 3,800-acre industrial complex—now appeared to have a basis in fact. Ludcke and PG&E did not appear to realize that their ambitious plans, coupled with Humble's own project, were fueling a healthy dose of what would in decades hence be referred to as NIMBYism (Not In My Backyard). Many bay residents simply did not want this much development in their area, and a latent backlash against the Moss Landing Area Development Plan would eventually lead to a burgeoning environmental movement.

In his talk, Ludcke offered rounds of praise for Humble. He listed a long statement of "Humble believes" that sounded as if he were a cheerleader for the oil company instead of an employee of PG&E. Newspaper accounts of the day do not report Ludcke expressing similar platitudes about PG&E.

"Humble believes ... in living by the rules of society; cooperating with government officials and agencies; participating in community and national affairs.

"Humble believes ... that it must manage wisely and scientifically the oil and gas deposits it owns ... Humble recognizes its responsibilities to protect such natural resources as water, forests and wildlife.

"Humble believes in hiring applicants ... on the basis of their qualifications. Qualifications means ability, actual and potential, and has no reference to religion, birthplace, race or color.

"Humble believes ... in providing each employee an opportunity to use his potential to the fullest; in compensating each employee fairly."

Ludcke also praised Monterey County Industrial Development Corp., especially Executive Director Vince Moore, for "quiet and efficient work" in bringing industry to the county. A few weeks earlier, it was Moore who reported at a Salinas City Council Meeting on the excellent conditions surrounding an oil refinery not far from Waikiki Beach in Hawaii and adjacent to agricultural fields that showed no damage from air pollution.

For MCID, this was the apex of its existence. Little did anyone know that this private, county-subsidized business promotion organization was about to become one of the early losers in the Humble affair. In 1963, MCID played an integral role in bringing Humble to Monterey County by aiding in the site selection. But just days after MCID's triumphant July 10 installment dinner, the Board of Supervisors eliminated the county's $15,000 annual funding to MCID, which represented a significant source of the organization's total income. Executive Director Moore, who had a $12,000-a-year salary, said MCID would fold in two years without those funds. Supervisors Tom Hudson and Warren Church took Moore to task on MCID's spending and support of Humble's refinery. The supervisors claimed that the subsidy was intended solely for advertising and not salaries, although Church questioned the appropriateness of even that.

"Should county money be used for lobbying private industry?" queried Church, referring to Moore's efforts to bring Humble to Moss Landing.

The board's vote was 3-1 with Harold Henry wanting to continue the funding, and Arthur Atteridge abstaining. Church's opposition to one of Humble's prominent supporters raised hopes among some Humble opponents that he might cast his lot with Hudson and Andy Anderson in opposing the refinery when it came to a vote by the Board of Supervisors. The *Monterey Peninsula Herald* called the vote "punishment" for MCID's lobbying for Humble.

While county officials had made field trips to refineries over the last few months with more to come, the prospect of a nuclear power plant at Moss Landing prompted the supervisors to pack their bags for yet another trip, this time to Eureka. Anderson, Atteridge and Church, accompanied by Sanitation Director Ed Munson and officials from San Benito and San Luis Obispo counties, toured PG&E's Humboldt nuclear facility. At that time, it was one of only 15 nuclear power plants in the United States.

The media was not invited, and the *Herald*'s Stanley Cloud raised concerns that the trip set a bad precedent for possible Brown Act violations. The Brown Act is a requirement that elected officials conduct public business openly, without deals being cut by a majority behind closed doors. It has gone through many permutations over the years with increasing restrictions. County Counsel William Stoffers claimed that as long as county business was not conducted there was not a violation of the Brown Act even though three supervisors took part in the trip. The laxer rules of the Brown Act of that age allowed Stoffers to make that curious determination even though the trip by the supervisors was solely for county business and constituted a majority of the board.

Beauford T. "Andy" Anderson, in his official portrait as Mayor of Seaside.
City of Seaside

Anderson came back from the two-day trip a strong supporter of nuclear power, declaring the Humboldt facility "spotless" and "quite interesting." He contrasted it with conventional power plants using fossil fuels while emphasizing the cleanliness and safety procedures. Anderson marveled that even in areas of potentially dangerous radiation, the Geiger counter carried by the group did not register.

Anderson was quite interesting himself, lacking the pretension found in many public officials. Although referred to as a "regular guy" who would use homespun analogies to make a point, Anderson was much more than that in at least one respect: He possessed extraordinary courage.

Beauford T. Anderson, known as "Andy" to all, grew up in Wisconsin where he had a trucking business at age 19 hauling milk to cheese factories. Drafted in 1942, he was assigned to the Pacific theater in World War II. At the Battle of Leyte in the Philippines in 1944, he crossed fifty yards through an open field under enemy fire and proceeded to drag two wounded comrades to safety and render first aid until help arrived to carry them away. He was awarded the Bronze Star. That is heroic, but only the beginning of his unparalleled bravery.

On April 13, 1945 at Okinawa, Technical Sergeant Anderson's unit was attacked in a predawn Japanese raid. Most of the soldiers under his command were wounded. He ordered them to safety. What happened next, without regard for his own well-being, is legendary. For his heroism, Anderson would receive the Congressional Medal of Honor, the nation's highest honor for valor. While the citation uses a now-derogatory phrase for Japanese people, it captures the essence of Anderson's bravery.

"He displayed conspicuous gallantry and intrepidity above and beyond the call of duty. When a powerfully conducted predawn Japanese counterattack struck his unit's flank, he ordered his men to take cover in an old tomb, and then, armed only with a carbine, faced the onslaught alone. After emptying 1 magazine at pointblank range into the screaming attackers, he seized an enemy mortar dud and threw it back among the charging Japs, killing several as it burst. Securing a box of mortar shells, he extracted the safety pins, banged the bases upon a rock to arm them and proceeded alternately to hurl shells and fire his piece among the fanatical foe, finally forcing them to withdraw. Despite the protests of his comrades, and bleeding profusely from a severe shrapnel wound, he made his way to his company commander to report the action. T/ Sgt. Anderson's intrepid conduct in the face of overwhelming odds accounted for 25 enemy killed and several machineguns and knee mortars destroyed, thus single-handedly removing a serious threat to the company's flank."

Anderson, a man of enormous modesty, rarely spoke of his heroism, even to those who knew him well. "The real heroes never came back," Anderson once said. After the war, Anderson returned to Wisconsin where he started a floor sanding business, married and then re-enlisted in the Army where he served as a recruiter, eventually ending up in California at Fort Ord. Medically discharged, Anderson started another floor sanding business in Seaside. Eventually, he ran for city council in Seaside where he served two terms, then ran for mayor in 1959 on a reform ticket promising harmony and progress. He was elected to a second term and credited with a substantial list of accomplishments. In typical fashion, he deferred the credit to the "teamwork" of city government.

In 1964, Anderson ran for supervisor in a seven-candidate free-for-all with no incumbent. In the primary, the Seaside mayor ran a surprisingly weak second against retired Army Major Gerald McGrath, who served as a trustee on the Monterey School District Board. McGrath pulled 34% of the vote to Anderson's 22%. McGrath was a relative newcomer to the area and the only one of the seven candidates not to have played a role in Seaside's incorporation a few years earlier. District 4 at the time included Seaside, Del Rey Oaks and most of Fort Ord. It was a working-class area heavily influenced by the presence of the military.

Anderson and McGrath, as the two-top vote-getters, headed to the November election. Anderson worked tirelessly to make up the ground between him and McGrath. In a reversal of the June primary outcome, Anderson narrowly defeated McGrath 4,253 to 4,072.

Anderson took office on January 7, 1965 with the other freshman board member Church, just a little over a month before Humble announced its plans to build an oil refinery at Moss Landing.

While the supervisors took stock of what nuclear power might mean for the county, speculation over the proposed refinery continued to be stoked by a mysterious flurry of phone calls that peppered Monterey County residents with questions about the Humble project. The *Californian* claimed that more than 500 households were called. Besides inquiring about the respondent's demographics, the pollsters also asked how long the person had been a resident of the area. The polltakers did not divulge the identity of their client. When questioned, both Humble's Salinas attorney Paul Hamerly and Citizens for Clean Air chair Charles Kramer denied any knowledge of the phone survey.

With the upcoming July 28 Planning Commission meeting looming, water pollution became a more prominent matter of debate. The California Department of Fish and Game sent a letter to the Planning Commission requesting that conditions be placed on the Humble permit to protect marine life. The letter listed standards and limits for water discharges, and that Humble submit monthly reports to the county. This was followed by two fishing organizations that also backed the Fish and Game letter.

The Monterey County Sportsman's Council and Ike Walton Club threw their support behind the Humble permit on the condition that the fish habitat be protected. The Ike Walton Club in Salinas was the local chapter of a national anglers' group formed under the name of a 17th-century Englishman known for his authorship of *The Compleat Angler*. The two groups asked the county to adopt an ordinance requiring those who killed fish in Monterey County habitats through pollution, contamination or siltation to replace the dead fish with those of equal value.

President Truman presents the Medal of Honor to Andy Anderson for extraordinary bravery during Anderson's service in World War II.

Courtesy of Jim Anderson

The tepid support of the fishing groups belied the concerns of many individual anglers. J. Kleiser of Salinas noted that striped bass caught near the Point Richmond refineries in San Francisco Bay had to be skinned to remove the taste of oil. Even then, Kleiser said, one in four of the fish had to be tossed because of a "crude oil taste."

In Santa Cruz County, representatives of the county Parks and Recreation Committee listened to Carvel Baldwin of Carmel, a retired Los Angeles banker, explain that "there is certain to be water and air pollution with any refinery." Baldwin spoke of Southern California beaches clogged with oil, specifically mentioning that oil tankers had the habit of washing out their empty holds with seawater, depositing a "grimy mess" on the beaches.

Shortly after July 4, the Monterey Bay Division of the League of California Cities met in Carmel. Invited were two significant speakers: Arthur Atkinson, chief deputy control officer of the Los Angeles County Air Pollution Control District, and Dr. John Middleton, the nationally known botanist from the University of California, Riverside whose groundbreaking research revealed the deleterious effects of pollutants on vegetables in the Los Angeles basin. Atkinson and Middleton's talks alerted the audience that pollution was not always controllable. Their comments contradicted the comments of Matthew Walker, legal counsel for the San Francisco Bay Area Air Pollution Control District, who a month earlier expressed the opposite opinion—that controls in the San Francisco Bay area had successfully limited air pollution. Middleton stated that the last place to put a refinery was the place Humble selected.

"No oil refinery, no power plant belongs at the throat of any valley," warned Middleton.

Both Middleton and Atkinson contended that PG&E's power plant pollution would only worsen with the presence of the Humble refinery. PG&E burned natural gas, but the presence of fuel oil next door would prompt officials at the power plant to switch to the cheaper, more noxious fuel. This inexpensive high-sulfur fuel had contributed significantly to the deteriorating air quality surrounding Los Angeles. Both men stated that imposing regulations on refineries was not as easy as it seemed, since any significant regulations would face court challenges by the oil companies. However, Atkinson did admit afterward that placing controls on a new refinery was much easier than imposing new controls on existing refineries. The warning was clear for Monterey County. If a refinery was to be allowed, then make sure that all the necessary regulations were in place before it was built.

The strong efforts by Citizens for Clean Air to mobilize opinion against

Humble continued to gather steam. Margaret Smith announced that the group had collected more than 13,000 signatures against the Humble project. Citizens for Clean Air's Kramer called the massive number of signatures "unprecedented."

On the other side, Humble supporters gathered 1,140 signatures in favor of the refinery from Castroville alone. These signatures were gathered from the immediate area surrounding Humble's proposed development. Peter DiMarco, spokesman for the Castroville Chamber of Commerce which organized the efforts, stated, "Residents of the area involved should have more to say than people living 20 miles away."

Most agriculture leaders in the Castroville area remained doubtful about Humble, and now those doubts were rising elsewhere in the Valley. With Bruce Church Inc. still expressing reservations, and various outside experts weighing in on the damage that air pollution could cause to many of the region's crops, more farmers were beginning to speak out.

The Monterey County Agricultural Advisory Committee presented a report that raised concerns of agriculture towards industrial development, but nodded approval of Humble if it did not pollute—an impossible requirement. The report stated that "industries which do not contribute pollutants damaging to the agriculture industry be allowed in Monterey County." The 17-member committee failed to reach a quorum while submitting their report, as only six members showed up. That was barely larger than its three-member subcommittee that looked at the Humble matter. The committee also urged that standards no less stringent than those in Los Angeles be implemented in the county and that no permits be granted for industry until "a countywide method of control" was established. Although the advisory committee did not mention Humble by name, and hinted that the Humble oil refinery was not a serious concern in itself, the committee was clearly looking at the bigger picture of a growing industrial presence in the county. However, the committee remained skeptical of an air pollution control district, obviously worried that polluting farm equipment could become the next target.

W.H. Wilbur, who headed the subcommittee, and whose wife sat on the Planning Commission that was scheduled to review the Humble proposal, took a favorable view of Humble's plans.

"Humble has certainly put the mark high on the wall for other industries to shoot at. They said they would build a clean plant," Wilbur said, but then added, "We want to do everything we can to protect our agricultural industry."

However, second thoughts by agriculture and related businesses were growing. David Scott, technical director of Soilserv, an agricultural chemical and fertilizer company, publicly announced Soilserv's opposition to Humble, saying the refinery would be "contrary to the present and future interests of the area and to the people who live in it." Scott denounced the idea that Humble could provide "clean industry" as an "impossibility." Referring to the marine air currents that flowed from Moss Landing down the Salinas Valley, Scott used the colorful analogy that "the installation of an oil refinery in such a position would be tantamount to a dead cat in your air conditioning system."

It was in the latter half of July that prominent produce company Bruce Church Inc. ran its advertisement in the *Californian* with the controversial aerial photo of Salinas that the *Herald* and *Californian* wrangled over as smog or fog. Although Bruce Church Inc. claimed only that the photo showed an inversion layer over the city, the company appears to have run the advertisement as a response to the ambivalent Agricultural Advisory Committee report. The company disputed that Los Angeles air pollution standards were adequate. The ad and anti-Humble position of the agricultural giant was significant enough to warrant newspaper coverage by itself as it hinted that agriculture's lukewarm support for Humble was wavering.

"Our agricultural industry cannot exist under levels of air pollution acceptable under Los Angeles County standards," stated Bruce Church Inc., calling for the county to be selective in its industries and to "establish control measures" to protect agriculture.

Not to be outdone, the pro-Humble farmers and landowners in the Castroville area responded with their own ad in the Salinas newspaper. A few days later, their response blared:

"Castroville-Moss Landing Agriculturists and Property Owners Say …. Agricultural crops will not be in danger because of the Humble Oil and Refinery Co."

The ad urged readers not to be "misled" and cited Monterey County consultant William O'Connell and "nationally known expert" on air pollution Fred R. Ingram assuring that the Humble refinery would not damage agricultural crops.

As the July 28 decision by the Planning Commission approached, County Counsel William Stoffers, Planning Director Ed DeMars, Sanitation Director Ed Munson and pollution consultant William O'Connell prepared recommendations for the Planning Commission to consider. Their report listed 31 conditions, a substantial increase from the 18 conditions originally suggested by the special subcommittee of the Planning Commission that ventured to Los Angeles in March. The document required that the permit be used within five years. It required that Humble comply with any regulations by the Central

Coast Regional Water Pollution Control Board, State Department of Fish and Game, U.S. Coast Guard and Monterey County Health Department. The regulations also included the right of the county to revoke the permit if any of the requirements in a permit were violated.

The proposed conditions included basic restrictions on landscaping, road dedications, setbacks and design control, but also standards for noise, vibrations, illumination, fire and explosion hazards. However, the heart of the requirements rested on air and water pollution. One of the major requirements included "continuously operating air monitoring stations in sites furnished by the county of Monterey." Items to be monitored included sulfur dioxide, hydrogen sulfides, oxidants, dust, wind direction and velocity. Later, organics and nitrogen oxides could be included. The conditions included complying with any reports that the county health officer required on air contaminants, and allowed county officials to inspect the refinery premises for any matters that the county was investigating. The document also bound Humble to comply with future "amendments, additions and substitutions." Coking operations were required to be enclosed to maintain a "dust free" environment. Humble would be required to prevent significant discharges to the atmosphere or sewers of hydrogen sulfides or mercaptans, a substance with a rotten cabbage or egg smell. Humble also would be restricted in the burning of solids or liquid waste. The conditions limited storage to tanks of 40,000 gallons or less unless the tanks were equipped with vapor controls. Containment of vapors included loading of trucks, trailers and railroad cars. Also included was a limitation on the size of oil effluent water separator compartments. Marine operations were to be conducted in a manner to avoid petroleum and petroleum product spills and leaks. Furthermore, the conditions also included broad regulations such as, "No activities shall be permitted which emit dangerous radioactivity at any point, or electrical disturbance adversely affecting the operation ... of any equipment other than that of the creator of such disturbance." Since railroad expansion was anticipated in the operation of the refinery (the railroad ran close by the building site), Humble was required to make any rail expansion accessible to surrounding businesses in the industrial area. In addition, the property could only be used as an oil refinery and related operations.

While the conditions laid forth only dealt with Humble, it was expected that whatever recommendations were eventually imposed would lay the groundwork for all refineries and air or water polluting industries in the nearly 4,000-acre industrial zone that ran from the banks of the Elkhorn Slough to the borders of Castroville.

   Although not finalized by any means, the 31 conditions represented a major step in the regulation of oil refineries, not at just the county level or even the state level, but nationally. Humble had come into Monterey County just a few months earlier, enticed by the possibilities of an industrially zoned area with a deepwater port and essentially no local regulations. Now the company faced a persistent and growing local opposition with an expanding list of regulations rivaling anywhere in the United States. Amid all this, Humble had yet to pass its first hurdle—the Planning Commission.

13

HUMBLE'S FIRST DEFEAT

July 27–29, 1965

*"You are dealing with an atom bomb, that's what you are
dealing with. For God's sake, keep your air clean."*

Mits Nakishima, Pajaro Valley flower grower

As July 28 approached, county officials prepared for one of the largest
crowds ever to attend a meeting at the courthouse in Salinas. Letters,
petitions and telegrams with a total of 15,330 signatures had already been
submitted to the county opposing the Humble refinery. On the other side, a
lesser but still staggering tally of 7,938 stood in favor.

Altogether, 23,268 people had expressed their support or opposition to
Humble. This represented about one in ten of the county's residents. While
most of the opposition came from the Monterey Peninsula, almost half the
population of Castroville, the town bordering the refinery site, put their
names forward in support of Humble. Altogether, it was an unprecedented
outpouring of public expression.

The individual correspondence to the Planning Commission divulged a
badly divided county:

- **Monterey Peninsula:** 83 in favor; 702 against.

- **Salinas (includes the Salinas Valley and some of North Monterey County):** 3,397 in favor; 3 against.
- **Watsonville (includes some of North Monterey County):** 1,794 in favor; 0 against.
- **Castroville:** 527 in favor; 0 against.
- **Moss Landing:** 57 in favor; 0 against.

The *Monterey Peninsula Herald* and *Salinas Californian* noted that at the last Planning Commission meeting in May with Humble as a topic, there appeared to be six of the nine commissioners in favor. Rumors now floated that it was a tossup, with Humble either getting the nod by a six to three vote, or rejected by a five to four vote. However, the Planning Commission's vote was more akin to an exhibition game than a championship showdown. Whatever the planners decided, the Humble matter would end up with the supervisors as the final arbiters. The Planning Commission possessed powers to grant use permits, but for a special permit such as Humble's, the ultimate authority rested with the Board of Supervisors.

Nevertheless, the influence of the vote was not to be taken lightly. Both opponents and supporters fought desperately for the momentum a vote for their cause would signify. Going into the meeting, the opponents fought hard to stake the claim that Humble was a dangerous proposition. Citizens for Clean Air bantered the mantra that "dirty industry breeds dirty industry." Furthermore, they contended that many of the air and water pollutants lacked any known controls.

One of the most prominent opponents on the Monterey Peninsula stepped forward shortly before the Planning Commission meeting to use his influence to halt Humble. Famed photographer Ansel Adams wrote a lengthy letter to the *Herald* in which Adams pleaded for Humble's project to be rejected.

"The admission of this refinery to the Monterey Bay area would, I believe, turn the tide towards industrialization. A particular illusion of our time supports the contention that industrialization is the Alpha and the Omega of Progress," wrote Adams.

"There are many other foci of progress, and here in the Monterey Bay area we have them to a gratifying degree. I believe we must support the vast potential of what we have in relation to the land and to the established (and potential) culture, which is developing rapidly and positively around us.

"Conservationists and far-seeing citizens are not opposing for the mere sake of opposition! We have other objectives, other plans for a balanced and productive society working in harmony with its environment.

"We do not want our environment ruined because of any commercial expediency—which, in the case of the Humble Oil Refinery seems nothing more than that ...

"Smog, water and air pollution, urban sprawl—these are the obvious results of industrial development. The Humble Oil Company chooses not to join with a smog-control program—unless we accept their project. This is an attitude of true impertinence and should serve as the turning point in public opinion towards their project."

Famed photographer and Humble opponent Ansel Adams.
National Park Service

Although opposition on the Monterey Peninsula appeared to rest on environmental issues, most of the leaders of the Humble opposition were men of industry (the few prominent women were an exception). Their opposition came not as true conservationists, but more as faux environmentalists. Charles Kramer, for example, had a manufacturing background and lived next to Stillwater Cove by the golf links at Pebble Beach. While he and others spoke of pollution and oil spills, there is no evidence that earlier in life, while they were building their fortunes, that they harbored similar views. Reading between the lines of criticism against Humble, it is evident that Kramer was just as concerned, if not more so, that an industrial center in Moss Landing would be a personal eyesore instead of an environmental hazard. Yet Kramer and the other leaders of Citizens for Clean Air were not alone. The environmental movement was still being birthed, and the concept was unclear to many. America was just awakening to the need to protect its environment. Monterey County and the surrounding environs were no different.

On the other hand, Adams was not one of those just realizing the beauty of nature. He was a long-time, hardcore environmentalist. His living came not from industrial affairs, but capturing nature on film. It was the uneasy alliance of those with authentic environmental credentials like Adams, cooperating with former industrialists like Kramer, which built a firewall of opposition against Humble.

During a midday lunch on that Tuesday afternoon in July at the Rotary Club in Watsonville, Humble's assistant district manager for manufacturing, R.A. Winslow, sounded upbeat. He dismissed the possibility of smog and relegated water pollution as a "rare emergency." Winslow dismissed flower grower Mits Nakishima's concern that nitrous oxide could damage plants. He denied that the refinery would emit any obnoxious odors, claiming the odors from the fishing boats bringing in their haul at Moss Landing would be much worse. Winslow even assured his audience that the requirements for freshwater in the refinery would not exceed what the farmland on the site currently used.

"To us a refinery is a thing of beauty," testified Winslow while offering appealing paint color schemes for the buildings and lush landscaping along the highway.

As the sun sank over the Pacific Ocean on July 28, members of the Monterey County Planning Commission gathered for a special meeting at 8 p.m. Attuned observers gathered a clearer picture of the commissioners' allegiance as the meeting approached. They pegged the vote 4-3 in favor of Humble with two commissioners undecided. The undecided included Leon Stutzman of Monterey and Peter Cailotto of Salinas. In May, Cailotto had expressed support for Humble, but his support was wavering.

The Planning Commission would have two votes that night. First came the vote on the 31 conditions proposed by county staff. After that, the permit itself faced consideration. Planning Director Ed DeMars led off the evening as he proceeded down the list of conditions that had been beefed up from the original recommendations released a couple of weeks prior. The county's pollution expert William O'Connell reported one of the last-minute substitutions as the submerged loading of petroleum products in the bay to avoid noxious vapors escaping into the air. The question of how possible violations might be handled arose and was addressed by County Counsel William Stoffers. Stoffers said that it would take "about a month" between detecting a violation and imposing an injunction on the cause of the infraction. But, he insisted, that delay would only happen if Humble resisted.

Attorney Paul Hamerly, representing Humble, spoke after the presentation of the conditions: "These are conditions which Humble can live with. These aren't quite as Humble would have written them; some things we feel are very strict."

As the two sides laid forth their case, opponents consumed most of the time. Kramer started, introducing his fellow co-founder of Citizens for Clean Air, Earl Moser. Moser must have been an unsettling opponent for Humble. Moser spent 32 years in the oil industry, and had served as an executive. He would dominate the opposition's case. The media that day noted that following the arguments of Moser and others required an advanced course in chemistry—"parts of oxidants per million parts of air," nitrogen oxide, carbon monoxide, hydrocarbons and sulfur oxide recovery were the standard phrases of debate over the 31 conditions. Moser supplied an array of statistics showing that despite pollution controls in Los Angeles and San Francisco, the areas' refineries still dumped hundreds of tons of pollutants into the atmosphere every day.

Kramer and Moser successfully added some technical details to the 31 conditions, although it appears many in attendance found the science a bit beyond their familiarity. The Humble representatives remained largely silent, except for the occasional interjection disputing a point of the opposing speakers. However, O'Connell took issue with many of the opposition's claims, such as the lack of ability to control sulfur oxides, which he rejected as false.

Members of the agricultural community took their turn expressing opposition. Farm superintendent Dave Williams of Bruce Church Inc. followed Moser, supporting Moser's assertion that pollution "cannot be controlled." He focused on the release of nitrous oxide, a particularly damaging pollutant to crops like lettuce and celery, as lacking any known controls to limit its damage. Watsonville flower grower Nakishima followed next, claiming that 2½ million square feet of flower growing in Monterey County existed because of the "god-given asset of clean air." Nakishima maintained that if clean air was preserved then the area could become the "flower bowl of the nation, if not the world."

"You are dealing with an atom bomb, that's what you are dealing with. For God's sake, keep your air clean," appealed Nakishima.

At 11:25 p.m., Chair Keith Evans called for an end to public discussion despite several opponents still in line to speak. In a surprising vote of unity, all nine commissioners voted for the amended 31 conditions. The unity started to break down after that. Each of the commissioners spoke on how they intended to vote with some referring to the 31 conditions.

Willard Branson of Carmel Valley declared that he was voting against Humble as he expressed concern that the process for monitoring air pollution was inadequate. In a couple of years, Branson would be appointed to the Board of Supervisors by Governor Ronald Reagan, and retain his seat in a close 1972 election against John Sigourney who, with his wife, would be the publishers of the extraordinary Monterey County political journal *the advocate*.

David Krishun of Castroville, a longtime supporter of Humble's refinery but also an backer of stringent controls, expressed his support as expected.

"I don't feel one refinery breeds another," Krishun said. "The Moss Landing area is a limited industrial area. We can control industry by regulating the amount of land used for industry.

"The biggest problem is not industry, but people, houses and automobiles," Krishun continued, using an argument that would have considerable influence later when the Board of Supervisors eventually took up the matter. "How many pollutants are emitted from cars in Monterey's tourism?"

Kenneth Mansfield of King City, Perry Henderson of Salinas and Charlotte Wilbur of Salinas, whose husband had chaired the agricultural advisory committee that gave a nod to Humble only if it did not pollute, all joined in favor of Humble with Krishun. Mansfield pointed out the geographical divide between the county and tossed a jab at Monterey Peninsula residents with "The peninsula is populated by people who have no other requirements than their own needs."

On the other side, Chair Keith Evans of Carmel joined Branson. Evans took a similar position to Branson: "Under present regulations, I could vote in favor of controls if the controls were adequate. But I don't think the controls are adequate."

Stutzman, one of the two undecided votes on the commission, also threw his vote with Branson and Evans while using the same language regarding concerns over adequate regulations. "I'm not sure the conditions can be enforced. It appears to me that policing ... is going to be an extremely difficult task."

Although Branson, Evans and Stutzman all expressed reservations about the enforceability of the conditions, none of them proposed changes to make the regulations more workable. All three were from the strongly anti-Humble Monterey Peninsula. A vote for Humble would have been politically dangerous. More likely, the excuse of weak regulations was an out for them to vote as their neighbors wanted. Opponents like Branson, a conservative and normally pro-business Republican, needed protection to whitewash their unusual anti-business position on Humble. The probable lack of sincerity over their position was further borne out by Evans later commending Planning Director DeMars on the fine work he had done preparing the conditions that Evans earlier belittled as inadequate.

"MOTHER AND CHILDREN DOING NICELY, THANK YOU."

Monterey Peninsula Herald editorial cartoon by Eldon Dedini.
Courtesy of the Monterey Herald

Joining Branson, Evans and Stutzman in a 4-4 deadlock was Dr. E.P. Marcucci of Carmel Valley. That left only Peter Cailotto of Salinas. A well-known hardware store owner, Cailotto had run against Arthur Atteridge in the 1964 election, when Atteridge was seeking a full four-year term after being appointed by Governor Edmund Brown. In a three-man race, Atteridge handily defeated Cailotto and avoided a run-off with a 2,000-vote victory margin.

Cailotto knew he was in the hot seat as a wavering supporter of Humble in a pro-Humble town. He came prepared that evening to fully explain himself and distributed a statement that he also read. Ironically, of the nine members on the Planning Commission, only Cailotto remained from the 1956 commission that approved the Moss Landing Area Development Plan. In addition, none of the current five members of the Board of Supervisors were in office when the 1956 report was approved. Only Cailotto remained as a link to those who created the development plan to allow oil refineries at Moss Landing.

"Is Moss Landing the right place for heavy industries?" Cailotto began in his statement. Cailotto placed his concerns on the air shed, an issue that he admitted had never been fully considered until Humble arrived.

"It seems that winds blow from the ocean inland through the Salinas Valley. We must recognize that the studies are limited and that only exhaustive wind tests would be the only proof of wind direction . . .Would a reasonable person, lacking these studies, allow any further industry at this location ... would he allow a smelting operation, stockyards, garbage dump, a refinery or any other industry that could cause odors and air pollution?

"I believe that Moss Landing has all the attributes for a highly complex industrial area provided that those industries wishing to locate there are of such a nature that they will not create air pollution, odors or noise, etc. ... How do we ascertain whether or not this refinery can meet those standards? It appears that expert opinion cannot be the basis for fact."

To Cailotto, as it must have been for many in the Monterey Bay area, it must have seemed that experts disagreed and fudged. Both sides claimed knowledge, but neither could prove it unequivocally. Part of the reason is that one side spoke of a 50,000-barrel refinery while the other considered "a parade of smokestacks." The truth lay somewhere in the middle, but every passing week muddied it. Yet Cailotto was in an especially difficult position as he had a hand in creating the predicament the county and himself were now in.

Cailotto, who had been on several field trips to refineries, took issue with the idea that refineries were not dirty. He took umbrage at coking operations in particular, declaring that it was economically "impossible" to have a "clean coking operation." Cailotto commented that trips to refineries in Nipomo and Los Angeles revealed dirty conditions. Cailotto then called the coking operations at Rodeo "the worst of all."

"The area around the plant was covered with black coke dust—there was a high degree of soot or coke in the air—everything you touched was black—there was a strong wind blowing the coke onto nearby hills and grazing lands ... personal observation of cattle grazing approximately ½ mile away showed white face cattle with black faces!"

Cailotto pointed out that the many favorable comments about the refineries at Kingston, Jamaica and Hawaii failed to note that the planners specifically placed the refineries so that the wind blew industry pollutants out to sea. Cailotto did not spare the water conditions at the refineries either. He pointed out the "iridescence of oil on the water" from a Los Angeles refinery's effluence line.

Cailotto presented a reasoned argument, but bailed to a preposterous conclusion. He proposed that Humble build its refinery nearly 100 miles down the Salinas Valley near the San Ardo oil fields. Cailotto was seeking to find a middle ground in a contentious issue lacking a clear compromise position. He failed.

Winslow scoffed at Cailotto's suggestion. Humble needed marine access, a fact that had existed since Humble first expressed interest in Moss Landing's deepwater port. The other problem was that Standard Oil of New Jersey did not own the San Ardo oil fields. The oil fields were first discovered in 1947 by Texaco, and by 1965, Mobil was the owner and operator with their own distribution channels in operation.

Cailotto concluded by expressing that the granting of a permit "would establish an unrevocable precedent not in the best interest of Moss Landing or Monterey County." He then cast his vote against Humble's permit.

At a little past midnight, a "jubilant" crowd of Humble opponents made their way home relishing the triumph of their upset. Those who supported the refinery were stunned, but none as much as the Humble representatives. Shocked Humble officials tried to make sense of the aftermath. Humble engineer Jack Gardner made it clear Humble still hoped that the Board of Supervisors would grant the special permit. Before leaving, a baffled Winslow held an impromptu news conference. He could not understand why the Planning Commission disregarded the county's own expert—William O'Connell.

"They have the expert evidence, but they won't accept it," said an exasperated Winslow.

While Humble might not make significant changes in its tactics, Winslow said some of the questions raised at the meeting would be addressed. Regarding the 31 conditions, Hamerly expressed that Humble could "live with" them, but officials were not happy. Winslow exclaimed that the conditions were "beyond what Los Angeles and San Francisco have even considered."

"Some are stronger than in Los Angeles, but in general we could live with them," Winslow admitted.

"You know, we looked all over for a site," the *Watsonville Register-Pajaronian* reported a Humble official, most likely Winslow, saying. "Then we found this zoned industrial. We thought that was just fine," as he shook his head. "And the Long Beach people were down on their knees asking us to build it there."

As dejected as the Humble officials felt, there was one other person who was about to experience difficult times. Cailotto left the Planning Commission meeting that night probably expecting some disagreements with Humble proponents. It turned out to be much worse than that. The next day, The *Californian* spread the headline across the entire front page: "Humble Oil Permit Rejected." The fourth paragraph down, in bold print, declared Cailotto as the decisive vote.

"The fifth vote, however, came from Commissioner Peter Cailotto of Salinas, where there was overwhelming citizen and organizational support for Humble Oil."

On the editorial page, the *Californian* called the Monterey Peninsula opponents "propagandists" and accused them of spreading fantasy, not facts. While not mentioning Cailotto by name, the editors accused him of surrendering to the opponents and using "facetious" arguments.

A supporter in Salinas excoriated the *Californian* for treating Cailotto as a "whipping boy." Instead, the supporter said, Cailotto should be "commended for the guts he had" and risking his reputation as the inevitable "black sheep" in the community.

For Cailotto, the fallout was immediate and devastating. People he called friends refused to talk to him. Eight customers who held accounts at his hardware store immediately closed them. The bitterness was so great that it took years for some who scorned Cailotto to apologize.

The battle over Humble was more than a community grappling with an oil giant now. It was personal.

14

AGRICULTURE'S GROWING

CONCERN

*"Annual leafy vegetable crops, forage crops and grasses,
and field and glasshouse-grown ornamentals and flowers
are among the most seriously damaged plants (by air
pollution)."*

John T. Middleton

Agriculture and tourism are the twin engines of industry on California's
Central Coast, and both are dependent on the environment. The proposed Humble Oil project brought this into sharp focus for many residents
and business leaders, who had to consider what impact an oil refinery would
have on the unique conditions that agriculture relied on to grow food for the
rest of the United States.

In the mid-1960s, Salinas was truly living up to its 20th-century nickname,
"The Salad Bowl of the World," a phrase so well known that even local television station KSBW took its call letters from the phrase. Yet the growing and
shipping of lettuce and other row crop vegetables was just the latest evolution
during a century of innovation in the Salinas Valley, and also in the adjacent
Pajaro Valley, which lies across both Monterey and Santa Cruz counties.

Both valleys benefited from the peregrinations of ancient rivers as they swelled, diminished, and changed course over millennia. Wetlands captured nutrients and enhanced the valleys' biomes, and sediments built up and blew down from the mountain ranges. This resulted in unusually rich, deep soils. Not only that, but the Goldilocks climate—seldom too hot or too cold—is due to the location of these valleys very close to the Pacific Ocean. Cool breezes and fog are regular features of local weather patterns, enabling fragile crops like lettuce and strawberries to thrive without burning. And as manmade irrigation came into vogue, several huge natural aquifers happened to be situated right under the valleys that farmers could tap into as needed.

The Salinas Valley had been renowned for its lettuce and leafy green crops since the early 20th century.
It was these same crops that were most in danger of being damaged by smog.
Kathryn McKenzie

Central Coast agriculture began with cattle and grain, not large-scale vegetable growing. Before the United States took over California, much of Monterey County was used as grazing land. The first recorded crop grown for market in the Salinas Valley, in 1853, was wheat. By the 1870s, in Gonzales and Chualar south of Salinas, a surveyor noted "a most excellent yield was obtained, reaching in favorable seasons 30 sacks per acre."

Sugar beets were introduced as a vital cash crop in the late 1800s, so much so that sugar king Claus Spreckels built a major processing plant southwest of Salinas and constructed an entire company town there. This caught the attention of grain farmers who began growing sugar beets instead. But sugar was not the most important industry in the Salinas Valley by any means. That title, in the 1920s, went to dairying, with more than 25,000 milk cows in Monterey County.

But change was coming to local agriculture as modern refrigeration methods were developed that could keep produce fresher longer. A wagonload of lettuce was shipped from the Pajaro Valley to San Francisco in 1916 to great acclaim, and then ice-bunkered railroad cars were developed, taking advantage of the Southern Pacific line that ran through the Salinas Valley. By 1931, Monterey County lettuce production had risen to 20,000 freight cars a year. During the decades to come, there were some periods when Salinas was supplying 90 percent—or more—of the nation's iceberg lettuce.

Cole crops such as broccoli and cauliflower also increased dramatically in the Salinas Valley during this time as urbanization pushed farms out of the Santa Clara Valley, going from hundreds to thousands of acres between 1951 and 1961. Celery, strawberries and artichokes also made gains during this period. Large national companies like Dole and Del Monte moved in, and local companies grew and soon became national brands themselves, like Driscoll's Berries, D'Arrigo Bros., Ocean Mist and many others.

With all that fresh produce being grown in the area, it was only natural that related industries would spring up as well. Cooling, shipping, packing and food processing businesses all become other important pieces of the agribusiness hub in the Salinas and Pajaro valleys. Other spinoff industries included container manufacturing, waxed paper, commercial ice and farm machinery sales and service.

By the time the 1960s rolled around, agriculture in the Salinas and Pajaro Valleys was unquestionably a large-scale enterprise with big companies, rather than family farms, growing produce for markets throughout the United States. Reports for 1965 put Monterey County's crop value at a whopping $160.7 million and Santa Cruz County's at $42.8 million. But in actuality, there were many more millions of dollars coming into the counties from agriculture support industries, which would not exist except for these crops.

When the Humble project was announced, there was immediate concern on the part of some ag business people that having a refinery in their neck of the woods would be bad for crops. They knew that Southern California agriculture had been decimated by smog. Air pollution had also left its mark on agriculture in the Bay Area and Santa Clara Valley by this point. Smog was not just a problem in the Southland; it had been observed for several decades in Northern California, where the Bay Area Air Pollution Control District was formed in 1955 to try to impose controls. But, as was noted in the BAAPCD's history, air pollution was not a city or county concern, but a regional one. Smog could not be contained to just one city or county.

Photo of a packing shed crew in Watsonville from 1953.
Authors' collection

John T. Middleton of the University of California at Riverside studied the effects of air pollution on crops in the urbanized areas of the state. His 1956 paper, "Response of Plants to Air Pollution," reported that plants are most greatly affected during periods of severe smog, just as people were also most impacted. Leaves on many plants would become discolored, curl up, or shrivel away in the face of air pollution. "Annual leafy vegetable crops, forage crops and grasses, and field and glasshouse-grown ornamentals and flowers are among the most seriously damaged plants," he wrote. Sugar beets, spinach and celery were among the most sensitive plants—all important crops in the Salinas Valley.

Middleton also found in controlled experiments exposing plants to airborne pollutants that leaves could become visibly damaged and stunted. But less obvious was the destruction on the cellular level—plants that didn't appear to be injured had still been tainted, becoming less able to take up water and nutrients, which would affect their health and eventually crop yield.

Smog's effects on Bay Area agriculture during the mid-20th century were striking. Air pollution was blamed for causing $5 million in damage to everything from citrus and salad crops to fir trees, spinach, orchids and garden flowers, in an area just 100 miles north of the Salinas Valley. Flower growers were particularly grieved by the effects of ethylene, which caused orchid petals to dry up, carnations to close prematurely, and snapdragon petals to drop. It was the reason why some flower growers relocated to the Salinas and Pajaro Valleys to seek cleaner air.

And it was why now, with Humble looming, that the flower growers would become some of the most vocal opponents of the project.

15

AN AUGUST OF DISCONTENT

July 30—September 1, 1965

"Oppose this refinery project with all your strength of mind and heart! ... It is, truly, now or never."

Ansel Adams

For nearly two decades, the industrialization of Moss Landing had wide-spread support in Monterey County. If Humble had arrived with plans for an oil refinery even one year earlier, the opposition would have been fainter and the Board of Supervisors far more favorable. However, a developing environmental movement was growing as pollution worsened. The old notion of more growth and jobs without consideration for quality of life faced serious questions for the first time. The growing recognition of industrialization's deleterious effects was a national awareness that Humble would have encountered in many places. The Monterey Bay area was not unique by any means in this regard. What helped awaken this consciousness even further in the region was PG&E's expansion, which had highly visible results, in addition to plans for several nuclear power plants.

By August 1965, as the debate heightened over Humble, PG&E construction workers were erecting the twin 500-foot concrete smokestacks at "Mighty Moss," hovering like monoliths at the center of the Monterey Bay's coastline.

Immediately adjacent to an August 25 *Monterey Peninsula Herald* article regarding vegetation damage that a Humble refinery might cause was a photo of the smokestack construction at PG&E. Moreover, these rising towers could be observed from points all around the bay, from Santa Cruz to Monterey.

For those who saw progress and prosperity in the Humble project, PG&E was another example of a brighter future. For those who feared a blot on the landscape and a destruction of tourism and agriculture from pollution, PG&E represented a foreboding nightmare of industry to come. It is hard to know how much the smokestacks galvanized opponents, and perhaps it is mere coincidence that opposition to Humble began to jell as the stacks climbed upward, but those twin towers stood as a daily stark reminder of Humble's ambitions, and the broader plan of a massive industrial complex, busy deepwater port and planned recreational and residential communities.

"The PG&E is itself already in the process of expanding its Moss Landing plant considerably," wrote Robert Western in a letter to the *Herald*, "and it is interesting, when driving by, to note the gigantic smoke stack in construction right now. This new stack is just one more that will add its ugly pall of smoke and irritants to our atmosphere, which is bad enough already on certain days."

In spite of the construction's poor timing, PG&E remained a reliable ally to Humble. Its representatives, who continued to speak in favor of the refinery for PG&E, must have seen its fate clearly tied to the oil company. A rejection of the refinery could portend a rejection of PG&E's future projects. The decision by the Planning Commission must have sent some shudders through PG&E's corporate headquarters.

For Humble, the consternation felt by its representatives over the Planning Commission vote contrasted with some positive news. Humble admitted that the mysterious survey conducted in Monterey County between June 25 and July 2 was its own. On August 6, Humble released the results. R.A. Winslow of Humble explained it was conducted in secret to achieve a response that was as accurate as possible. In his announcement, Winslow stated that the survey revealed a two-to-one edge in support of the refinery. He also explained that portions of the Monterey Peninsula were two-to-one against the refinery—the only geographical area in the county opposed to the project. Winslow reported the error rate as plus or minus 3 percent.

If Humble could prove that most of the county wanted the oil refinery, then it would be harder for the supervisors to turn down the will of the people. Some may have questioned the legitimacy of a poll conducted by the subject of the poll, but the results aligned with what most people expected and what public opinion had expressed through meetings, letters and petitions. The poll was a public relations boon for Humble. It revealed that the opponents of Humble were but a vocal minority.

Humble surveyed 985 individuals. The results cited 58% of the county in favor of Humble's plan, with 43% of those strongly in favor. The opponents numbered about half with 27%, and 22% labeled themselves strongly against. Another 15% of the respondents were undecided.

As expected, Tom Hudson's district, the heart of the Monterey Peninsula, flipped with 58% opposed and 26% in favor. Next door Seaside, Andy Anderson's district, was considerably more amenable to Humble. Filled with working-class families, many Seaside residents apparently saw the economic benefits that Humble might bring. The area registered 53% in favor and 37% opposed. In South County, the growing apprehension by agriculture toward Humble did not register much outright opposition. Only 5% of the respondents expressed their opposition, compared to 66% in favor. A considerable 29% remained on the fence. These numbers came from late June and early July, but by August there were growing indications that South County was shifting toward a less favorable view. In Arthur Atteridge's district of Salinas, a whopping 58% were strongly in favor of Humble, forging a total of 75% in support. Only one in ten of those surveyed in Salinas spoke against Humble. In North County, the site of Humble's project, even Salinas' support looked weak in comparison. In Warren Church's district, 82% of the people favored Humble with 72% of those strongly in favor, 11% were against, and a paltry 7% remained undecided.

The refinery's support placed several of the supervisors in politically risky situations. Anderson, in particular, was in a highly vulnerable position. He had already announced his opposition, putting him at odds with his constituents. Both Atteridge and Church's districts strongly backed Humble, boxing both supervisors into narrow political paths. They were the only two Democrats on the board, and might be inclined to more conservationist positions if three-quarters to four-fifths of their constituents had not been supportive of Humble.

Atteridge, an attorney, knew his district of Salinas well. He had served on the city council and as mayor before appointment to the vacant supervisorial seat left open when former Monterey County Supervisor Burt Talcott was elected to Congress in 1962.

As mayor, Atteridge sought to bring industry to Salinas as it grew from a population of 15,000 to 35,000, and played a significant role in bringing industry to Salinas in the late 1950s and early 1960s: Firestone, Peter Paul, and Nestlé. His time as mayor was marked by a building boom that included construction of the John Steinbeck Library, a new police station and the city's meeting chambers, known as the Rotunda. There was a boom in residential and commercial ventures as well. Atteridge is also credited with a strong urban renewal program that replaced dozens of substandard buildings. His mayorship was the beginning transformation of Salinas from a small town to a modern city.

Born in Watsonville, Atteridge attended Santa Clara University, where he played basketball, then went on to Hastings College of Law in San Francisco where he graduated at the top of his class. Atteridge was drafted into service during World War II. Despite never having been on a horse, he was placed in a horse cavalry unit in the Pacific theater where he rose to captain. After the war, degree in hand, he returned to Watsonville but had a problem. The only judge in Santa Cruz County was his uncle, with whom he did not get along with all that well anyway. Atteridge's solution to this was to move to Salinas, where he operated a law practice. He took office on the Salinas City Council in 1955.

Atteridge was known for his dry humor and genial nature, but he was not hesitant to lay down a challenge when needed—as often happened when he and Hudson diverged on opinions. Perhaps no one described Atteridge better than *the advocate*:

"Atteridge is an almost Faulknerian country lawyer with bushy and unruly eyebrows and a hard-headed wit. He seems sincerely to be concerned with what he conceives to be in the best interests of Monterey County, but he tries, if he can, to cover his bases and protect himself in his own district."

Throughout much of the Humble controversy, Atteridge appeared to take a back seat. He did not attend as many of the refinery field trips that the other supervisors did. While he was willing to inject himself in issues as they came to the board, the Humble matter was a different story. He appeared more willing to watch the other supervisors carry the ball on questions, although he took a significantly more active role when the conditions for Humble's permit were addressed before the board. While Atteridge had developed a reputation as pro-industry, his relative silence may have betrayed some differences between his personal beliefs and those of his constituents. It is also worth noting that in later years Atteridge would recount the many issues that came before him as an elected official, but he never mentioned Humble. At this time, Atteridge and Church were also developing a strong alliance that would last for years as both were fiscal conservatives and social liberals.

While Humble's survey appeared generally accurate, the widespread support in South County could be challenged as outdated based on developments in August. First, a second major grower in the Salinas Valley, D'Arrigo Brothers, joined with Bruce Church Inc. by opposing a permit for Humble.

"We very strongly oppose the granting of a permit to Humble or anyone else whose would emit, under the best conditions, the volume of nitrogen oxides with relation to the size of the plant, taxes paid and the wealth it will produce for the county," wrote Andrew D'Arrigo to Hudson in his capacity as board chair. D'Arrigo noted that the company left the Santa Clara Valley because vegetable crops had been damaged by pollution drifting from San Jose.

"We gave up those leases ... because when during the season the nitrogen oxides level of the air on a single warm day with less than normal wind can turn acres of lettuce golden bronze in color and stop celery growth for weeks, render beans unmarketable, we feel the necessity of moving to an area where these risks were not prevalent even at higher costs ... We want both agriculture and industry—not one at the expense of the other."

Days later, Harry Casey, the editor and publisher of the *King City Rustler* in South Monterey County, countered the *Salinas Californian*'s editorial that criticized the surprising 5-4 Planning Commission vote recommending a denial of Humble's permit. Casey called out *Californian* publisher Francis Cislini for kowtowing to Salinas business interests when the newspaper attacked the commissioners who voted against Humble. Casey further commended all the commissioners for voting their consciences.

More importantly, Casey openly questioned the worth of Humble's refinery to South County residents. Moss Landing was 65 miles away from King City. All the hubbub in the northern part of the county concerned those in the south about as much as an issue in a foreign country. However, the comments by air pollution experts meeting in the Salinas Valley about prevailing winds and crop damage began to ring in Casey's and others' ears. Agriculture is what founded King City. Anything that might threaten agriculture threatened the livelihoods of all.

Casey also noted that the nearly $1 million in tax revenues that Humble promised to fill the county's coffers for fire protection, schools, hospital expansion and even a cemetery district were all intended for North County. South County would get only a pittance of the tax base, but the brunt of the pollution. The tax dollars Humble promised were a sacred cow to many of the refinery's proponents, but Casey laid that promise out as more of a Trojan Horse, benefiting only those living near the refinery.

"Since refineries can mean air pollution and air pollution means crop damage, we Valley residents are being asked to take a chance. When we are invited to support Humble Oil's application we are, in effect, being urged to jeopardize our basic economy—our crops—so that Salinas can collect another plum ...

"If it can be positively proven that the restrictions placed on Humble—or any subsequent industry—absolutely guarantee there'll not be one iota of air pollution, we say fine ...

"But if there is a remote possibility that the location of Humble—and the location of similar operations that would be bound to follow—could jeopardize the clean air of the Salinas Valley, our basic livelihood and our living conditions, we think it incumbent on ... the board of supervisors to vote 'no.'"

Casey was an influential figure in the Salinas Valley. As the publisher of four weeklies, in each of the four small Salinas Valley towns, Casey represented an influential voice. Casey played a significant role in backing the construction of the Nacimiento and San Antonio dams which are vital for recharging the acquifers supplying the water to thousands of acres of rich agricultural farmland. His powerful editorials and backing led to 80-95% approval in the Salinas Valley for construction bonds to finance the dams. With Casey taking an anti-Humble position, a huge crack in the wall of support for Humble in South County began to develop.

Casey was not the last significant voice in the area to shout against Humble. A group of thirty farmers and businessmen in the Salinas Valley announced the formation of another "Citizens for Clean Air Committee," identical in name to the one on the Monterey Peninsula, but under different leadership. Headed by Tom Thwaits and L.A. Hearne, a former planning commissioner, the group met at Memorial Hall in Greenfield just north of King City to announce a campaign against the refinery with newspaper, radio ads and through contact with service clubs.

Although Charles Kramer, Earl Moser and leaders of the Monterey Peninsula group of the same name were in attendance, Hearne was adamant that the groups were separate with separate funds. While true, the increasing presence of Kramer and Moser in the Salinas Valley presented a change in strategy by Monterey Peninsula's Citizens for Clean Air. They had widespread support at their home base, plus two supervisors voting no. The Salinas Valley was now their target at hopes of swinging a third vote on the Board of Supervisors, Harold Henry.

"We are primarily interested in agriculture, where on the peninsula they are interested in clean air for residential purposes, you might say," Hearne explained. Hearne stated that the tardiness in forming a committee to oppose Humble occurred because "We didn't realize the importance of it. Agriculture is our bread and butter. We are very much afraid we would be seriously hurt with a smog condition. Our object is to defeat the granting of a special permit to Humble."

"We grow crops that cannot be grown in other parts of California or other parts of the United States," Hearne would later say. "We want to preserve our agricultural heritage, not only for ourselves and for our children, but for others who are following us."

Planned Industrial Growth In Monterey County Is Necessary To Lessen YOUR Tax Burden

The Proposed $50,000,000.00 Humble Oil and Refining Company Facility At Moss Landing Will Benefit Our County Tax Base.

HUMBLE . . . . Will Add One Million Dollars In County Taxes . . . . This Amount Equals The Taxes Being Paid By All Industrial Firms Which Have Located In Monterey County Since 1952.

This Informational Brochure Has Been Paid For By Independent Citizens Vitally Interested In The Economic Growth Of Monterey County

Pro-Humble Oil mailer sent to residents of Monterey County.
Authors' collection

In the Salinas area, yet a third group began forming, calling itself Individuals for Clean Industry. Dave Williams, farm superintendent for Bruce Church Inc., de-emphasized that opponents from the Monterey Peninsula were involved. Williams pointed out that the fears of following the path that led to the destruction of agriculture in Los Angeles were paramount. Williams' group included other prominent members of the agricultural community including Howard Eckhart of Eckhart Seed, William Clark of Speigl Farms, Robert Grainger and Jack Armstrong. Williams disagreed with the notion that pollution was not currently threatening agriculture. He charged that emission levels were approaching dangerous concentrations damaging to crops. Williams, like other opponents, feared that Humble would open the door to similar industries, further exacerbating the problem. Williams warned that the "gradual additions from many sources" was the real threat to agriculture, and that pollution "does not suddenly come upon us."

"We cannot control all sources of air pollutants, and we think the best control is to not knowingly add another major source of contamination to our area," Williams concluded.

The growing opposition even crept into the heart of support for Humble. A group of North County residents gathered at the Franco Hotel in Castroville and selected rancher Gene Boggiatto and Vincent Catalano of the Castroville Marketing Association as their co-chairs. North County opposition had been muted, probably because the area was so firmly in support of Humble. Those who were against it did not want to raise the ire of their neighbors. Instead, they were willing to look on as spectators.

"I'm against it," one North County resident said, "and if anyone asks me, I will tell him; but I don't want to get involved. We have been letting the Peninsula carry the ball on this."

Elsewhere, many farmers continued to back Humble. The split was significant enough that the Grower-Shipper Vegetable Association, which usually presented a united front for agricultural interests, declared it would remain neutral.

"To date we haven't been into it, and we haven't taken any position," stated Jack Bias, executive vice president of the association. "It is problematical that we have to represent our members equitably. We have members who feel both ways, and as a result, each grower and each shipper has a right to his own opinion. It is not up to the association to influence the thinking of its members."

The Monterey County Farm Bureau was far less circumspect. Representing 700 growers, its board voted 6-3 to reject Humble's project. Farm Bureau President Wayne Bowman expressed its members' concerns in a letter to the supervisors: "It appears illogical to invite into the Salinas Valley any industry that is known to emit air pollutants which will have an adverse effect on the existing, clean airshed so vital to the continued prosperity of Monterey County."

While Humble supporters in the agricultural community did not form their own groups, they did generally align with the pro-Humble groups with business ties. One of the agricultural supporters for Humble, Don Barsotti of the California Artichoke and Vegetable Growers Corp. in Castroville, explained why many in the farming community continued to support Humble. It was Barsotti's land that Humble, through a middleman, purchased for its site. Barsotti said when he learned that Humble was coming, he was concerned about damage to his crops, but the California Department of Agriculture told him that there was nothing to worry about. Barsotti paid attention to what the experts had been saying. All the experts, even those who warned against Humble, agreed that the major polluter was automobiles, and would remain automobiles. The disagreement in agriculture and the public was about what would happen after Humble. More industry would be a problem, but for many supporters that was a concern to be dealt with at a future date, project by project.

"I'm more worried about the exhaust from the millions of cars going bumper to bumper to the Monterey Peninsula," exclaimed Barsotti.

What Barsotti was most troubled about was taxes. Therein lay the basis of support for Humble in both the agricultural and business communities—an increasing tax burden was squeezing operations. Many saw Humble as a way to ease or at least slow the rapidly increasing tax rates.

"We own about 10 ranches out here, which we farm," Barsotti said. "The farthest is 10 miles from the Humble site. Our taxes are getting to the point it's hurting the farming picture. It's getting so it's not economical to farm anymore. Humble will help, and we need help. Humble is using up the bad land. We can live side by side."

Barsotti also dismissed the growing concerns about Humble's water needs. He said that he had been assured by Humble that the plant would use less water than farming the land, with an adequate supply from the three wells on the property.

However, that was not the entire story. The Humble refinery would have required a tremendous amount of water. To operate, it needed 1,300 gallons a minute 24 hours a day, seven days a week, twelve months a year. Altogether this was half a billion gallons of water annually. This was an enormous volume for an area that was beginning to experience serious saltwater intrusion from an overdraft of underground aquifers. At the time, the Humble site was used for growing artichokes. Humble made the argument that farming used 2,000 gallons a minute and that the two uses for water were roughly comparable. They were not. The agricultural water use was only for 11 hours a day, five months a year. While both uses of the property might use approximately the same amount of water for those five months, the refinery would continue to suck water out of the ground year-round. The refinery would use one-third of the water that the city of Watsonville used annually. The *Castroville Times and Moss Landing Harbor News* called for the supervisors to put limits on the amount of water that could be pumped from the ground if the permit was approved.

With the farmers divided, Supervisor Harold Henry started to feel some heat. Henry had been an outspoken supporter of Humble from the beginning, but at the Greenfield Chamber of Commerce, he toned down his support to what was described as "generally favorable." Henry claimed experts told him pollution would not be a problem, and he advocated the advantages of an increased tax base, which Casey had days earlier attacked as inconsequential in Henry's district.

Increasingly, awareness of the Humble affair stretched beyond the boundaries of the Monterey Bay region. In Monterey, the week that the Planning Commission voted against the Humble project, state Controller and future U.S. Senator Alan Cranston stepped into the fray.

"I applaud the decision," said Cranston. "[W]e also must consider the beauties of California before they are all vanished and our air is polluted and our water is polluted and our coastal areas are destroyed."

More fodder for opponents of Humble drifted into the public conversation when Standard Oil of New Jersey, Humble Oil's parent company, was fined $5,000 for polluting waters in New Jersey. At the same time, news from the San Francisco Bay Area came that 90,000 striped bass died from oil refinery operations in Suisun Bay, the area near the Martinez refineries.

Brought into the debate was Philip Leighton, professor emeritus of chemistry at Stanford University and one of the top air pollution experts in the country. Leighton was no stranger to the Monterey Bay, stating that he had visited the region more than 200 times in the last few years while witnessing an increase in smog during those trips. Leighton was invited to speak in Greenfield but prior to that, wrote a two-part article for the *Herald* prognosticating doom for the county's air quality.

Leighton mentioned that the three most easily visible signs of air pollution appear in stages: visibility reduction, plant damage and eye irritation. He noted that the time period between visibility reduction and plant damage is ten to twenty-five years. Leighton felt that the Salinas area had already passed the ten-year mark on visibility reduction, and proclaimed that the Humble refinery produced the nitrogen oxides and hydrocarbons needed for smog to initiate. He also pointed a finger at the expansion of the PG&E power plant, and spent considerable time discussing the burning of fuel oil. Many opponents to Humble argued that once completed, PG&E's power plant would likely switch to burning fuel produced by Humble. Leighton claimed that Mighty Moss and its new additions would produce the same amount of electricity as currently being produced in the Los Angeles area, where those plants spewed 150 tons of nitrogen oxides into the atmosphere every day.

Leighton further warned that the Salinas Valley was at the threshold of plant damage, implying that the construction of Humble's refinery or expansion of PG&E's power generation could be the tipping point. Leighton elaborated on the deleterious effects, suggesting that other unwanted consequences were to be expected. Nitric oxide, a colorless and relatively inert substance, part of the chemical brew released into the atmosphere in these types of industrial plants, becomes visible and toxic when mixed with hydrocarbons and sunlight as it converts to nitrogen dioxide. The release of sulfur dioxide, another invisible substance when produced, grows visible over time as it interacts with other elements. This happens slowly as it expands over a large area. Leighton reported that sulfur dioxide released in Los Angeles County spreads as far away as Ventura or Catalina Island. Leighton also pointed out that as these chemicals spill out into the air, they eventually condense into water droplets that cause plant discoloration similar to an acid burn. The burning of fuel oil in power plants also results in the formation of tiny carbonized particles known as cenospheres. Lifted into the atmosphere, they eventually settle onto plants, creating ulcer-like damage. The cenospheres corrode fabrics and metal, permanently discolor paint, and leave an oily film on windows. Leighton also added his voice into the long debate that industrial plants at the mouth of the Valley were undesirable.

"Indeed," wrote Leighton, "if one were asked to be specific, from the standpoint of photochemical air pollution, the most unfavorable locations imaginable for an oil refinery and a power plant, a juxtaposition of the two at the upwind of a long agricultural valley, already suffering from visibility reduction, would be close to the top of the list. The question of preserving the priceless heritage of clean air, versus the broadened tax base and jobs provided by industrialization has been faced by many other communities and resolved in favor of industrialization. These communities are now paying the price in terms of smog. Can Monterey County, with its agricultural and recreation resources at stake, afford this price?"

While Leighton's argument played on the worst of outcomes for both Humble and PG&E, his conclusions were plausible. For the agriculturally concerned audience in Greenfield, the expert information must have been deeply troubling.

At Greenfield, the panel included E.F. Darley, the plant pathologist from the University of California at Riverside who had made multiple trips to

Monterey County warning of the damage oil refineries could wreak on plant life. Darley's influence in persuading the agricultural community of the dangers Humble presented was not to be underestimated. His regular presence and persuasive arguments were critical for Humble's opponents. Also present at the forum was James Mattison, chair of the Monterey County Medical Society Public Health Committee, and George Haltiner, chair of the Department of Meteorology and Oceanography at the Naval Postgraduate School in Monterey. Haltiner spoke earlier at one of the first panels in May, and again he stressed the dangers of the inversion layer.

"In the event contaminants are loosed into our air, they will tend to be stuck," Haltiner stated. The Salinas Valley "is somewhat of a boxed-in canyon ... and there will be a tendency of air pollution to stay confined."

Mattison was not the only M.D. to speak against Humble. His fellow physician from Salinas, Rex Whitworth, described the dangers of smog in a letter to the *Californian*:

"Anyone who is honest enough to admit basic facts and who possesses average intelligence must know that smog is a euphemism for poisonous chemical effluents. Smog kills the human animal and causes permanent and progressive damage to the highly specialized tissues of the nose, sinuses, bronchial tree and lungs (apart from the merely irritating effects on the sensory organs of the eyes and nose) just as it surely kills and damages living vegetable matter, lettuce, citrus, etc. This can be adequately shown from the records in smog bound industrial areas of the U.S.A. and other industrialized countries which do not have the same automobile problem that the U.S.A. has."

The pro-Humble side had always insisted that Humble would bring more prosperity and not conflict with existing industry, for industrialization was the future for the Monterey Bay region. That argument took a blow when Green Giant Corp., a major vegetable processor, suggested that it might not build its Salinas plant after all.

"We have become aware of the warm debate concerning the issuance of a land use permit for an oil refinery in Moss Landing," C.J. Tempas, vice president of production for Green Giant, wrote to Supervisor Hudson. "We join others in your community who express concern as to the consequences of such an action. We are confident that the action of your board will be in the best interests of all concerned and that the Salinas Valley will be held clean and continue as the last major coastal valley reserved for the agricultural industry."

Just as he had prior to the Planning Commission meeting that voted to reject Humble's application, photographer Ansel Adams weighed in with another persuasive and lengthy letter to the *Monterey Peninsula Herald*:

"A crucial decision is facing the Board of Supervisors of Monterey County. The handwriting is on the wall for all to see. Everywhere we note the tragic evidences of polluted water, polluted air, malignant freeway growth, urban and suburban ugliness and the depletion of agricultural and recreational areas ...

"We are now awakening to the need for salvaging what we can from the unholy mess our industrial civilization has created. Serious concern and alarm is now voiced in all parts of our country—in fact, in all civilized parts of the world ...

"The responsibility is very great indeed: are we to permit industry to proceed with extravagance in the use of the earth's resources and pollution of our water and air—which can only result in the extermination of life, rather than its betterment? ...

"It is not too late to postpone—if not avoid—disaster, not only in our country but throughout the world. Look a little beyond the appealing edifices of 'prosperity' (which may crash upon us because of our own mania for exploitation) to the more rewarding vistas of a balanced society living in an environment of beauty, rich rural production, education and appropriate recreational development.

"Oppose this refinery project with all your strength of mind and heart! Urge everyone you know or will meet, everyone in your family, all members of your organizations, to take heed of the potential disaster facing us if this Humble Oil Company refinery is accepted in our community. It is, truly, now or never."

16

CITIZENS FOR CLEAN AIR

August 23 –September 2, 1965

"Your action will determine the future of the entire Monterey County area."

George Faul, Monterey Peninsula College president

No recounting of the opposition against Humble Oil is complete without a thorough discussion of Citizens for Clean Air. This group, formed on the Monterey Peninsula, operated in textbook style at organizing opposition to confront and challenge the Moss Landing refinery proposal. At its core were its two principal leaders and founders, Charles Kramer and Earl Moser, but countless others were involved from the beginning of its formation in early April 1965 until the Humble affair ended late the following year. There was Gus Bauman of Carmel Highlands, one of the first people to speak against Humble; Carmel Councilmember Gunnar Norberg; Del Monte Properties President A.G. Michaud, who also led the Committee to Form an Air Pollution Control District; William Howard Church, the professor from the Naval Postgraduate School; and many more.

Citizens for Clean Air operated as a launching pad for Humble opponents in the Salinas Valley. Kramer and Moser made repeated visits there, meeting with early opponents like Dave Williams from the Bruce Church Inc. Together, they coordinated the development of new opposition groups that began to appear in August up and down the valley from Castroville to King City. Citizens for Clean Air also provided a foundation for the creation of the Six Cities Fund in September that coincided with the emergence of Carmel City Attorney Bill Burleigh as a diligent foe of Humble.

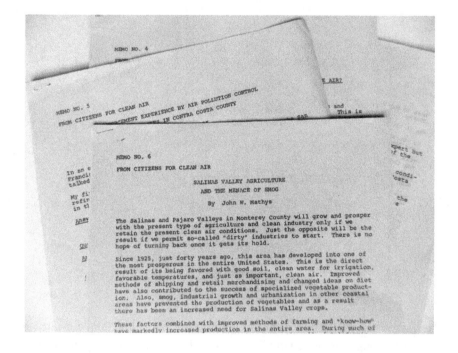

The anti-Humble group Citizens for Clean Air sent a series of blue memos to supervisors and county staff in their efforts to stop the refinery project.
Authors' collection

However, Kramer and Moser were unlikely heroes for what most saw as an environmental cause. Kramer was formerly in the manufacturing industry as a financial executive, and Moser a former Chevron executive. Both retired to the picturesque Monterey Peninsula, living lives of luxury derived from successful business careers doing things not so unlike what Humble President Charles Jones and other Humble officials were doing by putting a refinery in Moss Landing. It is perhaps the richest irony in the entire affair that two of Humble's most stubborn opponents made their fortunes doing essentially what Humble was trying to do.

The Humble controversy was a turning point for both men, as they would pursue environmental causes for years afterwards. The mounds of information on water and air pollution they prepared and submitted to the public and government agencies undoubtedly affected them. There was no insincerity in their beliefs, at least nothing shared publicly, but it was an evolution for them. Their initial concerns were of smokestacks despoiling their view at the gateway to the Monterey Peninsula. If the refinery was planned for somewhere south of Salinas, out of sight of their daily lives, their involvement might have been very different. Yet that is a statement that might apply to most of Humble's opponents, except for the few true environmentalists of the day, like Ansel Adams and Ruth Andresen. Whether Kramer and Moser ever sat down and regretted their past roles in the industrialization of America will never be known, but both of these smart, intelligent and forward-thinking men must have had some self-reflective moments at some point in their fight against Humble.

Once Kramer and Moser had finished stirring opposition in the Salinas Valley, they turned their attention to the Board of Supervisors. Moser with Monterey Peninsula College President George Faul, agriculturist John Mathys, former advertising executive Vincent Bliss and Naval Postgraduate School professor William Howard Church formulated an extensive series of papers, referred to as memorandums and printed on blue paper, which addressed the major issues of the Humble project.

In the weeks leading up to the September 2 Board of Supervisors meeting, Citizens for Clean Air blitzed the supervisors with information and counterpoints to Humble's impressive public relations tactics. The group sent ten separate memorandums to the supervisors using data presented by the many experts who had testified at community forums against Humble as well as original information gathered by group members. The papers were an attempt to assemble a comprehensive summary of the concerns that the organization raised since its inception in the spring.

"We have unbiased testimony from world renown(ed) men of the highest character and reputation that even a modern refinery with the most advanced controls system will add significant contaminants to our air supply," Kramer explained in describing the group's preparation to persuade the supervisors. "There are no regulations or enforcement measures which can prevent this."

The first testimony was a letter from Phillip Leighton, formerly dean of physical sciences and head of the chemistry department at Stanford University, highlighted in red and summarizing Leighton's concerns that the Salinas Valley was on the threshold of damaging pollution.

The second memorandum came from Faul, recently hired as president of Monterey Peninsula College, who had previously lived in Richmond near the array of refineries that dotted that part of the San Francisco Bay. Faul's argument focused on the concern that one refinery will breed more refineries. His paper included a foldout map identifying the five refineries of the eastern San Francisco Bay as a hub with all refineries within 20 miles of each other. Faul compared it to the refinery concentrations in El Segundo in Southern California, and similar areas in southern Lake Michigan and Houston.

Faul's presentation included a second map, this one highlighting a vast array of satellite industries at the refinery hub on the rim of San Francisco Bay. Faul identified 21 different petroleum byproduct businesses and 33 chemical companies using the products produced by the refineries. The maps suggested that for every refinery, more than 10 satellite businesses would pop up nearby to consume the refinery products.

"Some of these industries are even harder to control than a refinery," Kramer emphasized in his opposition comments.

Faul quoted D.J. Callaghan, chief administrative officer of the Bay Area Air Pollution Control District, that these refineries and satellite industries were major polluters. "Contra Costa County produces 40% of the particulate and organic pollution in the Bay Area," concluded Callaghan in a July 8, 1965 article in the Oakland Tribune. Faul noted nearly 200 complaints received by the air pollution control district during the previous year from both refineries and associated businesses.

"As I see it," Faul wrote of Humble to the supervisors, "the issue is monumental in nature. Your action will determine the future of the entire Monterey County area. It is not a question of one plant, or of one refinery. It is a question of permanent, irretrievable commitment to a certain type or industrial growth . . .

"Mr. Laurance Rockefeller was quoted as saying in Monterey recently, 'There is a place for Conservation and there is a place for Oil Refineries.'

"Let us agree on that. Let Contra Costa and El Segundo be the place for Oil Refineries.

"Let Monterey County be the place for Clean Air—and Clean Industry."

The third memorandum focused on people who lived near refineries in the San Francisco Bay Area. This was clearly an attempt to counter the many news stories that emerged when officials visited a refinery and happy neighbors gave glowing summaries. Altogether, 79 people were interviewed for the memorandum. Of those, 61 declared that they "have ... been bothered by air pollution or smog," an 86% confirmation rate. Of those who complained of air pollution, 86% identified smell as the problem, 59.5% labeled smog and 48% singled out dust. Significant majorities identified each of these air pollution elements as severe. Furthermore, 61% stated that air pollution caused property damage while 18% cited health problems.

Other memorandums readdressed the potpourri of chemicals that a refinery produced, complaints submitted to air pollution authorities in the San Francisco Bay Area, a summary of the dangers pollutants threatened to agriculture, a review of how the inversion layer worsened the smog menace, and recommendations on how to improve the conditions proposed by the oil refinery.

Memo No. 9 dealt with the promise Humble supporters made that the extra tax base of the refinery would ease the growing local property taxes. A comparison drew distinctions between select industrial and rural counties in the state. Monterey County was used as a base, with 23 manufacturing jobs per 1,000 people. Counties with more than 23 manufacturing jobs per 1,000 people, like San Francisco with 83 per 1,000, were considered industrial while those with fewer than 23 per 1,000, like San Luis Obispo with 8 per 1,000, were considered rural. The comparisons found that the industrial counties had 25% to 37% higher property taxes than Monterey County while the rural counties had 18% to 50% less. The paper also took issue with the idea that Humble was a tax boon for Monterey County. While county, Humble and independent sources confirmed that the $70 million refinery would generate close to $1.4 million in taxes each year, Citizens for Clean Air countered with $320,000 as the county's share, with the remainder going to other government entities such as districts. The group then subtracted the estimated cost of infrastructure maintenance, such as roads and an air pollution control district, to show an annual net loss for the county.

The last memorandum, prepared by Professor Church, addressed the economic impact on the county. Church dismissed the promise that half the 2,000 construction jobs would come from the Monterey Bay area. Instead, Church countered, companies hired to do the construction, such as Bechtel, would bring their own employees into the area to build the refinery. Church went on to theorize that if Humble's refinery had even a minor adverse impact an agriculture and tourism, the economic consequences would be severe. He claimed that a 1% loss of employment in agriculture, service or trade industries would result in the loss of 4,680 jobs, far exceeding the 200 to 300 that Humble claimed the refinery would generate.

One of the other submissions from Citizens for Clean Air included the picture of the Salinas area debated hotly by both the *Herald* and the *Californian* in early July. The *Herald* called it smog; The *Californian* called it fog. Weeks later Bruce Church Inc. claimed the photograph as its own, while emphasizing that it was not about smog or fog, but to prove that an inversion layer existed that would worsen any smog conditions that developed. Supervisor Warren Church noted that the photograph was submitted as evidence of smog by the "anti-Humble group" during the September 2 Board of Supervisors hearing. Whether Humble and its allies challenged the validity of the claim that it was smog is unknown. The photograph by Citizens for Clean Air, just like many of the claims by Humble, were examples that neither side was purely in pursuit of the truth.

Overall, the materials presented by Citizens for Clean Air constituted a formidable array of data and assertions pushing back on all the favorable claims that Humble and its supporters made to county officials. While the information's impact was minor at best, it represented the diligence, thoroughness and organization of Citizens for Clean Air that led it to challenge and effectively delay Humble from building its refinery on the timeline that the oil giant originally planned. Without Citizens for Clean Air, it is doubtful that public opinion against the refinery would have begun to shift in the summer of 1965.

17

H U M B L E ' S   S U P P O R T E R S

R E G R O U P

August 13 – September 1, 1965

"If we can put a man on the moon, we can control smog coming out of smoke stacks."

Chester Deaver, former Monterey County Supervisor

Despite the growing opposition, Humble Oil still had many support-ers, and they began to coalesce throughout the county. A new group emerged, gathering at Andersen's Pea Soup restaurant near the airport in Salinas, comprised primarily of members of various chambers of commerce but also including a representative of a carpenters' union, which stood behind Humble "100 per cent." The Planned Growth for Monterey County Committee, headed by members of the Salinas, Seaside and Marina chambers of commerce, announced a campaign to back Humble's refinery plans. The group then split into Seaside-Marina and Salinas-Castroville chapters.

"The establishment of Humble Oil at Moss Landing is in keeping with the progress of our times," said Jim Hendricks, head of the Seaside Chamber of

Commerce. "With the tremendous increase of population in California we must be prepared in all areas of industrial development."

Around the middle of August, a locally printed mailer by an undisclosed group known only as "Independent Citizens Vitally Interested In The Economic Growth Of Monterey County" appeared widely in mailboxes. The mailer asked for supporters to contact their supervisor and included a postcard to mail their elected representative.

The mailing boldly stated, "Planned Industrial Growth In Monterey County Is Necessary To Lessen YOUR Tax Burden." It warned the reader, "DON'T BE MISLED BY THE SCARE TACTICS OF THE OPPONENTS."

The mailer laid forth the same economic arguments that Humble and its supporters had touted since the spring—construction jobs, high-salaried permanent refinery jobs, and economic stimulation for the county. It assured those concerned about Humble's submarine pipeline unloading supertankers in the bay that it was the same process as PG&E had done for years to supply fuel to its power plant. The mailer further assured residents that Humble's water use would not exceed the demands of agriculture on a similar piece of land. The mailer also referenced two air pollution consultants who attested that "there will be no danger of damage to crops" from the refinery. There was the implied reference that the conditions currently under consideration for the refinery were acceptable to Humble and "will adequately prevent any contamination to air or water."

More support for Humble came from the Castroville Chamber of Commerce. During a two-and-a-half-hour meeting attended by 50 people, regular business was set aside to discuss Humble's permit. Not a single person in the crowded meeting spoke against Humble.

On August 13, Supervisor Warren Church appointed an ad hoc ten-person committee to visit the modern Union Oil refinery at Rodeo in the San Francisco Bay Area. This was the oil refinery that Planning Commissioner Peter Cailotto scourged as dirty and unpleasant during his visit. However, Cailotto was not in this two-car convoy arranged by Church. The group included business owners, neighborhood residents and adjacent property owners to the Humble project, as well as two members of the Monterey County Air Pollution Advisory Committee. The group spent an hour and a half touring the facility and then headed to the nearby town of Crockett where the group questioned nearby residents and businesses on any deleterious effects from the refineries. Also on the itinerary was a visit to the less modern Standard Oil refinery in Richmond for comparison.

Peter DiMarco, who represented the Castroville chamber on Church's committee, reported that all but one of the committee members favored Humble's proposal after visiting the refineries and the adjacent neighborhoods. Five committee members were present at the Castroville meeting and spoke in favor of the Moss Landing refinery. DiMarco's comments summed up the group's conclusions.

"There was no odor," said DiMarco, "and it was a bright sunny day. I asked Union Oil what would pollution, if any, do to vegetation. It was pointed out that vegetation is growing within a refinery near Santa Maria. One person told me he couldn't understand the fuss over a refinery in Monterey County. 'If you guys don't want that refinery, we'll take it,' he said. 'We need the plant here. We need the jobs.'"

One of the committee members and speakers was Paul Tripp of Elkhorn, who had managed Church's 1964 supervisorial campaign and was credited by the supervisor as "the single most important person" in helping him get elected. Tripp noted that he had worked for a refinery in Toledo, Ohio, and that he was "impressed" with the Union Oil facility that the committee visited.

Jack Simon, a civic leader in the Castroville area and one of the candidates in the 1964 supervisorial race that elected Church, introduced Humble chemical engineer George Swisher to take questions after the committee's report. Simon would run against Church for supervisor in the future, ultimately failing, but running strong, credible campaigns.

Simon was not the only candidate from the 1964 North County supervisorial race to back Humble. Douglass Allmond, who ran a strong third in the primary, a few hundred votes behind Church and a few hundred votes ahead of Simon, strongly advocated for Humble. Coincidentally, Allmond purchased property for retirement in Anacortes, Washington, where two modern oil refineries operated. The Anacortes refineries were to be a site of a visit by the supervisors later that month. Allmond, who subscribed to the local Anacortes newspaper for two and a half years, reported that he could find only one instance in the paper through letters or an editorial that had anything negative to say about the refineries. However, Allmond was realistic about industry's possible side effects.

"[W]e must accept some detrimental effects in order to receive the much greater benefits Humble refinery will bring to the area," wrote Allmond in a letter to the editor in the *Salinas Californian*. "[I]t is my considered opinion that it would be the height of folly to refuse to accept the proposed Humble Oil Refinery when they accede to all reasonable safeguards."

There was one more prominent voice in North County standing in unshake-
able support of Humble. Three-term former supervisor Chester Deaver, already
considering a rematch against Church in 1968, stated that if he were still on
the Board of Supervisors, then he would vote for Humble. After all, it was
Deaver who was on the Board of Supervisors in 1956 when the Moss Landing
Area Development Plan was enacted. This plan was in Deaver's district, and he
claimed strong support for it. It was Deaver who had been one of the county's
strongest voices in favor of industrialization during his tenure as a supervisor.
If Humble failed, then Deaver's legacy of Moss Landing industrialization was
in jeopardy.

"Humble has more to offer than Firestone," Deaver said, noting that the
oil company would draw allied industries into the county—one of the fears
of Humble opponents. "We have this scientific know how to control those
conditions we seem to be concerned about. If we can put a man on the moon,
we can control smog coming out of smoke stacks."

Deaver had been a strong advocate of the Firestone Tire and Rubber plant
that settled near Salinas in the late 1950s. The Firestone permit was approved
by the Board of Supervisors on a 4-1 vote. The only supervisor to vote against
it was Tom Hudson. During the Humble affair, the *Salinas Californian* would
constantly hark back to the Monterey Peninsula's and Hudson's opposition to
Firestone as an example of how the Peninsula kept trying to gum up Salinas
Valley matters.

As opposition mounted, supporters of Humble began to fear that the
supervisors might reject the project. The Castroville-Moss Landing area was
the center of Humble's support. For some years, debate over the incorporation
of Castroville had been a lively and viable matter. Incorporation of Castroville, and even the greater North County area, had been a major issue in the
supervisorial election of 1964 that featured six candidates and elected Warren
Church. Now, Humble supporters raised the issue of incorporation again.

"The minute this thing (the board hearing) is over—if the permit is not
granted—we will begin incorporation procedures," Frank Faustino of the Castroville Chamber of Commerce announced. Faustino was adamant. The refinery will be built "whether or not the board of supervisors grants the permit."

County Counsel William Stoffers threw cold water on the idea that incorporation was a quick process. Incorporation involved five steps: approval by
the Monterey County Local Agency Formation Commission, approval by
the County Boundaries Commission, filing of a notice of intent to circulate
petitions for incorporation, a hearing before the Board of Supervisors and

an election on incorporation. Stoffers estimated that process would take at least six months. Faustino countered that everything could be done in three to four months.

Humble never weighed in on the incorporation question, or if it would be willing to wait three to six months, or longer, if the supervisors rejected the oil refinery. Humble's attorney Paul Hamerly stated that the question of incorporation had never been discussed by Humble. Even Castroville's incorporation would not guarantee an immediate permit for Humble. A new city must have a process to accept and grant permits. That would add more time. Humble was already edgy about the delay since February. The new Castroville incorporation timeline put approval well into the following year.

Throughout the Humble controversy, one of the biggest supporters of the oil company came from unions. With at least half of the 2,000 construction jobs coming from Monterey County, the refinery promised an abundance of good-paying work. An even higher proportion of the jobs would have come from Monterey County except for a lack of skilled workers. The unions also saw an opportunity for employment, not just in the building of the plant, but in its maintenance. They were not without concerns regarding pollution, but felt, as many in the business community did, that a balance was achievable.

"We are in favor of Humble building this at Moss Landing with strong ordinances guarding air and water pollution," Leslie Dollins of Electrical Workers Local 243 said. "We're not just interested in the money."

Others began to speak out against the data presented by the increasing number of experts warning of damage from Humble. Edward Gribi, a petroleum geologist from King City, called the "Humble refinery controversy … fundamentally a scientific problem and conclusions should be reached by rigid adherence to the disciplines of the scientific method." Gribi blasted opposition to Humble on "emotional grounds" as "illogical, unreasonable, (an) almost hysterical position." Furthermore, Gribi felt that many of the experts quoted had their words taken out of context.

Humble was not sitting idly by as opposition began to climb in previously supportive areas. The oil company began an aggressive public relations campaign with visits to community groups and service clubs. Humble also began placing prominent ads in the local papers.

One ad in the *Watsonville Register-Pajaronian* prominently featured "Yvette," a goldfish. Yvette was stationed at Humble's Baton Rouge refinery where she swam around in wastewater before it was released into the Mississippi River. According to Humble, Yvette's ability to stay alive in wastewater was an

indicator that the water would not harm fish when released. Humble claimed
Yvette as part of its $6 million annual program to prevent pollution.

Yvette helps Humble keep our rivers clean

Yvette, a goldfish, is a full-time employee at Humble's Baton Rouge Refinery. Her job is to swim around in the waste water from the refinery, before it goes into the Mississippi River, to make sure it won't harm the fish.

For more than 35 years, Humble has been developing new and more efficient methods to solve one of industry's most critical problems—

preserving the purity of our air and water. Yvette is one of the least sophisticated and least expensive parts of our $6,000,000 yearly program to prevent pollution wherever we operate.

To Humble, this investment in clear air and water is another opportunity to fulfill the responsibility of leadership.

HUMBLE OIL & REFINING COMPANY...AMERICA'S LEADING ENERGY COMPANY (ENCO)

A goldfish named Yvette starred in one Humble ad, representing Humble's measures to prevent water pollution.
Authors' collection

Another series of ads involved a "pledge" by Humble that it would not
violate any laws and that its emissions would be less than the levels determined
harmful to "crops, flowers and marine life." Humble claimed that its refinery

49

would not "impair the gainful or pleasant use of the natural resources or the man-made living and recreational advantages of Monterey County."

Still another ad reprinted an editorial from the *Grand Junction Daily Sentinel* in Colorado espousing the clean refinery at Humble's Baytown facility near Houston. "... [N]o visitor would know from the smell or smoke that he was anywhere near a refinery," asserted The *Daily Sentinel.* "The affluent from this gigantic refinery is dumped into the Houston canal—which is badly polluted—but where this particular affluent goes in, the fish grow prolifically and to a large size."

Humble sent Jack Gardner, manager of planning for its manufacturing division, to the Salinas Lions Club where he and opponent Earl Moser spoke at the Jeffery Hotel in Salinas. Moser, a retired Chevron executive, knew the dangers and language of Humble. Moser commented that hundreds of tons of the three most noxious and plant-damaging pollutants from oil refineries were released every day into the air above the San Francisco Bay Area—49 tons of nitrogen oxides, 141 tons of sulfur oxides and 108 tons of hydrocarbons. Moser said that no controls could effectively limit these pollutants.

Gardner took issue with Moser, and for the first time by a Humble official, proposed hard numbers on the pollutants that the Moss Landing refinery would produce. Gardner said that Humble would release in Moss Landing only about 1/8 of the emissions produced by all the refineries in San Francisco Bay Area or 1/15 of those in Los Angeles. Gardner asserted that these numbers were "a rough ballpark estimate" and were inconsequential when compared to the "astronomical amounts" of air in the Salinas Valley. Gardner insisted that all three compounds Moser warned about were contained at acceptable limits. He further claimed that hydrocarbons were the worst offender and that automobiles were the primary cause of their release, and that a comparably sized enterprise to Humble would have many more than the 200 employees planned for their refinery. The addition of extra employees traveling to work by car would create far more hydrocarbons detrimental to Monterey County crops than Humble's refinery. Members of the Lions Club bought into Gardner's argument and took it a step further by claiming that tourism on the Monterey Peninsula was a greater threat of hydrocarbon pollution than anything Humble might produce. The members directed their questions toward Moser while ignoring Gardner, stating that Humble was necessary for the continuing development of the county.

The *Monterey Peninsula Herald* broke down Gardner's fractions from Moser's figures based on a 1963 report to estimate that 6.5 tons of nitrogen oxides,

17.6 tons of sulfur oxides and 13.5 tons of hydrocarbons would be released into the air every day by Humble's refinery. Those figures brought a quick response from irritated Humble officials.

"Humble disclaims the tons per day of air contaminates attributable to its proposed Moss Landing refinery as contained in yesterday's *Herald* article," the company declared. Humble also disputed that Gardner quoted "any tons per day of hydrocarbons, nitrogen oxides or sulfur oxides that would be emitted from its proposed refinery."

"The fractions, based on ratios of refining capacity, of one-eighth of the San Francisco Bay Area refineries and one-fifteenth of the Los Angeles refineries, were never intended as a basis for estimating the actual emissions from a modern grass-roots refinery. They were simply intended to illustrate the point that a small fraction of the refinery capacity in these two areas, when combined with the tremendous volume of air in the Salinas Valley, would result in such diluted concentration of contaminates that absolutely no harmful effects would result. It should further be pointed out that the calculations by the *Herald*, not Humble, were based solely on the San Francisco Bay data where refineries do not meet the strict controls as in Los Angeles. If the *Herald* had made the same calculations on the Los Angeles data, they would have shown only one-fourth the amount of hydrocarbons, one-third the amount of sulfur dioxides and three-fourths the amount of nitrogen oxides, and this is still for old existing refineries."

While Humble disputed the *Herald* numbers, and provided fractions for Los Angeles, it never provided the Los Angeles data that it based its fractions on, nor did it provide the tonnage that could be extracted from such data to show specifically where the *Herald* was incorrect. In response, the *Herald* retorted that it never claimed that Gardner provided those numbers, but estimated the totals from Moser's and Gardner's statements—the only data it had.

In the weeks leading up to the September 2 showdown at the Board of Supervisors' chambers, Gardner became the go-to man for Humble in the public eye. Gardner visited whoever would listen to him, including the Castroville Chamber of Commerce, and the Kiwanis Club in Castroville where a film on Hawaii's refinery "Fuel for the Fiftieth" was shown about the construction of the refinery at Barber's Point. In addition, there were two other movies—"Refinery at Work" about the inner workings of a refinery, and "Wild Rivers," an attempt to promote Humble's protection of rivers.

At the Kiwanis Club, Gardner dismissed the notion that the refinery would consume too much freshwater. But saltwater intrusion was becoming a serious problem in the Castroville area. The depletion of groundwater aquifers, primarily from agriculture, was allowing saltwater to creep steadily inland. Coincidentally, the first saltwater intrusion reports for the area came in 1946, around the time when Moss Landing's harbor was dredged. Humble proposed drawing out just under two million gallons a day of freshwater. Many critics questioned this as unsustainable. Gardner adduced that 85 percent of the cooling at the refinery would be by air with the remainder using reclaimed water that could be run through the cooling process multiple times.

Because of the concerns about air pollution, water was an underplayed issue. Saltwater intrusion was a problem neglected for decades and increasing as a threat, with the potential to contaminate drinking water sources and to harm plant life irreparably. An oil refinery needs massive amounts of water, but so does farming. Humble estimated its water use at 1,872,000 gallons a day. Sucking that much water out of the ground every day stirred fears that as the freshwater levels were depleted, saltwater would rush in to fill the void. One solution proposed was building a canal from the Salinas River to Humble in Moss Landing roughly along the path that the old Salinas River flowed prior to the turn of the century. However, that proposal received a less than enthusiastic response. Despite continuing concerns over the long-term viability of consuming that much freshwater, the problem was never adequately addressed throughout the entire Humble controversy.

Humble claimed that its facility would use no more water than agriculture used on the 444-acre tract. The three wells on the property produced 1,700 gallons per minute. Humble needed 1,300 gallons per minute. As Humble was prone to do from time to time, this assertion was disingenuous, if not an outright falsehood. William Carnie, the editor of the *Castroville Times and Moss Landing Harbor News*, called out Humble's claim, noting "This is the same thing as saying that if you turn on the faucet to wash the dishes, you will use no more water if you let it run all night."

"There is a big difference," elaborated Carnie, "between pumping these wells to capacity for perhaps 10 hours a day intermittently during five months of the year and drawing the same amount of water 24 hours a day for 365 days a year."

Also raised was the issue of Humble dumping its wastewater into the Monterey Bay. Gardner stated that wastewater dumping would occur one to one-and-a-half miles from shore "so no one can say we put it into the Moss Landing Harbor or sloughs." Gardner also claimed that the more distant dumping would not have any detrimental affect on marine life.

Air pollution remained the primary concern in public debate. Gardner pushed that automobiles were the real source of pollution in the state, not industry. He claimed that in Los Angeles 70 percent of the pollution was caused by automobiles, 20 percent by dry cleaning and painting, and just 2 percent from refineries. According to Gardner, the average vehicle produced 3,850 pounds of pollution per year. Gardner's computations are based on one gallon of gasoline causing 20 pounds of carbon dioxide. While it seems illogical that one gallon of fuel, which weighs 6.3 pounds, can produce 20 pounds of pollution, the increase in weight develops after the release of carbon atoms when burned. A carbon atom then combines with two oxygen atoms, which are individually heavier than carbon, to make a carbon dioxide molecule that is 3.7 times heavier than a single carbon atom.

"I can't say whether Monterey County will ever have smog—but if it does, it will be caused by automobiles, not refineries," charged Gardner.

The *Californian* remained steadfastly in Humble's corner and followed up Gardner's comments with an editorial on the same theme. It also blamed the bulk of pollution on automobiles, clearly meant to deflect attention from the growing concern that smog might destroy the lush and profitable crops of the Salad Bowl of the World. Once again, the *Californian* pointed its pen toward the Monterey Peninsula and tourism as a source of emissions that threatened those crops.

The Salinas newspaper also expressed outrage that Monterey County was developing a reputation as an unfriendly place for industry. The editors mentioned that a leading recruiter of industry in Northern California listed 33 locales as welcoming to industry. None of those were in Monterey County. The recruiter said Monterey County was not recommended because of delays and criticism endured by industries, complaining that "industry literally has to fight its way in." The *Californian* mocked the opponents of Humble who claimed the county had the right to "pick and choose" its industries. The editorial then rolled out a long list of denied companies: Wrigley, Sylvania, Hershey, Columbia Broadcasting Records, American Brake Shoe, Goodyear Tire and Rubber, and Birdseye Food Company as a few examples. The newspaper declared this was not an example of "pick and choose" but outright hostility to industry.

One of the outspoken critics of Humble in the North County area, Leonard Mattson, took the *Californian* to task for those examples in a letter to the editor. Mattson questioned if Birdseye, Wrigley's and Hershey ever applied for a permit. He also noted that several manufacturers were well-established locally and faced little if any opposition, including Chicago Printed String, Smuckers, Streater, Nestlé and Peter Paul.

The *Monterey Peninsula Herald* countered in an editorial that also disputed the *Californian's* contentions. The *Herald* noted that industry was not avoiding Monterey County and that two dozen companies had located in the county in recent years. The *Herald* also pointed out that opposition to the Firestone tire plant was not so much from the Peninsula as from the Salinas Valley. The editors drew a stark contrast with the *Californian* stating that "We MUST pick and choose" industries to protect both agriculture and tourism—the lifeblood of the region.

With less than two weeks before the Board of Supervisors would determine the future of Humble's refinery, Humble announced that its $50 million state-of-the-art refinery was going to cost $70 million. The cost increase wasn't from expansion but from an internal study that found cost increases in labor and materials to build the refinery. A demand for higher-quality gasoline also pushed up costs with more elaborate and expensive processing methods. Gardner insisted that the conditions proposed by the county to regulate Humble had little to do with the increased costs.

The increase in cost meant a big increase in taxes. The original cost would bring nearly $1 million to the county's coffers. The new cost boosted that toward $1.4 million. For those who touted the economic bonus Humble would bring, this provided further justification that industry was the future of Monterey County. The *Herald* sniffed out this increase in taxes as "added bait" to maintain support for Humble. In an editorial, Ted Durien made the unsubstantiated claim that the extra $20 million would create a larger refinery with more production and more pollution, all charges that Humble denied. A larger refinery would have meant a revised application, but Humble made no attempt to expand beyond its 50,000 barrels-a-day plan.

While Humble sought to halt the hemorrhaging of support from the Salinas Valley to North County, its focus was on the supervisors and the anticipated close vote. The upcoming trip to Anacortes, Washington, by the supervisors would be one last attempt to prove that a modern refinery was a clean refinery.

18

THE BOARD INVESTIGATES

July 29 – September 1, 1965

*"The days of the old robber barons are over. Today, industry
has civic responsibility."*

Bechtel Engineering Corporation official

With the final decision now in sight, reporter Stanley Cloud of the *Monterey Peninsula Herald* summarized the stakes on the table as the Board of Supervisors considered the Humble refinery:

"The future is much the same as past, except that—as the matter goes to the board of supervisors—the debate will intensify, will become even more political, even more regional, even more bitter—impossible as all that may sound after five months of one of the most heated debates in the history of the county.

"In this case, however, with public opinion at a fever pitch, the supervisors will, in a sense, be voting for their individual political lives when they decide on the Humble application."

After the Planning Commission rendered its decision, Board Chair Tom Hudson said that he expected the supervisors to take the matter up very quickly and render a decision in just one meeting, perhaps even within two weeks. After five months of struggle, the possibility that the battle was nearing its end only intensified the anxiety and tensions rippling through the county's political circles. However, North County Supervisor Warren Church, in whose district Humble planned its refinery, balked. Church made it clear that he was unprepared for a decision for at least three to four weeks, and said he had not seen a final draft as passed by the Planning Commission. He also stated that he felt the 31 conditions that the Planning Commission placed on the project were too weak and that "One or two points may need revising." Church, as tight-lipped as ever, refused to reveal those changes.

When the supervisors met the first Tuesday in August, the discussion was brief. Church made a short motion to review the Humble project on August 31. The rest of the board consented. Both Humble and its opponents announced their intention to submit new information. Supervisor Andy Anderson requested all available information on the economic impact of the $50 million facility and a history of Humble's oil spillages. Arthur Atteridge requested all information presented to the Planning Commission over the last six months.

The following week, the supervisors shifted the hearing date back to September 2 when Humble officials announced that they were unavailable for an August 31 meeting. The supervisors also placed discussion of an air pollution control district on the September 14 agenda, now possible under state law because of legislation introduced by State Senator Fred Farr. The shift from August 31, a Tuesday, when the Board of Supervisors regularly met, to September 2, a Thursday, meant that the supervisors would hold an unusual special meeting for the Humble permit. The supervisors probably realized that Humble would devour most of the day, hence the need for a special meeting. Nevertheless, that the meeting would run a marathon 17 hours was never anticipated by anyone.

The pro-Humble editors at the *Salinas Californian* lashed back at the supervisors for delaying Humble again. Calling the action of the supervisors "embarrassing," the *Californian* declared that Humble deserved better treatment. "MORE STUDY? For what?" demanded the newspaper. Belittling the calls for another review, the editors said that if the supervisors had not made up their minds after six months, what good was another four weeks?

With major farmers, the *King City Rustler* and several new anti-Humble groups probing the worth of the refinery, cracks in the once indomitable support for Humble were starting to show. The *Castroville Times and Moss Landing Harbor News* noted that the refinery was becoming increasingly controversial. The *Times* said the August delay gave the county time to tighten its regulations and time for residents to second-guess if Humble really was the best neighbor for their community. The newspaper credited one person in particular for the time of reflection.

A collection of refinery brochures and guides from the supervisors' field trips in 1965.
Author's collection

"A good deal of credit for bringing the refinery question into the open for full public debate must go to Supervisor Warren Church of North County. Church displayed considerable courage in insisting on a 30-day delay after the Planning Commission decision before bringing the matter to the Board of Supervisors. At the time of the planners' decision, North County appeared almost unanimously in favor of the oil company. Church received a good many brickbats from the pro-Humble camp for his pains.

"Church is by no means anti-Humble. He may well vote to overrule the planners if he believes that this is what the majority of his constituents want. He simply wants to be sure that everyone has a chance to be heard and that the people of his district are fully aware of what they will be getting."

The shifting political winds in the third supervisorial district during August made for some uncomfortable times for Harold Henry. Henry had a long history as a supporter of agriculture, a prerequisite to being a supervisor in the South

County district, home to some of the richest farmland in the world. However, Henry's long advocacy for Humble placed him at odds with his most important constituency. It was an unfamiliar position for the Salinas Valley native.

Henry was born in 1908 to George and Minnie Henry, part of a pioneer family in South Monterey County. His father served on the first city council in King City. George Henry's role in local politics spurred the younger Henry onto a similar civic path in life. Harold Henry worked in management with milling companies before becoming a bean and grain broker, as well as in civilian defense, and served on the southern district rationing board during World War II. He was elected to city council in 1945 and selected as mayor of King City, a position he held for the entire eight years he served on the council. In 1958, he won election to the Board of Supervisors and reelection in 1962. Despite describing Henry as a "genial and friendly man," the Californian's editors noted that his directness "made him a controversial figure."

Henry was somewhat of a foil to the interests of those on the Monterey Peninsula. Although he and Hudson agreed on many business matters, their differences in style, upbringing and experience put them at odds.

"The Peninsula and the rest of the county are just not compatible," Henry said during his first term on the board of supervisors.

While Henry was a strong supporter of agriculture, he also favored diversifying the county's economy so as to enlarge its tax base. That placed him as a strong supporter of the planned industrial complex at Moss Landing. Since most of his constituents viewed Moss Landing as a faraway place, there was not much concern or strong support for Humble in his district when the long battle began. It was easy for Henry to leap into the debate by fully backing Humble's plans without fears of political repercussions. Henry probably never considered that pollution could be a threat to the livelihood of the farming communities that he represented. Yet as expert after expert from around the state warned Monterey County of the dangers that lay ahead, Henry clung to the words of the county's hired pollution expert W.J. O'Connell. O'Connell said pollution could be controlled. That was good enough for Henry, but the opposition in South County slowly crept forward until it exploded. While it appears that most people still backed Humble in Henry's district, it was a tepid support. The opposition of refinery opponents in the agricultural community was anything but tepid. Their livelihoods were at stake. Although probably a minority, they were vocal, growing in numbers and representing the political power in South County. Unexpectedly, Henry was walking on landmines, especially with his seat up for reelection the next year.

Henry had opportunities to change his position on Humble, but either out of stubbornness, conviction or ignorance, he did not. Described by The *Californian's* Ray March as a "rube," Henry may not have totally grasped the sophisticated intricacies of the Humble issue. The technical operations of oil refining, the alphabet soup of chemicals and the still developing science of understanding pollution's direct and indirect effects were not easy subjects. None of the five supervisors had a background in science, and two of them did not have a college education—one of those being Henry. Henry may have been the least prepared to handle an issue as technical as Humble.

Henry's vacillating became evident again when he motioned at a Board of Supervisors meeting on August 17 that the supervisors should visit a modern, clean refinery such as Humble proposed to build. He suggested one in Puget Sound. The motion died without a second when Tom Hudson said, "Can't you think of a better place than Seattle?" Hudson suggested that the county pay for the trip instead of Humble, but the discussion broke down into disorganized comments until Hudson moved onto another item on the agenda, leaving the motion to die on the floor.

The following week, Henry pushed a visit to Puget Sound again. This time the other supervisors were more receptive. An agreement was made to visit the refineries in the town of Anacortes, which Humble claimed held one of the four sites where modern refineries existed, similar to what it proposed for Moss Landing. The other sites were in Hawaii, Norway and the Bahamas. Scheduled for the two-day trip were Supervisors Henry, Hudson, Anderson and Church. Atteridge demurred, stating that he had seen enough refineries in two tours of the San Francisco Bay Area. Besides the four supervisors, Sanitation Director Ed Munson came along on the trip. Church accepted the trip on the condition that Humble or refinery officials would not control the tour. He demanded that the supervisors and Munson be free to inspect wherever they wanted. Also on the trip were reporters Ray March of the *Salinas Californian* and Stanley Cloud of the *Monterey Peninsula Herald*, who would both write detailed accounts of the excursion.

The supervisors were to visit the 65,000-barrel-a-day Texaco and 72,000-barrel-a-day Shell facilities at Anacortes. Both refineries were approximately the same size as Humble's proposed Moss Landing plant. Ten miles away in neighboring Ferndale was a Mobil refinery, but it was not on the itinerary and only viewed from the air. Bechtel Engineering Corporation built all three. Bechtel, with its association with Humble, already planned on constructing the Moss Landing plant. As the supervisors conducted their trip, the Gemini

5 capsule splashed down from its record-breaking eight-day journey in orbit around the earth with astronauts Gordon Cooper and Charles Conrad. The marvels of science, from space exploration to modern, clean refineries, were now on full display.

The organization of the trip fell to Henry and Bechtel engineer Ted Dungan. The first day involved an inspection of Texaco's refinery followed the next day by a visit to Shell. Greeted by a handpicked selection of refinery supporters, the Monterey County delegation enjoyed lunch at the Skyline Marina in Anacortes with a manager from Shell, two representatives from Texaco, two from Bechtel, three newspaper representatives, the current mayor and a former mayor. The chatter during lunch bore the same story Humble had presented for months—modern refineries are clean. In Anacortes, the mayor—who happened to be an employee of the Shell refinery—spoke of the tax dollars that built schools and other infrastructure. Special attention was paid to the oyster beds, apparently unaffected by the effluent released back into the Pacific Ocean from the refineries. After the tours, the group met with Anacortes residents without the presence of oil company officials. However, many of these residents worked for the refineries.

Bechtel's experts emphasized that a modern refinery was defined by the control exercised over the release of chemicals from the production of petroleum products. The refineries were designed to meet Los Angeles-level pollution standards, according to Bechtel.

"The days of the old robber barons are over. Today, industry has civic responsibility," declared one Bechtel official.

March of The *Californian* reported that crops growing around the refineries appeared to have no damage, nor farmers concerned about any. The lack of agricultural damage was confirmed a few days later to Sanitation Director Munson by an official at the Northwestern Agricultural Experimental Station in nearby Mount Vernon.

Munson, aware that there was no air pollution agency and that air pollution monitoring was "not done routinely," pointed out that the nearly continual overcast skies were a big help in controlling smog. Direct sunlight and higher temperatures promote smog, which even in fog-laden Monterey County were far more likely weather conditions than in Anacortes. This was especially so the farther one traveled south through the Salinas Valley.

Humble officials claimed that the Moss Landing refinery would match the two Anacortes refineries in appearance and internal controls for pollution. When pressed on the effectiveness of the design, Bechtel deferred to the refinery officials. As Cloud of the *Herald* discovered, that was a "dead-end street." No official from either Texaco or Shell would reveal how many pollutants were released into the environment.

"They give assurances that the amount is well below tolerable limits," Cloud wrote, "... and point with pride to the obviously clean air around Anacortes."

"I think we're doing everything that's reasonable and economical," said Harvard Hicks, a Shell manager.

However, the *Herald* also highlighted a visit by a Monterey Peninsula resident less than two weeks earlier to the Anacortes area. Carmel resident L.J. Fletcher, another retired industrialist opposed to Humble's project, visited Anacortes in mid-August. the *Herald* ran Fletcher's letter to the editor as a front-page story. Fletcher witnessed an entirely different scene.

"If the Shell refinery at Anacortes, Washington is a 'modern' oil refinery, as indicated in your front-page story on Aug. 25, we of Monterey County are in for real trouble if such a refinery should be located here ...

"As we left the ferry slip, we looked over to the large Shell refinery, about one mile distant. It was completely covered with a thick, brownish smog. The smog covered the surrounding area, filling every depression ...

"Returning later on the ferry, I asked members of the crew about the morning smog. They said it was only bad when the air was still, which was not often."

Fletcher questioned if "every modern device is employed to eliminate smog, fumes, odors, etc." and smog was not eliminated, could Monterey County take the "undoubted risk" of a refinery to spoil the region's clean air?

Wally Funk, former owner of the *Anacortes American* newspaper and now owner of a neighboring town's newspaper, informed the Monterey County group that Anacortes was once a failing fishing and lumber town. The town had been losing residents for some time, but with the refineries, it bounced back, gaining 2,000 people in 10 years. Funk appeared befuddled about the antagonism to Humble in Monterey County, expressing that none of that existed in Anacortes.

"I can't understand why there's opposition (in Monterey County)," Funk said. "After all, we have scenic beauty to protect too."

"During the tour Monterey County officials had a difficult time finding anyone with a bad word for the refineries," March recounted. "One waitress admitted she occasionally caught an odor. A commercial fisherman said he knew of no water pollution damage to the salmon."

Cloud, in his story on the trip to Anacortes, confirmed March's thoughts.

"If there is anyone in this Pacific Northwest town who hates refineries, he is a difficult person indeed to find ... The support these people express ... for the oil refinery industry in general, was notable for its enthusiasm—an enthusiasm which is very nearly a mystique. The attitude apparently has affected the whole town. It is as though every citizen feels a very deep personal debt to the oil companies which built the refineries here ... The people are grateful, although several of them admitted that their situation was unique and that refineries may not be desirable in other more wealthy—and more smog prone—areas. Eye-smarting, plant damaging air pollution is not a problem, according to the unanimous opinion of all who were interviewed."

Cloud noted significant differences between Moss Landing and Anacortes that would explain the lack of pollution and discomfort. There was not an inversion layer. The wind blew away from Anacortes. The population was small and other industries were few, both which limited other contributing factors to smog. Overcast skies predominated throughout the year. Both March and Cloud attributed the lack of water pollution to the very stringent water quality regulations existing in Washington state. Both writers also confirmed that no one complained of any odors from the refineries. Cloud stated that the only odor concerns came from the handful of small lumber mills belching heavy smoke.

Henry's goal in proposing the trip to Anacortes was to find similar refineries in similar situations as the one planned for Moss Landing. Humble and Bechtel obliged, as they saw Anacortes as a winning presentation for their cause. The overwhelming support for the refineries in the area certainly made that case, and the fortunate breezy days for the supervisors' visit, unlike the stillness when Fletcher visited, added to the clean air image that Humble presented as the hallmark of modern refineries.

However, Hudson was not going to let Humble control the narrative. "There is almost no similarity between the Anacortes situation and the one in Monterey County," Hudson said. "If I lived in Anacortes, I would welcome the refineries too."

Henry pushed back against Hudson's position. He stated that Anacortes did favorably compare with Monterey County. However, one of the Texaco officials admitted that temperature inversions are rare in the Anacortes area. That was an important admission and a significant blow to the suggestion that Anacortes and Moss Landing were similar. The statement did not seem to faze Henry, though.

Back in Monterey County, the supervisors had just a few days to analyze their trip and to prepare for the critical meeting on September 2. It seemed that Humble was on the minds of everyone in the Monterey Bay area. Sharp disagreements emerged between friends and family members, but most of the debate was still lobbed geographically. The battle lines had shifted somewhat, but support remained strongest with those closest to the refinery and opposition stronger as one moved away from the focal point.

The *Watsonville Register-Pajaronian* looked at all the disparagement and scolded those who criticized supporters or dissenters like Planning Commissioner Peter Cailotto. In an honorable, but not politically realistic editorial, the editors appealed to a higher calling.

"It seems to us that the Monterey County Supervisors ... deserve to be considered as honorable men who will be motivated by the public good, not by multitudes of signatures on a petition saying "no" nor a Humble-financed public opinion poll saying "yes" ...

"Warren Church, the North County supervisor, may hold the deciding vote in this matter. If the polls are to be believed, most of his constituents want a refinery. But Mr. Church has access to more information than most of them, and he bears the obligation of making a decision which will have a long-range effect on the entire area, including Santa Cruz County. He is a man of ability and integrity, and we think he can be counted on to vote the way he sees the question, without regard to applause or condemnation."

19

WARREN CHURCH'S

CONUNDRUM

"I understood both sides."

Warren Church

Of the five men who sat on the Monterey County Board of Supervisors in the summer of 1965, one remained a mystery to watchers of the Humble controversy.

Tom Hudson was undeniably the most strident supervisor opposing Humble. Andy Anderson never wavered in his opposition either, although his district remained split and was probably pro-Humble. Harold Henry, initially as strongly in support of Humble as Hudson was opposed, toned down his support as the agricultural community rose against the refinery, but he never publicly entertained any opposition. Arthur Atteridge threw in his lot in support of Humble early and then went relatively quiet, giving some the thought that he might switch, but Atteridge never gave any overt indication that he would do so. That left only Warren Church as the unknown and swing vote in his first year as a supervisor.

Supervisor Church refused any hint at how he would vote until he began to pepper proponents and opponents with questions late into the night of

September 2 at the Board of Supervisors' Chambers at the Salinas Courthouse. But his silence was not from indecision. He made his mind up early, but Church saw Humble's refinery as more than a simple yes or no. It was complicated, and this meant a more intricate, measured decision.

Warren Church was an intensely private man for a public official. The 35-year-old had few close friends, and even then rarely shared all his thoughts with them. He was not one to easily trust someone, and once deceived he never accepted anything at face value from that person again. He was determined and thorough at whatever he tried to do, and preferred to rely on himself rather than others. Those traits would show themselves in the months of the Humble Oil controversy.

To understand Church, it is important to understand his love of North Monterey County. Church's grandfather imprinted a deep legacy on him even though Church never knew him. L.W. Church came from Massachusetts at the age of sixteen in 1852 and crossed the Isthmus of Panama on foot before making his fortune in the gold mines of the Sierra Nevada. He then settled in the Elkhorn area in 1868. Warren Church took to heart the many stories that his father told of life in 19th-century North Monterey County, especially about the Elkhorn Slough and its surrounding environs.

It was there that the Church family with an uncle, Zadock Karner, established a large dairy that ran nearly the entire length of what is now Castroville Boulevard and Dolan Road. Coincidentally, the property bordered Moro Cojo Slough, and the property line was not much more than a stone's throw from where Humble planned its refinery. Church's father, who was still alive in 1965 as the Humble affair played out, retained many family heirlooms for his son—a post-Civil War accounting ledger of business activities along the slough, 19th-century letters and pictures, bird eggs and rattlesnake rattles from Elkhorn—but most importantly, passed on an abiding love for rural life.

The Karner and Church dairy was lost when the cattle died one harsh winter in the 1870s, and the farm slowly pieced off as the family moved to a new site, directly across from where the headquarters of the Elkhorn Slough Reserve now sits. When L.W. Church died in 1905, the remaining land was split among Church's father and aunts. Church's father continued to farm his inheritance. That came to an end when a well drilling accident broke his back, and he was swindled in a loan that took the family farm from him. Family lore has it that he threw a curse on the property when he left it for the final time.

That story of dishonesty and that the more powerful prey on the powerless was one that the father never let his son forget. Throughout his life, Warren

Church strenuously avoided placing his fate in the hands of another, whether it was something as simple as a car ride or the grandiose promises of prosperity and purity from an oil company.

Warren Church, born days before the 1929 stock market crash, grew up in the tough economic times of the Great Depression. Although he said his family never went hungry, sometimes all they had to eat was beans. His mother and maternal grandparents came from Kansas around 1920 and carved out a small farm in the Elkhorn area. There they grew popcorn in the 1930s while Church's father kept bees and produced honey. Church recounted his family peddling and bartering bags of popcorn and jars of honey to Dust Bowl immigrants who worked the fields of the Salinas Valley and lived in Alisal, now part of East Salinas, or on the banks of the Salinas River in Hoovervilles that popped up to house them just south of the little town of Spreckels. As tough as times were, Church saw there were people far worse off than he and his family. Those experiences created an empathy for the underprivileged, and also a drive to better himself.

Warren's mother and father also ran a vegetable stand near present-day Highway 101 in Prunedale. Their neighbor was a young farmer named Chester Deaver. The Churches and Deaver never got along, but the Churches had to drive through Deaver's farm to get to their property. One day, Deaver put up a gate, supposedly to keep his chickens contained. Church's mother, a strong-willed woman who in her youth had packed up her belongings and moved by herself to teach native peoples in Hawaii, muttered that she wasn't going to put up with handling a gate every time that she came to the property. She promptly put her car in gear, hit the accelerator and drove straight through it. Deaver never replaced the gate. Thirty years later, Church would do the same to Deaver's political career in the 1964 election.

Church took up his father's profession as a beekeeper in his teens, owning 500 beehives and dabbling in land purchases at the age of 18. By the time he was drafted into the Korean War, he had branched into a new business venture as a nursery supplier. Returning from Korea, where he had been struck by shrapnel in a Chinese artillery bombardment, Church was awarded the Purple Heart. He also brought home the determination to enter politics.

In 1956, Church ran a weeks-long write-in campaign against Republican Assemblyman Alan Pattee. No Democrat filed to challenge Pattee so Church put his name forth in the last weeks of the campaign. He received nearly 2,000 votes, but Pattee swamped him as the only candidate on the ballot. It was the same year that Tom Hudson was elected to the Board of Supervisors.

Two years later, Church would again seek office. This time it was an unlikely race for county tax collector. At just 28 years of age, operating his nursery supply business and teaching elementary school in Pajaro, Church placed a respectable third in a four-person contest. The *Herald* called it a "surprisingly strong" race that initially had Church leading in the early returns, befuddling television commentators about the political newcomer.

In 1962, Church was elected to the Monterey County Board of Education. It was the same year in which Ruth Andresen was elected to the same board, and she would hold that seat for the next 48 years.

Later the following year, Church announced he would challenge Supervisor Chester Deaver, who was seeking his fourth term on the Board of Supervisors. Unlike his previous races, Deaver drew a crowded field of challengers. Besides Church, other candidates were Douglass Allmond, a cattle rancher; Jack Simon, a businessman and civic activist; Don Coffill, a businessman and fisherman; and Art Bayer, a retired cattle auctioneer.

Deaver faced a crowded field because a new interim zoning ordinance and building code in North Monterey County had agitated many residents. While cities had long embraced zoning laws, most rural areas had few zoning restrictions. Most of rural Monterey County was zoned "U" for Unclassified. That meant businesses, farms and residences could mix side by side. In 1963, the Board of Supervisors passed an interim zoning ordinance which began to designate areas for residential and business use and the enforcement of the first building code for unincorporated rural communities. The restrictions were lax, but for residents used to building and doing whatever they wanted to on their property, it was a disturbing intrusion.

As senior member on the Board of Supervisors, Deaver exerted considerable influence. Deaver had long advocated adding more industry to the county's tax base and played a crucial role in getting the Firestone plant to locate in Salinas. In the 1964 campaign, he touted his efforts on the relocation of Highway 1 over the Elkhorn Slough as that "which would allow industrial development there to become a reality." It is not a coincidence that the third largest contributor to Deaver's 1964 campaign was the law firm of Hamerly and Noland. In early 1965, Humble Oil publicly announced Hamerly and Noland as their attorneys to shepherd their oil refinery through the Board of Supervisors. Unfortunately for Humble, Deaver was out of office by that time.

Allmond primarily garnered support from those upset with the new zoning laws. Simon, Bayer and Coffill all assumed pro-business and development stances that were like Deaver's position, but Simon also strongly pushed for increasing the area's limited recreational facilities. Deaver had lost touch with many of his traditional bases of support, which gave the other candidates an opening. Of these four candidates, only Allmond and Simon, an energetic campaigner, were serious contenders.

An important issue in the 1964 campaign was incorporation. Castroville and Moss Landing seriously discussed incorporating and enjoying the fruits of the expected expanding tax base from the Moss Landing industrial complex. None of the six candidates spoke against that incorporation. The idea simmered for years, so it was not a surprise to see the matter arise in August 1965 as approval of Humble tottered. Incorporation supporters, like Peter DiMarco of the Castroville Chamber of Commerce, saw a potential Humble rejection as another opportunity to rally incorporation.

However, incorporation support did not stop at the borders of Castroville and Moss Landing. Opposition to the new zoning laws inspired the creation of the North Monterey County Incorporation Study Committee. The group advocated that incorporation would allow North County residents to control their own zoning laws instead of supervisors from the rest of the county imposing restrictions on them. It was a questionable position to take since incorporation invariably leads to further government regulations, including zoning. The committee even drew up plans for a 150-square-mile city named "Great Oaks."

Allmond was a member of the committee and a strong supporter for incorporating the entire North Monterey County area as a whole, including Castroville and Moss Landing. This put him at odds with Castroville and Moss Landing incorporation supporters who wanted separate cities in North County for their communities. Allmond even called the Castroville incorporation efforts "a stab in the back." The other candidates either supported the incorporation of North County, or like Deaver, did not declare a position. The only candidate to openly oppose the incorporation of North County was Church.

Church's platform also included creating a park system for Monterey County with "two or three" parks. His goal was to kickstart the county into developing a park in North Monterey County and another south of Salinas on the lower slopes of Mount Toro. Church's support for parks and maintaining the rural nature of North County seemed to contradict his later support of Humble Oil, an incongruity that the *Monterey Peninsula Herald* once noted along with several of his political acquaintances outside of his supervisorial district.

When Church officially filed to run for supervisor on February 24, 1964, he made an interesting comment as he outlined the differences between himself and Deaver. According to the *Salinas Californian*, "Church said that he is also vitally interested in making certain that the county's prime agricultural land is preserved. 'We can't have industrial development helter skelter,' he said. 'We have to draw the line somewhere.'" Those comments, and Church's platform on protecting prime agricultural land, squarely placed him as one of the more skeptical supervisorial candidates regarding industrial development for the county. A year later, those concerns would take a backseat as support for Humble's refinery took firm root in North County. As it was, the refinery was planned on prime agricultural land, just as most of the industrially zoned 3,880 acres was.

North Monterey County Supervisor Warren Church in the 1960s.
Authors' collection

Church also made one other major campaign promise, something a bit unique from other candidates of the day. He proposed an unofficial referendum on important issues affecting the district where he would conduct an informal "opinion vote" at his own expense. It was a concept that Church would rely on time and again as controversial issues arose during his twelve-year tenure on the board.

"Commenting on his unofficial referendum plan,' Church said, 'When our laws do not provide an opportunity for the people to vote on matters, we can do it unofficially. The most important ingredient needed is a supervisor for the district who will conduct an election and abide by the will of the majority.'"

The June 1964 primary put Deaver into a comfortable lead with 2,927 votes, but he was short of the 50% needed for a runoff. In a distant second place was Church with 1,374, followed closely by Allmond with 1,116 and Simon at 938. Bayer and Coffill trailed far behind.

Of the six candidates in that election, Deaver, Allmond and Simon would take strong positions in support of Humble the following year. Bayer's position is unknown, but he had advocated for industrial development in Moss Landing during the campaign, which would appear to put him in the Humble camp. Only Coffill expressed concerns about Humble the following year when he suggested that many Humble supporters would regret their position because of the odors that would develop from the refinery. However, Coffill came in last in the election and did not even get re-elected to his Moss Landing Harbor Commissioner position later the same year.

The November election pitted Deaver, who did little campaigning except by surrogates, against Church, who conducted an extensive door-to-door campaign that covered 99% of the voting households—an enormous feat in the spread-out, hilly and somewhat undeveloped area, of which parts had acquired electricity only in the previous 15 years. On Election Day, as President Lyndon Johnson rolled to an easy victory over Barry Goldwater, The Californian declared Church's "surprising upset victory" in an above-the-fold banner across its front page. Church won a relatively comfortable 5,456 to 4,390 victory over Deaver.

Church had no idea that in a little over three months, his campaign promises would face a test in one of the most pivotal and controversial issues ever to face the Monterey Bay region. Throughout the Humble Oil debate, Humble conducted a sophisticated and effective campaign about the benefits of its Moss Landing refinery. Humble representatives generally stayed focused, factual and persistent with a few exceptions. One of those exceptions happened in the days following Humble's February announcement of its intention to build a refinery. The chief representative for Humble at that time was J. Prince Warner, vice president for manufacturing. Some of Warner's answers to a few basic questions from the supervisors were so untruthful as to be condescending, as if he assumed that the supervisors were uneducated bumpkins from a cow county.

A particularly strong falsehood came when Church asked Warner, "What about the clean air of Monterey County?"

"We can build a good, clean, sweet-smelling refinery," Warner responded, adding that smoke from the refinery would be undetectable by instruments.

It's unlikely that any supervisor believed that line. For Church in particular, Warner's words appeared as a deliberate attempt to deceive. Claims of a "sweet-smelling refinery" with no detectable emissions sounded like a con man's swindle. For Church, that was enough to question everything about Humble.

Humble's refinery was an excellent chance for Church to use the "unofficial referendum" promised from his campaign, although it was more of an unscientific poll of his constituents. In spring 1965, Church asked the voters of his district if they supported or opposed Humble. Church's poll found 75% support in his district, which mirrored Humble's later June survey that found 82% of the residents in North Monterey County supported the refinery. Initially, the Humble survey aroused some suspicion about the veracity of its results. However, if it was accurate in Church's district, then it was likely accurate for the entire county.

Whatever Church's initial feelings about the refinery, it was now clear to him that he had only one path. There was no question what an overwhelming majority of his constituents wanted on the Humble Oil question. During the campaign, Church strenuously promised to abide by the will of the majority. This painted him into a corner, for there was no ambiguity among his constituents in regard to Humble. Indeed, the strongest support in the entire county was in Church's supervisorial district.

Church's political support and future was already at a critical juncture just months into his term. His position had weakened despite his November election victory. The interim zoning ordinance that contributed significantly to Deaver's defeat came back to the supervisors for review and permanent implementation in the spring of 1965. Church voted for it. Those who opposed government's intrusion on their property rights complained strongly to the new supervisor. Church was well aware that if he opposed Humble, he would face recall and certain defeat.

Despite his other campaign promises to preserve the rural nature of North County, Church did not necessarily see that Humble's refinery was at odds with those promises. He did not buy into the slippery slope argument that one refinery would beget another until the whole countryside was dotted with factories. He saw Humble as one entity, not as a gateway to more refineries and satellite petroleum industries. Perhaps it was a bit naïve, and an imperfect rationalization, but it kept him alive politically.

Church would often mention in his recollections that he "understood both sides." He was one of the few people who tried to find a middle ground in a polarizing issue. It was a particularly narrow tightrope to walk, and one of the driving reasons that he put the brakes on the Board of Supervisors Humble vote after the Planning Commission decision. Church said some of the conditions needed revisiting, but true to his tight-lipped stance, he refused to reveal which conditions. In fact, Church was still formulating his plan until just a few days before the September 2 showdown. Despite his decisiveness and conviction in backing Humble, and his actions that followed the September 2 hearing, Church's thinking leading up to that point included more doubt than it may have appeared.

Although there was widespread support in Church's district for Humble, there was also widespread support for tight controls to prevent pollution and other disturbances. Church chose not to reveal his position on Humble until he knew what those controls should be. Why he did this is not known, but he must have been aware of the problems Harold Henry had created for himself by supporting Humble early. It was also Church's nature to act deliberately and carefully. Church's search for the right operating conditions would be a months-long education culminating in a meeting in late September when the supervisors finalized Humble's permit.

Monterey Peninsula Herald reporter Stanley Cloud, writing later in the year in his surreptitious role as editor and writer of *the advocate*, commented on Church's decision-making process in the November issue of *the advocate* that followed the Humble votes.

"Church is extremely cautious and not always effective, but he is keenly aware of the issues before him. He performs a prodigious amount of research—a habit the others could do well to emulate. Veterans, like Hudson and Henry, too often rely on faulty memories when they are seeking precedent in past board decision. Church *knows* because he has *checked*.

"As a freshman supervisor, Church is unusual in that he declines to accept tradition as reason and refuses to knuckle under to Hudson's power plays.

"He is sincere, if soft-spoken. He thinks of himself as a conservationist in spite of his vote for the refinery. He is also something of an iconoclast, and he doesn't hesitate to anger the 'gods' of county politics."

In his education on oil refining, Church was the only supervisor to take

part in every field trip by county officials to examine refineries in Los Angeles, the San Francisco Bay Area and Anacortes, Washington, except for one
visit solely conducted by the Planning Commissioners. Church was involved
heavily in the selecting of W.J. O'Connell, Monterey County's hired expert on
refineries. Church compiled and retained folders of information for his review
from both the opponents and supporters of Humble. As August rolled around,
following the vote by the Planning Commission rejecting the Humble project,
Church stayed in close contact with County Counsel William Stoffers and
Director of Sanitation Ed Munson on the conditions required if the Humble
permit was granted.

The opposition to Humble urged complete rejection, but initially, and up
until the Planning Commission meeting in July, opponents also urged strict
controls if the refinery was approved. After the planners rejected the project,
opponents, perhaps sensing victory, hardened and urged that the supervisors
unilaterally reject the proposal. It would make the meeting where the board
set the final conditions for the Humble permit an odd political juxtaposition
for the supervisors, supporters and opponents of the refinery.

Church's request to delay came partly from his discomfort that the conditions approved by the Planning Commission were not restrictive enough.
This created a strange political paradox. Church, who supported the refinery,
contrasted with the Planning Commission, which had rejected the refinery,
but laid out 31 conditions in case Humble gained approval. Church found
the conditions prepared by the opponents of Humble to be an inadequate
safeguard. It is an unusual and incongruous situation in politics when a supporter of a project presents tougher restrictions than the opponents. In this
case, it was fortuitous for the Monterey Bay area. Yet Church also had another
reason to delay, and that was to make sure his constituents knew the ins and
outs of the issue.

"I did not want to rush into the Humble decision," Church wrote in notes
summarizing the Humble affair, "because of need and responsibility to study
the matter thoroughly and in particular to make sure we have adequate conditions in which the refinery would operate under. Also, persons need to be
made aware of some of the ill-effects of the refinery even under the best of
conditions."

Crucial in Church's thinking style was respect for process. When opponents
raised concerns that an oil refinery was inappropriate for Monterey County,
Church dismissed the concerns as irrelevant for the Humble discussion. In
Church's mind, the objections about the appropriateness of an oil refinery

should have been raised before Humble's application. Moss Landing was a planned industrial area. The approved Moss Landing Area Development Plan encouraged the very industry Humble proposed. Thus, Humble should be evaluated according to those standards. It had been that way for years and no one complained. Indeed, people spoke of the importance to bring in industry. Church even pointed out that at his first board meeting on January 4, 1965, a month before Humble dropped its plans on the county, that the supervisors extended the Moss Landing interim zoning that included heavy industry such as oil refineries. He even mentioned that there was a moral obligation to approve Humble because of past board decisions approving other industrial projects. In other words, the protest against Humble at this point was the "right place, wrong time." If the people decided that future refineries and petroleum-related industries were inappropriate for the Moss Landing industrial development, then the zoning should be changed to reflect that. Church even took a sympathetic stance toward Humble in acknowledging the company as a "whipping boy" for industrial development while Kaiser Refractories and PG&E faced no significant opposition to expand during the same time.

Church also carefully noted that opponents and supporters agreed on one key point—a 50,000-barrel oil refinery at Moss Landing wasn't going to tip the scale of pollution to destroy agriculture or degrade the health of the area's residents. Church underlined in his notes summarizing the September 2 meeting that "no one said this one refinery would cause damage or pollution in itself." For Church, this was essential. He had seen refineries all over the West Coast, the new and the old ones. The new ones such as those at Anacortes impressed him. It convinced him that oil refining was generally not a "dirty industry," although a "contributor to smog." Years later, it was a position that Humble opponent Ruth Andresen would convince him to reverse during the time they served on the California Coastal Commission. But even if he had believed otherwise in 1965, Church was not going to break with his constituents. He had just made a campaign promise the previous year that he would abide by the will of the majority, and a super-majority supported Humble's refinery.

Another important factor in Church's decision-making was the determination that equivalent industries to replace Humble's promised $1.4 million in tax revenues would most likely be labor-heavy. All those workers would need cars, which had already been determined to be the worst pollution emitters. Workers would also need homes and support businesses which would mean more jobs and more people—and more polluting cars. Church noted that from 1952-65 there had been many light industries that came to the county. He estimated they employed about 4,000 people, with up to 15,000 more people living in the county if their families were counted. That brought another 8,000 cars and a lot more pollution and other problems, including a need for infrastructure like schools. All this impacted the county far more than Humble could. It was clear to Church that Humble's small refinery by itself was not a problem and far preferable to the damage that other industries with an equivalent tax base might bring.

While Church's pollution analysis was thorough and logical, his thought process did not succeed in persuading the opposition. Gus Bauman of Citizens for Clean Air took exception to Church's argument. Without mentioning the supervisor by name, Bauman dismissed his car example. "How ridiculous can we get!" Bauman exclaimed at the thought that people traveling "to and from work" could cause more pollution than Humble's refinery. In fact, Citizens for Clean Air had held multiple forums where outside experts expressed that cars were the primary source of pollution.

Church's arguments paralleled Planning Commissioner Daniel Krishun's in many ways. Although there is no record of the two strategizing, Krishun was a constituent of Church's—although a holdover appointee from Deaver's time as a supervisor. In general, Krishun advocated early what Church would later place in detail on the Humble permit. Krishun strongly supported the refinery, but also strongly supported tight controls, although he did not identify the specifics of those controls. Krishun's early positioning was significant, and he should be credited for trailblazing the path that Church would follow.

After the trip to Anacortes, Church firmed up his list of conditions. While there, Church ventured on a solo fact-finding excursion, ostensibly to review tax records of its two oil refineries, but also to break away from the county group and conduct his own research with the community's inhabitants. What he discovered exactly is unclear, but his notes remark that both refineries at Anacortes were small, producing 65,000 and 70,000 barrels a day, like Humble's proposal at Moss Landing of 50,000 barrels. Those notes highlighted that Anacortes had strict water pollution controls, but none for air emissions. He also reviewed the population growth in Anacortes since the refineries arrived, extent of pollution, effects on crops, real estate values and school enrollment. Church also noted was that two chemical satellite facilities were placed near the oil refineries.

Church became aware during this trip that oil refineries can ramp up their production 50% or more beyond their stated capacity. This observation appears to have inspired one of the critical conditions that Church would propose when the supervisors would meet later in September.

20

THE OPPOSITION STRIKES

BACK

September 3 - 22, 1965

"The matter should be decided by the people and laid to rest forever."

Bill Burleigh

Humble, despite having won approval from the Board of Supervisors, still did not have its permit in hand. The conditions for the permit were to be determined on September 24. A gloomy and bitter *Monterey Peninsula Herald* editorial, written by Allen Griffin, doubted that the three supervisors who rejected the Planning Commission's recommendations would make the effort to strengthen the conditions put forth by the commission.

"The same supervisors who refused to look into the future—which part or, in some cases, most of their constituents don't give a damn about anyhow, will pass upon the restrictions that are to be placed on Humble Oil. They want to pass on them quickly, too, so Humble Oil may roar ahead in this conquered province.

"What three supervisors are vitally interested in is that the restrictions imposed on Humble will be the sort the oil company 'can live with.'

"This newspaper doesn't want to disillusion anybody, nor does it want to discourage the many fine citizens who have fought and will continue to fight for clean air. But it does want to point out that the battle will continue to be as tough as Humble can make it and that in the end the air is going to be fouled up anyhow ...

"And by that time there may be more refineries, chemical plants, more synthetic plants. We have departed from the ways that made this county rich and great—in favor of the looters, big and little. In this wonderful county, we proved the correctness of the title of the book 'California Destroyed.'"

In the Salinas Valley, anger turned toward Supervisor Harold Henry. During the meeting to approve Humble, mumblings floated of a possible recall. The next day more rumors emerged of a committee forming to initiate the action. However, the rumors quickly died. Henry was up for election in just nine months anyway. The consensus seemed to be that the voters could decide then. Wayne Bowman, president of the Monterey County Farm Bureau, pointed to the challenges Henry would face encountering the voters the next June. "I just think at the next election he's going to have an awfully tough time getting elected. That's what I think."

"Mr. Henry's support has been waning anyway – even before this issue," another member of the agricultural community, who remained anonymous, said. The agriculturist stressed that public opinion in South County had turned against Humble: "There are many people down here who simply feel he is not adequately representing them."

However, Henry had an opportunity for a little fence-mending, as efforts to establish an air pollution control district in Monterey County were delayed until after a decision on Humble's permit. Ten days after the vote on the permit, Del Monte Properties President A.G. Michaud appeared before the supervisors for a vote on the formation of the new district. Expecting to see a vote on the matter, Michaud was disappointed to learn from Chairman Tom Hudson that the supervisors would only engage in an informal discussion at this time, with a final decision delayed until December. Bowman, expressing agriculture's concerns for more pollution controls, presented a request for further studies and a six-month delay. He was quickly backed by Henry, but only got three months.

Opposition to the air pollution control district arose from the Monterey County Farm Bureau and Monterey County Agricultural Advisory Committee. Agriculture, which had begun to coalesce around opposition to Humble because of fear over air pollution damage to crops, now felt less concerned with controlling the pollution threat if they bore responsibility for some of it. The ag community raised concerns about the creation of a new district with its own taxing powers, possible prohibitions on brush burning, agricultural burning, working of summer fallow and other farming activities. The farmers joined with PG&E and Kaiser Refractories which frowned on the district while complaining that they were already enduring high taxes.

"There is no urgency to establish a district at this time," Bowman from the Farm Bureau said—a departure from his statements during the Humble hearing.

Humble, on the other hand, expressed support for the creation of a district, a promise the oil company had made in July if it received a permit. Paul Hamerly, Humble's attorney, even argued for the "advantages" of a countywide air pollution control district with separate taxing powers. Humble made its preference known that it preferred one regulatory agency, a countywide district, instead of multiple smaller jurisdictions imposing air pollution standards. With Humble weighing in, the debate over the district created a bizarre realignment of alliances. Humble and its longtime adversary, Citizens for Clean Air, now joined in arguing for the creation of the district while the pro-refinery PG&E and Kaiser Refractories joined with anti-refinery farmers in the Salinas Valley to push against a district.

At the Board of Supervisors meeting, all the supervisors, except Henry, expressed support for a district. Henry, in a clear effort to reinforce his standing with the agricultural community said, "I want to know more about it. I want more details. I was accused last week of letting down the farmers and now I'm going to back them up."

"There may be a little face-saving going on here as far as agriculture is concerned," responded Hudson.

With yet another delay and another date for a hearing, Michaud left frustrated. "The moment of truth has been delayed," he said.

However, the moment of truth for Humble was still at hand. Although a few people, including Charles Kramer, urged that the county must come together and heal the divide splitting it, the pause was only momentary. The wounds from months of battle were too fresh. Even more important, there was yet another strategy concocted by Humble's opponents. Citizens for Clean Air began to take a back seat as a new strategy initiating legal and political challenges to the county's approval of Humble's permit unfolded.

The beginnings of this new strategy could be traced all the way back to May when a new city attorney was hired in Carmel. A young lawyer, Bill Burleigh, received the nod from a list of five candidates for the part-time position. Burleigh, still a relative newcomer to the area, noted years later that being unknown worked to his advantage.

"I was the only one they didn't know," said Burleigh, now a retired Monterey County judge. "They knew something bad about all the other applicants but they didn't know anything at all about me because I was new."

A newspaper ad urged local farmers to oppose the Humble refinery.
Authors' collection

Sandwiched between Humble's approval on September 3 and the meeting to set conditions on September 24, Burleigh announced the circulation of petitions for a referendum to overturn the supervisors' decision. The mayors of six Monterey County cities collaborated to use Burleigh as their legal counsel for what would later be known as the Six Cities Fund—Carmel, Monterey, Pacific Grove, Seaside, Del Rey Oaks and King City.

"This is the one (Humble controversy) that ... my city council raged about," Burleigh recalled. "I remember how outraged they were that they'd even consider that, a refinery in Monterey County, and they turned me loose." Burleigh later noted that he was just out of law school: "I got my feet wet on Humble Oil."

Burleigh, a native of Virginia, graduated from high school in Idaho, then with honors from the University of Colorado and received his law degree from the University of California, Berkeley. Before arriving on the Monterey Peninsula, Burleigh spent three years in the Marines. As the first phase of opposition to Humble began to ease, it was Burleigh who carried the baton of opposition into the following year. Burleigh would remain a thorn in the side of Humble for that entire time.

"I didn't get paid. I didn't get anything extra for it," Burleigh said, referring to the work he did on Humble, other than his $450-a-month position as Carmel City Attorney. "It was a labor of love. I was fighting for something I believed in."

As Burleigh announced the petition drive for the referendum, two leaders of the Citizens for Clean Air, Earl Moser and Gus Bauman, began organizing a plan to collect the needed signatures. The petition drive caused the formation of still another committee. This one was named Committee-for-Referendum, with Burleigh as chair. The group ran full-page newspaper ads and gathered a massive assortment of volunteers to staff tables at every major shopping center on the Monterey Peninsula. Although it was little acknowledged in the media, women were an important part of the drive opposing Humble, staffing the signature-gathering tables as well as making phone calls, writing letters and raising awareness about the issue.

The petition demanded that the Board of Supervisors rescind its action or submit the matter to a vote of the people. To gain ballot status, the petition would need 10% of the total who voted in the 1962 gubernatorial election, or 5,331 signatures. The referendum supporters set a goal of 7,000 and hoped to submit the signatures when the supervisors met to decide on the conditions.

"The matter should be decided by the people, and laid to rest forever,"

Burleigh said. "Let the voters determine what they want in the way of industry at Moss Landing."

In California, boards of supervisors have considerable power in county government. They act legislatively, administratively and even quasi-judicially. In their legislative role, they can set laws, generally referred to as ordinances, or establish county policies on a wide range of issues. On most other matters, the supervisors utilize their administrative powers. They grant permits, oversee county programs, and approve budgets among many other things. In their administrative role, the supervisors are not making new policy, but merely fulfilling their obligations under existing policy. Simply put, legislatures make laws while administrators carry them out. The quasi-judicial powers of supervisors are essentially the powers to settle claims against the county and handle appeals on land use and tax matters.

The basis for the referendum rested on the claim by Burleigh and the others that the Board of Supervisors acted legislatively in granting a permit for Humble. Only legislative actions are subject to a referendum, and administrative actions are not. Examples of legislative actions include the formation of the Moss Landing Area Development Plan, or when the interim and later permanent zoning ordinance in North Monterey County was passed. Claiming that the granting of Humble's permit was legislative, and not administrative, was a challenging proposition that not everyone agreed stood on firm legal ground.

A building permit is normally considered administrative and not subject to a vote by the people, and essentially this is what Humble's special permit represented. Burleigh, as the referendum's counsel, took a creative and expansive view, suggesting that the permit was so precedent-setting with potential new conditions that it was actually legislative. The Humble controversy was certainly opening new laws and enforcement mechanisms, such as the looming creation of an air pollution control district, but the legality of the referendum remained questionable. Even the anti-Humble *Santa Cruz Sentinel* reported that most observers viewed the referendum as "grasping at straws" and "another delaying tactic."

In Monterey, the referendum was much more than an attempt to delay or overreach. As the *Monterey Peninsula Herald* called it, the referendum was "a second chance, one which gives the people, not just five supervisors, an opportunity to express themselves."

Delay or not, the legality of the referendum immediately faced criticism from County Counsel William Stoffers. Stoffers disagreed with Burleigh by labeling the Humble permit as "administrative or executive" and not legislative.

Stoffers had more bad news for the referendum supporters as well. Stoffers stated that the permit was not official until the conditions were approved. This meant that the petition gathering was premature, in seeking to overturn a board of supervisors' decision that was not yet finalized.

For the supervisors, the pressure was clearly upon them in the hypercharged political environment. Tom Hudson responded with a "No comment" when questioned if he supported the referendum. Henry battled lingering rumors of a recall and opposition to his coming reelection. Warren Church encountered refinery opponent Ruth Andresen on the steps of the Salinas courthouse, and the two former colleagues on the Monterey County Board of Education would strain their friendship in a heated exchange over Church's vote to approve the Humble permit.

With only a week left in their self-imposed deadline, Humble's opponents quickly began to gather thousands of signatures. A day before the September 24 Board of Supervisors meeting, Burleigh announced that he had 6,300 signatures in hand, more than needed, but short of the 7,000 they hoped to achieve. However, Burleigh said that he expected more petitions bearing an additional 2,000 signatures, delivered to him before the day was out. If so, that would place the total over 8,000 and a remarkable number gathered in less than a week.

As the 24th arrived, the supervisors met for their second special meeting of the month. This one came on a Friday with expectations of another marathon session of pro and con refinery speakers. Burleigh brought a huge stack of petitions and presented a total of 12,572 signatures, far exceeding his own optimistic expectations the day before. The number was astounding for four and a half days of signature gathering. Burleigh continued to argue that the permit was legislative and that once the signatures were verified, a referendum must be held. The meeting then launched into an hour-long discussion between the supervisors, Stoffers and Burleigh.

Stoffers countered Burleigh, opposing almost every point made. He declared the petitions "null and void." Stoffers emphasized, as he had previously done in comments to the media, that the board acted administratively, not legislatively. Once again, he also raised that since the permit had not been officially granted, the petitions were invalid as they were collected before a permit was issued.

"In my opinion," said Stoffers, "the granting of the special permit is merely carrying out the policy of the board that has existed for 20 years."

Despite opposition from the county counsel, Hudson moved for the supervisors to accept the petitions as Burleigh requested and forward them for verification to County Clerk Emmet McMenamin. Surprisingly, the motion ended deadlocked and failed 2-2. Church abstained, declaring that the petition had not been properly submitted. Hudson, commenting that the deadlocked vote was a "sad thing," then tried another tactic. He moved to assign the petitions directly to the county clerk for verification. This time Church voted, but against the motion, defeating it on the same 3-2 majority that granted Humble its permit. Hudson and Anderson tried yet another approach, informally proposing delaying discussion of the conditions until a resolution on the referendum was decided. That was too much for Arthur Atteridge.

"If you feel the way you do," Atteridge said, "why don't you make a motion or get someone to make a motion? I'm going to vote against it. Let's get this show on the road."

The supervisors voted down the motion 3-2, but that only pushed Hudson to inquire if Humble opposed the referendum. Humble's representatives, which included attorney Paul Hamerly and R.A. Winslow, assistant manager of manufacturing, emphasized the many delays since earlier in the year and demurred on accepting any further ones. Hudson and Anderson proposed more motions, even one by Anderson to rescind the permit. Again, the motions went down 3-2. Once again, Hudson reached into his bag of parliamentary tricks and tried to impose a directive, not requiring a vote, to instruct McMenamin, a separate elected official not appointed by the board, to verify the signatures. The county clerk pushed back, responding that even if the chair and board directed him to verify the signatures, he would not unless county counsel confirmed it was appropriate.

The always process-respecting Church ended the debate: "If the opponents had been on the ball six months ago, they could have circulated a petition to change the zoning at Moss Landing."

Burleigh, frustrated by the supervisors' rejection, left the meeting aware that the only recourse for the referendum now was with the courts.

21

MONTEREY COUNTY SETS A

NEW STANDARD

September 7 – October 29, 1965

"Generally, the most restrictive (permit) we know of."

Unknown Humble Oil Official

The 36 conditions that the Monterey County Board of Supervisors took up on September 24 were a mix of regulations gathered primarily from the Los Angeles and San Francisco Bay regions. Both areas had a long history of dealing with pollutants whereas Monterey County had little experience. Nevertheless, Monterey County officials were already constructing conditions with a flavor tailored for the region's special needs.

When Humble Oil approached Moss Landing for its refinery, the prospect of a deepwater port was a major enticement, and the lack of air and water regulations—or any regulations at all for an oil refinery—was also appealing. Humble tried to persuade the local communities that it was a great steward of the environment and that no new regulations were necessary. As conditions were slowly added to the permit, Humble feigned surprise and discomfort, suggesting that it might have to look at other locations when some of the most basic regulations were proposed. Humble officials estimated that the conditions might cost $2 million for compliance. Yet as the Board of Supervisors gathered to make the final determination, Humble officials, while not happy at the growing restrictions they considered stringent, felt that they could "live with these conditions."

The first 18 conditions came from the Planning Commission subcommittee that visited Los Angeles in March with other county officials. The county hired W.J. O'Connell as its consultant to analyze Humble's plans and the necessary controls needed. In the background, County Counsel William Stoffers, Zoning Director Edward DeMars, Director of Sanitation Edward Munson and county supervisors, primarily Warren Church, worked to put the finishing details on the conditions adopted by the Planning Commission in July. Church's greater involvement was not a surprise for the Humble project was in his district. His notes and correspondence show engagement from when the initial conditions were proposed in March 1965 until the final decision in September 1965. Much of Church's involvement was nudging and suggesting behind the scenes, clearly aware that he would ultimately have his own opportunity to cement the final conditions.

By the time of the Planning Commission meeting at the end of July, the original 18 conditions had grown to 31 with McConnell's tinkering. All were unanimously accepted by the Planning Commission. A week later, DeMars added five more for a total of 36. The genesis of the new conditions is not known, but county records, newspaper accounts and the notes of Supervisor Church suggest a flurry of activity as it was expected the Board of Supervisors was going to act on the Humble permit in early August. Despite the additions, Church continued to feel the regulations were inadequate and wanted more study. Now, nearly two months after the Planning Commission gave a green light to the conditions, the supervisors were ready to consider the conditions for Humble's permit.

Going into the September 24 meeting, most observers did not expect many changes. Some, like the editors of the *Monterey Peninsula Herald*, feared that the 36 conditions might be watered down. Others heard of Church's comments that there were "certain conditions that needed revising," but no one expected anything significant. The writers at the *Salinas Californian* predicted the proposed regulations "will remain essentially the same as adopted by the Planning Commission."

Pressure from outside Monterey County, especially in Santa Cruz County, continued for more restrictions. Debating their concerns over the possible conditions that the Monterey County Board of Supervisors would decide upon, the Santa Cruz County Board of Supervisors agreed to send one of their members to the September 24 meeting in Salinas as an observer and to raise concerns that the conditions were inadequate. The Santa Cruz supervisors also continued to push for an air pollution district that would encompass Santa Cruz and Monterey counties, and even suggested that one of the three air pollution monitoring stations, intended to evaluate Humble's compliance to regulations, should be placed in Santa Cruz County. Also present for the setting of conditions were representatives of PG&E and Kaiser Refractories. Both industrial giants feared that the new restrictive conditions placed on Humble would eventually apply to their industries as well.

The supervisors then proceeded to review every one of the 36 conditions line by line while considering the changes offered by the staff and with public comment after each condition.

The 36 conditions reviewed by the supervisors included six major categories:

1)   Compliance with Local, State and Federal Agencies – This required following the rules and regulations of Monterey County ordinances, Central Coast Regional Water Pollution Control Board, California Department of Fish and Game, U.S. Coast Guard, Bay Area Air Pollution District, Monterey County Department of Health, Monterey County Planning Department and compliance of county ordinances established within the next five years regulating sulfur or organic compounds.

2)   Pollution Safeguards – These required limits on air emissions; waste-water discharges; safe loading and unloading of petroleum products in the Monterey Bay's waters, such as requiring marine loading of gasoline by submerged line only; and disposal of sanitary waste and refuse. Particulate matter emissions were to be tied to the limits imposed by the Riverside County Air Pollution Control District. Also included were the installation of three air monitoring stations to ensure air emission compliance.

3)   Infrastructure Upgrades – Development and expansion of county roads and Highway 1, including curb, gutter and sidewalk improvements around the proposed Humble Oil refinery, and an "extensive and attractive" landscape program. Any expansion of rail facilities into the refinery were to be constructed in a manner that those facilities could be made available to other industries too.

4)   Industrial Processing – These were specific restrictions on the plant operations requiring that coking operations be dust-free and enclosed,

forbidding the release of hydrogen sulfides and mercaptans into the atmosphere or sewers, limiting the burning of liquid or solid waste to a specific incinerator, operating equipment to prevent hydrocarbon release into the atmosphere, vapor pressure restrictions on storage tanks and vapor control devices on oil effluent water separator compartments.

5)   Permit – The Board of Supervisors had the power to revoke the permit if conditions were not met or corrections were not initiated within 10 days of notification.

6)   Miscellaneous Conditions – These included guarantees that the site would only be used for a refinery as the permit laid forth; exempting Humble from violations that were a result of a breakdown in air pollution control equipment; equipping flares with pilot lights; and performance standards regarding noise, illumination, fire and explosive hazards.

This was not going to be a meeting of dramatic statements, flashy promises and gloomy fears. It was about gritty, time-consuming details over words, phrases and scientific details cloaked in bureaucratic minutiae.

The three county officials most active in reviewing and proposing alternative text before the supervisors were Stoffers, DeMars and Munson. They identified five, mostly minor changes, from the Planning Commission's recommendations. These included painting tanks "white or a light pastel color" to keep the temperature cooler and elaborations on language to make the conditions clearer. One notable change was striking a limit of regulating five compounds in the permit.

After the supervisors dismissed the referendum petition, they recessed for lunch and then returned to the discussion. Citizens for Clean Air's Earl Moser called for water cleanliness standards at least as restrictive as those in Anacortes, considered some of the strictest in the nation. Munson discussed Moser's request by calling the water standards in Washington "equitable" and achievable. Longtime Humble opponents Dave Williams and Wayne Bowman spoke on protecting crops and devising conditions "no less strict than those imposed by the Los Angeles County Air Pollution District." The demands for strict regulations had been an integral part of the opposition's plan since March. While advocating a rejection of the permit, they had also pushed for the strictest regulations possible if the permit was approved. That tactic changed when the Planning Commission rejected the permit, but now that the supervisors had voted favorably for Humble, the strategy of creating strict conditions was back.

That day, every supervisor appeared to have a different agenda. Andy Anderson wanted to keep the meeting short and prevent another marathon meeting like the September 2 one that approved Humble's application. Tom Hudson tried repeatedly to delay a final decision, but always ended on the losing end of a 3-2 vote. When other supervisors tried to hurry the process along, it was Hudson who pushed back, calling for a review to go over the conditions word by word, declaring it "inconceivable" to do otherwise. Hudson proposed some minor clarifications on lighting, landscaping and building placement, but sometimes even Anderson abandoned him. Both made efforts to clarify permit details during which Humble proponents accused them of "nitpicking." Arthur Atteridge scoffed at delays and pushed that a final decision should be made at that meeting. Harold Henry seemed to disappear from the discussion unless it was to exchange an angry word with Hudson. On the other hand, Church came to the meeting with a three-page typed list of proposals and reasoning to back his positions.

The meeting would extend past midnight, although it was not quite as long as the September 2 meeting that approved the permit. However, the minute details, and the knowledge that all parties were nearing the end of the year-long struggle, made this meeting a particularly grueling one. It lacked the intensity and levity of previous meetings. An example of how easy it was to get lost in detail came when Hudson spent 30 minutes trying to determine who would hold title to the three air pollution stations meant to monitor Humble's refinery. When the meeting began, the board chambers were packed to capacity, but unlike the September 2 meeting that kept most participants glued to their seats, the crowd slowly dwindled until adjournment. When the meeting finally ended, the only ones left in attendance were Humble officials, two members of Citizens for Clean Air, a few refinery supporters from Salinas and Castroville and a handful of farmers.

"In contrast to past hearings on the issue before the planning commission and the board," wrote Stanley Cloud of the *Monterey Peninsula Herald*, "there was little emotion, tension, humor or drama connected with this final, anti-climactic round."

With the meeting grinding into the evening, Hudson tried to delay a vote as the supervisors broke for dinner. Hudson moved for an adjournment until 10 a.m. the following Monday. Anderson supported the action. Atteridge, who had developed a reputation during the Humble affair of discouraging delays, resisted, urging that the board wrap things up by 10 p.m. that evening. With support by both Church and Henry, Atteridge halted Hudson's efforts.

Hudson eventually gave in when he learned that W.J. O'Connell, the county's expert on oil refineries, was not available on Monday. Anderson, however, continued to resist. He declared that he was not interested in another marathon meeting and that he was heading home after dinner. When the board reconvened after dinner, Anderson was in his seat, with no explanation about why he changed his mind.

The county's permit for the Humble refinery became official on September 25, 1965. But the battle was not yet over.

Courtesy of Salinas Californian

While it seemed anti-climactic, it was far more than that. The conditions were the meat and potatoes of the permit. To the opponents, the battle tottered on the edge of being lost at the September 2 meeting. However, a permit is only as good as its conditions. Early in the process, it became painfully obvious to Humble Oil that Monterey County was not going to roll over and acquiesce. The conditions kept piling up. By the time of the September 24 meeting, Monterey County had compiled a list of regulations that rivaled anything in Los Angeles or San Francisco. What Humble did not know is that there were more restrictions to come. Contrary to the fears of many opponents that the conditions might be weakened, the opposite occurred. Many of the 36 conditions were enhanced and more were added as the list increased to 39 conditions. It was not simply adding the five suggestions from staff that increased the number, since some of those were rejected. It was comments from the audience and suggestions that the supervisors raised themselves that added the three new conditions and strengthened many of the others with new language.

While the supervisors came with suggestions to alter the conditions, suggestions from the audience drove the final wording of many changes. It was then that the agricultural community exerted a powerful influence. Although there were many strong opponents to Humble in agriculture, once it became clear that the permit was going to be granted, agriculture jumped on board to restrict the deleterious effects of Humble. It was agriculture, more so than the opponents on the Monterey Peninsula, such as Citizens for Clean Air, who embraced the notion of enhanced permit conditions.

The Peninsula opponents were still smarting from the bitter defeat of the permit votes on September 2 and now the rejection of their petition for a referendum. The referendum had primarily been a Peninsula phenomenon anyway. It is unknown how many signatures came from the Peninsula as opposed to the rest of the county, but all the petition tables were at shopping centers and social gatherings on the Peninsula. It would not be out of reason to assume that upwards of 90% or more of the signees were residents there. Peninsula opponents were still trying to find a way to shut down Humble completely. The agriculture community was looking for a way to live with it.

At the forefront of agriculture's demands stood Jack Bias, executive vice president, and James Houseberg, assistant manager of the Grower-Shipper Vegetable Association. Bias and Houseberg dominated the discussion of conditions from the audience. That was an unusual development. Unlike the Farm Bureau, which opposed Humble, the Grower-Shipper group took a neutral stance just a month earlier. However, there was nothing neutral about Bias' and Houseberg's stance that night. They pushed strongly for stricter controls. They were not alone as more outspoken opponents from the Salinas Valley joined them.

Dave Williams of Bruce Church Inc. broached if it was possible for the refinery to be limited to the 50,000-barrels-a-day Humble stated in its permit. O'Connell responded that it was "unrealistic to assume a refinery will remain the same." That set the supervisors into a three-hour discussion on how to limit the future expansion of the refinery, and an opportunity for Church to raise a condition that he had long considered. Church, although a solid vote in favor of the refinery, wrote in his notes that Humble needed to "prove" that it would not be a significant polluter before expanding.

During the supervisors' trip to Anacortes, they learned that a 50,000-barrel refinery could generate an output up to 80,000 barrels. The ability to considerably expand output caused consternation. Discussion turned to limiting Humble's 50,000-barrel refinery to 65,000 barrels. If Humble wanted to exceed that, then it needed to come back for another permit. R.A. Winslow, Humble's assistant general manager, responded that Humble be allowed to expand its facility by 10% of the initial investment per year without seeking a new permit. At $70 million to construct the facility, that would allow $7 million a year for future expansions. O'Connell countered that the Board of Supervisors should set a limit of $2 million to be able to control the expansion.

As the meeting wore on into the evening, Atteridge, ever vigilant of the circles the other supervisors kept talking themselves into, noted that the discussion had returned to the same topic they discussed nearly four hours earlier. With patience wearing thin, Hudson and Henry once again began sniping at each other.

"We know you're against it (Humble)," Henry said. "You've been against it all day."

"I'm just looking out for agriculture in your district," charged back Hudson.

Church, who had originally stated that he had "one or two" changes, outlined seven conditions that he "had a strong interest in and worked for strengthening." Some were minor, some were aligned with the staff recommendations, including enhancing the stop operations condition proposed by Stoffers, but others were more substantial. Church notes that he was the only supervisor to raise three of the seven conditions that most interested him. All three conditions were adopted with support from Atteridge and Henry. The other four conditions received support from the other supervisors, primarily Atteridge who often defended Church's position. Indeed, nearly every time Church raised a condition, Atteridge would soon lend his support.

O'Connell included in his recommendations to the Planning Commission that the county retain the power to shut Humble down within 10 days if it violated the terms of the permit. This gave Humble time to correct the problem while still operating or tie up the demand in court. Church felt this gave Humble a way to continue operating even if their operations were hazardous. He requested as early as August 24 in a letter to Stoffers that the recommendations include a Dade County, Florida, condition that if the refinery violated the permit in a manner endangering the community, then a cease operations order could be enacted immediately. A special three-person committee, including the county health officer, had the power to make that decision.

Church's notes also included two other major additions. One would require Humble to bear the cost of cleanup for any oil spill. While Church was the only supervisor to argue for this condition, he found support from Atteridge and Henry, who appeared willing to go with whatever Church proposed as long as the permit was granted. While the cleanup may not seem like an unusual recommendation, the language was such that Humble would hold initial responsibility for a cleanup even if a third party, such as a tanker or railroad company, was responsible for a spill.

The second condition spoke to Williams' concern about restricting expansion of the refinery. For Church, this was an essential condition. Other members of the board expressed strong support. Humble promised that it was a clean industry. Requiring a new permit every time an expansion occurred would force Humble to fulfill those promises or risk a denial of their expansion and limit their operations to a far less profitable 50,000- to 65,000-barrel refinery. Humble probably saw this much differently. The arduous, time-consuming and acrimonious battle of the last six months promised a repeat every time an expansion was planned. Humble's initial 50,000-barrel proposal before the county only involved as little as a quarter of the entire property slated for eventual development. Expansion was part of the business plan. While Humble might have been able to squeeze 80,000 barrels a day out of its refinery initially, the county clamped that limit at 65,000 barrels. Anything more required a new permit.

As before, nearly every vote made by the Board of Supervisors that day was 3-2, just as it had been since the meeting earlier that month. Atteridge, Church and Henry voted together; Hudson and Anderson voted on the opposing side. Those votes created an anomalous situation where the three supervisors voting for the Humble permit responded to fears by the opponents for tougher restrictions while the two supervisors who opposed Humble voted against the tougher restrictions. Observers reasoned that Hudson and Anderson cast negative votes more in general protest than opposition to the strengthened conditions. In the end, the final vote was also 3-2 to grant the permit with the 39 conditions with a smattering of conditions pulled from around the nation, and, as the *Salinas Californian* reported, "a few original ones for good measure."

Humble officials tried to put on cheerful faces, saying that they could live with these restrictions, but, outside the meeting, their expressions were grimmer. At the Planning Commission meeting in July, Humble officials remarked that those 31 conditions were strict. When the supervisors gave a nod to Humble in principle at the marathon September 2 meeting, J. Prince Warner, Humble vice president for manufacturing, called the then proposed 36 conditions "more restrictive and more complete than any in existence today in Los Angeles or San Francisco—or in the entire United States."

Now there were 39 conditions. One unidentified Humble official said, "They (the conditions) are very restrictive." Another moaned about the county-imposed restrictions as "Generally, the most restrictive we know of," echoing Warner's frustrations three weeks earlier before even more stringent conditions were added. This was a particularly revealing comment as Humble had touted its faithful compliance with regulations on oil refineries throughout the United States, as well as in Jamaica, Norway and other places around the world.

The regulatory scheme that the Monterey County Board of Supervisors developed over six months went from nothing to what Church would later describe in his notes as "possibly the strongest in the nation"—another echoing of Warner's words. Humble Oil representatives, part of the largest oil company in the world, Standard Oil of New Jersey, appeared to take those conditions a step further, suggesting that they were stronger than anything they knew anywhere in the world.

The *Californian* made note that these regulations were precedent-setting: "It is conceivable in the future that other areas debating the admittance of an oil refinery will look at Monterey County as an example of strict regulations. The conditions imposed are that unique."

What is known is that the Monterey County regulations immediately caught the attention of the petroleum industry. McGraw-Hill and the *Oil and Gas Journal* immediately requested copies of the conditions of Monterey County's special permit. McGraw-Hill, in particular, asked for "quick attention" because of the news importance of the conditions.

For those who had witnessed the grueling political debate of the last six months, it seemed that this historic struggle was reaching its final stages.

"If this had been a boxing match, the referee would have thrown in the towel long ago," observed one wag as the hearing drew to a close.

But the towel was not to be thrown in quite yet. Although the intensity of debate would lessen, there were still nine long months before a final resolution.

22

THE REFERENDUM GOES TO

COURT

September 24 – November 24, 1965

"We'll go down fighting. If we go down."

William Howard Church

A t the end of September 24, the petition calling for a referendum on the Humble Oil permit had been rejected and the Board of Supervisors had approved a permit for a 50,000-barrel refinery, although not quite the one Humble had expected, as it was limited to 65,000 barrels a day in production and weighed down by 39 permit conditions, some that had never been imposed on a refinery before. Deflated but not defeated, the growing opposition to Humble's refinery planned its next steps.

On September 27, Carmel City Attorney Bill Burleigh announced that opponents were organizing to continue the fight against Humble. Burleigh himself seemed in a fighting mood, stating that the opponents would "definitely have to go to court as our next move."

With Burleigh was Humble opponent Professor William Howard Church, who announced the creation of the Six Cities Fund for legal and political action.

Church said his group would fund Burleigh's legal efforts while a nationwide campaign to oppose the refinery was organized. Professor Church further stated that the group sought $30,000 to cover its legal costs and another $30,000 for "support and pressure building." Church mentioned that a similar strategy defeated an oil refinery on the East Coast. "We'll go down fighting," Church said. "If we go down."

"This is going to obtain the building of support for our program from national figures—both political and business leaders—and from national organizations, especially those interested in conservation," declared Professor Church.

Burleigh followed with the announcement of a letter-writing campaign to Michael Haider, the president of Standard Oil of New Jersey, and to the president of its subsidiary, Charles Jones of Humble Oil and Refining. Letters to members of Congress were also urged.

Stirrings of a boycott on Humble products, rumored for months, were also afoot. One proponent proposed that in a letter to the *Monterey Peninsula Herald*. "Starting with a public burning of credit cards, we could all take an oath to refrain from buying Humble products for the rest of our natural lives," wrote Shirlie Stoddard of Pacific Grove.

Longtime Humble opponent Gus Bauman, now representing the Six Cities Fund, noted that the issue was not just clean air, clean water, jobs, agriculture, health or "the beauty of nature." Bauman wrote in a letter to the *Herald* that the Humble matter was now a legal issue over whether the people have the right to force a referendum.

On October 19, Burleigh filed a petition for a writ of mandate in Superior Court to require County Clerk Emmett McMenamin to accept and verify the petition signatures gathered for the referendum. The writ also stated that the Board of Supervisors should either reconsider the granting of the Humble permit or place the issue before the voters. Burleigh represented two plaintiffs in the suit—William Howard Church of Pebble Beach and Helen Lyons of Castroville. Burleigh based the lawsuit on the grounds that the Board of Supervisors acted legislatively and not administratively. The county's position was that the granting of a permit to Humble was an administrative act. The board's legislative action had occurred years earlier when the land around Moss Landing was zoned industrial. Humble's permit was administrative because it was in compliance with the legislative act of that zoning. Burleigh's position held that the permit to Humble opened new regulatory boundaries beyond the granting of a permit for industrial zoning.

"The power to be exercised is legislative in its nature if it prescribes a new policy or plan; whereas it is administrative in its nature if it merely pursues a plan already adopted by the legislative body itself," explained Burleigh.

Burleigh noted that the new air and water pollution regulations were legislative because they had not existed before. In his view, that meant that the supervisors acted as legislators, not administrators. Burleigh also denied that the petitions were submitted prematurely. On the other hand, Stoffers and McMenamin said that referendum petitions could only be accepted as valid if they were submitted *after* the conditions were set and the permit granted. Burleigh argued that past court cases determined that signatures must be submitted prior to the setting of conditions for a permit.

The suit was presented to Judge Gordon Campbell, who set November 24 for a court date, but did not designate a court to hear it, an unusual action in writ of mandate petitions. It was widely expected that Campbell, a resident of Carmel, was intending to recuse himself from the suit. Campbell did issue an alternative writ of mandate which required the Board of Supervisors to either rescind Humble's permit, set a date for a public vote on a referendum, or instruct County Counsel William Stoffers to explain on November 24 why Monterey County had not reversed its decision.

Also in November, Western Oil and Gas Association, a trade organization, filed suit in Los Angeles questioning the constitutionality of county smog control districts, such as the one under discussion for months in Monterey County. State Senator Fred Farr broke new regulatory ground when he authored a state bill allowing counties to develop anti-pollution districts before pollution became a problem—a novel approach for the time, at least for California. The association's lawsuit was likely under consideration for some time, but Monterey County's aggressive new regulations on oil refineries must have sent shivers through the oil and gas industry. The fossil fuel industry clearly did not want Monterey County's air pollution control plans to become the new standard. Professor Church immediately latched onto the consequences of the lawsuit as justification for opposing the Humble permit.

"This suit, by Western Oil and Gas, which seeks to invalidate county smog rules that restrict or prohibit burning certain fuel oils when natural gas is available, points out the precise reason that we oppose the Humble Oil use permit," Humble opponent Church said. "We want to avoid the incidents of pollution by avoiding the cause."

"Our committee opposed the smog control ordinance adopted by Monterey County Board of Supervisors because we felt the provisions were weak and inadequate," Church continued. "The repercussions of the Los Angeles or any future suit should it be decided in favor of the company, would leave us with no means to controlling air pollution from any stationary source."

"We feel that this issue will give additional impetus in our efforts to obtain a referendum. Let's let the people of this county decide on the quality of the air they will breathe. I personally feel that many of the people who favored the Humble Oil permit, with the provision that heavy smog control restrictions would be enforced, will think again in view of these facts."

Carmel City attorney William "Bill" Burleigh proved to be a tenacious foe of Humble Oil's refinery project.
Courtesy of Carmel Pine Cone

On November 16, Humble responded in Superior Court with a "complaint in intervention" as an affected third party to Burleigh, Church and Lyons' complaint against Monterey County's granting of a permit to Humble.

Declaring itself as having "substantial interest," local attorney Paul Hamerly, representing Humble, filed a complaint in intervention. Although the complaint basically reinforced the county's position that the supervisors' action was administrative and not legislative, it also argued that the area had been designated for industry like Humble's since 1945. Hamerly also argued that a referendum would cause undue hardship on the company with a "lengthy, expensive campaign" for something that had already been granted legally by the Board of Supervisors.

Professor Church took advantage of Humble's complaint to emphasize that the oil company did not really care about the wishes of the people of Monterey County. He said Humble once touted its survey that showed an overwhelming majority of people backing the refinery, but now complained about the burden of dealing with a process that would allow them to express that opinion with votes.

"This action on the part of Humble Oil indicates their reluctance to allow this issue to come before the people," Church said.

"To us this means several things," continued Church. "First, Humble is afraid to let this matter be determined by the people because they are afraid that the use permit would be rescinded. Second, it is a good indication of what future obstruction we would encounter from Humble in regard to the enactment of constructive pollution controls should the refinery be established at Moss Landing."

With the court hearing just a week away, another delay in the marathon Humble matter arose. Judge Gordon Campbell disqualified himself from the case because he had already formed an opinion on the writ of mandate. That was followed by Judge Stanley Lawson also disqualifying himself for owning property at Moss Landing across the highway from the proposed refinery. That left only Judge Anthony Brazil, but he was on vacation and would not return by the time of the hearing. With no judge in Monterey County to hear the case, the Judicial Council appointed San Luis Obispo County Superior Court Judge Richard Harris to hear the case.

On the day of the court hearing, Stoffers, Hamerly and Burleigh appeared before Judge Harris in a nearly packed courtroom in Salinas. Stoffers called for the court to accept his demurrers, which are objections to the case proceeding because the plaintiff lacks a valid claim. In this case, Stoffers claimed that the Six Cities Fund lawsuit lacked a valid basis for relief because an administrative act cannot be put to a vote. Stoffers and Hamerly both proceeded to argue, as expected, that the Board of Supervisors acted in an administrative and not legislative manner.

Burleigh took a broadly aggressive position. As Burleigh first began to present evidence, Stoffers objected, calling for the court to act on his demurrers. Judge Harris rejected the request, stating that he would take the demurrers under submission but would not rule until the evidence had been presented. Burleigh then called Hudson to the stand and asked him if the board's action was legislative. Before Hudson could answer, Stoffers objected and was sustained by Harris. Stoffers would continue to make multiple objections during Burleigh's presentation with many of those objections upheld. Burleigh continued to try to use Hudson's words to show that the granting of a permit to Humble was a change in policy.

Burleigh based his argument on the fact that interim zoning had been put in place shortly before Humble sought a permit. Interim zoning does not allow a referendum. Thus, Burleigh contended, the granting of a permit to Humble was the first opportunity that the people had to express their opposition to the board's actions. Burleigh read from a transcript from the board hearing on Humble where the words "change" and "policy" were widely used. He then read where Hudson stated, "this is a legislative hearing and we will conduct it as such." Burleigh also noted that the Planning Commission is empowered with the power to grant permits, but that during the adoption of the interim zoning the board also reserved the right to grant permits in the industrial zoned area. Burleigh argued the interim zoning was approved to halt "dirty" industry so that the board "could make up its legislative mind" for permanent zoning.

"Why did they take it away from the administrative board?" asked Burleigh. "Because they decided they are the legislative body. They are the ones who should decide."

Stoffers countered that Burleigh was wrong. Prior to the interim zoning, the Moss Landing area was zoned unclassified. The interim zoning, Stoffers contended, was to halt subdividing the land for homes. The area had allowed heavy industry, including oil refineries, since 1945. It was specifically zoned for industrial, commercial, recreational and residential use in 1956 with the Moss Landing Area Development Plan. The board, by developing an interim zoning, was merely trying to protect the industrial status of the area. Stoffers made the argument that the proper time for a referendum was during the legislative zoning process over the last 20 years, not during the administrative granting of a permit—the same argument that Supervisor Warren Church had been a strong proponent of throughout the Humble affair.

Burleigh challenged Stoffer's position: "To argue that the people could have sought a referendum in 1930 or 1945 is a meaningless privilege because we didn't have the (refinery) problem then."

Burleigh also called Donald Compton, a chemistry instructor at Monterey Peninsula College. In an attempt to prove that an oil refinery would be a new source of pollution so as to heighten the unique nature of its permit, Burleigh asked Compton if an oil refinery would create different pollution from PG&E or Kaiser. Compton affirmed that an oil refinery "would produce different pollutants in larger quantities."

Hamerly responded by calling Jack Gardner from Humble's manufacturing division. Gardner said, as he had at public hearings many times before, that Humble's oil refinery was not a "threat" and would add a "relatively small contribution" of pollutants.

As Burleigh ended his case, he left with these remarks: "I think it would be a bad situation if the legislative body of any city or any county could avoid the basic right of referendum by the process of adopting a temporary emergency ordinance."

"I think it is only fair to tell you," Judge Harris said after both sides finished their arguments, "that you shouldn't look for a quick decision in this case. I do not think it's the kind of case that can be decided as quickly as some people think it should."

Harris informed the parties that he should have a decision in 60 days.

23

TOM HUDSON – HUMBLE'S

BANE

"(Hudson) put on a good show."

Arthur Atteridge

When the Monterey County Board of Supervisors met at the beginning of 1965, prior to Humble Oil filing its permit application, the board was in the midst of major changes. Thomson Jay Hudson assumed the position as chair and undisputed leader of the board. Two new supervisors took office that day. Andy Anderson, in the newly reconstituted fourth supervisorial district, replaced Frank Echeberria of San Ardo, who had served only a single term. Prior to the 1964 election, District 4 represented only the underpopulated area south of King City where just a few hundred voters resided. A court challenge earlier in the decade headed by *Monterey Peninsula Herald* publisher Allen Griffin caused the district to be redrawn to include parts of the Monterey Peninsula. The other supervisor elected in 1964 was Warren Church, who defeated the current senior member of the board, Chester Deaver, who had been in office since 1952. Arthur Atteridge had only taken office in 1963 and Harold Henry in 1959. That made Tom Hudson, in office since 1957, the new senior member.

Hudson would leave an impression decades after his service as one of the most flamboyant politicians ever to serve in Monterey County. Often sporting a Stetson hat and a large cigar, and always a bowtie, likely made by his wife, Hudson could be seen driving a Cadillac convertible or biking up the hill from Point Lobos to his office, even later in life while in his 50s. Hudson also possessed a pilot's license and was known to ferry supporters, associates and even journalists to and from state meetings.

In the midst of his tenure on the board, the *San Jose Mercury* reported that a Peninsula resident once commented about Hudson, "Sure he gets a lot done. He's charming. But my gosh, did you ever see such ambition?"

"I don't object to being called ambitious," replied Hudson. "You don't get anything done without being ambitious."

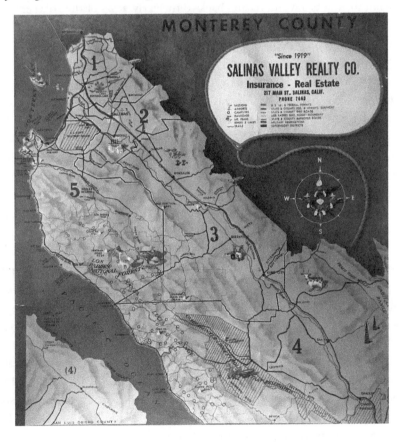

This pre-1964 map of Monterey County shows the five supervisorial districts.
Authors' collection

Hudson was either deeply admired or strongly disliked. He was known to have a temper and a sharp tongue at board meetings when someone rose to question his motives or disagree with him strongly. Then, just as quickly, he would try to appease the target of his ire with a plea to be friends.

"He is one of those rare birds who can fight (you) tooth and nail over an issue and then take you to lunch," said Harry Casey, publisher of the *King City Rustler*.

Hudson was a shrewd politician and master political manipulator. He was as sly as everyone thinks a politician should be, but with the goal of getting things done. A Republican with strong conservation ties, his aim was to preserve scenic Monterey County as industry arrived and the population grew. Hudson's family had long played a role as environmentalists before environmentalism was a word, dating back to the early years of the 20th century. The Hudsons were branded with the same Republican ideological streak as Theodore Roosevelt's conservation policies.

"I hope my children and their children will live to enjoy Monterey County as we have known it," Hudson described his vision for the future.

Opposition to Humble Oil was a natural for Hudson, especially since his district was adamantly against it. He was also pro-business, but like his conservation record, those positions were malleable in search of a better deal. Some called him a political scoundrel because of his backroom deal making, and that was by those who liked him. Yet without Tom Hudson, the Humble Oil controversy may have turned out much differently. Although not formally part of Citizens for Clean Air, Hudson attended and spoke at their forums. Undoubtedly, he was involved in scheming with its leaders, because Hudson was always scheming. He repeatedly called for public votes to rescind the Humble permit or support the failed referendum attempt. Behind the scenes, he pleaded, cajoled and pressured the other supervisors to see his way. It is probable, if not likely, that it was Hudson's endless efforts, many which will never be known, that eventually tipped the scales. Without a doubt, no single person played a greater role against Humble.

While Hudson's conservationist views and support from his constituents for opposing Humble drove him to oppose developing heavy industry in Moss Landing, he had a more personal reason as well. By the time he was supervisor, Hudson had an interest in a company that owned half of Cannery Row. The city of Monterey was already examining how to turn the smelly canneries into something more attractive for tourists. The site of more smokestacks in Moss Landing was not an appealing vista.

Stanley Cloud, the *Monterey Peninsula Herald* journalist who covered Humble Oil and then quit the newspaper to helm *the advocate*, described his interactions with the supervisors and Hudson in particular:

"The supervisors used to have a monthly (I think) lunch meeting to which the three or four reporters who covered them regularly were invited. It was absolutely off the record, and so the politicians were unusually relaxed in their discussions. It was at the Jeffery Hotel, which was just a few blocks from the courthouse. It had been around since the days of horses, and there was an old hitching post still outside. The lunches were held in a private dining room whose walls, as I recall, were green And, for me, sitting there and listening, those off-the-record meetings were better than a Ph.D. course in political science, and Hudson, of course, was almost always the dominant figure."

At another time, Cloud recalled a chance encounter with Hudson at the County Counsel's office on the day of the vote for Joan Baez's Institute for the Study of Nonviolence in Carmel Valley. At that time, Cloud was still writing for the *Herald*, which usually treated Hudson favorably, and explains why Hudson was unconcerned by the Cloud the journalist's presence. The Board of Supervisors had recessed for lunch when an agitated Hudson suddenly appeared.

"Do I have immunity as a member of the board?" Hudson asked the assistant county counsel.

"My guess is that you do have a certain degree of immunity, but I'm not sure how far it extends," came the reply.

"Are you sure it is not absolute immunity?" asked Hudson.

"Who are you planning to attack, Tom?" a curious Cloud asked.

"I'm writing a little speech for this afternoon."

Cloud surmised the speech was about the Baez school vote and inquired. Hudson smiled and said that he liked Baez, but that she was too close to the Sigourneys. John and Mary Sigourney were political opponents of Hudson, and also were the publishers of *the advocate*, which Cloud operated surreptitiously as editor.

"McCabe had a good article in this morning's (San Francisco) Chronicle," stated Hudson. "Did you see it?"

"No," replied Cloud.

"He wrote about the idiot left. That's a pretty good phrase, you know. The idiot left. You ought to read it."

Hudson then went over to the law books, glanced over the titles and took one out. He flipped through the pages.

"Here it is. It says I have absolute immunity."

A couple of hours later, back at the board meeting, Hudson listened to the testimony on the Baez hearing, and then read from a prepared speech he had worked on during lunch.

"The people of Monterey County should know the players in the game ... (Miss Baez) takes pride in refusing to even stand, let alone join in the traditional pledge to our flag ... (Her attorney, Francis Heisler is) one of the leaders, like Miss Baez, of the ... idiot left. They've even used the great Sigourney wealth to finance *the advocate*, the new house organ of the idiot left ... hiding behind the respectability of money and property to attack whenever possible.

"I'm making this statement so that when we hear from Sigourney-Brown-Strathmeyer-Larsen fringe we know their sentiments and loyalties ... We have before us the masters of their trade of the idiot left movement; that is; those who teach young Americans in civil disobedience."

As Cloud described it, the Baez school was not the main target of Hudson's wrath. The school had already received approval from the Upper Carmel Valley Advisory Committee and the Monterey County Planning Commission, showing broad support from among various ideologically differing views. None of those who approved the school on those committees were the target of Hudson either. Instead, this was an opportunity to strike back at his foes in Monterey County and attempt to brand them as either unpatriotic or politically foolish.

Later, when Hudson learned that Cloud wrote anonymously for *the advocate* at that time, it did not appear to bother him that one of his primary critics had a front row seat as he jockeyed with the limits of his immunity. Hudson never disparaged Cloud for reporting that afternoon's encounter, just as he never tried to kick Cloud out of the County Counsel's office that afternoon. For Hudson, publicity of any type always seemed a good thing.

The next week, two of the people Hudson targeted appeared before the board demanding apologies. Hudson sat silent, probably content that he had stirred the hornets' nest enough to disrupt them without getting stung.

Two reporters approached Hudson afterwards. "Will you retract or apologize?"

"Neither."

"Do you have any comments on the remarks made today."

"No comment."

Later, Hudson walked to the press table.

"I'm sorry I couldn't make a comment a while ago," Hudson said, "but the board had just adjourned. My immunity is only good when the board is in session. I'll answer any question you ask while the board is in session."

The irony in the bombastic attacks on the supporters of the Baez school is that when a final vote came to approve or reject the school, it passed by a narrow 3-2 vote with Church, Atteridge and Hudson voting yes. Hudson sided with Church and Atteridge that Baez's school was a free speech issue.

In the fray of a political debate, Hudson had a knack for playing both sides of a controversy and finding a new controversy in it as well. Whatever the situation, Hudson somehow ended up standing at center court. Again and again, throughout the Humble affair, that same talent for behind-the-scenes machinations coordinated with his public aggrandizement. Only a Tom Hudson could make those intertwine effortlessly.

For Hudson, the attention-seeking and incessant desire to prevail was natural. His prominence was ingrained in his DNA. Hudson's family history runs deep, not just in Monterey County, but prominently in American history. He was a descendant of a long list of overachieving and remarkable individuals.

In 1898, Hudson's maternal grandfather, Alexander MacMillan Allan, a builder and architect, but also one of California's first preservationists, purchased 640 acres of land from the failing Carmel Land and Coal Company, which included what is now known as Point Lobos State Natural Reserve. A.M. Allan would eventually expand his holdings to thousands of acres. He ultimately sold Point Lobos to the state to preserve it. That land would play a major role in Hudson's life.

Hudson's great-grandfather, also named Thomson Jay Hudson, was a journalist, editor, principal examiner at the U.S. Patent Office and unsuccessful U.S. Senate candidate. Hudson reached prominence in 1893 with the publication of *The Law of Psychic Phenomena*, which is still available. The book made the senior Hudson "famous throughout the English-speaking world." His theories were an interesting mix of science, reason, and psychic abilities. Hudson asserted that people had two minds the objective (conscious) and subjective (unconscious). He debunked mediums but promoted telepathic abilities between people as subconscious minds connecting. His writings still have followers to this day. Ironically, while in his 20s in Michigan, Hudson's great-grandfather found work during an oil boom of the 1860s. At that time, he developed some equipment and processes to extract oil that still have relevance.

Hudson's paternal grandfather, Charles Bradford Hudson, took part in the Spanish-American War in Cuba. He moved to the Monterey Peninsula in the early 1900s and was a noted impressionist painter, muralist and etchings artist during Carmel's Bohemian days. His paintings are still sought and valued at thousands of dollars. Charles Bradford Hudson also took part in many studies for the U.S. Bureau of Fisheries, creating illustrations of fish species. The artist Hudson has been described "as the world's finest illustrator of marine life."

Supervisor Thomson J. Hudson was known for his love of the limelight and flamboyant style.
Courtesy of the Hudson family

Hudson's father, Lester Jay Hudson, was a man of distinction as well. He served in the Navy for 30 years, rising to the rank of rear admiral. He received the Legion of Merit award with a gold star and the Navy Commendation ribbon for his service during World War II. Hudson captained the USS San Diego, an anti-aircraft ship used to protect aircraft carriers, during many of the island-hopping invasions against the Japanese forces. The San Diego was the second-most decorated ship of World War II, excepting only the USS Enterprise.

With this succession of highly successful forefathers, it is not surprising that Tom Hudson had great confidence and drive. It was Humble's misfortune that it stumbled onto such an intractable and competent foe.

Hudson was born in 1922 at the Pacheco Adobe in Monterey. He studied at the University of California, Berkeley, and later at Hastings Law School, and would go on to practice law in Monterey. He joined the Army in World War II, faked a vision test to qualify as a paratrooper for the 101st Airborne, and took part in the Normandy invasion. Hudson had to tape his glasses to his head whenever he prepared for a jump. Later, he was wounded in Holland.

After the war, at the age of 32, he challenged incumbent Republican Congressman Charles Teague, but Hudson failed to get the Republican Party's endorsement. Two years later, he emerged victorious, defeating the incumbent in the fifth district supervisorial race.

His grand gestures never seemed to cease. At one point, he rode his horse into the *Monterey Peninsula Herald's* office on election night. The horse slid on the smooth floor, causing Hudson to spur a quick retreat. In 1971, after Hudson left the Board of Supervisors, he staged a challenge on horseback with the state of California over Point Lobos Park. Hudson claimed that a proposed outfall involving Carmel sewage would violate the environmental protection provisions of the agreement under which his grandfather sold the land. He arrived with two of his children, hammers, tacks and "No Trespassing" signs to symbolically protest the outfall.

While he would fight mightily on major issues, he would direct the same energy to seemingly mundane matters. One of his passionate fights was to halt the establishment of a traffic light near his office at the corner of Polk and Hartnell streets in Monterey. A landscape island near the area of dispute eventually was taken over by Hudson as a personal flower garden.

"(Hudson) had a lot of aggressiveness and put on a good show," Arthur Atteridge said years after they had served together. Atteridge was probably the supervisor who was least impressed with Hudson's style. He voted right before Hudson and often used his time to focus on Hudson's intent.

"His (Hudson's) usual method is to reveal the problem (which sometimes has been undercover for some time), flush out the parties interested, appoint a committee to let tempers simmer down, then spring a solution," wrote Jack Fraser of the *San Jose Mercury* to describe Hudson's tactics.

Humble Oil, with its competing interest groups and political intrigue, was the perfect plot for Hudson to play a starring role. The opposing sides were still developing in April 1965 when Hudson announced during a board meeting that Humble was leaving for Benicia. Monterey County had just returned a delegation from Los Angeles where air pollution rules combined to make 18 recommendations to the Planning Commission with permit conditions for the refinery. With what would happen in September, when the supervisors eventually imposed 39 conditions, the initial 18 conditions now appear almost quaint. Yet Humble bristled publicly with those original 18 conditions, and the delay of a Planning Commission decision for nearly 45 days until May.

The inquiries into a Benicia site had nothing to do with those early recommendations, though. While Hudson was wrong that Humble was leaving for Benicia in April, he was on the right track. Humble Oil was in contact with the San Francisco Bay city of Benicia and top United States government officials regarding the century-old Benicia Arsenal that the Army had just closed. However, those discussions had been ongoing since 1964. Humble was not putting all its stock into Moss Landing or anywhere; there were other alternative sites. However, the fact that Hudson knew what Humble was doing during secret negotiations was an indicator that he constantly probed behind the scenes. Hudson always seemed in the know about Humble. Sooner or later, he let the public know what he knew as well.

In May, he opened a Citizens for Clean Air forum. While other supervisors were still weighing where to throw their lot or keeping their decisions low-key, Hudson was fully on the side of the burgeoning anti-Humble group. The leaders of the opposition—Charles Kramer, Earl Moser, William Howard Church, A.G. Michaud and Ansel Adams—were Hudson's constituents and allies. It is inconceivable that Hudson was not attempting to orchestrate how Citizens for Clean Air should influence the county and Hudson's fellow supervisors. If he was in the middle of a political issue, Hudson never restrained himself from becoming directly involved. It was not going to be different with Humble. It seemed that behind every rumor was a trail leading to Hudson. Exactly what Hudson did between February and September of 1965 is not fully known, but Hudson was not going to sit out the biggest political issue of his tenure as a supervisor. After September 1965, many of his actions became more transparent, but there is still much that remains hidden.

Surprisingly, there is little indication that Hudson delved into the specific conditions of the Humble permit. Perhaps it was too detail-oriented for Hudson, who wanted the splashy headlines and public attention or the intrigue of clandestine secrets. Putting together the nuts and bolts of something that he opposed was not flashy enough for Hudson. For someone like Warren Church, those details were right up his alley, especially since his young political career was on the line. Hudson was willing to let Church tinker in the minutiae while Hudson took the headlines.

By September, Hudson was a prominent face of the opposition. He chaired marathon board of supervisor meetings late into the night. He tried motions, worded slightly differently, multiple times during a single meeting as he desperately tried to find an anti-Humble motion that would bring a third vote to his side. He tried to use agriculture to pressure Harold Henry into changing his Humble support. He tried to engage Atteridge to see his legal points of view. He tried to overpower freshman Supervisor Church into following his lead, and when that failed, he turned to their shared vision on conservation issues.

After the permit was issued to Humble Oil, Hudson engaged anew with more covert plotting. This is known because of his occasional public announcement of a previously unknown fact, or a private meeting that Hudson admitted to having with a Humble official. As he was working to dissuade Humble privately, Hudson was at the same time coordinating public opposition in a last-ditch effort to stall the refinery permanently. Those efforts would continue right until the end.

The sudden rise of a well-organized and politically astute opposition was an unanticipated setback for Humble. Its officials also never expected to encounter a Tom Hudson, and that became clear as they would routinely call out interference by local politicians, finger pointing intended directly at Hudson. None of this was more evident than from the fall of 1965 to the first half of 1966. Hudson's fingerprints were everywhere as he played the role of puppet master, directing events to their final conclusion.

24

SHIFTING POLITICAL WINDS

September 29 – December 15, 1965

*"A proposed oil refinery located where the Salinas Valley
joins the Monterey coast will change this area's future from
fair and clear to filthy and foul."*

Placards distributed by the Six Cities Fund

At the next Board of Supervisors meeting following the approval of the
Humble Oil's permit conditions, Supervisor Warren Church called for
setting up "almost immediately" three air pollution monitoring stations, which
had become a focus of discussion by both opponents and proponents of the
Humble refinery. Both sides agreed on the danger of air pollution, and the need
for monitoring stations to track emissions from the Humble Oil operations. The
monitoring equipment was also desired by Santa Cruz County which hoped
to have one stationed within its boundaries. However, the timing and placement had not been decided, and Church wanted that handled straight away.

"I personally feel these stations should be set up before Humble goes into
operation," Church said. Furthermore, he argued that the monitoring stations
should go into operation two years before Humble refined its first barrels of
oil so that a baseline of clean air standards could be established. Since Humble

planned on beginning operations in a little over two years, there was little time to waste, according to Church's timeline.

Supervisor Tom Hudson immediately latched onto Church's idea, giving it his wholehearted support. Hudson ordered Sanitation Director Ed Munson to bring the matter to the Air Pollution Advisory Committee's attention and bring it back to the board as soon as possible.

In about a month, Munson was back with proposals to set up two permanent air monitoring sites at Castroville and the newly built Moss Landing School. The equipment would be placed on 50-square-foot plots. A third mobile unit was also planned for use where needed. The units would measure sulfur dioxide, hydrogen sulfide, carbon monoxide, dust fall, wind direction, and wind velocity among other things. Humble was to assume responsibility of the units within 180 days of sites being established. Around this same time, Humble announced it was in the design phase with refinery construction to begin in late 1966 and slated for completion in 1968.

However, the significance of Supervisor Church's request was multifold. Prior to this point, the board had been divided 3-2, with Church aligned with Harold Henry and Arthur Atteridge on the pro-Humble side. Church, now supported by the always strongly anti-Humble Hudson on the air pollution monitoring equipment, represented the first crack in the wall of support for Humble that the board had maintained throughout its votes.

Yet the Humble affair represented something larger as well. The Humble project opened a flood of issues regarding zoning, pollution, health and other issues that were the beginning of a transformation to modern Monterey County. In the past, concerns over these issues were often minor and the county's response even trivial. Those issues were already coming to the forefront before Humble, such as the new zoning laws in North Monterey County that dominated the 1964 supervisorial election. Similar new laws were developing in other parts of the county as well, and throughout the state and the nation. In the 1960s, America was moving toward greater regulation, environmental protection, health and safety laws and social services. In some areas, Monterey County was now setting the pace for the nation, especially on some matters of industrial regulation and environmental protection.

Although Supervisors Hudson and Church saw eye to eye on the pollution monitoring stations, for now, they had more to disagree about. At the first board meeting in October, Hudson once again tried to get a majority vote in favor of the referendum previously rejected by the board, perhaps hoping that Church was vacillating in his support of Humble. Hudson announced that thousands more signatures had been gathered. The petition calling for a vote of the people through a referendum now had more than 15,000 signatures. Hudson asked the board to reconsider its previous vote and submit the petition to the county clerk "so that the people will have a chance to be heard on this subject."

"The people have spoken and have probably spoken more strongly in a period of 10 days to two weeks than I think they ever have before in the history of the county," stated Hudson as the supervisors engaged in an hour of discussion.

Church stated he would not object to a referendum election "if it were legally justified." Hudson countered that it was merely a "technical" point over whether the board's action was administrative or legislative standing in the way of a vote. Church then suggested that the refinery opponents should prepare an initiative to rezone the industrial area of Moss Landing to exclude refineries. Church also expressed support to a point raised by Hudson during the Humble debate suggesting that the Moss Landing industrial zoning be changed to exclude "dirty industry." He then added that "this is too grave a matter" to decide with Supervisor Atteridge not present. With that, Hudson's motion died on a 2-2 vote. Once again, Hudson found only support in Anderson, but he vowed to try again when Atteridge was back.

After Carmel City Attorney Bill Burleigh filed a writ of mandate in Superior Court, Hudson brought the referendum back to the board for another vote. Hudson vowed to continue to bring it to a vote every week if necessary.

"This is the last opportunity that the board has to recognize the democratic forces that exist in Monterey County," Hudson said. "And I hope the board will see fit to brush aside some of the technicalities the board has used not to give the people a vote."

Try as he might, Hudson could never persuade a majority of the board to reconsider its action against the referendum and give the people of Monterey County the chance to vote yea or nay on the Humble refinery. He tried again, for what would be a fourth time, on October 26, but predictably, lost again on a 3-2 vote. On that day, he signed the Humble permit as board chair. Stymied but undeterred in his approach to halt Humble, Hudson had other less public options available.

Besides Hudson, Burleigh and Professor William Howard Church, other opponents were still organizing to deny Humble its permit. Comically, some did not quite understand what they were doing. Professor Church said that a task force had formed in Salinas to stop Humble, and word spread that other groups were forming in Watsonville, Castroville and King City. However, when the Salinas group was contacted by The *Californian*, none of the five members knew what their group was going to do.

Then, as had occurred back in April, seemingly out of nowhere came rumors that Humble was pulling out of Moss Landing to head toward the city of Martinez in the San Francisco Bay Area. Humble announced it was meeting with representatives in Martinez only as a "courtesy" and that Moss Landing was still its favored site. The story died down shortly thereafter, but it left many unanswered questions. Why would Humble even consider another site since it now held a permit for Moss Landing? Further studies on the site and design of the refinery were just gearing up. Nothing in that work was consequential enough yet to raise issues with a Moss Landing refinery. The only significant developments at this time were the stalled referendum, a lawsuit which many observers felt was based on a weak pretense but threatened to become an impediment to Humble's plans, and the 39 conditions attached to the permit. Perhaps Humble still did have Moss Landing as its top choice, but something was causing second thoughts.

Later in the month, Humble representative Jack Gardner appeared at a luncheon in Soledad on behalf of Monterey County Industrial Development Inc. to reassure the group of Humble's commitment to Monterey County. However, Gardner made no comment regarding the recently filed lawsuit by Burleigh and the Six Cities Fund.

"We're even more confident than ever that we will build a plant that will be an asset to Monterey County, and that we will meet the 39 conditions," attested Gardner.

By November, Gardner announced that the Humble refinery was in its design phase. The continuing opposition, court challenges and restrictive permit conditions did not seem to dissuade Humble's resolve at all. Gardner set 1968 as the date the refinery would open, and once again, tried to ease pollution concerns.

"We would not build if we thought the plant would do any harm," Gardner said at the Alisal Chamber of Commerce's annual meeting at the Italian Villa in Salinas.

Air pollution had been a growing concern in Monterey County before Humble. In 1960, an air pollution ordinance was adopted and passed by the Board of Supervisors, and took effect in 1961. While some parties were initially cited for violating the ordinance, such as Firestone, which had conducted regular burning at its Salinas plant, others came into compliance with the new law, and still others failed to comply while begging for more time to change business practices. Coincidentally, this issue came to a head in November 1965. Observers viewed it as the first indicator of how determined the county was to combat air pollution. Humble's opponents looked on intently, and had much in which to be disappointed.

Three major violators remained: Berman Steel in Salinas, Kaiser Refractories in Moss Landing, and the Monterey County Road Department, which operated seven landfills. All three asked for more time to implement acceptable air pollution controls. While all were able to get variances from six to ten months, all variances came on a split vote. An earlier variance had been granted to a fourth violator, the City of Salinas, for a landfill it operated outside of town. Hudson voted against each of the three variances. Harold Henry and Church voted in favor of each variance. Arthur Atteridge and Beauford Anderson split, voting for some variances and against others. Despite the close votes, there was no serious consideration given to requiring immediate compliance to the county's pollution ordinance.

Multiple individuals stepped forward to complain of dust from Kaiser's dolomite quarry off Old Stage Road outside of Salinas. One of the complaints came from W.H. Wilbur, a member of the Agricultural Advisory Committee that had given a tepid endorsement to Humble in the summer. His wife, Planning Commissioner Charlotte Wilbur, had also voted for Humble. However, Wilbur brought samples of white dust covering the leaves on his and his neighbor's gardens. Others complained of dust layers on their homes, cars and vegetation. Gus Bauman of Carmel Highlands, an active and vocal Humble opponent, asked Sanitation Director Ed Munson if Kaiser was complying with the county's air pollution laws.

"[T]here are indications that they are in compliance some of the time," Munson responded.

Hudson turned to the Kaiser representative at that point and said, "It's as if you really didn't care if we have an ordinance or not. I don't see how you have gotten away with it as long as you have."

Supervisor Church complained that if Kaiser was forced to immediately comply, jobs would be lost. Both Kaiser's quarry and plant were in Church's district. Atteridge and Henry supported Church—both their districts were also near the quarry. The variance passed 3-2.

Berman Steel said it was looking for a furnace to comply with the county ordinance, but gave no explanation why one had not been found in the four and a half years the ordinance had been in effect. Berman mentioned that it was a contractor in producing steel for the war effort in Vietnam. That was enough to garner Medal of Honor recipient Anderson's vote. Again, the variance passed on a 3-2 vote with Henry and Church voting with Anderson.

The third violator was the county itself. At that time, the county road department operated the landfills. Road Commissioner Bruce McClain said the county's violation was small and provided a necessary refuse service to county residents. To dispose of trash, the county incinerated it. The solution was to switch to a cut and cover operation. McClain said that cut and cover would require a five-fold increase in the landfill budget. Since the supervisors were the officials responsible to setting the county budget, the violations were clearly attributed to policies set by the supervisors and not McClain's department. The embarrassing negligence of the supervisors led to a 4-1 vote for another variance—the longest one approved of the three. Only Hudson dissented.

After the final variance was approved, Supervisor Church stated that he felt the board had "been tough" on the offenders. "We drew a line," Church explained later to the *Monterey Peninsula Herald*—the line being a time limit to comply. Humble's opponents were not impressed by that position. The *Herald* took particular displeasure with the supervisors' lack of backbone to enforce the law or even fund county programs to comply with its own regulations. The *Herald* felt this acquiescence played smugly into Humble's plans.

"We suspect that Humble put too much stock in the county's negligence in enforcing its own standards of pollution—including delays not only to Kaiser Refractories and Berman Steel, but to its own county dumps. . .Such postponements, after a liberal five years to cleanup, hardly can discourage Humble from assuming that it can expect similar lackadaisical treatment. And delays cannot help but encourage the inevitable dirty satellite plants which are waiting for the refinery's dregs."

To the anti-Humble observers, it did not seem that the supervisors were tough at all. "What we witnessed here was a perfect example of civil disobedience condoned by the board," noted one observer. If this was how the county was planning on enforcing pollution standards when Humble's refinery violated them, then the 39 conditions on Humble's permit looked rather toothless. What Humble's opponents saw in the county's lack of enforcement would only stiffen their resolve to fight until the end.

While the county hesitated at enforcing its air pollution ordinance, efforts to form a control district were still under consideration. Santa Cruz County still hoped to make it a multi-county district, but air pollution control advocate A.G. Michaud of Pebble Beach had switched to supporting a district that included just Monterey County, at least for the period of formation. At the end of November, Santa Cruz County supervisors voted on Supervisor Robert Burton's motion "to start a cooperative move to start an air pollution control district." Santa Cruz County then proceeded to reach out to Monterey County to create a district. That plan ran into problems because the politically powerful Salinas Valley farmers saw this as a dilution of their influence.

Race for Poverty Funds, P. 8

Monterey County's Incredible Kooks Discover the advocate

It has begun. We knew it would, of course, but nevertheless it is always a shock in America.

The editors of the advocate have begun receiving late-night telephone calls from the anonymous little people who cower in fear before an idea.

So far, there have been no threats. For now, the electronic night riders are only in a mood to harrass. Their courage must yet be boosted by their fear.

One wants to laugh; but it has been going on so long in this country and it has happened to so many.

Nelson Rockefeller told the 1964 Republican National Convention about threatening phone calls and obscene letters.

The delegates who nominated Goldwater laughed at him and booed him.

Thomas Kuchel knows about them, too, and has tried to fight. So has John Lindsay. So has Mark Hatfield. So have countless others warned and fought and tried to expose this underworld, this frightened little band of bigots.

When will all the rest of us quit giving them the benefit of the doubt? When will we quit listening to the excuses issued in their behalf by the Reagans and the Murphys and the Rousselots?

When will we at last realize that these people will not rest until they have broken the fine thread that connects them to the hope that is America?

the advocate

VOL. I. NO. 3   NOVEMBER, 1965   MONTEREY, CALIF.   20 CENTS

A Bettor's Guide to the Monterey County Board of Supervisors

These days—as county issues seem increasingly to dominate the local headlines—it has become all the rage to try to predict how the County Board of Supervisors will vote. During the Humble Oil debate, such predictions replaced television as a favorite parlor pastime. Now people are asking what will be the outcome of the hearing on the Institute for the Study of Non-violence.

Here, then, is the advocate's interpretation of the board and how it votes:

From such factors as their seating arrangement at the courthouse, their individual personalities and their party affiliations, it is possible on occasion to predict what the supervisors will do.

Who's On First?

The roll call votes usually proceed from left to right with the chairman (Thomson Hudson of Point Lobos) voting last. This puts the pressure on Seaside's Beauford Anderson, the first to vote. He is safe, however, and predictable, if Hudson's position on the motion at hand is known. The two usually agree. Nevertheless, Anderson has been known to try an occasional independent stand of his own—with rare success.

Second to vote is Warren Church of North County. His vote is his own, and he rarely agrees with Hudson and Anderson on matters of basic political philosophy.

With two votes cast, Harold Henry of King City has a choice of sides. He can go with either Anderson or Church. Although he agreed with Church on Humble, he is philosophically more akin to Anderson on most matters.

Salinas' Arthur Atteridge is fourth to vote. He likes to interpret the plays called by Hudson, making them easier for everyone to understand. He, too, is a frequent opponent of Hudson's on controversial issues.

Ruffles and Flourishes

Finally, there is Hudson, chairman of the board this year. He can often be relied upon to make a speech before he votes. He doesn't like to admit it, but he is a believer in strict district representation.

That is a brief introduction to the full course in "supervisor watching." Let's go down the roster again—in a different order—for another view.

Church is extremely cautious and not always effective, but he is keenly aware of the issues before him. He performs a prodigious amount of research—a habit the others would do well to emulate. Veterans, like Hudson and Henry, too often rely on faulty memories when they are seeking precedent in past board decisions. Church knows because he has checked.

As a freshman supervisor, Church is unusual in that he declines to accept tradition as reason and refuses to knuckle under to Hudson's power plays.

He is sincere, if soft-spoken. He thinks of himself as a conservationist in spite of his vote in favor of the refinery. He is also something of an iconoclast and he doesn't hesitate to anger the "gods" of county politics—such as the chambers of commerce.

Henry is a bean broker and his allegiance is to agri-
continued, p. 4

A "Bettors Guide" to the voting habits of the Board of Supervisors published in the advocate. Authors' collection

However, there was no guarantee that any district would be formed. Six months had passed since serious discussion began on creating an air pollution control district and the Monterey County Board of Supervisors had still not acted. Henry, trying to beef up his support in the agricultural community, announced that he opposed the formation of a district. The South County supervisor, who was up for reelection the next June, needed to do some fence-mending with his divided agricultural community. Although some farmers and others had slowly grown to oppose Humble, many remained supportive of the refinery. That divide extended to an air pollution control district, but Henry saw it as an opportunity to regain support.

"We ought to wait until we have a real problem," Henry said in dismissing the need for immediate action.

The county's current air pollution control ordinance that businesses had run afoul of earlier that month had an exemption for agricultural burning. Continuing that exemption was critical for agriculture's support. Yet as the air pollution control district appeared on the supervisors' agenda again, some support began to turn in the agricultural community. The county's Agricultural Advisory Committee voted 8-0, with one abstention, to support the formation of a countywide air pollution control district. The previously hostile reaction by the committee was eased when the head of the state Air Resources Bureau, John Maga, informed the committee that agriculture was exempt from district regulations. Committee members then warmly embraced the idea that universal air pollution regulation in the county could benefit crops by reducing crop-damaging smog from non-agricultural sources. A further clarification of state law found that not all agricultural activities were exempt, but that agriculture might have a ten-year grace period to comply with some regulations. The scenario seemed acceptable to most farmers.

"Certainly, if we're afraid of air pollution, then, by controlling the cities, it will be a benefit to agriculture in the county," explained county farm advisor William Huffman.

The support of the ag committee for an air pollution control district did not alter Supervisor Henry's views, though. He had long advocated the formation of the advisory committee, which had been created just a year before and was over half-filled with Henry appointees. Yet Henry broke from their recommendation. He continued to oppose an air pollution control district, just as he had when it was first proposed.

At the December 7 supervisors' meeting, eyes were once again on air pollution regulations. The possible creation of a countywide air pollution control district was one of the many consequences of the Humble controversy. If the supervisors voted to create a district, it would make Monterey County the first local government in the state, possibly the nation, to develop regulations to prevent air pollution *before* it was a problem. Previously, state law required a finding of "significant" air pollution contamination before a district could be activated to address the pollutants.

Prior to Monterey County's dealing with Humble, local governments in the United States had only intervened in pollution a couple of dozen times since the 1880s. It is doubtful that any local government embraced it with the thoroughness and gusto that Monterey County did. This was an alarming development for the oil and gas industry, as well as to industry in general. It was one of the reasons that Western Oil and Gas Association filed a lawsuit in Los Angeles in November to prevent local government from conducting preemptive regulations against pollution. Humble's travails in Monterey County were beginning to ripple through the industry.

Once again, a badly split Board of Supervisors was dealing with a Humble-related issue. No one was quite sure if the vote would approve or once again delay an air pollution control district. Finally, a 3-2 vote approved the district—Hudson, Anderson and Church voting yes.

"The vote marked the first time that Church, Atteridge and Henry did not stand together against Hudson and Anderson on a matter related directly to the debate over Humble Oil Co.'s proposed refinery at Moss Landing," wrote Stanley Cloud in the *Herald*.

The *Herald's* editorial board embraced Church's vote. "We welcome Mr. Church to this good company" (the new board majority on air pollution of Hudson, Anderson and Church). Church's vote should not have been a surprise, as it was he who pushed for more anti-pollution conditions on the Humble permit than any other supervisor, and who just a few days after the permit was granted called for air pollution monitoring stations to be immediately set up."

If anything, the faltering vote on the Board of Supervisors was now Hudson. Henry had already stated his opposition, declaring that the district was not economically feasible. Atteridge opposed the district too, but declared that his opposition rested on the enforcement penalties being criminal when he preferred that they be civil. Anderson and Church both took strong positions for immediate adoption.

Hudson, the indefatigable Humble opponent, appeared to be having second thoughts, and spoke of the need to protect agriculture from unnecessary regulatory burdens. While it appeared that Hudson might be leaning against the air pollution control district at that point, agricultural representatives like Wayne Bowman, president of the Farm Bureau, and Jack Bias, executive vice president of the Grower-Shipper Vegetable Association, spoke in favor of agricultural exemptions, contradicting Hudson on some points. Representatives of Humble Oil and PG&E also spoke in support of a district, although with clear hopes of tamping down the regulations. Also speaking in favor was Earl Moser of Citizens for Clean Air, completing a strong coalition of business, agricultural and environmental supporters on the same side.

Included at the meeting was a Santa Cruz County delegation of Supervisor Robert Burton and Planning Director Louis Muhly, urging the adoption of a multi-county district. The Monterey County supervisors rejected the Santa Cruz idea outright. Burton returned to his board, requesting that Santa Cruz County create its own district while lobbying the state legislature to create a regional district for the Monterey Bay area.

One of the topics of debate was the structure of the air pollution control district. State Senator Fred Farr authored the legislation that allowed the county to form a district before there was a pollution problem. However, disagreement arose between Henry and Atteridge, who wanted a structure similar to the performance-based San Francisco Bay Area Air Pollution Control District and suggested waiting for up to a year to get it right. This district measured emissions for compliance while a permit-based district approved specific anti-pollution devices. On the other side were Church and Anderson who warned that the real issue was the immediate need for a district.

In the unusual position of playing down the middle was Hudson who seemed to lean towards supporting the position of Henry and Atteridge. Perhaps Hudson was trying to protect his pro-business credentials, but it was an odd position to take after his strident opposition to Humble. With the supervisors teetering on another delay, a 15-minute recess was called. In that time, Hudson was seen talking to Church. When the board reconvened, Hudson announced that he had changed his mind, and the air pollution control district was activated.

A week later, the Board of Supervisors had the entire Moss Landing industrial zoning plan before them. An interim zoning law had been in effect for the last two years, and it was time to renew it or develop precise zoning for the area. In what the *Watsonville Register-Pajaronian* described as a "sharp fight," many of the old issues and alliances regarding Humble boiled over, but positions were not as hardened nor the alliances as firm as earlier in the year. Church, who six weeks earlier had expressed interest in changing the Moss Landing zoning to something more limiting, now seemed unenthusiastic about the idea. Hudson and Anderson sought to exclude any pollution-causing industries in the new interim zoning, but that motion failed 3-2 with the old Humble wall of Henry, Atteridge and Church prevailing. As Hudson was prone to do when facing defeat, he tried yet another motion, worded differently, to try and create a majority for his side. He failed again.

When County Counsel William Stoffers informed Hudson that the industries to prohibit would need to be specifically excluded, Hudson then focused his attention only on refineries. Church said he did not support that position, but also said that he did not want to vote on another oil refinery permit. Church preferred that the 50,000-barrel Humble refinery be up and running as a test case before other large industrial projects came for review, but was not willing to go as far as Hudson to ban them without any consideration.

Hudson then turned away from the oil refinery exclusion and backed Church's motion to extend the interim zoning without any changes. The motion passed 4-1 with Hudson leaving Anderson as the only vote in dissent. Hudson did not abandon only Anderson, but also Humble opponents Gus Bauman, Charles Kramer, Gunnar Norberg and Dave Williams, who all spoke on various alternatives to prevent pollution-causing industries. Although Hudson tried again to amend the motion for more restrictions and failed, it must have been baffling for longtime Humble opponents to see the stalwart anti-Humble Hudson begin to waver.

As tumultuous 1965 drew towards an end, there was one more interesting development in the ongoing fight over Humble's refinery. The Six Cities Fund began distributing placards on the Monterey Peninsula with the warning: "Danger: Smog Ahead." The placards were placed at centers of tourism—hotels, motels and restaurants. The placard read: "Join the Monterey County Six Cities Fund to fight oil refinery smog and pollution. . .A proposed oil refinery located where the Salinas Valley joins the Monterey coast will change this area's future from fair and clear to filthy and foul." The placard also contained more anti-refinery comments and an envelope for those moved to contribute.

"Visitors who come here to enjoy the pure and crystal-clear air that we have are concerned too," William Sefton, spokesman for the Six Cities Fund, said, "and this is giving them an opportunity to express themselves."

Humble supporters such as Carol Leino attacked the placards as a "smear campaign" against Humble. Leino, while suggesting that the attacks were "slanderous" to Humble, also pointed out in a letter to the editor of The

Californian that drawing this attention to visitors might have the undesirable effect of them going elsewhere.

"[L]et us keep our problems in the Monterey County 'family,'" Leino wrote. "The tourists and visitors come here to enjoy themselves and spend their money on such enjoyment. They most certainly do not come to Monterey County to be begged for money to assist in our problems. But, you can bet on one thing, if signs are placed throughout the area saying "Danger—Smog Ahead," the tourists will start looking for the road that doesn't go Ahead."

25

HUMBLE WINS AGAIN

January 22 – May 10, 1966

"We expect to begin construction near the end of the year."

J. Prince Warner, Humble Vice-President

The year 1966 arrived with many of the same problems of 1965. President Lyndon Johnson affirmed the United States' commitment to the war in Vietnam, and sent more troops to fight, sparking anti-war demonstrations. The USSR completed a soft moon landing with an unmanned spacecraft, putting the Russians ahead in the Space Race. The Salinas Valley was preoccupied with massive flooding from storms, causing more than $6 million in damage to crops. On the radio, Barry McGuire's song "Eve of Destruction" haunted the airwaves with its lyrics: "If the button is pushed, there's no running away/ There'll be no one to save with the world in a grave."

Humble Oil, permit in hand, continued to evaluate the soil and sea conditions around its proposed refinery. Yet a final resolution remained unsettled. While Humble's opponents continued attempting to sway public opinion, most observers saw the fate of Humble resting with courts. Nevertheless, for many residents, if not most, Humble's arrival seemed inevitable.

In January, Vince Moore, executive director of Monterey County Industrial Development Inc., espoused the advantages of a "diversified economy." At a

MCID meeting, he spoke of the benefits a single refinery might bring to the region. While pondering the fear of opponents who warned that one refinery would beget many more, Moore continued, "My personal feeling is that we don't want eight or ten refineries." Moore did not express what he considered an ideal number of refineries, but it was just that type of proliferation that Humble's opponents feared.

A.G. Michaud, who championed the formation of a local air pollution control district, to the right of his boss, S.F.B. Morse, at the opening of Spyglass Hill Golf Course at Pebble Beach in 1966.
Courtesy of Monterey Herald

As the Crosby golf tournament came to Pebble Beach in early February, one of the visitors to Pebble Beach was Supervisor Harold Henry. Henry, who squabbled with Supervisor Tom Hudson over Humble and agriculture, took the opportunity while watching some golf to smack back at the Monterey Peninsula, which had so often criticized him over his Humble support. Henry called the sewage conditions at Pebble Beach "really deplorable." At that time, overflow sewage was dumped into the bay at Pebble Beach.

"You could have Humble Oil sitting on Cypress Point and it couldn't pollute the air and water any more than it already is," said Henry.

Henry demanded that A.G. Michaud, president of Del Monte Properties, and County Sanitation Director Ed Munson get together for a solution. However, Henry had forgotten that a few months earlier the Board of Supervisors approved the creation of a new district in Pebble Beach to build a sewage treatment plant. The matter was already on its way to being resolved.

During this time, famed photographer and ardent Humble opponent Ansel Adams revealed that he had been in contact with Charles Jones, president of Humble Oil. Adams, speaking on behalf of all the opposition groups, sought to persuade Jones that despite Humble's noblest intentions and most effective pollution controls, there could be no "guarantee" against careless or accidental oil spills.

Finally, in early February, the legal decision the Monterey Bay area had been waiting for since November 24 was released. Superior Court Judge Richard Harris denied the petition for a writ of mandate to the Six Cities Fund. In a 14-page decision, Harris ruled that the county had operated administratively, not legislatively. The judge determined that the permit conditions for an oil refinery had been in effect "for over 20 years" and the Board of Supervisors retained the right to grant permits. Harris refuted every point of plaintiff attorney Bill Burleigh's case, but noted the "ingenious" arguments Burleigh presented. Harris then countered Burleigh's argument that board action in the past two decades had changed the county's policy on oil refineries.

"This court is unable to follow petitioners' contention that there has been any 'change of policy' relative to the construction of oil refineries in Monterey County," wrote Harris. "In fact, what petitioners here seem bent on doing is to prohibit the construction of any oil refineries anywhere in Monterey County."

Harris did leave a slight opening for Burleigh and the Six Cities Fund. They were given 15 days to amend the petition so as not to direct it at individual supervisors, but at the board in general, and to present any new arguments.

However, the door was not left much ajar, as courthouse observers noticed the near impossibility of devising a new argument in such a short time span.

"The fight isn't over," Burleigh said. "If there are valid grounds for an appeal, then we will probably appeal."

"I'm bitterly disappointed over this temporary setback," said Supervisor Tom Hudson, "but I hope that the various groups working so hard to combat the situation will continue their job."

Harris' ruling exposed what most observers had felt about the Six Cities Fund case. It rested on the specious argument that Humble's permit was a legislative act instead of an administrative one. The result was simply another blow to the opposition and one step closer to a refinery for Humble. Plaintiff William Howard Church promised that regardless of an appeal, organized efforts would continue so as to prevent another polluting industry from settling in Monterey County.

"Meanwhile," said elated Humble executive J. Prince Warner, "we have been going ahead actively with engineering studies and the design of an ultra-modern clean refinery which will operate well within the rigid restrictions of the permit. Several hundred thousand dollars have already been spent. Recent work has included detailed land surveys, investigation of soil characteristics at the site, and wave and current studies in the offshore loading and delivery area. Arrangements have been completed for the purchase of additional land adjacent to the site for suitable rail connections. In general, all work is on schedule; and, assuming that no complications develop, we expect to begin construction near the end of this year. On this basis, the refinery should be in operation early in 1969."

At this point, Humble looked nearly unstoppable. The opposition had been thwarted at every angle, politically and legally. It seemed that the groundbreaking was only months away. Nevertheless, the next day the Six Cities Fund came out swinging. Speaking for the group, Professor Church said they would either amend the complaint or file an appeal.

"We will continue to fight to keep dirty industry out of the area," vowed Church. "The fact it took the judge so long indicates there must have been considerable soul-searching there on the law and the facts. We believe a higher court may feel differently."

To the surprise of some, the opponents did not appeal. Instead, within the 15 days' deadline that Judge Harris gave the Six Cities Fund, Burleigh and his plaintiffs were back in court with an amended case. Burleigh's new argument charged that the equal protection and due process clauses of the

U.S. Constitution were violated. He centered the constitutional challenge on the interim industrial zoning ordinance passed in 1963, that the presence of a refinery threatened local agricultural and tourist economic interests, that the Planning Commission failed to consider the permit in the 30 days required by law. Burleigh contended that the interim ordinance was "unclear and uncertain," and that the ordinance "does not provide for uniform enforcement and administration." A hearing was set for April 11.

"[V]ictory is in sight," proclaimed Church of the Six Cities Fund in a statement released with the new complaint. Professor Church asked for another $50,000 in donations to pay for the legal bills and continue the public relations fight that he claimed was bearing fruit. He pointed to recent stories in the *New York Times*, *San Francisco Examiner* and Scripps-Howard Newspapers on the Humble Oil struggle, and said the Humble battle was putting Monterey County at the forefront of national attention in the battle of clean air versus smog.

By all signs, it did appear that opposition was growing beyond the Monterey Bay region. The California State Parks Commission took an interest in Humble's Moss Landing project in March, spurred by Commissioner Margaret Ownings of Big Sur. The move surprised local officials who had not been forewarned. Observers felt that the state parks agency became involved because the county was seeking more state parks, especially beachfront parks, and Moss Landing was a prime site for one.

When the parks commission met in April, Commissioner Ownings proposed a resolution against Humble's refinery because it presented a threat to the "abundance of marine life" and the white sands of neighboring beaches. However, her resolution ran into opposition from Harold Zellerbach, whose family owned Crown Zellerbach Corporation. A part-time Carmel resident, Zellerbach had expressed his opposition to the refinery earlier, but now took the procedural position that it was too late for the parks commission to act. Zellerbach said it should have been done before the Monterey County Board of Supervisors approved the permit. Ownings' motion was continued to May.

Elsewhere, even the national and influential Sierra Club passed a resolution against Humble Oil's Moss Landing refinery, calling out Humble's refinery as "a grave threat to the unique biological, recreational and esthetic values of the surrounding land and sea." As organized support for Humble had withered away since its permit was granted, the opposition seemed larger and stronger than ever—and growing.

Questioned if the amended lawsuit was simply a delaying tactic to harass Humble, Professor Church rebutted that they had "sound legal advice" and "ultimately will be successful." Yet Church also embraced the benefits of a delay. "At least this has kept Humble from beginning the refinery. Any construction is at their own risk," stated Church. While his statement about delaying construction was questionable, Humble had long said it would take a year of onsite studies before building, and the threat that continuing legal action might impede construction was real.

William Stoffers, Monterey County counsel, agreed with Professor Church that if Humble "got underway with a refinery and a majority against it, they would be out of luck." In that scenario, Humble would be forced to dismantle its facility.

Before the April 11 hearing, opponent Church announced on March 9 that the Six Cities Fund was changing its name. The organization now called itself the Anti-Pollution Association of Monterey County. The name change was to broaden the membership of the group and develop an organization with a long-term purpose to combat "the rising tide of mass pollution." The group included a seven-member committee ranging from farmers to medical personnel to business leaders, with prominent citizens from both the Monterey Peninsula and Salinas Valley that included long-time Humble opponents from the agricultural community, Dave Williams and Larry Hearne, as well as Professor Church and Gus Bauman.

The April 11 hearing was short. It was over in an hour. Judge Harris took demurrers, a motion to strike and the arguments of both sides under submission. Burleigh staked his amended case about due process on four points: any future refinery could be put to a vote by referendum, the interim ordinance did not allow a referendum or provide guidelines for administering the zoning as a permanent ordinance would, if the court did not rule in favor of the plaintiffs then the Board of Supervisors would be "allowed absolute, total discretion" under interim zoning, and the failure of the Planning Commission to act in 30 days removed the option of the Board of Supervisors acting on the permit. Judge Harris expressed a lack of enthusiasm for Burleigh's last point regarding the Planning Commission delay.

"I don't place much stock in this particular phrase or your argument, Mr. Burleigh," Judge Harris said.

County Counsel Stoffers questioned if the Anti-Pollution Association even had the right to sue the county and argued that upending the right of the Board of Supervisors to grant a permit for oil refineries would remove any regulatory restriction. Burleigh countered that invalidating one part of the ordinance would instead invalidate the entire document.

Harris announced that he would have a ruling as soon as possible, promising that it would come much quicker than the 76-day wait of the last hearing. This time the ruling came after a month. On May 10, Judge Harris presented his decision, but the conclusion was the same as before—the Board of Supervisors acted administratively and not legislatively. However, Harris ruled against Stoffers' argument that the plaintiffs did not have the right to sue the county, denying the defendants' claim that the lawsuit was "frivolous" and a "sham." Then, in one of the biggest surprises in his decision, Harris once again allowed Burleigh to amend his complaint and bring it back to the court within ten days.

Although Humble's opponents were losing badly in the courts, they kept nipping at the heels of Humble and obstructing firm plans for building the refinery. Years later, Burleigh said that delaying tactics were out of the ordinary for him. But that was effectively what his lawsuits would have achieved if the case continued. Nearly six months had passed, Humble had won on motions in two hearings, but the legal morass remained unresolved.

Nevertheless, time and options were running out for Humble's opponents. Every legal defeat left one less option. Unless Burleigh could come up with an amended pleading with a viable theory that would allow the court to set aside the permit, the last legal hope rested on an appeal. With the time for construction of the refinery drawing near, the Anti-Pollution Association had to hope that its lawsuits were harassing Humble Oil enough that it might look elsewhere.

26

A HUMBLING EXPERIENCE

February 14 – May 9, 1966

"The scope has changed from what we originally had in mind."

Michael Haider, chairman of Standard Oil of New Jersey

At the one-year anniversary of Humble Oil seeking a permit for a Moss Landing refinery, the changes the battle brought the county were substantial and remarkable. Monterey County now had a template on how to regulate oil refineries and other heavy industry. That template was setting a new standard of regulation, especially for local governments, for the nation and even the world. In addition, the county had an air pollution control district with teeth and a purpose not only to reduce air pollution but to prevent it—an unusual, if not unique, action by a local government for that time. With nearly 3,500 more acres of Moss Landing industrial zoned land still to be allocated for industry, that template had an important role ahead.

During this time, Humble commissioned another public opinion survey. Humble announced that the poll results would not be released, but that its purpose was to "update" the data from the survey conducted the previous summer. The first survey showed county residents favoring the refinery two to one. The second survey, conducted by Field Research Co., ran seven pages, asking residents about their knowledge on industrialization, taxes, local newspapers and the economy. Why Humble felt compelled to invest further in a survey when it had a permit is unknown, but it probably played a role in assessing support in Monterey County in case a referendum was ordered by a court or if Humble needed to come back to the county for an alteration in its permit. Whatever the purpose, Humble was not talking about it.

"We're going full speed ahead," affirmed Humble spokesperson D I Bolding, who added that construction should begin in December 1966 or January 1967.

As the legal battle wove its way back and forth through the court of Judge Richard Harris, organized efforts against Humble continued on many fronts. In early March, Carmel City Councilmember Gunnar Norberg pushed through a motion requesting special legislation from the state that would allow a city to spend public money to fight pollution that originates in other communities. The appeal asked State Senator Fred Farr to put the item on his legislative agenda.

For some time, Tom Hudson had been telling people that Humble was not going to build in Monterey County. In March, the buzz Hudson spread began to intensify. As the rumor gathered steam, Hudson refused to divulge his source or reasonings. While Hudson was often in the know, he had suggested that Humble was pulling out of Moss Landing for Benicia almost a year earlier, and that had not happened. Nevertheless, when Hudson had something to say, there was usually some fire behind the smoke.

What followed next was a series of confusing, surprising and extraordinary events. The exact details remain somewhat of a mystery. On March 31, the *Salinas Californian* broke the story with the near shocking headline: "Humble Fan Club Backed by Hudson?" According to The *Californian*, Hudson, the ardent foe of Humble, proposed a "gold card club" or "Buy from Humble Club" to support the oil giant's products. Membership in the club would come from names supplied by Hudson, presumably dyed-in-the-wool Humble opponents. Hudson expressed his hope that when Humble pulled out of Monterey County that the people could be unified in their support of Humble products. He then elaborated on his bizarre business proposal that the Sierra Club should back Humble products because the oil company's reputation had been badly damaged by the struggle over a Moss Landing refinery.

The Sierra Club quickly squelched the proposal, but not before Hudson refuted major parts of The *Californian's* story. The next day, the *Monterey Peninsula Herald* ran a story with Hudson denying that he proposed any type of "club." However, Hudson did reveal that he told Humble's president that he was encouraging people to buy Humble products when the company left Monterey County.

The reaction by Humble opponents in Monterey County was also immediate. "Our directors do not share the optimism expressed by Supervisor Tom Hudson that Humble Oil is ready to pull out of Moss Landing," said William Howard Church, president of the Anti-Pollution Association. Professor Church went on to say suggestions of any consumer support for Humble before it pulled its permit were damaging and misleading.

An editorial cartoon that appeared in the Monterey Peninsula Herald.
Courtesy of Monterey Herald

At this same time, word leaked out that Hudson had been involved in private negotiations with Humble for months or even a year. The *Salinas Californian* reported that a month after Humble applied for its permit in February 1965, Humble officials held a brunch with Assembly Speaker Jesse "Big Daddy" Unruh. Unruh, a Democrat, often clashed with Governor Pat Brown, also a Democrat. Unruh is "often regarded as the most powerful Assembly Speaker in California history," according to his 1987 obituary in the *Los Angeles Times*. President Lyndon Johnson was less complimentary, calling Unruh "one of the most selfish men" he had ever encountered in politics. In other words, if Unruh was involved, something big was happening for his own benefit. The time of the Humble and Unruh meeting was near the date when Hudson announced that Humble was moving to Benicia. That could be written off as coincidence except for growing signs of an Unruh-Hudson connection.

That connection became clearer months later. In January 1966, Hudson, a Republican, was Monterey County chair for ticket sales to Democrat Unruh's testimonial dinner—a highly unusual alliance between two well-known deal-makers. By April, the talk floating through the state legislature in Sacramento was that Hudson had cut a deal with Unruh. Hudson sold tickets to Unruh's dinner, and, in return, Unruh promised to persuade Humble to move elsewhere in the state. At the dinner, Hudson was seated next to Humble Oil officials. When questioned about the seating arrangements, Hudson called it a "coincidence," which was unlikely since Hudson was in close contact with Humble and Unruh. Also around the time of the dinner, Hudson admitted flying to Houston to meet with Charles Jones, president of Humble Oil.

"I don't think that warrants a comment," Hudson said to The *Californian* when asked if a deal was made with Unruh.

Humble also had its own denial. The oil company said its only contact with Unruh was at the brunch shortly after the permit application in Monterey County, apparently forgetting the tickets they purchased at the Unruh testimonial dinner. Humble also denied that any political group had proposed other sites for the Moss Landing refinery, coyly ignoring that Unruh was an individual and not a group.

For Hudson to suddenly go quiet about such an intriguing backroom deal was out of character, and gives some credibility to a secret agreement. Hudson probably realized that he was publicly revealing a little too much. A few days earlier, Hudson, confident that Humble was leaving and trying to let the public know of his role in that development, spilled a story to the media that conflicted with his and Humble's comments. "I ... told Charlie Jones (Humble's president) that I will work with Jesse Unruh to help them find another location if they decide to move," Hudson told the *Herald*.

As all this was breaking, another story unfolded and captured attention throughout the state. At the end of March, local and state media, including the *San Francisco Examiner* and *Los Angeles Times*, reported that Humble Oil had "abandoned" its Moss Landing site because soil and shore studies revealed the site as "unsuitable." Almost immediately the media backtracked, stating that Moss Landing was still under consideration. Local newspapers followed up with more detail.

Humble spokesperson Bolding announced that the soil conditions were "poorer than anticipated originally, requiring more piling." Furthermore, wave surges would also delay tankers' unloading for days, an additional cost increase. Bolding said that preliminary studies prior to Humble purchasing the Moss Landing property did not reveal these problems.

Bolding stated that Humble had taken out options on two properties in the San Francisco Bay Area as alternative sites. These were in the same places that rumors had floated over the last year: Martinez and Benicia. The Martinez location was identified as the Crockett-Rodeo area, but was not the same spot as examined the previous October. Bolding said the options were taken out so engineering studies could be conducted at the two sites. From Humble's perspective, officials must have hoped that the preliminary studies this time were more accurate than the ones at Moss Landing, which initially were satisfactory and compelled Humble to seek a permit there. Bolding also announced another problem for Humble's Moss Landing refinery.

"Economic changes affecting the industry and our participation in it have occurred which necessitate our planning for a considerably larger refinery than originally intended," Bolding commented.

Although a recent survey found strong support for the refinery, Bolding hoped county residents would understand the necessity of Humble looking at the other sites. "If the economics are better somewhere else, we may go there."

Is this how the great Humble Oil controversy was to end, not stopped by public opposition, legal action, permit conditions or political maneuverings? It seems that Mother Nature had simply played a dirty trick on Humble. Preliminary studies at Moss Landing were inaccurate for both the soil and sea, and this was only discovered through extensive studies after the land had been purchased and permits secured. The permits and the studies had at least cost several hundred thousands of dollars by this time. Unfortunately, according to Humble, that tantalizing deepwater port was too rough for super tankers to unload in a timely and cost-effective fashion. Even if the tankers did unload, the crude oil would have to be processed in a refinery, driven uneconomical because additional pilings were required to stabilize the soil.

The *Watsonville Register-Pajaronian* snickered at the thought in an editorial:

"Is it possible that an oil company, whose very life comes from underground, made a mistake in its early tests, or is this just an excuse?

"Humble says the wave action in Monterey Bay is more severe than it thought, perhaps posing the problem of having 175,000-ton supertankers lying idle offshore for days before they can hook up to a pipeline. Could the company's engineers have failed to measure the waves beforehand?"

If there was a problem with the waves, Humble should have known long ago. All it had to do was talk with its neighbor, PG&E. The power company had been unloading oil tankers for years with a pipeline that extended 3,600 feet offshore. At this time, the Mighty Moss power plant was the main source of electricity for California. It was essential to keep it operating, and it used lots of fuel—up to 50,000 barrels of oil a day—the amount Humble's refinery was scheduled to process. The wave surges did not stop PG&E from unloading oil tankers so it was baffling that waves could interfere that severely with Humble's tankers. PG&E would continue to unload fuel offshore for many years more. In 1976, the Army Corps of Engineers examined pipeline delivery systems off the Moss Landing coast and deemed that "Wave and tidal conditions are considered good." The Army expressed more concern about the fog than waves.

At the time that Humble was raising these questions, Hudson announced that he had been meeting with Humble President Charles Jones. Hudson stated that Jones saw "a great deal of interest in this problem as the opposition saw it." Hudson's words undercut Humble's statement as he was not talking about poor soil tests and wave surges.

Supervisor Andy Anderson suggested another problem: "The condition (to enlarge the plant) sounds like it might be an important one." The condition Anderson mentioned required a new permit if Humble needed to expand to a larger facility than the original permit allowed. That would require Humble going back to the Planning Commission and Board of Supervisors all over again. Ironically, Anderson and Hudson, staunch Humble opponents, had voted against that regulation.

Humble also followed up with a somewhat contradictory statement on the poor soil tests and wave action. Humble said that more research was ongoing but that construction bids were being taken for the project—a curious act if the sea and soil conditions were unacceptably poor. Some observers felt that Humble was simply trying to plant a decoy for the opponents, that the refinery construction was going elsewhere. The opposition was not buying that and stood united, except for Hudson's increasingly conciliatory gestures.

"My advice to refinery opponents," said William Howard Church, "is to keep their powder dry until Humble Oil has actually withdrawn its permit requests."

In an interview with the *Santa Cruz Sentinel*, Humble again contradicted itself. J. Prince Warner, Humble's vice president of manufacturing, told the *Sentinel* that Humble was not "junking" its Moss Landing project, but again elaborated on the need for more pilings—this time for the loading and unloading of ships. Warner absolutely denied that local opposition had any influence on the recent hesitation by Humble.

Despite the soil and wave problems that Humble claimed just a day earlier threatened the project, Warner stated that Moss Landing met all the qualifications and Humble would need to "adapt" the refinery to the Moss Landing location. However, Warner said that Humble needed a refinery bigger than the one the permit allowed, and Humble spokesperson Bolding admitted that Humble might need to start the permit process over for a larger refinery. Although Humble expressed the need for a 70,000-barrel-a-day refinery during this time, Bolding took it a step further. He said that Humble already envisioned a refinery producing 100,000 barrels a day in a few years.

Elsewhere a new contender emerged as a possible Humble site. M.H. McDonald of the Economic Development Committee of San Luis Obispo County Chamber of Commerce wrote in a letter to Fred Kimball, the chair of the San Luis Obispo Board of Supervisors, that Humble West Coast production manager W.F. Eiting Jr. had told him that Humble was not going to build at Moss Landing. The San Luis Obispo supervisors wrote to Humble inviting them to build there. However, the Sierra Club, which had already opposed the Moss Landing Humble project, said it would oppose a San Luis Obispo refinery, especially if it was placed at Nipomo Dunes—one of the primary locations under consideration. Bolding reacted immediately, refuting the suggestion that Humble was pulling out of Moss Landing. Bolding said that McDonald "conned" Eiting into a false statement.

Amongst the confusion and contradictions with Humble underlings, Michael Haider, chairman of Standard Oil of New Jersey, Humble Oil's parent company, made his own public comments to the *Herald*. Haider said that Humble officials had not yet made up their minds on whether to stay with

Moss Landing or relocate. More studies needed to be done, clarified Haider. "The scope has changed from what we originally had in mind," Haider stated.

The studies Haider spoke of were not soil and wave studies. The studies were economic—markets, location, size and so on. Haider shrugged off the opposition to the refinery as "exaggerated" and pointed that many people in Monterey County wanted Humble to build. Haider made no suggestion that there were significant problems with the soil or sea conditions.

There was yet another behind-the-scenes act being played out, and a significant one at that. If Humble wanted to build a larger refinery, it was not only the opposition and lawsuits against it that stood in the way. It appeared that Humble no longer had the votes on the Monterey County Board of Supervisors to get a permit for a larger facility.

At the end of March, in one of the articles in the *Herald* describing the soil and wave problems and the need for a larger refinery, a paragraph wrapped in parentheses suggested that one of the three supervisors who had backed Humble on the 3-2 vote to grant a permit was not looking fondly at a larger refinery.

"(It is by no means certain that Humble would get a permit for a plant larger than 65,000 barrels. At least one supervisor who voted for Humble's permit, has indicated he might not look with favor on a larger plant)," wrote Stanley Cloud.

Fifty-four years later, Cloud could not recall who that supervisor might be. He even suggested that the parenthetical statement might have been inserted by one of his editors who was in the know. Regardless, it was an impassable roadblock for Humble unless the oil giant could remain content with a small refinery. That did not seem to be the case.

One of the three supervisors who voted for the permit—Harold Henry, Arthur Atteridge or Warren Church—was signaling publicly to Humble, "Do not bother coming back for another permit because you will not get it." Whoever that supervisor was, he did not want his name attached to his opposition to a larger refinery. There was good reason for that. Feelings of support still ran high and all three supervisors were in districts that were pro-Humble. But which one of the three was it?

Cloud's counterpart, Ray March of the *Californian*, also inserted parentheses in one of his articles at that time, although the hint was a bit vaguer. "(Observers predict a new application would meet considerable opposition)," wrote March. Was March speaking of the same topic as Cloud? Or was he suggesting that Monterey Peninsula and agricultural interests would come after

Humble with a vengeance? Both conclusions might be true. But if a supervisor was switching allegiance, then nothing else mattered anyway.

At the same time, the *Watsonville Register-Pajaronian* had more to add to the intrigue. Watsonville lies just outside the northern border of Monterey County and within Santa Cruz County, so the local paper was intently interested in Humble's fate as it expected to house many of the workers from the refinery. Church's supervisorial district was the only district to serve the Monterey County side of the Watsonville community. The *Pajaronian*, in search of a response to the contradictory signs from Humble, reached out to Supervisor Church. The usually tight-lipped Church, who had kept his support for Humble undisclosed from March to September of the previous year, turned a bit loquacious as he analyzed the new developments. As he had also said to The *Californian*, Church found "no surprise" in Humble's desire to look elsewhere.

Church credited the ongoing opposition to Humble by the Monterey Peninsula as the key factor in Humble's hesitation. He noted the legal efforts by Carmel City Attorney Bill Burleigh as part of that opposition. The court battles kept "things hanging" for Humble, impeding their plans to begin building. But Church had something more to add.

"I doubt if they could win a fight to get another permit," Church said. "So they are limited to the size of plant allowed by the original permit. They may want a larger plant, and I don't know if they could get it."

Church's reference that Humble was unlikely to get a permit for a larger refinery matched the parenthetical comment in Cloud's article. Was Church referring to himself, or to Atteridge or Henry? Whoever it was, it was a secret limited to Cloud, Church and perhaps a few others. It might also explain why Hudson had spent the previous weeks spreading the word that Humble was leaving Monterey County.

All the talk of Humble pulling up stakes stirred the latent supporters of Humble into belated action. The Moss Landing Chamber of Commerce initiated a letter-writing drive to reassure Humble that the refinery was still wanted for growth, jobs and a "diversified economy." The Salinas City Council also got into the act, approving Councilmember Jack Barnes' motion that the city restate its "support of their (Humble Oil's) plan to locate in this area. Monterey County Industrial Development reaffirmed its support for Humble as well, but went a step further in supporting the plans for a larger refinery of 75,000 to 100,000 barrels a day production. Despite these efforts, the supporters of Humble were spent from the year-long battle, too disorganized to rouse a united response, or sensing that any efforts were too late to make a difference. Their efforts were half-hearted at best.

Lending support to Humble's opponents was State Controller Alan Cranston, a Democrat. Cranston, who had already voiced his opposition to the Humble project, expressed his disapproval once again. Calling the oil refinery a "folly," Cranston said that it "threatens not only to pollute the water but the air as well and in this place, of all places—one of the most beautiful areas of the state—it is a tragic idea."

Cranston was not the only state politician to begin weighing in on Humble. The building of the oil refinery was starting to shape up as a matter of statewide interest in the coming June primary. Robert Finch, a Republican candidate for Lieutenant Governor, said the oil refinery should not be allowed in Monterey County because "There is not enough hard evidence that anti-pollutant measures will work effectively." Finch and Cranston's statements demonstrated that Humble opposition was genuinely bipartisan at even the state level.

Nevertheless, not all the state's politicians were willing to weigh in on Humble. Ronald Reagan, making his initial bid for public office in the Governor's race, spent two days campaigning in Monterey County in early May 1966. At a gathering of 30 people at the Mark Thomas Inn in Monterey, Charles Kramer rose to pose the Humble question to Reagan. Reagan demurred that it was a local issue, but Kramer said air pollution was a state issue and the locals were fighting a "goliath." Before Reagan could answer, attorney Harry Noland, whose law firm with Paul Hamerly represented Humble, jumped in to chastise Kramer for putting Reagan on the spot. Reagan, smiling, backed away from the question and tried to shift to another topic, suggesting that if he could get away with it, he would move the state capital back to Monterey.

Suddenly and tragically, another shoe dropped against Humble. Supervisor Harold Henry, probably Humble's strongest voice on the Board of Supervisors, faced a tough re-election bid. Although always a firm supporter of agriculture, Humble had divided Henry's constituency, placing the supervisor in a tough race with three opponents. On April 23, he had been campaigning hard; upon returning home, he sat down and suffered a fatal heart attack. Henry's death only added more uncertainty to Humble's fate. If he was the wavering Humble supporter opposed to a larger refinery, that would still leave two votes in favor of Humble. If he was not, and either Church or Atteridge swung their vote to the other side, that left only one vote for Humble among the supervisors. Humble must have taken notice.

Even the *Herald*, which butted hard against Henry on Humble and other issues, noted his dedication and conviction, but also the alienation that he had caused on the Monterey Peninsula. Ted Durien of the *Herald* contemplated if Henry's support for Humble was because he supported Humble's plans or if it was a kneejerk reaction to Humble's opponents on the Peninsula.

Henry's unexpected death foreshadowed the end of the Humble affair. The curtains on the great Humble Oil drama were starting to close, and a final decision soon to be announced.

27

HUMBLE'S PLAN B

*"Nothing else is being given equal consideration (to Moss
Landing) now, but I hesitate to say we are closing the door
on another site."*

Jack Gardner, Humble Oil official

Almost from the beginning, rumors floated of Humble Oil moving its
refinery to another location. Humble started its search for a West Coast
refinery by scouting sites from Washington state to San Diego. One of the
primary alternatives was the San Francisco Bay Area. It was already heavily
industrialized with infrastructure and multiple oil refineries, including one
built by Chevron in the 19th century. The problem with the Bay Area was the
bay. It was shallow, far too shallow for a supertanker. That is what made the
deep submarine canyon just a few hundred meters off the Moss Landing shore
such an ideal site.

The Humble controversy was barely starting to spark controversy when
Supervisor Tom Hudson announced in April 1965 that Humble was pulling
out for the small city of Benicia, tucked well inside the San Francisco Bay.
Benicia did not have any oil refineries but there were many around in the
nearby cities. Hudson's "scoop" was quickly dismissed by Humble officials and
fell from the news. Still, Humble officials would periodically float rumors of
other sites, probably intended more as a scare tactic to press Monterey County
into lightening its growing list of permit restrictions.

One of the more serious alternatives arose in early October, just a couple of weeks after the Monterey County Board of Supervisors approved the 39 conditions for the Humble permit. The *Monterey Peninsula Herald* announced that Humble officials had been investigating an alternative site near Martinez, just on the other side of the Carquinez Bridge from Benicia.

Martinez was already in the middle of a heavily industrialized area on the northeastern edge of the San Francisco Bay. In the mid-1960s, more than 20 oil refineries and plants producing petroleum-derived products could be found along the Carquinez Strait, in a string of cities from Richmond on up to Pittsburg, as well as heavy industry that included shipbuilding, canneries and tanneries. Benicia was also among these centers of industry.

The *Oakland Tribune* broke the Martinez story with confirmation coming from Paul Hughey, the city manager of Martinez. A Humble spokesperson in Houston also confirmed the discussions. Hughey noted just how inviting Martinez was compared to Moss Landing.

"We have 2,000 acres zoned for heavy industry along the river," Hughey stated. "Humble would not have to go to the planning commission or the board of supervisors."

Hughey said the only problem was that the San Francisco Bay was only 25 feet deep at the Martinez location, but dredging was going to open it to 45 feet soon. Nevertheless, that was nothing near what the deepwater port of Moss Landing offered. Word of the uprising against Humble in Monterey County was generating considerable attention, and Hughey made sure that Humble officials knew that it would be different in Martinez.

"We reminded these people (Humble engineers) what the public reaction would be down your way in case of an oil spill in Monterey Bay," Hughey told the *Herald*. "There would be no danger of that here."

"We are in touch with the Humble office in Houston," Hughey continued, "and we are continuing to bombard them with information about the various advantages."

Jack Gardner of Humble's manufacturing division discounted that Humble was seriously considering moving to Martinez. Gardner said that the meeting with Contra Costa County and Martinez officials should not be taken as a "threat" by Monterey County. He emphasized that Martinez was simply a backup in case there are "further delays."

"Nothing else is being given equal consideration (to Moss Landing) now, but I hesitate to say we are closing the door on another site," Gardner said. Gardner continued, emphasizing that "harassment, complaints, fault-finding, and the attitude of public officials all enter into Humble's reasons for considering an alternate location for its refinery."

Essentially, Gardner had just informed the opposition that it was having an impact. Charles Kramer, William Howard Church, Bill Burleigh and others had reason to be hopeful. Perhaps just a little more pressure would wound Humble enough to make it leave, but Humble was not about to show its cards. It still held firm in its Moss Landing plan as clarified in a statement released by Gardner a few days later:

Undated photograph of men loading cartridges for big guns at the Benicia Arsenal.
G.G. Bain, U.S. Library of Congress Prints & Photographs Division

"The discussions between Contra Costa County and Martinez officials and Humble representatives were at the instigation and invitation of the people of Contra Costa County. While Humble feels it desirable to keep current on information on alternate sites, they are not giving serious consideration to any location other than Moss Landing for their West Coast refinery. The discussions were primarily a courtesy to the people of Contra Costa County, who have approached Humble."

Whatever discussions were going on in the Martinez area with local officials and Humble Oil, it was clear that not everyone was on the same script. James Ritch, general manager of the Contra Costa Development Association, directly contradicted Gardner, stating that Humble was not there at a local invitation, but "on its own volition" had developed an interest in the area.

Ritch also contradicted Gardner on another point. Ritch said that Humble might "hedge on its bets" because it might not be able to "live with" the conditions that Monterey County placed on the permit. Gardner admitted that a refinery in Martinez would have "somewhat less stringent" conditions, but dismissed it as "an extremely minor consideration" as Humble had already stated that it could live with the Monterey County conditions.

If the conditions were not a serious consideration, it is odd that Ritch would know about them. Ritch would have little interest of the conditions for a permit in another county over 100 miles away—unless the conditions had created such uneasiness in the industry that officials at other refineries had confided in Ritch, or Humble officials had expressed their own concerns to him directly.

For those watching Humble closely, the Martinez foray left questions and raised doubts. Was Martinez simply a backup plan or a serious contender to Moss Landing? Humble opponents like William Howard Church expressed skepticism a few days later when he announced the lawsuit against the Board of Supervisors. For others, it was just another sign that the struggle over Humble had more twists and uncertainties to come.

The local principals involved in working with Humble continued their contacts with Humble over the winter. However, by late March of 1966, the Martinez site had fallen from favor. Humble turned its attention away from Martinez and to its neighbor, Rodeo, also in Contra Costa County. Most of the discussions at Rodeo were done surreptitiously. Yet the publicity that the Martinez site generated in October presented a peek at what Humble was thinking.

Before the Martinez site gained attention in October 1965, there was the Benicia rumor in April of the same year, and that rumor would gain more substance the following year with the Rodeo site. Humble announced what almost nobody in Monterey County realized. Even as controversy swirled around the proposed oil refinery at Moss Landing, Benicia was desperate to woo Humble, and secret negotiations had been under way for some months even as oil officials began pressing their case with Monterey County in February 1965.

Benicia had a special problem, one that its city officials had been grappling with since the beginning of the 1960s. The city was drying up and dying with the departure of its largest employer, the U.S. Army. Benicia's economy was in free fall, and officials there were ready to take drastic action.

Benicia had not always been so overlooked. The city, founded in 1849 and the third city to incorporate in the new state of California, was considered a gateway to the Gold Rush during the mid-1800s. Benicia briefly became the state capital in 1853, and its citizens quickly constructed a red brick Capitol building with impressive Greek columns. The capital designation did not last long, since only 13 months later, Governor John Bigler decided he would rather attend the state's business in his hometown, Sacramento. Over the next century, the U.S. Arsenal in Benicia would swell from a small depot to a massive facility with thousands of acres and hundreds of buildings.

And then came a fateful decision.

On March 30, 1961, the teletype machine at the arsenal clattered out a message from the U.S. Army Chief of Ordnance that left personnel stunned and shaken. "Benicia Arsenal, Benicia, California, will be inactivated by closeout and/or transfer of mission to Tooele Ordnance Depot, Tooele, Utah. After inactivation, Benicia will be declared excess." The date for closure: March 30, 1964.

It was all part of an effort by the Kennedy administration to modernize and streamline the armed forces, with funds to be put into nuclear weaponry rather than outdated arsenals, a remnant of the past century. It was part of a wave of base closures, more than 600 in all, that was to sweep the country. Almost immediately, a reduction of force took place, with arsenal workers transferring to other nearby bases, such as Mare Island Naval Shipyard and Travis Air Force Base. Still other employees decided to make the move to Utah.

Reg Page remembers that time in Benicia history. Now an author and Benicia historian, Page worked on the construction of the Interstate 680 freeway between Cordelia and Benicia in 1964. Benicia was by then rather sad and run-down; said Page, "It made quite an impression on me. The town didn't look too good then."

Page noted that the highway construction bypassed Benicia, leaving it with fewer economic opportunities, on top of the fact that the arsenal was pulling out. Benicia historian Dr. Jim Lessenger noted that, "They just dedicated 680, bypassed Benicia and left it in the lurch."

An article that Lessenger wrote for the *Benicia Herald* details much of the history of this period, and in an interview at his home, he filled in additional details that he has gathered through years of effort, digging for lost paperwork and documents and talking to locals.

After so many years of living cheek by jowl with the arsenal, the city of Benicia was almost wholly dependent on it economically. Military and civilian employees of the arsenal shopped at its stores, sent their children to school there, went to its churches and patronized its eating and drinking establishments, Lessenger wrote. Soon after the closure was announced, a "Save the Arsenal" movement was launched, but to no avail.

As the months went by and downsizing at the arsenal progressed, matters became more desperate. The city council debated in open session whether there was enough money in the budget to afford a new police car. Lessenger said that in 1960-61, the city didn't even have enough money to pay its employees.

As mentioned earlier in this book, it was then that Benicia City Attorney John Bohn and Mayor James Lemos came up with a grand scheme to save the city. Their audacious idea was the Benicia Plan, which would allow the city to buy the arsenal property on an installment plan—something that the U.S. government had never before allowed. The city would then lease the property to a private investor. The lease fees would go to pay off the mortgage with the federal government.

Lessenger said that Humble didn't originally consider Benicia, but was considering the site in nearby Rodeo, and of course Martinez was also a possibility. But once the arsenal was set for closure, the wheels started to turn. "There began a multi-tiered negotiation between Humble Oil, Governor Brown, the GSA, McNamara, Sen. Luther Gibson and Sen. Clair Engle from 1964 to 1965," Lessenger said.

The process was by no means an easy one, since many agencies and utilities wanted a slice of the arsenal property. Some locals didn't like the conversion idea and fought against it. But ultimately, the plan prevailed. A new problem cropped up: the land beneath the Carquinez Strait was owned by the state, and in 1964, the state legislature passed a bill to convey the "submerged and tidal lands" around the former arsenal's pier in perpetuity to the city of Benicia. The pier, which would be rebuilt by the city, was essential to industry.

As it turned out, only Benicia Industries was interested in working with the city as a lessee, since all the other companies that expressed interest wanted to buy the property outright. The deed for the arsenal, conveying the property from the U.S. government to the city of Benicia, was signed in February 1965. Benicia Industries and the city signed the Master Lease the following month. Thanks to State Senator Gibson, state legislation was passed to create a new agency called the Surplus Property Authority, which had the ability to assume the debt for the arsenal property. The stage was now set for businesses to come in and buy pieces of the property.

28

A TIGER TURNS TAIL

May 3 –19, 1966

"I am very happy. It looks as though we are reasonably safe now."

Samuel F.B. Morse

At the beginning of May, Humble Oil opponent State Senator Fred Farr confirmed what had been fueling Supervisor Tom Hudson's optimism since March. Farr announced that Humble was "definitely" leaving Monterey County, explaining that "reliable sources" in Sacramento had confirmed that development with him. According to Farr, his sources were connected to Humble Oil. What Farr did not say was that he, too, had been doing some lobbying behind the scenes. He had been in contact with his colleague State Senator George Miller Jr. about finding another site for Humble, perhaps in Miller's district or a nearby one. Miller's district included Contra Costa County in the East Bay, an area that was already home to refineries.

However, Humble spokesperson D I Bolding acted baffled. Bolding said if Humble was leaving, then that was news to him. Bolding said that he had no idea what sources Farr was referencing. "We have not abandoned the Moss Landing site," said Bolding.

As Humble secretly began to look north toward Benicia and Contra Costa

County, a familiar problem developed. The Contra Costa County Planning Commission issued a continuance on a rezoning hearing for property near the town of Rodeo to change it from agricultural to industrial. Humble was eyeing this as an alternative to Moss Landing, but Humble officials must have wondered if they were experiencing déjà vu.

Rodeo residents rose in protest of Humble's plans. Fears that the city would be ringed by oil refineries, with an increasing air pollution problem, stirred opposition. Others warned that if Humble built at the proposed location, the city would be boxed in with no room for expansion. The protests in Rodeo likely unsettled Humble officials as they clearly were not looking forward to jumping from one oil controversy in Monterey County to another in the San Francisco Bay region.

The following week, the Contra Costa Planning Commission granted a change in zoning on a 7-0 vote. While a victory for Humble, it was not a guarantee. The county's general plan had stipulated that the site be designated for industrial use. The vote simply ratified that. Recommendation would need approval from the county's supervisors, though, and that was scheduled in the coming weeks. Beyond that, Humble still needed to conduct engineering studies, similar to the ones being conducted at Moss Landing. George Swisher, project coordinator of Humble's manufacturing division, said that this did not impact continuing studies at Moss Landing and a final decision rested solely on economics. The Contra Costa County Board of Supervisors finally granted the rezoning Humble desired on June 11, but by then it was too late. The Rodeo site was destined to be a bridesmaid.

Despite the news that Humble might relocate, opponents were still waging a fierce battle. Humble was scoring victories against Bill Burleigh and his allies in the courts. Other opponents, including Tom Hudson, were preparing to take the battle straight to Humble. Hudson, with Kramer, began to organize an opposition effort for May 18 in Cleveland at the Standard Oil of New Jersey stockholders' annual meeting. In many ways it was strange to see Hudson back to engaging in this opposition since he was suggesting the fight was won, except for the formality of a Humble announcement. Perhaps Hudson was not as confident as he publicly pretended or, perhaps, he saw one last opportunity to be at the forefront during the demise of Humble's Moss Landing project. Always on the lookout for some good publicity, challenging Humble in Cleveland would put him straight in the spotlight. Hudson planned on gathering 200,000 proxy shares of Standard Oil of New Jersey stock to force a vote.

What had started as a local issue ramped up to a regional and then a state issue. Now, Humble's refinery stood on the brink of becoming a national issue—a development that the *Monterey Peninsula Herald* noted.

"It (Humble's refinery) may have begun that way (a local issue), but it is nothing of the sort today," editorialized Allen Griffin in the *Herald*. "This is a statewide issue. It is becoming a national issue. The entire nation is concerned today about pollution of the air and of the water."

Senator Fred Farr with President John F. Kennedy and Vice President Lyndon Johnson in the early 1960s.
Fred Farr Papers, Digital Commons @ CSUMB

Packed for Cleveland, Hudson and Kramer departed with a suitcase full of proxies. Unfortunately, they were far short of 200,000. Hudson's suitcase carried only 44,000 proxies, valued at over $3 million. Hudson called the shares a "respectable number" but it represented one of the few times the opposition delivered less than it promised. To pressure a multinational corporation like Jersey Standard, as it was known, would take a lot more than a few thousand stockholder shares. Hudson dismissed the failure to get 200,000 shares as falling short of time. Hudson and Kramer planned to appear before the oil company's board of directors and present a resolution opposing the refinery's construction.

There was yet another demonstration against Humble, one of the first of its kind. Standard Oil of New Jersey credit cards were being returned to the company. Some were cut up and some were whole, but this was one of the nation's first consumer revolts involving the use of credit cards. The modern credit card and modern credit card practices had only come into being in the 1950s.

One of those early protesters was a Monterey dentist, Joseph Noto. Noto sent his credit card to Jersey Standard with a letter of protest. He urged others to do the same. Noto said his opposition was not over tourism or that the Monterey Peninsula was a retirement area, but because of agriculture.

"I do not wish to destroy this part of our economy," wrote Noto. For good measure, Noto offered to picket any Humble gas station in the county "two hours a day, seven days a week" if Hudson and Kramer's resolution was rejected.

The stage was set. Hudson and Kramer prepared to confront Humble Oil's board of directors. Back in Monterey County, thousands waited expectantly to hear what the next move might be. But on the morning of the Cleveland showdown, May 18, Humble Oil released a statement. All studies at Moss Landing and Rodeo were suspended. Humble's new refinery site was Benicia. The stated reason for choosing Benicia boiled down to engineering concerns and the need for a larger refinery which was not permitted at Moss Landing – a stunning admission that the 39 conditions that Humble had claimed it "could live with" for months were not so acceptable after all. At the same time, Humble dismissed the idea that local opposition had any impact on its decision. The statement even declared that the Moss Landing site was an "excellent industrial location," contradicting the earlier statements that engineering problems, including unstable ground, prevented the refinery's construction.

Standard Oil of New Jersey President J.K. Jamieson said preliminary results at Benicia "looks more promising" than the other sites. That Jersey Standard would bet all on preliminary results when previous preliminary results at Moss Landing, according to the oilmen, were significantly wrong, was not addressed.

Humble, which once seemed to have a unified message, now contradicted itself still again. Bolding, who just days earlier had brushed off Farr's comments that Humble was leaving, now confirmed that it was all true. In an interview with the *Salinas Californian*, Bolding admitted that the opposition did have an impact after all.

"I guess I would be wrong to say there hasn't been a great deal of thought

and concern about it," Bolding said. "Nobody likes to be called a dirty industry when we don't feel that we are. We were never given an opportunity to
demonstrate."

Humble's attorney in Salinas, Paul Hamerly, also conceded that the opposition had a "significant impact." Hamerly said he did not know if Humble
would have stayed in Monterey County if officials felt they could get a permit
for a larger plant.

The response from Humble's opponents was ecstatic as expected. A.G.
Michaud credited the Humble issue for prompting the formation of an air
pollution control district to protect the region's air. Other prominent opponents praised the outcome as well.

"This is a great tribute to men who persistently fought without any discour-
agement at any period of the game," responded Samuel F.B. Morse, chairman of
Del Monte Properties. "I am very happy. It looks as though we are reasonably
safe now."

"It was a victory for the people who felt Humble would cause smog in
Monterey County—the conservationists and agricultural people," said State
Senator Fred Farr.

"Naturally I am very pleased that this threat to our agriculture will not
develop at Moss Landing," Salinas Valley opponent Larry Hearne said. "I hope
that now the entire county can unite for progress and development of clean
industries that are compatible with agriculture and desirable."

"[W]e feel the battle has been won, but the war hasn't," William Howard
Church, professor at the Naval Postgraduate School and stalwart Humble
opponent, emphasized. Church felt the threat of another industry arriving
remained on the horizon.

Hudson and Kramer went forward with their presentation, but it was
anticlimactic. Humble's decision had been made between 3:30 and 4:00 p.m.
the day before. Their now 45,000 shares of stock were hardly a drop in the
bucket at the Cleveland meeting, which had more than 3,000 stockholders
and 180 million shares. Hudson and Kramer's shares represented less than
3/10,000 of the voting power present. Kramer pushed that the Moss Landing
refinery was a "hornet's nest" that would only get worse before it got better,
and then called for the oil giant to surrender its permit. Michael Haider,
President of Jersey Standard, sat politely through it all, although an official
later suggested that if everything worked out then the permit would likely be
withdrawn. Kramer hammered the directors on their opposition to a refer-

endum in Monterey County and their part in the court battle in Los Angeles against air pollution laws.

"When suit is filed to limit the people's powers of control, nothing but their resentment is gained," stated Kramer.

Supporters of the refinery were disappointed, to be sure. Salinas Mayor Sid Gadsby bemoaned that the business image of Monterey County had been damaged, especially the opportunity to attract heavy industry.

"I think Monterey County is going to miss this boost to our economy," lamented Robert Elking, secretary-manager of the Salinas Chamber of Commerce.

One of the biggest boosters of Humble Oil, the *Salinas Californian*, turned its disappointment into a bitter diatribe at those who chased Humble away. The editors called State Senator Farr unwise for playing a part in stopping "the orderly industrial progress of Monterey County." While accepting Humble's argument that engineering and marine studies were less than desirable, the editors also dismissed that was the sole reason for Humble's departure, blaming the Monterey Peninsula for having Humble's "image tarnished by half-truths, distortions and dirty politics." The *Californian* called the result "a 'great victory' for the reactionaries, for the prosperously retired and the gullible."

The *Watsonville Register-Pajaronian* had long supported Humble, but not with the fervor of the *Californian*, for it also took up many of the opponents' concerns. The *Pajaronian* sensed that Humble leaving was a good thing, and that many good things had happened since its arrival. The *Pajaronian* mused that a smelly oil refinery might not be the best use for the industrial area of Moss Landing after all. There was now in place a mechanism to keep "the last remaining clean airshed in coastal California" safe from smog. The task now, according to the editors, was to welcome non-polluting heavy industry into the area.

"Moss Landing is designated on Monterey County's master plan, as a site for heavy industry," stated the *Pajaronian*. "It is a proper site for such use—with rail and highway connections and a port. Pacific Gas & Electric and Kaiser are already located there; and it would be folly for conservationists, however well-intentioned, to contend that Elkhorn Slough should be maintained as a permanent bird refuge."

The comment on the Elkhorn Slough was prescient. In a short fifteen years, the desire to protect the slough, the Monterey Bay and the area's natural beauty would dominate. In the span of a generation, the mood of the people changed from "develop at every opportunity" to "preserve as much as possible." It was a desire not limited to the Monterey Bay area, but rising in the nation as a whole.

King City Rustler publisher Harry Casey, a strong opponent of Humble in the Salinas Valley, praised the work of Humble opponents on the Monterey Peninsula and suggested this could be the beginning of a better direction for Monterey County.

"If one good thing came out of this Humble fight," said Casey, "it was this recognition on the part of Peninsula residents and leaders that farmers are important. Let's hope that this feeling of friendship will continue and that all elements involved will devote their interest to bring clean, compatible enterprises to Monterey County."

Finally, there was Burleigh and his lawsuit backed by the Six Cities Fund. Burleigh considered that Humble's announcement "could be the world's greatest con game." The feisty Burleigh said that he intended to continue with his appeal to Superior Court.

"I'll have 60 days to file an appeal and on the 61st day they could say that Benicia is worse than Moss Landing," warned Burleigh.

In Benicia, the locals were obviously ebullient. Humble was a knight on a white horse arriving just in time to save the city from oblivion. There were still details to be worked out and government permits to approve, but it was nothing like the tortuous road Monterey County sent Humble down.

Undoubtedly, Humble was pleased with that, buoyed by the fact that the city was prepared to accept the refinery with few, if any, conditions or restrictions. Benicia historian Dr. Jim Lessenger couldn't recall any conditions being placed on the Humble refinery when it was first built. It was also likely that the city of Benicia would not fight Humble on any proposed expansions, instead welcoming the jobs and the tax money that would flow in from an enlarged operation.

Benicia did not have the deepwater port of Moss Landing, but large tankers coming in could be "lightered," where they would transfer their cargo to smaller vessels for the final passage to the pier. Humble officials also saw that there was plenty of room in the new industrial park for spinoff industries, such as producing asphalt—a badly needed commodity for building all those new Bay Area freeways and highways. "They could see dollar bills flashing in front of their eyes," said Lessenger.

In many ways, Benicia was an ideal place to put a refinery, with well-traveled shipping lanes already in place, and a major highway system just outside the town, ready for trucking refined products to retailers. But even more importantly, there was a city there that was welcoming Humble with open arms, and no questions asked.

After fifteen months, Humble, Benicia and Monterey County all got what they wanted and needed.

29

THE AFTERMATH

"Of all the land use decisions for the California Central Coast, Humble Oil was the most significant. If it was successful, it would have ruined everything."

Congressman Sam Farr (Retired)

By the end of September 1966, Humble Oil had acquired a permit from the Bay Conservation and Development Commission to build two docks on the Carquinez Strait—the initial step in the construction of the Benicia refinery. Humble was finally ready to break ground and announced that it would immediately begin production of the $135 million, 70,000-barrel-a-day refinery. Compared to Monterey County, the Benicia permits lined up quickly.

At Benicia, Humble appeared to have learned a few things from its battle in Monterey County, and promised to build an environmentally-friendly oil refinery. In many ways it did. The refinery was painted and landscaped, much as the Monterey County permit required. The plant was designed for air and not water cooling, saving 90% of the water originally planned. The refinery minimized pollution by burning natural gas instead of oil. Altogether, Humble claimed to have spent an extra $10 million on making its refinery environmentally acceptable. The refinery was even designed to hide the pipes, tanks and equipment, as Benicia historians Reg Page and Dr. Jim Lessenger point out.

"They went out of their way to provide that the refinery blended with the topography they were presented," Lessenger said.

Back in the spring of 1965, Humble officials chafed and warned of moving to Benicia for the first time because Monterey County was daring to consider regulations such as painted tanks and other non-oil-refining regulations. Benicia never imposed regulations for an environmentally friendly refinery. This was Humble's own initiative, wisely taking steps to limit any future public outrage.

However, there were some problems, as there are with any new project. The Benicia refinery had a flare problem with burning gases lighting up the sky with a roar. The wastewater system broke down and Humble violated clean water laws. However, of the 77 major water polluters in the San Francisco Bay Area, Humble was only ranked 62nd—the other refineries were far worse. Then suspicions were raised when Appaloosa horses began to die nearby. People pointed their fingers at Humble. Tests revealed it was due to toxic lead, but someone pointed out that animals had been dying there from lead poisoning since the turn of the century. An old smelter existed nearby.

Air pollution tests claimed that Humble was dumping 56 tons of pollutants a day into the atmosphere, not an impressive figure for a modern refinery. Then it was discovered 56 tons were the entire emissions from the petroleum industry in Solano County where Benicia resides. A further breakdown found the Humble refinery kept air pollutant emissions to a low 24 tons per day, the lowest in the Bay Area, which was a fraction of what the Moss Landing PG&E plant might burn on occasion—up to 250 tons of sulfur dioxide per day.

Humble's refinery brought Benicia back to life. It quintupled the tax base, paying for schools, roads, parks and staffing the fire and police departments. Property taxes in Benicia were one-third those of neighboring cities. Humble and Benicia were made for one another, but that was not by design. It was the necessity of both. Today, Valero owns the former Humble refinery which is still in operation.

That leaves the long-pondered question: Why did Humble leave Moss Landing for Benicia?

The answer or, as better defined, answers, are now clear. There are five reasons for Humble to have left the Monterey Bay area but not all carry equal weight.

First and foremost was the large and vigilant opposition against Humble Oil. The widespread opposition in Monterey County was unparalleled and certainly shocking to Humble. The many forums and public hearings were always packed by opponents who wrote letters, signed petitions and called their supervisors. Hundreds, if not thousands, actively took part in the most basic grassroots organizing essential to fighting any political issue. The Humble opposition was a model of how to leverage public opinion against a political issue with grassroots organizing, political lobbying, litigation and backroom deal-making all a part of the equation.

Yet the Humble opposition had something else unique to grassroot movements. Indeed, few movements have this crucial advantage. It had former members of Congress, industrialists, financiers and nationally prominent environmentalists lined up against the refinery. Humble also faced an increasingly united and powerful agricultural community with its own methods of influence. Together, environmentalists, retired industrialists and agribusinesses coupled with hundreds of ordinary people—such as small business owners, laborers and housewives—created an unprecedented force of resistance that had contacts with government officials and private industry across the state and country. Humble ran into a buzz saw it never saw coming.

A second reason for Humble leaving was pressure on the oil company by the persistent litigation from Carmel attorney Bill Burleigh. The lawsuits were part of the opposition's well-developed strategy, but deserve independent recognition. The legal battles pursued an entirely different course of action than simply public pressure. Yes, Burleigh lost two court battles, but those court battles tied Humble down. If Humble had begun construction and a judge ruled adversely, then the refinery would need to be dismantled. That concern threatened to keep construction at bay. As decision time arrived for Humble in the spring of 1966, Burleigh latched onto Humble like a bulldog, with no intention of letting go. Burleigh's litigation could tie Humble up for months or even years. The legal battle that created modern environmental law with the Consolidated Edison power plant at New York's Storm King Mountain had lasted three years at this point. Storm King would eventually drag on for seventeen years.

As Humble withdrew to Benicia in May 1966, Burleigh prepared to appear before the U.S. Court of Appeals in San Francisco. Burleigh was continuing to appeal as late as September 1966. Four days later, Humble announced it was beginning construction in Benicia. We are still not sure when Burleigh finally gave up hounding Humble, but Humble representatives must have been grateful to finally have shaken him.

The third factor in Humble's decision were the soil and wave studies. Although the authors have doubted the significance of these, there were concerns that independent sources have verified. Ruth Andresen, a geologist, said that there were problems with the soil and the newly developed earthquake standards. The soil conditions were not ideal. The question is how poor they were. To accept that the soil conditions were severe enough in themselves to send Humble to Benicia is very unlikely. Humble gave conflicting testimony about its engineering studies. Sometimes Humble mentioned the soil studies as major concerns, and other times said it was only a minor problem. When Humble announced it was leaving, its officials still touted the site as a great industrial location, which is contradictory if the soil was a problem. The authors have concluded the soil issue was a consideration but not an insurmountable one. The PG&E and Kaiser buildings have endured to the present day, neighboring the old Humble site. Humble had the option of more pilings to stabilize any buildings that it constructed. Yes, that would have increased costs, and economics was the final arbiter in Humble's decision. It was something for Humble to consider in the scope of everything else, but it was not anywhere near the reason for Humble's departure from the Monterey Bay area. As the *Watsonville Register-Pajaronian* once noted, the soil studies seemed like an "excuse" rather than an obstacle.

The wave studies were even more questionable. PG&E had been unloading fuel for more than a decade with a submarine pipeline. True, Humble wanted a more sophisticated system for its supertankers, but again, if PG&E operated a marine unloading process, it is difficult to imagine that Humble faced an unresolvable barrier. More pilings were a solution that Humble considered, but like the soil problem, that would have increased costs. Humble's argument of unexpected wave conditions has another hole in it. The Army Corp of Engineers, which started dredging Moss Landing Harbor in 1946, had compiled detailed studies on wave actions during 1956-58. These studies appear to negate Humble's statements. The studies were still deemed reliable when further dredging was being considered in 1974. A company as large as Humble would not have been so incompetent as to not know of these studies before it conducted its own. The wave surges, like the soil conditions, were a consideration but also very unlikely to have been a deciding factor. If nothing else, the soil and wave concerns were enough to direct attention away from admitting that the public opinion turning against Humble had an impact.

Fourthly, the many regulations imposed on the permit placed a financial burden on Humble. Those "rigid" conditions were noted by a diverse group, including Harold Zellerbach, California State Parks Commission; James Ritch, Contra Costa Development Association; Humble attorney Paul Hamerly; and numerous others. At one time, Humble stated that complying with Monterey

County's permit would cost a "couple of million dollars." This is a considerable amount of money for that time, but an extra two million dollars is small when compared to a $70 million facility that could recoup those costs by unloading supertankers. It also pales in comparison to Humble's claim to have spent $10 million to make its Benicia refinery environmentally friendly. That is likely a lot more than soil stabilization, wave surge remediation and county regulations might incur.

The 444-acre parcel that Humble purchased in the 1960s was never developed, and today is still a farmer's field near Moss Landing.
Kathryn McKenzie

Still, the regulations were not to be taken lightly. The conditions broached new regulations not previously considered anywhere. There was one requirement of particular concern to Humble. Humble's initial plan included less than one-third of the 444-acre site. That left plenty of room for expansion. It was part of the business plan. Monterey County put a big monkey wrench into those plans when it required Humble to come back for a new permit every time that it wanted to expand past $2 million in improvements. Humble fought this hard, seeking a limit of $7 million, but failed.

Supervisor Andy Anderson focused on this condition as the reason for a Humble relocation when word first spread in March 1966 that Humble might move. At that time, Standard Oil of New Jersey Chairman Michael Haider made a comment that the "scope had changed" for Humble's expansion on the West Coast. That scope was a larger plant and the requirement for another permit stood right smack in the way, as Anderson noted. On the path to that permit was an enormously effective and battle-hardened opposition. Even if Humble wanted to tackle that opposition again, there was another problem—a big one. One of the supervisors that voted for the permit was not a supporter for a larger plant, as Stanley Cloud of the *Monterey Peninsula Herald* reported. There are only three candidates for who that supervisor might be: Harold Henry, Arthur Atteridge, and Church.

Henry, of all the supervisors, took heat for his vote. Perhaps Anderson did too as his district was pro-Humble or at least deeply divided, but the fallout to Anderson did not appear publicly whereas Henry's constituents were boisterous in their public disgruntlement. Henry had plenty of opportunities to withdraw his support, but never did. Indeed, as he campaigned for re-election in the spring of 1966, Henry still defended his support of Humble and inviting more industry. Of all the supervisors, it also seems strange that he would confide in Cloud of the *Herald* when there was lingering enmity between Henry and the Peninsula. With all this, it is hard to see a connection for Henry as the supervisor against Humble expansion.

Atteridge is a reasonable choice as a possible defector from the Humble cause. Although he had been an advocate of industrial development for many years, Atteridge never expressed the depth of enthusiasm that many of the Humble supporters did. When Humble started hinting that it was leaving at the end of March 1966, Atteridge would not commit to a position.

"I haven't any comment to make," Atteridge said. "I'd assume that Humble is a property owner that can go where it wants. If there is a change (in the size of the refinery), I would reserve a decision on that until it came up."

That neutral stance, and that Atteridge strongly backed Church during the hearing when the conditions were set, are enough to consider Atteridge as the vote turning against a larger plant, but there is no evidence beyond that. Atteridge had reasons not to want Humble to rise as an issue again, but Henry and Church also had reasons not to revisit Humble and perhaps even stronger ones as they were in potentially more vulnerable positions. Henry had already alienated many of his constituents. Humble was in Church's district, so he faced either the greatest blame or praise depending on the outcome.

That leaves Church as the final consideration for Cloud's mysterious third vote against a Humble expansion. When compared to Atteridge, the public record for Church breaking from a pro-Humble position is much clearer. Church was more heavily engaged in details than Atteridge or any other supervisor. He attended more refinery field trips than any other supervisor. It was Church who requested that the supervisors delay a decision in early

August for a month so that the public could be better educated and conditions refined. Church attended the all-important Anacortes trip where supervisors learned that a refinery's production can exceed the capacity for which it was designed. It was this trip that was the genesis for limiting the size of Humble in its initial permit. Atteridge was not there. Church actively pursued this restriction, according to his notes. It was Church who, days after the permit was finalized, demanded that monitoring stations be put in place immediately so as to measure air quality before Humble started operations. Church also broke with Atteridge and Henry on the establishment of an air pollution control district. Although Atteridge was not opposed to the concept (he wanted civil, not criminal penalties), he still voted no.

There are also the comments that Church made to the *Register-Pajaronian* where he did not believe Humble had the votes for a new permit. It would be highly unusual and politically unwise move for a supervisor to muse publicly that another supervisor is altering his position on such a highly controversial issue. Such an act would impact the close relationship that Church and Atteridge were developing on many issues. On the other hand, a supervisor trying to signal to Humble that he was not in their camp might do exactly this, and then tell Cloud of the *Herald* the same thing, so as to spread the word that Humble may as well not even try again because it would not have the votes. By doing this anonymously, Church would be protecting himself politically.

In addition, there are the many private papers and notes that Church kept. While this gives an unequal insight into his actions and thinking, the papers still reaffirm the public record that Church was more engaged than any other supervisor with the details of Humble's project.

The one argument against Church is that he admitted to not knowing why Humble left Moss Landing, crediting the opposition as the most likely reason. This is a valid argument, for without the opposition, Humble would have built. Yet as the end approached, the efforts of Kramer, Moser, Bauman and the others were not enough on their own. There was nothing stopping Humble from building once it got its permit besides the lawsuit and the need for a bigger refinery.

There is one last piece to this puzzle. Church recalled, a half century after these events, that he had received an "unusual" phone call from a Humble official months after the permit was granted. As Church recalled, he knew no reason to be contacted at that time by Humble, since nothing was coming before the board involving the project. The call was about modifying the permit, but Church could not recall the specific details of the discussion or

the name of the individual who called him. It is likely this call was around
February or March for Humble began to publicly express concerns about the
need for a larger facility that would require another permit after that. At this
time, Tom Hudson was spreading the word that Humble was leaving, and no
one knew where Hudson got the information. We do know that Hudson was
engaged in clandestine negotiations with Humble at this time. It is feasible,
even likely, that the ever-plotting Hudson knew of Church's concerns about
a larger Humble facility and saw an opportunity to drive a final stake into
Humble's plans by urging them to call Church. That is speculation, but so
much about Hudson and his deeds are shrouded in that.

Today, Valero operates the former Humble Oil refinery in Benicia.
Kathryn McKenzie

Finally, the fifth reason weighing on Humble's departure was Harold Henry's untimely death. By all accounts, Henry remained supportive of Humble
to the end. Henry was probably the strongest supporter of Humble among
the supervisors. Even if he had not died in April 1966, Henry was in a very

difficult race for re-election—one he was·likely to lose. Although it appears that the Humble issue was decided by the time he died, if Humble had any lingering hopes of a new permit, those were dashed with one less pro-Humble vote on the Board of Supervisors.

If Humble had sought to build its refinery in the 1950s, or even if it had gone to the Board of Supervisors a year earlier in 1964 when South County Supervisor Frank Echeberria, representing oil-rich San Ardo, was on the board instead of anti-Humble Anderson, and when Chester Deaver still held the supervisorial seat in North County, the vote would likely have been a 4-1 approval of Humble. It is also doubtful the permit would have been laden with the extensive conditions. But this was 1965. Environmentalism was coming to life. Rachel Carson's *Silent Spring* put those who abused the environment on notice, environmental activists were strengthening, governmental jurisdictions were coming to life to protect the environment, and two new supervisors were in office in Monterey County.

The battle over the Moss Landing refinery was a precedent-setting fight of national consequence. The involvement of state and national political figures as well as national environmental groups attest to that. Both the Sierra Club and the Audubon Society took positions against Humble. All this opposition must have been a shock to the oil company, especially since Moss Landing was zoned industrial. Kaiser Refractories and PG&E ran into no meaningful opposition when they were constructed, nor was there any during the expansions that PG&E announced in 1963. The county appeared waiting with open arms for industry. Even the Monterey Peninsula embraced the appropriateness of Moss Landing for industrial use just a few years earlier. All that changed with Humble.

30

E P I L O G U E

"It is regrettable that Mr. Henry, Mr. Atteridge and
Mr. Church cannot be made to grow up all over again,
20 or 50 years from now and possess the certain knowledge
of what life could have been like without
their short-sighted yes votes. "

Dr. and Mrs. Russell Pratt

Today, the Monterey Bay area is many things, but it is not a major industrial center, contrary to the plans that were made for it in the 1950s and 1960s. Instead, it is known the world over as a site of great beauty, a bustling focal point for marine research, and a place where people are firmly committed to the bay retaining as much of its natural state as possible.

If plans for the Humble Oil refinery had become reality, it's likely that the little fishing village of Moss Landing would have become a mass of hulking infrastructure, similar to that which exists in Long Beach or Martinez, with that "parade of smokestacks" that Humble opponent Charles Kramer predicted. Massive metal tanks, complex pipe systems, and warehouses would block the views of the water; it would certainly not be a place to stop and enjoy, but rather to drive quickly past.

It's possible that all along the Central Coast, there would have been a shift toward supporting business interests rather than protecting the environment, and that would have led to degraded air quality and water quality, dimming the bay's splendor and habitat.

But this dystopian view is all conjecture, because Humble Oil was defeated. What happened during those 15 months of conflict in the mid-1960s was a defining moment in the history of the Monterey Bay. Perhaps the ecology of the bay would not have been altogether destroyed by industry, but it certainly would not be what it is today.

One event probably did more than any other to harden many Californians against the intrusion of industry: the 1969 Santa Barbara oil spill, at the time the largest spill in U.S. waters. Images of befouled beaches and dying seabirds on television and in publications left a permanent and powerful impression on an entire generation of young people who saw the awful result of this offshore oil drilling accident. The following year, the first Earth Day was organized, calling attention to the pressing need for environmental protections.

The Monterey Bay today is home to marine research stations and organizations as well as being a federally protected sanctuary.
Kathryn McKenzie

As nuclear power fell slowly to the wayside, so did PG&E's plans for nuclear power plants at Moss Landing. PG&E, like other industry, never seriously looked at Moss Landing again. Today, the twin smokestacks still loom high above the landscape, but only as a landmark—they are no longer in operation. The power plant is a shell of its once grand self as more efficient energy sources have supplanted it. The former Mighty Moss is now part of a plan by

Tesla for the world's largest battery facility to store energy from wind and solar for later distribution.

Kaiser Refractories no longer exists. Its buildings remain, but as a grow house complex for cannabis. The Elkhorn Slough, once envisioned as a center for industrial, residential and recreational development, is a wildlife sanctuary and key stopover for bird migration. Sea otters, endangered amphibians and other creatures thrive in its waters, a far different fate than one as a repository for chemical soup from industrial plants. A few years after Warren Church retired as a supervisor, he became one of the original members of the Elkhorn Slough Foundation, which formed to preserve the estuary—a bit of twisted irony because his first vote on Humble Oil's refinery set in motion the demise of those environs, but his second vote put in place an opportunity to protect them.

The hard work and dedication of those anti-Humble forces have evolved into ongoing and enhanced protections for Monterey Bay. In the mid-1960s, an influx of marine science programs, by both UC Santa Cruz and the California State University system, began to take hold. Stanford University's Hopkins Marine Station, which had been in Pacific Grove since the late 1800s, grew and expanded. Today, more than two dozen additional research and government facilities, including offices of the National Oceanic and Atmospheric Administration, are dotted around the bay.

Following the passage of the federal Coastal Zone Management Act, Elkhorn Slough was designated as the very first National Estuarine Research Reserve in 1979, offering special safeguards for the slough as well as opportunities for conservation and research. Today, scientists study how tidal wetlands keep the bay healthy, something that was not well understood before, and how the slough provides important habitat for more than 100 species of birds and other wildlife.

Ed Ricketts' groundbreaking theories on marine ecological zones gave rise to the Monterey Bay Aquarium, which opened in 1984 with the novel idea of presenting marine animals in exhibits that resembled the environments in which they were found naturally. The Aquarium is now a premiere destination that attracts 2 million visitors a year, who visit it on Cannery Row and peer across the bay to view the old PG&E smokestacks that are a ghostly reminder of what could have been.

In 1992, the Monterey Bay National Marine Sanctuary was established after decades of lobbying efforts, ultimately carried out with legislation proposed by Congressman Leon Panetta, which guaranteed government protection of an area stretching from Rocky Point in Marin County to Cambria in San Luis Obispo County, including 276 miles of shoreline and 6,094 square miles of ocean. The Monterey Bay's submarine canyon, which once harbored dreams for industrialists as a major deepwater port on the West Coast, remains home to unique species studied by multiple marine research centers.

In the Salinas Valley, agriculture remains king. It still reigns as the Salad Bowl of the World, but now bordered on its edges by wineries that have diversified the local harvest. The feared damage of pollution never arrived as increasing controls reduced even the occasional haze of smog that once floated on the valley's inversion layer. Pajaro Valley and other agricultural areas around the bay are major producers of an astonishingly diverse array of crops, with organic farms an important mainstay in recent years.

Tourism is a multi-billion-dollar business which has succeeded a little too well, as holiday and summer traffic crowds the Pacific Coast Highway through Big Sur, and residents around the bay complain about short-term vacation rentals taking over their towns. For now, smog is still not a problem, despite the carbon footprint of visitors that fly or drive to the area year-round.

The acreage near Moss Landing where Humble Oil intended to build its West Coast refinery was never developed. All these decades later, the 444 acres are still just a farmer's field, usually planted in artichokes or row crops, anonymous to the thousands of vehicles that pass by it each day.

Then there are the many individuals who floated in and out of the Humble controversy. As one of our readers once commented, Humbled reads like a Russian novel with all the characters coming and going. The fates of some of the prominent players are worth noting.

The movement that rose against Humble was one of the early battles of the modern environmental movement, but also an early example of Not In My Backyard sentiment, or NIMBYism. The leaders of the opposition were hardly storied environmentalists. There were exceptions, though, like Ruth Andresen and the esteemed Ansel Adams. Andresen was carving out a legacy as an environmentalist, but she was in Salinas, away from the center of opposition. While Adams let others organize the opposition, he was a powerful symbol, the conscience of the movement, and a player that could not be ignored nationally. He wielded that influence as a moral club with arguments of conservation that the proponents could never answer.

The chief organizers—Charles Kramer, a former manufacturer; Earl Moser, a former oil executive; and Gus Bauman, a former industrialist—were skillful and resourceful opponents to Humble. The supporting list of opponents, prominent names like Zellerbach and Westinghouse, stood out. These people made their fortunes doing exactly what Humble Oil was doing: building industry and making profits. Yet the ugly sight of an oil refinery appearing in their front windows appalled these former captains of industry who previously had done exactly what Humble Oil was proposing.

Perhaps it was a sudden awareness of the evils of pollution, a guilt trip or just the selfish desire to not see the downside of their lifelong work materialize in their own front yard. Some, like Moser and Kramer, did become authentic conservationists. Moser has a trail named after him at the Monterey County park at Jack's Peak. Kramer went on to serve on the California Coastal Commission in the 1970s with Andresen and Supervisor Church. Others, like Professor William Howard Church of the Naval Postgraduate School, went back to their pre-Humble lives.

Not all the opponents were on the Monterey Peninsula. Watsonville flower grower Mits Nakishima, who pleaded to halt air pollution so that the burgeoning flower industry of the region could survive, stayed active and deeply involved in his community. The many opponents in Santa Cruz County also forged ahead, developing an air pollution district just as Monterey County did, with the two districts merging into a single regional agency in 1968.

Credit for the creation of these districts rests largely with A.G. Michaud of Pebble Beach who took a side issue of the Humble refinery, air pollution control, and turned it into a cause that embraced both opponents and supporters of Humble.

Dan Krishun, the planning commissioner who supported Humble but advocated for strong pollution protections, served as a Salinas High School District board trustee in the 1970s. Krishun's support of Humble, blended with his concerns about pollution, undoubtedly caught Supervisor Warren Church's attention, who represented Krishun's area. Church was able to see that his fellow North Countian was able to support Humble and demand strong pollution controls with no backlash from his neighbors.

Carmel attorney Bill Burleigh did not relinquish his grip on Humble until the company secured its Benicia permits and began construction there. Burleigh would remain a significant figure in Monterey County long after the others left the public eye. He was appointed a Superior Court Judge by Governor Ronald Reagan a few years after Humble. Burleigh credited the appointment to his friendship with Clint Eastwood. But Burleigh's best-known accomplishment was his founding of the Big Sur International Marathon in 1986.

Fred Farr, a pioneering conservationist in the California State Senate, legislated the bill that allowed Monterey and Santa Cruz counties to establish air pollution control districts. But Farr's legacy extends far beyond that. He introduced successful bills requiring toilets in the fields for farm workers, education for migrant farm workers' children, and development of California's scenic highway system. Farr worked tirelessly behind the scenes at the state capitol to find a new home for Humble. Like Hudson, no one really knows how much Farr did to bring about this. By 1966 Farr was redistricted into an unfriendly district for a Democrat and lost in a matchup against Republican State Senator Donald Grunsky.

Of course, there was also Tom Hudson, collaborating, pressuring and maneuvering political influence while cutting deals, but constantly hounding top Humble officials any way he could. Hudson, with his position as a supervisor and anti-Humble advocate, exerted his influence relentlessly. It would be the high mark of Hudson's political career.

Hudson's political ambitions were constrained in the 1960s because members of his party occupied all the higher offices, except for Farr, who had a firm hold on his office until he was redistricted out. Hudson also had a difficult position to balance as a supervisor. He was a Republican and pro-business, but also a strong conservationist. His family had staked that position for decades, starting from the sale of Point Lobos to the state. There were tensions in his political alliances and particularly among those on the left who felt Hudson's conservation policies were not pure enough.

Hudson had long advocated for parks in Monterey County, including the preservation of his family's land across the highway from Point Lobos. In 1957, the county created the Peninsula Area Planning Commission to develop a master plan for the usage, development and preservation of unincorporated land on the Monterey Peninsula. This included parks, especially for the creation of Monterey Pines Park. The commission spent about a decade holding hearings before submitting a master plan. In 1962, the commission recommended that it work with Hudson to develop the plan.

Reporter Stanley Cloud of the *Monterey Peninsula Herald* and later *the advocate* recalled that Hudson was not forthright in his goals at that time. It should be noted that *the advocate* was published by John and Mary Sigourney, political opponents of Hudson.

"In my opinion and looking back, he (Hudson) deliberately and deceptively maintained—for years—a publicly neutral position, striking a pose as an honest broker," Cloud wrote. "He would talk vaguely, but elaborately and deceptively, about opposing commercial development in particularly sensitive areas—even

as he knew that he and his family had specific plans for commercial development of their huge Point Lobos ranch property, which was some of the most
sensitive land on the entire Peninsula. Those plans went back AT LEAST to
October 1, 1962, which was the date on the plan that he had secretly filed in
defense of a land-use lawsuit against him and his family brought by a few Peninsula voters, who suspected (but didn't know for sure) that Hudson's public
stance in favor of the Area Planning Commission and against commercial
development was a bald-faced lie, at least where his property was concerned."

The plans Cloud refers to involved a commercial development with a motel,
gas station, golf course, guest ranch and residences. That Hudson did this
behind the scenes was not surprising. Hudson used the same process in fighting
Humble, and it was a tactic with which he was comfortable and successful.

Just as the Humble affair was ending, the Peninsula Area Master Plan
came before the board for final approval. By that time, thanks in large part to
Hudson's behind-the-scenes maneuvering, all proposals for public parks had
been eliminated, and Hudson voted to approve the revised plan—still with no
mention of his family's own plans for the commercial development of Point
Lobos. The *Salinas Californian* ran an article revealing those plans for the first
time, but the editors promptly told reporter Ray March that "no more on the
subject would be published." The *Herald* refused to run anything more than
a blurb stuck in the back pages, with *Herald* publisher Pete Arthur telling
Stanley Cloud that what Hudson was doing was a "good thing."

At the time, Hudson was concerned that when his parents passed, the "cash-
poor, land-rich" Hudsons would be strapped to keep the property. Hudson
planned to commercialize the property and "still have it maintain its environmental heritage," according to Hudson's son, also named Tom.

Hudson always denied that there was a conflict, but the issue followed him
as long as he served on the board. "If there was a conflict of interest, I would
tell you so," said Hudson.

On February 21, 1967, Hudson abruptly resigned. The official reason was
that he was taking a position as an unpaid consultant on conservation and
planning matters for Governor Reagan, but it was a job with no office in
Sacramento or even a desk. The resignation shocked the county. It was out of
place for Hudson to step away from the limelight, from a public position to
a relatively obscure one.

"My God," said one observer. "That's nothing. That's no job at all."

The curious actions of Hudson's last months in office had one more act
to play out. At his last Board of Supervisors meeting, just hours before he

was to leave office, three scenic easement proposals came before the board. Scenic easements result in lower tax bills and the deadline for that year was midnight. The first two passed the board when the third appeared on the agenda. It was for Point Lobos Ranch, presented by Hudson's mother. Hudson properly recused himself and the supervisors approved it on a 3-1 vote. The only supervisor to vote against the Hudson property scenic easement request was Warren Church, who sardonically commented that the easement would save the landowners $10,000 a year or more.

The real reason for Hudson's resignation is unknown, but Hudson may have finally grown weary of the battles, especially as they turned somewhat personal. The Reagan job was nothing. It was "intended to give him a way out." His district was changing as well. It was growing more liberal and a tough election was ahead if Hudson ran again in 1968. It seems that Hudson, always controversial, had lived the political life hard and fast and now had nowhere to go. He had many friends, but also his share of enemies ready to take him down. Hudson never again ran for public office, spending his time at his law practice and taking care of his family properties.

County politics tends to bleed the good intentions of men and women. Unlike state and national politics, county politics involves spats and tussles with neighbors and acquaintances. After 12 years on the board, Supervisor Warren Church felt he had shed a heavy burden when he decided not to run again. Hudson probably felt the same by 1967, especially with his style of flamboyant deal-making politics. The 1960s and 70s were an especially dramatic time of social upheaval, land use regulations, social programs and government expansion that created controversy, long meetings and bitter battles. Humble was just another one of those with meetings that dragged into the late hours, although it was by far the most intense.

Of all the people involved in the Humble affair, it was probably Hudson who made the biggest difference. There is much about what Hudson did to stop Humble that will never be known. What we do know is that Hudson simply outfoxed one of the world's largest corporations with a combination of seductive, beguiling charm, steely determination and devious plotting. Many leaders are replaceable, but there was no one like Hudson. He was, perhaps, indispensable to the fight.

Warren Church would continue to serve on the Board of Supervisors until 1977 when he retired. He considered higher office, particularly for the State Senate seat that a retiring Donald Grunsky held. He decided against that race because even a dozen years after he fought the Monterey Peninsula over Humble, he still had reservations that he would find support there. Throughout the 1960s, he encountered several people in the Democratic Party who expressed that they would never support him because of his yes vote on Humble. However, many did put Humble behind them eventually, like Ansel Adams, who was one of Church's largest campaign contributors in his 1972 re-election campaign.

Tom Hudson, ever the dealmaker, at Point Lobos with Pebble Beach founder S.F.B. Morse (left) and an unidentified man.
Courtesy of the Hudson family

While the three other supervisorial seats had a steady stream of changing faces, Church and Atteridge remained, often on the losing side of 3-2 votes. By 1972, those votes were 3-2 on the winning side with the election of Roger Poyner in Anderson's old district. Later, Fred Farr's son, Sam, was appointed to a vacancy on the board by Governor Jerry Brown—Hudson's old seat. Even though Atteridge was gone by then, the 3-2 majority remained. By 1976, the county made its first steps toward controlling growth. Church, who had opposed incorporation of North County in 1964, took pride in efforts to preserve its rural nature. He pushed for the preservation of Elkhorn Slough while limiting industrial growth and harbor expansion at Moss Landing, even clashing bitterly with the pro-industry Moss Landing Harbor Commission in 1973. Church is also credited with establishing controls that lowered the daily pollution levels of the PG&E power plant from 100 tons per day to 19 tons. But Church, considered the "father of the county parks system," viewed the parks as his proudest achievement.

Like Hudson, the years of service on the board during highly controversial times took a toll on Church. But the lifelong North County native would remain active in county matters, serving on a variety of boards and commissions until his death in 2017.

Humble also seems to have shortened the political career of Supervisor Andy Anderson. He resigned in September 1967, claiming ulcers made his remaining time on the board untenable. Anderson's son confirmed that his father did have stomach problems. He had been wounded in the war and endured "operation after operation after operation." While ulcers would certainly play a role in his decision, others have speculated that he was also uncomfortable with the job. Anderson credited "teamwork" for his accomplishments as mayor of Seaside. Church long lamented that the Board of Supervisors during this time was faced with agonizingly long meetings and highly controversial issues. It is not something that Anderson, or anyone, expected. Add in the ulcers and it becomes understandable that his service became unbearable. But his stand against Humble was instrumental in its ultimate defeat. Anderson was the only supervisor to vote against the majority wishes of his constituents. His steadfastness meant that only one other anti-Humble vote was needed to put the brakes on the oil company. Eventually, that vote came when Humble needed to expand. Anderson exhibited tremendous courage in opposing Humble, a courage none of the other supervisors dared test. The Medal of Honor winner served both his country and Monterey County well. He lived out the remainder of his life in South Monterey County and Salinas until his death in 1996. His wife died a month after him. They are buried at Arlington National Cemetery.

The fate of the final major player in the Humble affair was less dramatic. Arthur Atteridge, an affable, generally mild-mannered fellow, explained his reasoning for voting for Humble:

"(The refinery) would have brought a great deal of tax base to the county without doing what I thought would be a great deal of damage at the time. ... That's what this was all about, a small amount of acreage and large tax wealth," while noting that PG&E paid for one-quarter of Nacimiento Dam at the headwaters of the Salinas River.

Perhaps Atteridge had personal reservations about Humble. He was a Democrat who had conservationist leanings, but his district of Salinas was adamantly pro-Humble. Atteridge saw what happened to Planning Commissioner Peter Cailotto, who became a pariah for years in Salinas following his fateful vote, and that certainly left an impression. Atteridge remained on the board until he was defeated in 1974 by Edwin Norris.

Lastly, there is one final matter to note in the lives of two of the principal Humble players—Church and Hudson. It was their deaths. Church, always cautious and careful politically, choose as one of the first people in California to use its new right-to-die law in 2017. As his body withered away, he decided, with the same thoughtfulness that he used to craft conditions to limit Humble Oil's operations, to end his life legally and decisively. He died on the anniversary of the climatic September 2 Board of Supervisors meeting that approved Humble, and was laid to rest at his family plot at the Castroville Cemetery at Moss Landing, almost directly across the highway from where Humble intended to build.

Hudson, always active, vibrant and controversial as ever, continued as a well-respected community leader until his tragic early death. In his 50s, Hudson died in a small airplane crash in the high Sierra in 1975. His plane iced up and disappeared into a mountainside. Barely ten years after Humble tried to build its refinery, Hudson was gone, but not entirely forgotten.

In Monterey, at the corner of Polk and Hartnell Streets near Hudson's old law office, there still sits a small plaque. It reads, "Thomson J. Hudson, Attorney, Conservationist, Soldier, 'He fought the good fight.'"

END NOTES

1

HUMBLE WINS

"The people who stumbled out," Stan Cloud, "Oil Refinery Approved 3-2," *Monterey Peninsula Herald*, September 3, 1965, 1.

"When the vote was over," "Proponents Too Tired To Cheer," *Monterey Peninsula Herald*, September 3, 1965, 5.

"Death brings grief," Tom Wieder, "Pollution District Urged," *Monterey Peninsula Herald*, September 3, 1965, 5.

"Humble Oil, a powerful affiliate," James A. Clark and Mark Odintz, "Exxon Company, U.S.A.," August 31, 2015, Texas State Historical Association, https://tshaonline. org/handbook/online/articles/doe04, retrieved March 27, 2020.

"looking at various sites," author's email with James Lessenger, June 27, 2019.

"Long-time students of county politics", Cloud, "Oil Refinery Approved 3-2," *Herald*, 4.

"Media from all over the Monterey Bay area," Stan Cloud, "Oil Hearing Was Not Dull Despite Length," *Monterey Peninsula Herald*, September 4, 1965, 1.

"Board Chair Thomson J. Hudson," George Burkhardt, "Humble Oil Co. Permit Approved," *Watsonville Register-Pajaronian*, September 3, 1965, 1.

"A pro-business Republican with a strong conservationist," Jack Fraser, "Monterey's Supervisor a Man on the Go," San Jose Mercury, February 21, 1960, unknown.

"Joining with Hudson," "Andy Anderson Is First Mayor Named by the People," *Monterey Peninsula Herald*, May 28, 1964, A3.

"Although his district split," Ray March, "Board to Act on Humble Oil," *Salinas Californian*, September 1, 1965, 4.

"Anderson was concerned that the refinery,"

"Seaside Supervisor," *Monterey Peninsula Herald*, September 3, 1965, 4.

"Representing South Monterey County," Alan Pugh, "Multi-County Air Pollution Control District Formed To Oppose Proposed Oil Refinery," Santa Cruz Sentinel, May 25, 1965, 1.

"Henry strongly backed expanding the tax base," March, "Board to Act on Humble Oil, *Californian*, 1.

"Unlike the other four supervisors," Pugh, "Multi-County Air Pollution Control District Formed To Oppose Proposed Oil Refinery," Sentinel, 1.

"Church had run the year," Ray March, "Deaver is Defeated by Church," *Salinas Californian*, November 4, 1964, 1.6

"Church was the only candidate," "N. County Supervisor Aspirant Give Views on Incorporation Plan," *Salinas Californian*, undated article approximately December 1963;

"He also campaigned on the promise," authors' conversations with Warren Church.

"As the *Salinas Californian* reported," March, "Board to Act on Humble Oil," *Californian*, 2.

"The lengthy parade of speakers," Burkhardt, "Humble Oil Co. Permit Approved," *Register-Pajaronian*, 1.

"Hudson angrily denied," Ibid.

"Yet Hudson tried four times," Mac Bowe, "Humble Refinery Ok'd After Lengthy Hearing," San Jose Mercury, September 4, 1965, unknown.

"Although tempers flared," Stan Cloud, "Clean Air Advocates Comment," *Monterey Peninsula Herald*, September 4, 1965, 5.

"Atteridge, an avid baseball fan," Cloud, "Oil Hearing Was Not Dull Despite Length," *Herald*, 2.

"A doctor rose to talk," Ibid.

"A rancher from King City," Ibid.

"Hudson and Anderson posed questions,"

"Church mum as hearing on Humble refinery opens," *Watsonville Register-Pajaronian*, September 2, 1965, unknown.

"Humble officials tried to persuade," "Proponents Too Tired To Cheer," *Herald*, 5.

"There's no need whatsoever," Ibid.

"We feel strongly that agriculture," Ibid.

"Tom Dunne, city manager of Salinas," Ibid.

"Allmond pointed out," Burkhardt, "Humble Oil Co. Permit Approved," *Register-Pajaronian*, 1.

"Challenging Hudson's many critical comments," "Proponents Too Tired To Cheer," *Herald*, 5.

"Deaver had emerged as a strong advocate," "Deaver Supports Humble," *Salinas Californian*, September 1, 1965, 1.

"Deaver, who had also," Ibid., 2.

"Also in favor of Humble's," "Proponents Too Tired To Cheer," *Herald*, 5.

"It was bad enough," "PG&E Putting Up 500-foot Stack," *Monterey Peninsula Herald*, January 31, 1964, 30.

"Disreputable Cannery Row," Stephen R. Palumbi and Carolyn Sotka, Death and Life on the Monterey Bay: A Story of Revival (Island Press, 2011), 127.

"Smog had become an enormous problem," Sarah Gardner, "LA Smog: The Battle Against Air Pollution," Marketplace, July 14, 2014. www.marketplace. org/2014/07/14/la-smog-battle-against-air-pollution, retrieved March 31, 2020.

"The view on pollution was not unanimous," March, "Humble Wins 3-2," *Californian*, September 3, 1965, 2.

"Some, like George Hobbs," Ibid.

"$160 million business," Monterey County Department of Agriculture, Monterey County Crops Report, 1966, 8. https://www.co.monterey.ca.us/Home/ShowDocument?id=1395, Retrieved March 31, 2020.

"Williams, also chair of the group," March, "Humble Wins 3-2," *Californian*, 2.

"It was only in the last few weeks," Ibid.

"Andrew Frey, of King City," Cloud, "Clean Air Advocates Comment," *Herald*, 5.

"The burgeoning flower industry," Burkhardt, "Humble Oil Co. Permit Approved," *Register-Pajaronian*, September 3, 1965, 1.

"Don Barsotti, speaking for," "Proponents Too Tired To Cheer," *Herald*, 5.

"Monterey Peninsula residents like Charles Kramer," Cloud, "Clean Air Advocates Comment," *Herald*, September 3, 1965, 5.

"This (plan for a refinery)," Ibid.

"had endured a nightmare year," "Accident Kills Farr Daughter," *Monterey Peninsula Herald*, August 24, 1965, 1.

"to rise in defense," March, "Humble Wins 3-2," *Californian*, September 3, 1965, 2.

"Altogether 23 speakers," Ibid. 1-2.

"As one of Henry's constituents spoke," Cloud, "Oil Refinery Approved 3-2," *Herald*, 1.

"Hudson made repeated calls for breaks," Alan Pugh, "Humble Oil Wins Permit 3-2," Santa Cruz Sentinel, September 3, 1965, 1.

"Hudson questioned the premise," March, "Humble Wins 3-2," *Californian*, 2.

"When Hudson stated that Humble's refinery," Pugh, "Humble Oil Wins Permit 3-2," Sentinel, 1.

"groans and murmurs of no," Ibid.

"By the early morning hours," Burkhardt, "Humble Oil Co. Permit Approved," *Register-Pajaronian*, September 3, 1965, 1.

"Let's vote on the decision now," Ibid.

"He spoke that he was supporting," March, "Humble Wins 3-2," *Californian*, 2.

"Atteridge asserted that Humble," Ibid.

"A sharp verbal squabble," Cloud, "Oil Refinery Approved 3-2,' *Herald*, 1.

"There is the integrity of this county,"

Manuscript of Tom Hudson Speech, Monterey County Board of Supervisors Archives.

"Humble had grudgingly gone along," "36 Rules For Plant Outlined," *Salinas Californian*, September 3, 1.

"In an editorial, Ted Durien, managing editor," Ted Durien, "A Cow County Turns An Historic Corner," *Monterey Peninsula Herald*, September 3, 1965, 1.

2

A NATURAL WONDER

"But one theory is that," Robert Lloyd Allen Jr., *The Impact of Tectonic Activity in the Development of Monterey Submarine Canyon*, March 1982, https://archive.org/details/DTIC_ADA115717/, retrieved April 2, 2020.

"In the last few million years," Alan O. Allwardt and Gerald E. Weber, *The Geology from Santa Cruz to Point Año Nuevo—The San Gregorio Fault Zone and Pleistocene Marine Terraces*, retrieved April 2, 2020.

"A topographical map shows the canyon," Monterey Bay Fisheries Trust, "Mapping the Monterey Canyon," May 2, 2018, https://montereybayfisheriestrust.org/news/2018/4/6/mapping-the-monterey-canyon. retrieved April 2, 2020.

"A website for MBARI," Monterey Bay Aquarium Research Institute (MBARI), https://www.mbari.org/science/seafloor-processes/geological-changes/mapping-sections/. retrieved April 2, 2020.

"Great benefit for wind-driven upwelling," National Oceanographic and Atmospheric Administration (NOAA), https://oceanexplorer.noaa.gov/facts/upwelling.html, retrieved April 2, 2020.

"Early explorers to Monterey Bay," Stephen R. Palumbi and Carolyn Sotka, *The Death and Life of Monterey Bay: A Story of Revival*, 2011, 11.

"But some people were starting to take note," Paul Taylor, "*Silent Spring* Triggered an Environmental Movement," June 20, 2016. Permaculture Research Institute, https://permaculturenews.org/2016/06/20/silent-spring-environmental-movement/, retrieved April 2, 2020.

"Andresen, who had earned a degree," authors' interview with Ruth Andresen, Aug. 2, 2019.

"Air pollution had been a fact of life," Chip Jacobs and William J. Kelly, *Smogtown: The Lung-Burning History of Pollution in Los Angeles*. The Overlook Press, 2015. 19.

"On Memorial Day 1963, organizers released," James Daly, Sonoma Magazine, "Nuclear Fault Line—Bodega Head," February 2015, https://www.sonomamag.com/nuclear-fault-line/, retrieved March 22, 2020.

"One of the hardest-fought controversies," "The Scenic Hudson Decision," Marist Environmental History Project, Marist College, http://library.marist.edu/archives/mehp/scenicdecision.html, retrieved March 30, 2020.

"There was already some federal environmental legislation," Earth Days Timeline, PBS, https://www.pbs.org/wgbh/americanexperience/features/earth-days-modern-environmental-movement/, retrieved March 30, 2020.

3

THE GATHERING STORM

"just 482 pickers," "Crisis in Berry Labor In Valley Turns Worse," *Salinas Californian*, May 10, 1965, 1.

"In Santa Cruz, the University of California," Peggy Townsend, "The Birth of UC Santa Cruz: Audacious and academic," UC Santa Cruz, January 21, 2015. https://news.ucsc.edu/2014/12/birth-of-ucsc.html, retrieved April 4, 2020.

"At Moss Landing, PG&E," "PG&E Putting Up 500-foot Stack," *Monterey Peninsula Herald*, August 25, 1965, 30.

"expressed the apprehensions," Ray March, "Board Approves Baez Permit," *Salinas Californian*, December 1, 1965, 1.

"Baez's school was approved," Ibid.

"Also favoring the permit," Misc Activities, private papers of Warren Church.

"February 15, 1965, was a fair day," Eric C. Brazil, "Humble Oil Plans For County Site," *Salinas Californian*, February 15, 1965, 1.

"announced the purchase," Ibid.

"cost in excess of a million dollars," "$50 million refinery to be built in ML,": *Watsonville Register-Pajaronian*, February 15, 1965, 1.

"a year to design," Brazil, "Humble Oil Plans For County Site," *Californian*, 1-2.

"PG&E already had a submarine pipeline," "$50 Million Plant," *Monterey Peninsula Herald*, February 15, 1965, 1.

"As plans progressed," Alan Pugh, "Humble Oil Says It Will Meet 'Reasonable' Pollution Controls," *Santa Cruz Sentinel*, June 13, 1965, 8A.

"Local representatives, especially from," "$50 Million Plant," *Herald*, 2.

"Good refinery sites are hard," Brazil, "Humble Oil Plans For County Site," *Californian*, 2.

"Deep water inshore was a prime consideration," "$50 million refinery described as 'small,'" *Watsonville Register-Pajaronian*, February 20, 1965, 2.

"Three years earlier," "A New, Desirable Industry," *Salinas Californian*, February 26, 1965, 6.

"Humble had recently acquired," "'Clean' Refinery Plans Told MCID," *Salinas Californian*, February 20, 1965, 2.

"Humble estimated that three," Pugh, "Humble Oil Says It Will Meet 'Reasonable' Pollution Controls," *Sentinel*, 8A.

"Humble anonymously purchased," "$50 million refinery to be built in ML," *Register-Pajaronian*, 1.

"We want everyone to know," Brazil, "Humble Oil Plans For County Site," *Californian*, 2.

"bend over backwards," "'Clean' Refinery Plans Told MCID," *Californian*, 2.

"Monterey County Assessor" Brazil, "Humble Oil Plans For County Site," *Californian*, 2

"Tom Hudson, then chair," Ibid, 2.

"I have no position," "Close Study Of Refinery Is Urged," *Monterey Peninsula Herald*, February 17, 1965, 1.

"clean, sweet-smelling refinery," "Refineries smell sweet," *Watsonville Register-Pajaronian*, February 17,1965, 2.

"Warner claimed the water used," Ibid.

"leaving plenty of room," "'Clean' Refinery Plans Told MCID," *Californian*, 2.

"The Santa Cruz County Planning Commission, "Planners Concerned Over Refinery," *Santa Cruz Sentinel*, March 11, 1965, 1.

"Commissioner Bruce Woolpert's words represented," Ibid.

"Commissioner Erle Byer warned," "Planners' warning on Humble," *Watsonville Register-Pajaronian*, March 11, 1965, 5.

"What Humble thinks it may do," "Nothing particularly humble about this firm," *Watsonville Register-Pajaronian*, February 16, 1965, 14.

"Strong support was developing in Salinas," "A New, Desirable Industry," *Californian*, 6.

"The Salinas Chamber of Commerce," "Proposed Refinery Endorsed," *Salinas Californian*, March 17, 1965, 1.

"Castroville Chamber of Commerce," "Castroville Chamber Backs Oil Refinery," *Salinas Californian*, March 24, 1965, 2.

"The Marina and Seaside Chambers," "Seaside Chamber Backs Humble Oil Refinery Plan," *Salinas Californian*, April 22, 1965, 2.

"All the chamber of commerces," "Humble Decision Deferred To May 11," *Salinas Californian*, March 31, 1965, 2.

"already a bedroom community," "What Moss Landing plants mean to Watsonville," *Watsonville Register-Pajaronian*, March 12, 1965, 16.

"Stepping forward to express concerns," "Bardin Criticizes C of C Endorsement of Refinery," *Salinas Californian*, March 19, 1965, 4.

"The committee that traveled," Stan Cloud, "Air Group Endorses Humble Plant," *Monterey Peninsula Herald*, March 19, 1965, 28.

"Carmel resident Earl Moser", Ibid.

"John Maga, head of the air pollution," Ibid.

"The oil companies say they can build," Ibid.

"Maga did admit," Ibid.

"We assure you," "Tough LA Refinery Controls Sought by Air Pollution Unit," *Salinas Californian*, March 19, 1965, 4.

"Gardner and Winslow were both," Ibid.

"One hundred people piled," Stan Cloud, "Year Approval Recommended For Refinery," *Monterey Peninsula Herald*, March 31, 1965, 1.

"Humble attended in full force," "Humble Decision Deferred To May 11," *Salinas Californian*, March 31, 1965, 1-2.

"Cailotto presented the findings," Cloud, "Year Approval Recommended For Refinery," *Herald*, 1-2.

"Besides adoption of the Los Angeles regulations," Ibid, 2.

"Esso senior engineer Frank Church," "Humble Decision Deferred To May 11," *Californian*, 2.

"It seemed extensive and too restrictive," Cloud, "Year Approval Recommended For Refinery," *Herald*, 2.

"Hamerly said the current regulations," "Humble Decision Deferred To May 11," *Californian*, March 31, 1965, 2.

"What really had Winslow," Cloud, "Year Approval Recommended For Refinery," *Herald*, 2.

"In an editorial," "Let's Not Put the Cart Before the Horse," *Salinas Californian*, April 7, 1965, 6.

"Gus Bauman of the Carmel Highlands Association," "Humble Decision Deferred To May 11," *Californian*, 2.

"Carmel City Councilman Gunnar Norberg," Ibid.

"I have never seen a refinery," Ibid.

"William Howard Church, president of the Del Monte," Ibid.

4
FROM HUMBLE BEGINNINGS

"The black goo had been observed," How Products are Made: Kerosene, http://www.madehow.com/Volume-7/Kerosene.html, retrieved April 2, 2020.

"By 600 B.C., the Chinese were transporting," EKT Interactive, History of Oil, www.ektinteractive.com/history-of-oil/, retrieved April 2, 2020.

"the first oil wells were drilled," American Oil & Gas Historical Society, https://aoghs.org/petroleum-pioneers/first-california-oil-well, retrieved April 2, 2020.

"Whale oil had previously been used," Petroleum History Institute, http://www.petroleumhistory.org/OilHistory/pages/Whale/whale.html, retrieved April 2, 2020.

"Humble Oil, founded in 1911," Jordan Blum, "The March from Humble Oil to Exxon Dates Back More Than a Century," Houston Chronicle, May 25, 2016, https://www.chron.com/local/history/economy-business/article/The-march-from-Humble-Oil-to-Exxon-dates-back-7943392.php, retrieved April 2, 2020.

"What's remembered best today": "The History of Advertising in Quite a Few Objects: 43 Esso Tiger Tails," September 27, 2012, https://www.campaignlive.co.uk/article/history-advertising-quite-few-objects-43-esso-tiger-tails/1151980, retrieved April 2, 2020.

"Leading oil companies were aware," John Schwartz, "Pressure on Exxon on Climate Change Intensifies With New Documents," April 14, 2016, https://www.nytimes.com/2016/04/14/science/pressure-on-exxon-over-climate-change-intensifies-with-new-documents.html?_r=1, retrieved April 2, 2020.

"Oil and gas production," E. Allison and B. Mandler for AGI, 2018, American Geosciences Institute publication, "Petroleum and the Environment, Part 18: Air Quality Impacts of Oil and Gas," https://www.americangeosciences.org/geoscience-currents/air-quality-impacts-oil-and-gas, retrieved April 2, 2020.

"In addition to these compounds being toxic": National Geographic online Resource Library: Smog, https://www.nationalgeographic.org/encyclopedia/smog/, retrieved April 2, 2020.

"More than 6,000 products," Ranken Energy Corp., 2017, https://www.ranken-energy.com/index.php/products-made-from-petroleum/, retrieved April 2, 2020.

"One important step in the process," U.S. Energy Information Administration, https://www.eia.gov/todayinenergy/detail.php?id=9150, retrieved April 2, 2020.

"Petroleum coke is a byproduct," Oxbow Corp., 2015, https://www.oxbow.com/Products_Energy_Products_Petroleum_Coke.html, retrieved April 2, 2020.

"At the Richfield refinery in Long Beach,"

1960s Richfield refinery brochure, private papers of Warren Church.

"By the standards of the day," 1960s Anacortes refinery visitors' guide, Church papers.

5

THE SWORDS ARE DRAWN

"Supervisor Tom Hudson reported," "Humble to Abandon Refinery?" *Monterey Peninsula Herald*, April 13, 1965, 1.

"There are certain things," Ibid, 2.

"As far as I know," *Salinas Californian*, "Report Denied That Humble May Withdraw Application," April 13, 1965, 5.

"There were at least," email with Dr. Jim Lessenger, June 27, 2019.

"Oil refineries had been part," "The San Francisco Bay Area Oil Infrastructure," IWW Environmental Unionism Caucus, https://ecology.iww.org/PDF/misc/BayAreaRefineryInfrastructure.pdf?bot_test=1, retrieved July 10, 2019.

"In 1851, the Benicia Arsenal," Robert B. Roberts, "Benicia Arsenal" California Military Department, Military History and Museums Program, http://www.militarymuseum.org/Benicia.html, retrieved July 11, 2019.

"The post's garrison ceased," Ibid.

"When the Army announced the closure," Dr. Jim Lessenger, "How Benicia's Arsenal became the heart of the city's tax base," Benicia *Herald*, February 24, 2015, https://beniciaheraldonline.com/how-benicias-arsenal-became-the-heart-of-the-citys-tax-base/, retrieved July 14, 2019.

"Benicia was beginning," authors' interview with Reg Page and Dr. Jim Lessenger, Aug. 3, 2019.

"Both men would leave," Ibid.

"On a flight back from Washington," Ibid.

"This was called the Benicia Plan," Ibid.

"Seeking leasees for its new venture," Lessenger, "How Benicia's Arsenal."

"The GSA suspected fraud," Lessenger interview.

"Benicia Councilman John "Jack" Cody," Lessenger, How Benicia's Arsenal."

"The GSA demanded that Benicia," Ibid.

"The lawsuit fizzled," Ibid.

"Bechtel had another role," "A New, Desirable Industry," *Salinas Californian*, February 26, 1965, 6.

"When word reached Benicia," Lessenger interview.

"It also had no air pollution," email with Ray March, March 25, 2020.

"noting that the county lacked," "Misc. notes," private papers of Warren Church.

"suggested that the county," "Humble to Abandon Refinery?" *Monterey Peninsula Herald*, April 13, 1965, 1.

"The Planning Commission jumped," "Three-Man Group On Pollution Is Appointed," *Salinas Californian*, April 19, 1965, 1.

"The committee wasted no time," "Burlingame Expert Hired On Refinery," *Salinas Californian*, April 28, 1965, 2.

"Monterey County had some resources," "Area Atmosphere Sampled By County," *Salinas Californian*, June 30, 1965, 3.

"Back on the Monterey Peninsula," "Carmel Planners Ask Denial of Refinery," *Monterey Peninsula Herald*, April 29, 1965,18.

"A powerful citizens' group," "Clean Air Campaign By Citizens," *Monterey Peninsula Herald*, April 29, 1965, 1 & 16.

"The two co-chairs of Citizens," Ibid, 16.

"William Howard Church, a professor," Ibid.

"Professor Church stated," Ibid.

"Professor Church continued," Ibid.

"then described as the Moss Landing Area Development," Monterey County Planning Commission, Moss Landing Area Development Plan, September 1956.

"Church claimed that the Monterey," "Clean Air Campaign By Citizens," Herald, April 29, 1965, 16.

"In an inversion," "Glossary: Inversion," National Oceanic and Atmospheric Administration's National Weather Service, June 25, 2009 https://w1.weather.gov/glossary/index.php?word=inversion, retrieved July 12, 2019.

"400 people squeezed," "Experts on Pollution See Loss of Pure Air," Monterey Peninsula Herald, May 4, 1965, 1.

"They only had 300 cards," Ibid.

"In the 17 years of the district's existence," Ibid, 2.

"Darley called Monterey and Santa Cruz," Alan Pugh, "Smog Experts Warn – Don't Become Another LA," Santa Cruz Sentinel, May 4, 1965, 1.

"Weeks later, C.R. Thompson," "Polluting the Air is Costly," Monterey Peninsula Herald, May 26, 1965, 1-2.

"Haltiner pointed to the Salinas Valley," Pugh, "Smog Experts Warn – Don't Become Another LA," Sentinel, 1.

"Humble was not alone," "Letter to A.T. Vierra," private papers of Warren Church.

"Haagen-Smit warned that in ten years," Pugh, "Smog Experts Warn – Don't Become Another LA," Sentinel, 1.

"Both Haagen-Smit and Griswold said," Ibid.

"The Pacific Grove Chamber of Commerce," "PG Chamber Delays Refinery Approval," Monterey Peninsula Herald, April 29, 1965, 2.

"Towards Salinas, some people": "Carmel, Pebble Beach Fight Industry," Salinas Californian, May 5, 1965, 6.

"The divide was spreading," "The Refinery and The Bay, Santa Cruz Sentinel, May 5, 1965, 21.

"That prompted the Planning Commission," "Planners Urge SC Air, Water Pollution Controls," Santa Cruz Sentinel, May 6, 1965, 9.

"With growing opposition, Humble officials grew uneasy," "Refinery Officials Pledge Tight Lid On Air Pollution," Monterey Peninsula Herald, May 7, 1965, 30.

"The Californian also hit back," "Humble Oil Also Believes in 'Clean Air," Salinas Californian, May 7, 1965, 6.

"State Senator Fred Farr noted," "Farr Urges 'Care' on Refinery," Monterey Peninsula Herald, May 11, 1965, 1.

"Also weighing in was former California Governor," "'Humble Will Kill You,' Says Knight," Monterey Peninsula Herald, May 12, 1965.

6

FACE-OFF AT THE PLANNING COMMISSION

"packed to capacity with 200 people," "Humble Oil Co. Hearing Is Continued Until July," Salinas Californian, May 12, 1965, 1.

"As the meeting began," Ibid, 2.

"Humble brought forth its team." Stan Cloud, "Planners Delay Refinery Ruling: Stricter Pollution Law Asked," Monterey Peninsula Herald, May 12, 1965, 2.

"who drew laughter at his contention," Alan Pugh, "Oil Permit Appears 'In The Bag,'" Santa Cruz Sentinel, May 12, 1965, 1.

"Humble is extremely anxious," Cloud, "Planners Delay Refinery Ruling: Stricter Pollution Law Asked," Herald, 2.

"Humble's experts admitted," Ibid.

"When O'Connell spoke," "Humble Oil

Co. Hearing Is Continued Until July,"
Californian, 2.

"When Fred Naber of Carmel," "Planners
Delay Refinery Ruling: Highlights Of Oil
Hearing," *Monterey Peninsula Herald*, May
12, 1965, 2.

"Later in O'Connell's statement," Cloud,
"Planners Delay Refinery Ruling: Stricter
Pollution Law Asked," *Herald*, 2.

"It is not possible to make a decision," "Humble
Oil Co. Hearing Is Continued Until July,"
Californian, 2.

"The tool hasn't been forged," Ibid.

"on the motion of Commissioner Peter
Cailotto," Ibid.

"A head count of the nine commissioners,"
Cloud, "Planners Delay Refinery Ruling:
Stricter Pollution Law Asked," *Herald*, 2.

"The *Santa Cruz Sentinel* reported" Pugh, "Oil
Permit Appears 'In The Bag,'" *Sentinel*, 1.

"Humble representative R. A. Winslow,"
"Humble Oil Co. Hearing Is Continued
Until July," *Californian*, 1.

"Commissioner Dan Krishun of Castroville,"
Cloud, "Planners Delay Refinery Ruling:
Stricter Pollution Law Asked," *Herald*, 1.

"Krishun claimed Castroville," "Humble Oil
Co. Hearing Is Continued Until July,"
Californian, 2.

"Yet Krishun was also troubled," "Pollution Unit
Limits for Industry Control Proposed,"
Salinas Californian, May 25, 1965, 9.

"the specific number of air," "July Oil Hearing
Scheduled at 8 p.m. by county planners,"
Monterey Peninsula Herald, May 25, 1965, 2.

"proposed setting up an industrial committee,"
"Pollution Unit Limits for Industry Control
Proposed," *Californian*, 9.

"Other commissioners joined in," Ibid.

"How are you going to do it?," Ibid.

"the company was not stepping up," "Time

Is Set For Humble Hearing," *Salinas
Californian*, May 25, 1965, 1.

"Most of North Monterey County," author's
conversation with Warren Church.

"Many of Krishun's fellow commissioners,"
"Humble Oil Co. Hearing Is Continued
Until July," *Californian*, 2.

"On the same day the Planning Commission,"
"Monterey Bay Air Control District
Asked," *Monterey Peninsula Herald*, May
12, 1965, 1.

"The Santa Cruz City Council," Alan Jones,
"Council Takes Action On Major Issues,
None Final," *Santa Cruz Sentinel*, May 12,
1965, 7.

This was at least the third request," "Capitola
Planners To Meet," *Santa Cruz Sentinel*, May
16, 1965, 5.

"Another event happened the same day," "New
City Attorney For Carmel," *Monterey
Peninsula Herald*, May 12, 1965.

7
A PARADE OF SMOKESTACKS

"A week after the Planning Commission,"
Eric Hofeldt "Standard Oil's Help Asked
In Smog Fight," *Monterey Peninsula Herald*,
May 19, 1965, 1.

"Regardless of the outcome," Ibid, 2.

"Haider went onto claim," "Refinery Won't
Pollute Air, Oil Executive Says," *Salinas
Californian*, May 20, 1965, 4.

"Haider went onto claim in Jamaica," "Humble
Oil Protest Put To Board," *Santa Cruz
Sentinel*, May 20, 1965, 8.

"Kramer did not ask Humble," "Refinery
Won't Pollute Air, Oil Executive Says,"
Californian, 4.

"Kramer traveled to San Francisco," "Smog

Control District Urged," *Monterey Peninsula Herald*, May 20, 1965, 1.

"We want to seek the assistance," Ibid, 2.

"Kramer said legal opinion," Alan Pugh, "Multi-County Air Pollution Control District Formed To Oppose Proposed Oil Refinery," *Santa Cruz Sentinel*, May 25, 1965, 1.

"One oil refinery can't make much difference," C. D. Wheelock, "Don't Let Them In," *Monterey Peninsula Herald*, May 17, 1965, 16.

"The first signs of saltwater intrusion," "Seawater Intrusion Monitoring," Monterey County Water Resources Agency, https://www.co.monterey.ca.us/government/government-links/water-resources-agency/programs/seawater-intrusion-monitoring, retrieved April 9, 2020.

"Residents whose homes bordered," author's conversations with Nita Wells.

"Returning from San Francisco," "New Group Formed For Smog Pollution," *Monterey Peninsula Herald*, May 21, 1965, 1.

"Michaud announced that he would present" Pugh, "Multi-County Air Pollution Control District Formed To Oppose Proposed Oil Refinery," *Sentinel*, 1.

"was a highly influential and respected member," "Robert Allen Griffin," California Press Foundation, https://cal-press.wildapricot.org/hall-of-fame_robert-allen-griffin, retrieved June 11, 2020.

"The city of Monterey's Planning Commission," "Monterey Planners Urge Smog District," *Monterey Peninsula Herald*, May 26, 1965, 1.

"Days later, Monterey's call," "Pollution Controls Favored," *Monterey Peninsula Herald*, May 28, 1965, 1.

"Michaud's next appearance," "Smog District Urged," *Monterey Peninsula Herald*, June 1, 1965, 1.

"Unfortunately, the present air pollution," Ibid.

"The supervisors passed the matter" "steps taken

to form anti-pollution district," *Watsonville Register-Pajaronian*, June 3, 1965, 2

"The growing debate over an air pollution," "Farr Prepares Smog Bill in Legislature, *Monterey Peninsula Herald*, June 4, 1965, 15.

"While the Monterey Peninsula," "Castroville CC Endorses Humble Plan," *Salinas Californian*, May 26, 1965, 1.

"Citizens for Clean Air responded," "5,000 Oppose Oil Refinery," *Monterey Peninsula Herald*, May 27, 1965, 1.

"As the *Santa Cruz Sentinel* expressed it," Alen Jenes, "Pro And Con Petitions Out In Humble Conflict," *Santa Cruz Sentinel*, May 27, 1965, 1.

"Although months away from a vote," Pugh, "Multi-County Air Pollution Control District Formed To Oppose Proposed Oil Refinery," *Sentinel*, May 25, 1965, 1.

8

A PLAN FOR PROSPERITY

"The booming sardine canning," David Spradling, "Dreams of Cannery Row. After the Sardines, What?" Monterey Public Library, August 26, 2014, https://www.monterey.org/library/About-Us/Newsroom/dreams-of-cannery-row-after-the-sardines-what, retrieved April 10, 2020.

"Kaiser Refractories made munitions," William Harold Oliver, Jr, *Bricks from the sea: Kaiser Refractories*, Moss Landing, CA, (1951; United States; William Harold Oliver Jr. Productions, 1951,) 16mm.

"In December 1944, wartime legislation," Marina Public Library, Marina, CA, Moss Landing File, "Urgency Project Is Recommended At Moss Landing," December 13, 1944.

"In 1946, the U.S. Army Corp of Engineers,"

U.S. Army Engineer District, San Francisco, Corps of Engineers, Draft Environmental Statement, Maintenance Dredging (FY 1974), Moss Landing Harbor, Moss Landing, California. March 1974. 2.

"arrived in 1947 to construct a power plant," Mark Silberstein, Chela Zabin, Et al., "History of Land Use," http://digital. mlml.calstate.edu/islandora/object/ islandora%3A2450/datastream/OBJ/ download/Chapter_07-_History_of_Land_ Use.pdf, retrieved August 19, 2019.

"the second largest fossil fuel power plant," "History," Moss Landing Chamber of Commerce, https://mosslandingchamber. com/our-history/, retrieved May 31, 2020.

"PG&E planned a nuclear power," "Humble Oil Objectives, PG&E Plans for Use of Nuclear Power Plants Outlined," Salinas Californian, July 10, 1965, 18.

"Standard Oil of California in the 1950s," Lillian Woodward, "Big Change in Last Decade, Future Looks Even Brighter," Monterey Peninsula Herald, January 7, 1956, 9.

"On September 18, 1956, the Monterey County," "Moss Landing Plan Adopted," Monterey Peninsula Herald, September 18, 1956, 1.

"Monterey County Planning Commission submitted," Monterey County Planning Commission, Moss Landing Area Development Plan, September 1956.

"The Planning Commission assured the county," Ibid, ii.

"At the public hearings held," Ibid.

"Calling for the 'great potential,'" Ibid, 1.

"As the study progressed," Ibid, 2.

"The 1956 master plan was three years," "Moss Landing Plan Adopted," Herald, 1.

"Other than those who suggested minor," Planning Commission, "Moss Landing Area Development Plan," ii.

"Deaver's campaign literature focused," "Retain Chester 'Chet' Deaver," private papers of Warren Church.

"From a standpoint of forward thinking," "Moss Landing Harbor District Expansion Plan Being Studied, Monterey Peninsula Herald, August 8, 1954, 16.

"In 1946, the state granted," "Supervisors Agree to Help Pay Debts for Moss Landing," Monterey Peninsula Herald, December 2, 1954, 12.

"It was found that state law," "Supervisors Withdraw Moss Landing Loan – Found It Was Illegal," Monterey Peninsula Herald, December 7, 1954, 3.

"In 1949, it faced litigation," "Moss Landing Harbor Officials Win Reprieve From 'Writ,'" Monterey Peninsula Herald, August 12, 1949, 7.

"As if that was not bad enough," "Last Three Members of Harbor District Resign," Monterey Peninsula Herald, December 27, 1955, 1.

"I'm tired of this and want no more," "Last Three Members of Harbor District Resign," Herald, 1.

"desperate for funds," "New Harbor District to Be Detailed," Monterey Peninsula Herald, May 7, 1957, 1.

"At the forefront of this drive," "In Memory of Myron 'Doc' Etienne (1924-2016), Noland, Hamerly, Etienne and Hoss, https://www.nheh.com/articles/ remembrances/in-memory-of-myron- doc-etienne-1924-2016, retrieved March 3, 2020.

"a long-time activist," "Myron 'Doc' Etienne, ProRodeo Hall of Fame, http://www. prorodeohalloffame.com/inductees/ by-category/notablelifetime-achievement/ myron-doc-etienne/, retrieved March 3, 2020

"With a larger district, Etienne," "Plan Outlined in Marina," Monterey Peninsula Herald, May 9, 1957, 1.

9
WHITE KNIGHTS OF THE DUCHY

"The *Salinas Californian* lamented," "It's Past Time for Action on the Refinery Issue," *Salinas Californian*, June 3, 1965, 6.

"The *Californian* had another beef too," Ibid.

"Postponement and further postponement," Ibid.

"The *Californian* then accused the advocates," Ibid.

"He stated that he intended," Stan Cloud, "Stricter Pollution Controls," *Monterey Peninsula Herald*, June 5, 1965, 1.

"those recommendations would primarily," Ibid, 2.

"O'Connell would not make a recommendation," Ibid, 1.

"He added that the initial conditions suggested," Ibid 2.

"Director of Sanitation Ed Munson," "Stiff Air Pollution Controls Recommended," *Salinas Californian*, June 7, 1965, 4.

"constantly assured listeners that Humble," Alan Pugh, "Humble Oil Says It Will Meet Reasonable Expectations, *Santa Cruz Sentinel*, June 13, 1965, 8A.

"Rumors persisted that the was," "Air Pollution Consultant Defended on Employment," *Salinas Californian*, June 29, 1965, 4.

"He also consulted for the," "More Pay Voted for County's Consultant on Air Pollution," *Monterey Peninsula Herald*, June 29, 1965, 13.

"Supervisor Tom Hudson, who had already," Ibid.

"What did concern Humble," Pugh, "Humble Oil Says It Will Meet Reasonable Expectations, *Sentinel*, 8A.

"the Board of Supervisors reluctantly," "Air Pollution Consultant Defended on Employment," *Salinas Californian*, June 29, 1965, 4.

"They sought to hurt Humble," C. Edward Graves, "Better Than Zoning," *Monterey Peninsula Herald*, June 7, 1965, 22.

"this tactic would go further," "Peninsula Assault on Humble," *Monterey Peninsula Herald*, May 16, 1966, 2.

"Opponents also spread word," F. A. Bacher, Jr., "Writer Disagrees with Refinery Editorial," *Salinas Californian*, June 11, 1965, 6.

"Charles Kramer formed a new anti-Humble," "Smokestack Industry -- Yes or No?" *Salinas Californian*, June 9, 1965, 4.

"Kramer and Humble's Jack Gardner," "Jaycees Promised 'Clean' Refinery," *Monterey Peninsula Herald*, June 10, 1965, 2.

"We certainly don't want to have to explain," Ibid.

"Kramer hit back that it was about," Ibid.

"Matthew Walker, legal counsel for the San Francisco Bay Area," Tom Wieder, "Pollution Controls Vital, League of Cities Unit Told," *Monterey Peninsula Herald*, June 11, 1965, 5.

"Walker embraced the notion that pollution," "Refinery Control Plan Told," *Salinas Californian*, June 11, 1965, 4.

"He also expressed that Humble's choice," Ibid, 1.

"Walker urged that people pressure," Wieder, "Pollution Controls Vital, League of Cities Unit Told," *Herald*, June 11, 1965, 5.

"Walker stressed that the real issue," "Humble Oil Application in Proper Perspective," *Salinas Californian*, June 12, 1965, 4.

"the fear of one oil company's," "Oil Probe Linked to Refinery," *Monterey Peninsula Herald*, June 16, 1965, 2.

"Some people claimed they fled," Ibid.

"Others spoke of the economic benefits," Tony Azevedo, "Monterey County Needs Industry," *Salinas Californian*, June 16, 1965, 6.

"In another case, an independent petroleum

geologist," Edward Gribi, Jr., "Refineries Can Be Built Without Pollution," *Salinas Californian*, June 21, 1965, 6.

"At one of the earlier planning commission meetings" "Employes (sic) Sunbathe Right In Middle of Refinery!" *Salinas Californian*, June 17, 1965, 7.

"The nine visited a massive," Ibid.

"When we went through," Ibid.

"In Pacific Grove, the City Council," "Pacific Grove Council Urges Smog Controls," *Monterey Peninsula Herald*, June 17, 1965, 6.

"At the Salinas City Council," "Moore Describes Visit To Refinery in Hawaii," *Salinas Californian*, June 15, 1965, 5.

"Erle Byer of Watsonville," Erle A. Byer, "Baseless worries on refinery," *Watsonville Register-Pajaronian*, July 3, 1965, 14.

"Monterey County Industrial Development," "Monterey County Industry – Balance and Quality," *Salinas Californian*, June 19, 1965, 6.

"Moore and Monterey County Industrial Development announced," "Petitions Back Oil Refinery," *Salinas Californian*, June 26, 1965, 2.

"To the north, the Santa Cruz County," "Board Urged To Help Form Air Pollution Control Unit," *Santa Cruz Sentinel*, June 18, 1965, 11.

"The supervisors expressed concern," "Santa Cruz County Favors Smog District," *Monterey Peninsula Herald*, June 24, 1965, 16.

"Back in Monterey," Earl Hofeldt, "Chamber Board Hears Arguments on Refinery," *Monterey Peninsula Herald*, June 22, 1965, 5.

"Gordon Reid, one of the chamber's directors," Ibid.

"Kramer emphasized that smaller industries," Ibid.

"making the decision on a 9-3 vote," Eric Hofeldt, "Peninsula C of C In Favor of Smog District," *Monterey Peninsula Herald*, June 29, 1965, 1.

"(The resolution might) kill the stink," Ibid.

"With support for an air pollution," "Delay On Smog District," *Monterey Peninsula Herald*, June 28, 1965, 1.

"Munson responded that staff," Ibid, 11.

"Supervisors Harold Henry," "Air Pollution Control District Proposed," *Salinas Californian*, June 28, 1965, 2.

10

A TALE OF TWO NEWSPAPERS

"The *Monterey Peninsula Herald* ran the photograph," "A Smoggy View of the Salinas Valley," *Monterey Peninsula Herald*, June 22, 1965, 5.

"It's news to Salinas Valley residents," "*Californian* Checks Mystery 'Smog' Photograph of Valley," *Salinas Californian*, June 30, 1965, 5.

"That's right. Smog.," Ibid.

"The *Californian* tried more than once," Ibid.

"When The *Californian* contacted Smith," Ibid.

"The *Californian* then began to refer to the subterfuge, "Smoggy Thinking on the Peninsula," *Salinas Californian*, June 30, 1965, 6.

"While The *Californian* mused," Ibid.

"the newspaper also quoted Salinas Chamber of Commerce," "*Californian* Checks Mystery 'Smog' Photograph of Valley," *Californian*, 5.

"Sensing that it had caught Humble's opponents," "Smoggy Thinking on the Peninsula," *Californian*, 6.

"Yet The *Californian* was not without," Ibid.

"Another turn in the story," Bruce Church Inc., "This Is Our Picture," *Salinas Californian*, July 20, 1965.

"Bruce Church Inc called for the county," Ibid.

"In the 1940s, pollution vulnerable crops,"

Chip Jacobs and William J. Kelly, *Smogtown: The Lung-Burning History of Pollution in Los Angeles*, Overlook, 2015,49-51.

"In the book *Smogtown*," Ibid.

"the newspaper followed up with a more complete story," "Are Two Peninsula Groups Same Force," *Salinas Californian*, July 2, 1965, 2.

Amidst this consortium of Humble opponents "As efforts to form an air pollution control district"; *Salinas Californian*, July 8, 1965.

"When it was pointed out to Michaud," Ibid.

"perhaps sensing that he was included," Ibid.

"Monterey attorney Thomas Moore," "Humble Oil Declines Bid To Join Anti-smog Drive," *Monterey Peninsula Herald*, July 26, 1965, 4.

"Humble Oil Declines Bid," Ibid.

"Humble Oil Willing to Aid," "Humble Oil Willing To Aid in Pollution District Formation," *Salinas Californian*, July 26, 1965, 2.

"The *Herald*'s headline focused" "Humble Oil Declines Bid To Join Anti-smog Drive," *Herald*, 4.

"The *Californian*'s headline reflected" "Humble Oil Willing To Aid in Pollution District Formation," *Californian*, 2.

"Humble's position was not a clear," Ibid.

"On the front page of the July 1," Stan Cloud, "Smog Danger to Plants Told to County Growers," *Monterey Peninsula Herald*, July 1, 1965, 1.

"But on page three," "Air Pollution Caused Without Industry," *Salinas Californian*, July 1, 1965, 3.

"the Monterey Bay area will eventually," Cloud, "Smog Danger to Plants Told to County Growers," *Herald*, 1.

"Speaking with Darley at the advisory committee," Ibid, 2.

"Darley told the audience that the first signs," Ibid.

"Darley noted that ag had as much responsibility," "Air Pollution Caused Without Industry," *Californian*, 3.

"Agriculture should not be given a blanket exemption," Ibid.

"The subcommittee appeared to support," "Committee May Suggest Control of Industry Total," *Salinas Californian*, July 1, 1965, 3.

"As I see it, we need some radical changes," Ibid.

11

A TRIBUTE TO TOURISM

"Early visitors began," "Our Heritage & Timeline," 2020, Pebble Beach Co., www.pebblebeach.com/timeline/, retrieved April 2, 2020.

"Rutherford B. Hayes was the first," Pacific Bank Handbook of California, 1888, 66, https://books.google.com/books?id=vCSR9VK8lJUC, retrieved April 2, 2020.

"developers in Carmel began selling," Michael Chatfield, "A Century of Utopia," Carmel Magazine, Winter 2016, https://carmelmagazine.com/archive/16wi/a-century-of-utopia, retrieved April 2, 2020.

"Tourism kicked into high gear," National Council on Public History, https://ncph.org/wp-content/uploads/Monterey-History-on-the-Half-Shell.pdf, retrieved April 2, 2020.

"Visitor spending in 1966 alone," Review of Highway Beautification-1967, Hearings Before the Subcommittee on Roads, U.S. Government Printing Office, 1967, 1051. https://books.google.com/books/about/Review_of_Highway_Beautification_1967_He.html?id=60YMkX1cBukC, retrieved April 2, 2020.

"Today, close to $3 billion" James Herrera,

"Travel Impacts Report," *Monterey Herald*, May 13, 2019. https://www.montereyherald.com/2019/05/11/2018-travel-impacts-report-monterey-county-visitor-spending-up-5-8-to-3b/, retrieved April 2, 2020.

"Santa Cruz enticed visitors," Chandra Moira Beal and Richard A. Beal, Santa Cruz Beach Boardwalk: The Early Years, 2003, 15. https://books.google.com/books?id=h6KOXpTDFKUC, retrieved April 2, 2020.

"Coney Island of the West," Santa Cruz Economic Development Office, https://choosesantacruz.com/industries/tourism, retrieved April 2, 2020.

"In the 1960s, a national movement" National Council on Public History, https://ncph.org/wp-content/uploads/Monterey-History-on-the-Half-Shell.pdf, retrieved April 2, 2020.

12

PRELUDE TO BATTLE

"city councils in Seaside," "Seaside Council Opposes Oil Drilling in Bay," *Monterey Peninsula Herald*, July 16, 1965, 1.

"Pacific Grove passed resolutions," "P.G. Council Against Drilling," *Monterey Peninsula Herald*, July 22, 1965, 14.

"at the Monterey County Industrial Development," "Humble Oil Objectives, PG&E Plans for Use of Nuclear Power Plants Outlined," *Salinas Californian*, July 10, 1965, 18.

"After 1970, PG&E's plans," Ibid.

"Included in these plans were power plants," Ibid.

"In his talk, Ludcke offered rounds of praise," Ibid.

"Humble believes," Ibid.

"Ludcke also praised MCID," Ibid.

"one of the early losers in the Humble affair," Monterey County cuts off CID funds," *Watsonville Register-Pajaronian*, July 14, 1965, 2.

"Should county money be used for lobbying,' Ibid.

"The board's vote was 3-1," "Industrial group gets no money," *Watsonville Register-Pajaronian*, July 19, 1965, 11.

"While county officials had made field trips," Stan Cloud, "Supervisors Tour PG&E A-power Plant," *Monterey Peninsula Herald*, July 23, 1965, 6.

"Anderson came back from the two-day trip," Ibid.

"Although referred to as a 'regular guy,'" email from Ray March, August 15, 2019.

"use homespun analogies," "Andy Anderson Is First Mayor Named by the People," *Monterey Peninsula Herald*, May 28, 1964, A3.

"grew up in Wisconsin," Monterey Public Library Clippings File.

"At the Battle of Leyte," "Beauford T. Anderson," Arlington National Cemetery Website, June 11, 2015, http://www.arlingtoncemetery.net/btanderson.htm, retrieved August 22, 2019.

"a man of enormous modesty," Dave Nordstrand, "Remembering a Hero," *Salinas Californian*, February 15, 2012,11.

"Anderson returned to Wisconsin," Steve Hopkins, "Soldiers Grove Never Forgot World War II Hero," Wisconsin State Journal, June 16, 1992, 3B.

"Anderson ran for the city council," "Beauford T. Anderson," Arlington Website.

"ran for mayor in 1959," "Andy Anderson Is First Mayor Named by the People," *Herald*, A3.

"In 1964, Anderson ran for supervisor," "Hudson Wins Re-Election in Monterey," *Salinas Californian*, June 3, 1964, 1.

"Anderson worked tirelessly," "Andy Anderson Edges McGrath," *Salinas Californian*, November 4, 1964, 7.

"a mysterious flurry of phone calls," "Mystery Peninsula Poll Of Refinery Opponents," *Salinas Californian*, July 1, 1965, 4.

"The California Department of Fish and Game," "Humble Oil's Bid Gets New Support," *Salinas Californian*, July 13, 1965, 4.

"The Monterey County Sportsman's Council," Ibid.

"J. Kleiser of Salinas," J. Kleiser, "Trying to Prove We Are Stupid," *Salinas Californian*, July 16, 1965, 6.

"representatives of the county Parks and Recreation Committee," "County Parks Unit Warned Of Refinery Plan," *Santa Cruz Sentinel*, July 11, 1965, 2.

"Shortly after July 4 *Salinas Californian*," "LA Pair Opposes Site For Proposed Refinery," *Salinas Californian*, July 9, 1965, 3.

"No oil refinery, no power plant," Ibid.

"Both Middleton and Atkinson contended,' Ibid.

"strong efforts by Citizens for Clean Air," "Clean Air Committee Claims 13,000 Names," *Monterey Peninsula Herald*, July 17, 1965, 2.

"Humble supporters gathered 1,140," "1,140 Castroville Area Residents Favor Refinery," *Salinas Californian*, July 21, 1965, 2.

"The Monterey County Agricultural Advisory Committee," "Ag Advisory Unit Ask 3-Pronged Controls," *Salinas Californian*, July 15, 1965, 8.

"countywide method of control," "Group Favors Smog Controls," *Monterey Peninsula Herald*, July 15, 1965, 2.

"W. H. Wilbur, who headed the subcommittee," "Ag Advisory Unit Ask 3-Pronged Controls," *Californian*, 8.

"publicly announced its opposition to Humble,"

"Opposition Voiced to Oil Refinery," *Salinas Californian*, July 17, 1965, 6.

"Bruce Church Inc. ran its advertisement," "Salinas grower gives warning on pollution,": *Watsonville Register-Pajaronian*, July 21, 1965, 1.

"Our agricultural industry cannot exist," Ibid.

"farmers and landowners in the Castroville area," "Castroville-Moss Landing Agriculturists And Property Owners Say ...," *Salinas Californian*, July 26, 1965, 22.

"As the July 28 decision," "Refinery Controls Outlined," *Monterey Peninsula Herald*, July 14, 1965, 1.

"The document required that the permit," "Restrictions Given for Humble Plant," *Salinas Californian*, July 14, 1965, 1.

"The proposed conditions included basic restrictions," "Refinery Controls Outlined," *Herald*, 1-2.

"While the conditions laid forth," "Monterey Issues Report On Pollution," *Santa Cruz Sentinel*, July 15, 1965, 16.

13

HUMBLE'S FIRST DEFEAT

"county officials prepared," "Humble Hearing Set Tomorrow," *Monterey Peninsula Herald*, July 27, 1965, 1.

"almost half the population of Castroville," "Humble Plant Hearing To Resume Tomorrow," *Salinas Californian*, July 27, 1965, 2.

"The individual correspondence to the Planning Commission," "Major Opinion Split On Refinery," *Salinas Californian*, July 27, 1965, 2.

"rejected by a five to four vote," "Humble Hearing Set Tomorrow," *Herald*, 2.

"the opponents fought hard," "Humble

Plant Hearing To Resume Tomorrow," *Californian*, 1-2.

"One of the most prominent opponents," Ansel Adams, "Oppose Humble Oil," *Monterey Peninsula Herald*, July 28, 1965, 22.

"opposition on the Monterey Peninsula," email from Stanley Cloud, August 28, 2019.

"During a midday lunch at the Rotary Club," "Humble executive defends refinery," *Watsonville Register-Pajaronian*, July 29, 1965.

"To us a refinery is a thing of beauty," Ibid.

"members of the Monterey County Planning Commission gathered," Stan Cloud, "Planners Turn Down Refinery," *Monterey Peninsula Herald*, July 29, 1985, 6.

"two votes that night," Ray March, "Humble Oil Permit Rejected," *Salinas Californian*, July 29, 1965, 4.

"Ed DeMars lead off the evening," "Humble Oil Loses First Bid For Refinery," *Santa Cruz Sentinel*, July 29, 1965, 1.

"The county's pollution expert William O'Connell," March, "Humble Oil Permit Rejected," *Californian*, 4.

"addressed by County Counsel William Stoffers," Stan Cloud, "Planners Cover Bases With Smog Controls," *Monterey Peninsula Herald*, July 30, 1965, 4.

"Attorney Paul Hamerly, representing Humble," March, "Humble Oil Permit Rejected," *Californian*, 4.

"Moser must have been an unsettling," "Humble refinery loses first round," *Register-Pajaronian*, 1.

"The media that day noted," March, "Humble Oil Permit Rejected," *Californian*, 4.

"Moser supplied an array of statistics," Stan Cloud, "Jubilation Follows the Crucial Round-1 Vote Against Refinery," *Monterey Peninsula Herald*, July 29, 1965, 5.

"Kramer and Moser successfully added," Cloud, "Planners Turn Down Refinery," *Herald*, 6.

"O'Connell disputed many of the opposition claims," "Humble refinery loses first round," *Register-Pajaronian*, 1.

"farm superintendent Dave Williams," Cloud, "Planners Turn Down Refinery," *Herald*, 6.

"He focused on the release of nitrous oxide," "Humble Oil Loses First Bid For Refinery," *Sentinel*, 1.

"Watsonville flower grower Mits Nakishima," Cloud, "Jubilation Follows the Crucial Round-1 Vote Against Refinery," *Herald*, 5

"You are dealing with an atom bomb," "Humble refinery loses first round," *Register-Pajaronian*, 1.

"Chair Keith Evans," "Humble Oil Loses First Bid For Refinery," *Sentinel*, 1.

"all nine commissioners voted," Cloud, "Planners Cover Bases With Smog Controls," *Monterey Peninsula Herald*, July 30, 1965, 4.

"Willard Branson of Carmel Valley," March, "Humble Oil Permit Rejected," *Californian*, 4.

"I don't feel one refinery breeds another," Ibid.

"The biggest problem is not industry," "Humble Oil Loses First Bid For Refinery," *Sentinel*, 1.

"Kenneth Mansfield of King City," Cloud, "Planners Turn Down Refinery," *Herald*, 6.

"Mansfield pointed out the geographical divide," "Humble Oil Loses First Bid For Refinery," *Sentinel*, 1.

"Branson was joined by Chair Keith Evans," March, "Humble Oil Permit Rejected," *Californian*, 4.

"Stutzman, one of the two undecided votes," Ibid.

"That left only Peter Cailotto," "Atteridge Wins Second District," *Salinas Californian*, June 3, 1964, 1.

"only Cailotto remained from the 1956 commission," Monterey County Planning Commission, Moss Landing Area Development Plan, September 1956, iv.

"Is Moss Landing the right place": Peter Cailotto statement, private papers of Warren Church.

"Cailotto, who had been on several field trips," Ibid.

"Cailotto pointed out that the many favorable comments," Ibid.

"bailed to a preposterous conclusion," Ibid.

"Winslow scoffed at Cailotto's suggestion," Cloud, "Planners Turn Down Refinery," *Herald*, 6.

"Humble's assistant district manager for manufacturing," Rodney G. Colvin, "San Ardo Oil Field, Monterey County, California," AAPG Datapages, Inc., http://archives.datapages.com/data/pacific/data/008/008001/57_ps0080057.htm, retrieved September 2, 2019.

"At a little past midnight," Cloud, "Jubilation Follows the Crucial Round-1 Vote Against Refinery," *Herald*, 5.

"Cailotto concluded by expressing," Peter Cailotto statement, Church papers.

"Jack Gardner made it clear," "Humble Oil Loses First Bid For Refinery," *Sentinel*, 1.

"Winslow, baffled that the county's own expert," "Humble to Appeal to County Board," *Salinas Californian*, July 29, 1965, 1.

"Winslow said some of the questions," Ibid, 4.

"Hamerly expressed that Humble," Ibid.

"Winslow exclaimed that the conditions," "Company Poll Backs Refinery," *Monterey Peninsula Herald*, July 29, 1965, 5.

"You know we looked all over for a site": "Humble refinery loses first round," *Register-Pajaronian*, 2.

"The *Salinas Californian* spread the headline" March, "Humble Oil Permit Rejected," *Californian*, 1.

"On the editorial page, The *Californian* called," "Planners Surrender to Peninsula Propaganda," *Salinas Californian*, July 29, 1965, 6.

"A supporter in Salinas," John B. Parr, "Cailotto Commended for Stand on Humble," *Salinas Californian*, August 3, 1965, 6.

"For Cailotto, the fallout was immediate," '65 Moss Landing Refinery Battle Determined Future of the County," *Monterey Peninsula Herald*, October 20, 1985, 1B.

14
AGRICULTURE'S GROWING CONCERN

"Wetlands captured nutrients," Traci Rae Hukill, "The Gift of Salinas Valley Soil," Monterey County Weekly, Sept. 26, 2002, http://www.montereycountyweekly.com/news/local_news/the-gift-of-salinas-valley-soil/article_99074433-995a-5045-9944-3b87607be192.html, retrieved April 25, 2020.

"Before the United States took over California," Monterey County Farm Bureau, Salinas Valley History, http://montereycfb.com/index.php?page=salinas-valley-history, retrieved April 26, 2020.

"But change was coming to local agriculture," Monterey County Historical Museum, http://mchsmuseum.com/salinasbrief.html, retrieved April 26, 2020.

"Reports for 1965," Monterey County Annual Crop Report, 1965, 8, Monterey County, https://www.co.monterey.ca.us/Home/ShowDocument?id=1393, retrieved April 27, 2020.

"Santa Cruz County's," Agricultural Commissioners' Crop Reports, 1962-1969, Santa Cruz County, 48, https://ageconsearch.umn.edu/bitstream/99649/2/, retrieved April 27, 2020.

"John T. Middleton," "Response of Plants to Air Pollution," May 1956 Journal of the Air Pollution Control Association, https://

www.tandfonline.com/doi/abs/10.1080/0 0966665.1956.10467730, retrieved April 26, 2020.

"Smog's effects on Bay Area agriculture," Doug Haydel, "Regional Control of Air and Water Pollution in the Bay Area," California Law Review, 1967, https://pdfs.semanticscholar.org/ee13/ e00ed94d946f3306f45bf6136ec3c1e30b7d. pdf, retrieved April 26, 2020.

"Flower growers were particularly grieved," Air Pollution Aspects of Ethylene, prepared for the National Air Pollution Control Administration by Litton Systems Inc., 1969, 15, https://www.google.com/ books/edition/Air_Pollution_Aspects_ of_Ethylene/y1N7wAEACAAJ?hl=en, retrieved April 27, 2020.

15
AN AUGUST OF DISCONTENT

"as the debate heightened over Humble," "PG&E Putting Up 500-Foot Stack," Monterey Peninsula Herald, August 25, 1965, 30.

"The PG&E is itself already," Robert R. Western, "Humble Oil And Bad Air," Monterey Peninsula Herald, August 25, 1965, 24.

"The mysterious survey," "Humble to Appeal to County Board," Salinas Californian, July 29, 1965, 1.

"the only geographical area in the county," "Company Poll Backs Refinery," Monterey Peninsula Herald, July 29, 1965, 5.

"Humble surveyed 985 individuals," "Most County Voters Favor Refinery," Salinas Californian, August 6, 1965, 1.

"He had served on the city council," "Atteridge Wins Post as Chairman of Supervisors," Salinas Californian, January 4, 1964, 1.

"Atteridge sought to bring industry to Salinas,"

"Atteridge Can Provide Wise Leadership," Salinas Californian, January 5, 1966, 6.

"His time as mayor was marked," author's interview with Michael Atteridge, June 3, 2020.

"There was a boom in residential," Lisa Eisemann, Roll Call, The Mayors of Salinas. 2013. 55-56.

"Born in Watsonville," Ibid.

"where he played basketball," email from Michael Atteridge, June 6, 2020.

"Degree in hand," Atteridge interview.

"From 1939, he operated," Eisemann, Roll Call. 55-56.

"After taking office on the Salinas City Council," Atteridge interview.

"Atteridge was known for his dry humor," author's conversations with Warren Church.

"Perhaps no one described Atteridge," Stan Cloud, A Bettor's Guide to the Monterey County Board of Supervisors," the advocate, November 1965, 4.

"in later years Atteridge would recount," Atteridge interview.

"as both were fiscal conservatives," Atteridge email.

"and social liberals," Church conversation.

"a second major grower in the Salinas Valley," "Grower Opposes Refinery," Monterey Peninsula Herald, August 5, 1965, 1.

"We very strongly oppose the granting," Ibid 1-2.

"D'Arrigo noted that the company left," Ibid 2.

"Harry Casey, the editor and publisher," Harry F. Casey, "Thoughts On Humble," Monterey Peninsula Herald, August 12, 1965, 18.

"As the publisher of four weeklies," "Harry F. Casey," California Press Foundation, https://cal-press.wildapricot.org/hall-of-fame_harry-casey, retrieved June 11, 2020.

"A group of thirty farmers," "Valley Group

Organizes to Block Humble," *Salinas Californian*, August 13, 1965, 15.

"a former planning commissioner," "Refinery Foes Meet Tonight In Greenfield," *Salinas Californian*, August 26, 1965, 1.

"Hearne was adamant that the groups were separate," "Valley Group Organizes to Block Humble," *Californian*, 15.

"We are primarily interested in agriculture," Ibid.

"We grow crops," Ray March, "Agriculture Pollution Damage Feared," *Salinas Californian*, August 26, 1965, 3.

"yet a third group began forming," "Third Group Forming for 'Clean Air,'" *Salinas Californian*, August 13, 1965, 15.

"Williams' group included more prominent members," Stan Cloud, "Opposition to Oil Refinery Mounting in South County," *Monterey Peninsula Herald*, August 19, 1965, 1.

"Williams disagreed with the notion that pollution," March, "Agriculture Pollution Damage Feared," *Californian*, 3.

"A group of North County residents gathered," Cloud, "Opposition to Oil Refinery Mounting in South County," *Herald*, August 19, 1965, 1.

"I'm against it," "Humble Oil at Moss Landing – An Appraisal," *Castroville Times and Moss Landing Harbor News*, August 31, 1965, 1.

"To date we haven't been into it," Ray March, "Agriculture Divided Over Oil Refinery," *Salinas Californian*, August 25, 1965, 18.

"The Monterey County Farm Bureau was far less," "Refinery Decision Tomorrow," *Monterey Peninsula Herald*, September 1, 1965, 5.

"Wayne Bowman, President of the Farm Bureau," Wayne Bowman to Monterey County Board of Supervisors, August 31, 1965, private papers of Warren Church.

"One of the agricultural supporters for Humble," March, "Agriculture Divided Over Oil Refinery," *Californian*, 18.

"I'm more worried about the exhaust," Ibid.

"We own about 10 ranches out here," Ibid.

"Barsotti also dismissed the growing concerns," Ibid.

"This was an enormous amount," "Humble Oil at Moss Landing – An Appraisal," Times, 1.

"At the Greenfield Chamber of Commerce," "Gonzales Chamber Hears Henry Discuss Humble," *Salinas Californian*, August 13, 1965, 15.

"In Monterey the week of the Planning Commission," Earl Hofeldt, "Cranston Hails County Vote on Oil Refinery," *Monterey Peninsula Herald*, July 30, 1965, 1.

"More fodder for opponents of Humble," Wini Adams, "Distorted Idea of Refinery Operation," *Salinas Californian*, August 11, 1965, 6.

"Leighton was no stranger," Eric Brazil, "200 Hear Experts' Criticism of Humble Oil Refinery Plan," *Salinas Californian*, August 27, 1965, 1.

"Leighton mentioned that the three most easily visible signs," Philip A. Leighton, "Air Pollution Expert Tells of Refinery Perils," *Monterey Peninsula Herald*, August 24, 1965,

"Leighton further warned that the Salinas Valley," Philip A. Leighton, "Plant Damage, Human Hazard Told by Expert," *Monterey Peninsula Herald*, August 25, 1965, 30.

"the panel included E.F. Darley," Brazil, "200 Hear Experts' Criticism of Humble Oil Refinery Plan," *Californian*, 2.

"In the event contaminants," Ibid.

"Mattison was not the only M.D. to speak" Rex H. Whitworth, M.D., "Effect of Smog on Homo Sapiens," *Salinas Californian*, September 1, 1965, 6.

"That argument took a blow," "Oil Permit May Block Food Plant," *Monterey Peninsula Herald*, August 31, 1965, 1.

"Just as he had prior to the Planning Commission," Ansel Adams, "Feeling Runs Deep On Humble," *Monterey Peninsula Herald*, September 1, 1965, 34

16
CITIZENS FOR CLEAN AIR

"In the weeks leading up to the September," Stan Cloud, "Refinery Decisioin Tomorrow," *Monterey Peninsula Herald*, September 1, 1965, 5.

"Kramer was formerly in the manufacturing," Ray March, "Refinery Opponents Fear Contamination," *Salinas Californian*, August 23, 1965, 12.

"Moser with Monterey Peninsula College President George Faul," Memos from Citizens for Clean Air For Mr. Church, private papers of Warren Church.

"In the weeks leading up to the September 2," Ibid.

"We have unbiased testimony," March, "Refinery Opponents Fear Contamination," *Californian*, 12.

"The first testimony was a letter from Phillip Leighton," Memo No. 1, Church papers.

"The second memorandum came from Faul," Memo No. 2, Church papers.

"Some of these industries," March, "Refinery Opponents Fear Contamination," *Californian*, 12.

"Faul quoted D.J. Callaghan," Memo No. 2, Church papers.

"The third memorandum focused on people," Memo No. 3, Church papers.

"Other memorandums readdressed the potpourri of chemicals," Memos from Citizens for Clean Air For Mr. Church, Church papers.

"Memo No. 9 dealt with the promise Humble," Memo No. 9, Church papers.

"The last memorandum, prepared by Professor Church," Memo No. 10, Church papers.

"One of the other submissions from Citizens for Clean Air," Picture of Smog in Monterey County in 1965, Church papers.

17
HUMBLE'S SUPPORTERS REGROUP

"A new group emerged," "Group Formed to Back Humble Oil Refinery," *Salinas Californian*, August 10, 1965, 2.

"a locally printed mailer from an undisclosed group," Planned Growth For Monterey County, private papers of Warren Church.

"More support for Humble came from the Castroville Chamber," Gary Smart, "North County Backing Humble," *Salinas Californian*, August 25, 1965, 1.

"On August 13, Supervisor Church appointed," Oil Refinery Tour, Church papers.

"Peter DiMarco, who represented the chamber," Smart, "North County Backing Humble," *Californian*, 1.

"There was no odor," Smart, "North County Backing Humble," *Salinas Californian*, August 25, 1965, 2.

"the single most important person," conversations with Warren Church.

"Tripp noted that he had worke d," Smart, "North County Backing Humble," *Californian*, 2.

"Jack Simon, a civic leader in the Castroville area," Ibid.

"strongly advocated for Humble," Douglass Almond, "Refinery Rejection Would be Height of Folly," *Salinas Californian*, August 21, 1965, 6.

"already considering a rematch against Church," Church conversations.

"stated that if he were still on the Board," "Deaver Supports Humble," *Salinas Californian*, September 1, 1965, 1.

"Humble has more to offer than Firestone," Ibid, 4.

"The Firestone permit was approved," "Hudson Quits Board In Surprise Move," *Salinas Californian*, February 21, 1967, 4.

"During the Humble affair, the *Salinas Californian*," "'Smoggy' Thinking on the Peninsula," *Salinas Californian*, June 30, 1965, 6.

"debate over the incorporation of Castroville," Stan Cloud, "Refinery Site Incorporation Is Considered," *Monterey Peninsula Herald*, August 31, 1965, 1.

"The minute this thing (the board hearing)," Ibid.

"County Counsel William Stoffers threw cold water," Ibid, 2.

"Paul Hamerly stated that the question," Cloud, "Refinery Decision Tomorrow," *Herald*, 5.

"One of the biggest supporters," Ray March, "Refinery Would Bring Area Construction Boom," *Salinas Californian*, August 27, 1965, 7.

"We are in favor of Humble building," Ibid.

"Edward Gribi, a petroleum geologist," Edward Gribi, "Refinery Controversy Is Scientific Problem, *Salinas Californian*, August 25, 1965, 6.

"One ad in the *Watsonville Register-Pajaronian*," "Yvette helps Humble keep our rivers clean," *Watsonville Register-Pajaronian*, August 17, 1965, 4.

"Another series of ads," "Humble Oil and Refining Company Pledge to Citizens of Monterey County," *Santa Cruz Sentinel*, August 25, 1965, 6.

"another ad reprinted an editorial," "Humble:

An Example of Clean Operation," *Watsonville Register-Pajaronian*, August 27, 1965, 9.

"Humble sent Jack Gardner," Stan Cloud, "Gives Estimate of Air Pollution," *Monterey Peninsula Herald*, August 18, 1965, 35.

"Gardner asserted that these numbers," "Humble Oil Disclaims Pollution Estimate," *Monterey Peninsula Herald*, August 19, 1965, 36.

"Gardner insisted that all three compounds," Cloud, "Gives Estimate of Air Pollution," *Herald*, 35.

"The *Monterey Peninsula Herald* broke down," "Humble Oil Disclaims Pollution Estimate," *Herald*, 36.

"Humble disclaims the tons per day," Ibid.

"The fractions, based on ratios of refining capacity," Ibid.

"The *Herald* retorted that it never claimed," Ibid.

""including the Castroville Chamber of Commerce," "Refinery Topic Slated Tonight in Castroville," *Salinas Californian*, August 24, 1965, 3.

"the Kiwanis Club in Castroville," "Autos Cause Smog, Not Refineries," *Salinas Californian*, August 20, 1965, 3.

"Gardner dismissed the notion," Ibid.

"saltwater intrusion was becoming a serious problem," "Seawater Intrusion Monitoring," Monterey County Water Resources Agency, https://www.co.monterey.ca.us/government/government-links/water-resources-agency/programs/seawater-intrusion-monitoring, retrieved May 7, 2020.

"Humble estimated its water use," Ray March, "Humble Water Use Less Than Farming," *Salinas Californian*, August 30, 1965, 19.

"Humble claimed that its facility," Ibid.

"The editor of the *Castroville Times and Moss Landing Harbor News*," William Carnie, "Memo from the Editor," *Castroville Times and Moss Landing Harbor News*," August 1965, 4.

"Also raised was the issue of Humble dumping," March, "Humble Water Use Less Than Farming," *Californian*, 19.

"Gardner pushed that automobiles were the real source," "Autos Cause Smog, Not Refineries," *Californian*, 3.

"I can't say whether Monterey County will ever have smog," Ibid.

"The *Californian* remained steadfast," "What About the No. 1 Air Pollutant – Autos?" *Salinas Californian*, August 19, 1965, 6.

"The *Californian* also expressed outrage," "County Creates Unfavorable Industrial Climate," *Salinas Californian*, August 18, 1965, 6.

"One of the outspoken critics of Humble," "'Fallacious Reasoning' in Editorial Claimed," *Salinas Californian*, August 24, 1965, 6.

"The *Monterey Peninsula Herald* countered" "Who Says We Can't Pick and Choose?" *Monterey Peninsula Herald*, August 27, 1965, 1.

"With less than two weeks before the Board of Supervisors," "Humble Sees Bigger Investment," *Monterey Peninsula Herald*, August 20, 1965, 1.

"The *Monterey Peninsula Herald* sniffed," Ted Durien, "The Last Valley With Clean Air," *Monterey Peninsula Herald*, August 24, 1965, 1

18

THE BOARD INVESTIGATES

"reporter Stanley Cloud of the *Monterey Peninsula Herald*," Stan Cloud, "Tougher Fight Ahead Over Oil Permit," *Monterey Peninsula Herald*, July 29, 1965, 5.

"Board Chair Tom Hudson said that he expected," "Supervisors to Rule On Humble Oil Plant," *Salinas Californian*, July 30, 1965, 1.

"North County Supervisor Warren Church," "Supervisor Sees Delay For Humble," *Salinas Californian*, August 2, 1965, 1.

"When the supervisors met the first Tuesday," "Humble Hearing Set Aug. 31," *Salinas Californian*, August 3, 1965, 1.

"Supervisor Andy Anderson requested," Ibid, 1-2.

"The pro-Humble editors at the *Salinas Californian*," "New Delay on Humble Oil Embarassing," *Salinas Californian*, August 4, 1965, 6.

"noted that the refinery was," Memo from the Editor, *Castroville Times and Moss Landing Harbor News*, probably August 24, 1965, 4.

"A good deal of credit for bringing," Ibid.

"Born in King City in 1908," Steve Harrison, "Harold George Henry," Find a Grave, https://www.findagrave.com/memorial/23569974/harold-george-henry, retrieved September 18, 2019.

"His father served on the first city council," "One of Earliest Local Citizens, G.P. Henry Buried Saaturday," *King City Rustler-Herald*, May 18, 1950, 8.

"He worked in management with milling," "Supervisor Harold Henry Dies Suddenly in King City," *Salinas Californian*, April 25, 1966, 2.

"a bean and grain broker," "Harold Henry, South County Supervisor, Dies of Heart Attack," *Monterey Peninsula Herald*, April 25, 1966, 2.

"Henry worked in civilian defense," "Supervisor Harold Henry Dies Suddenly in King City," *Californian*, 2.

"He was elected to the city council," Harrison, "Harold George Henry."

"Despite describing him," "County Loses Dedicated Public Official," *Salinas Californian*, April 25, 1966, 6.

"The Peninsula and the rest of the county,"

"Harold Henry, South County Supervisor, Dies of Heart Attack," *Herald*, 1.

"He also favored diversifying," Ray March, "Board To Act On Humble Oil," *Salinas Californian*, September 1, 1965, 2.

"Henry clung to the words," "Gonzales Chamber Hears Henry Discuss Humble," *Salinas Californian*, August 13, 1965, 15.

"Described by The *Californian*'s Ray March," email from Ray March, August 15, 2019.

"Henry's wavering became evident again," "Harold Henry Requests View of Modern Refinery," *Salinas Californian*, August 18, 1965, 8.

"The following week, Henry pushed a visit," "Northern Refinery Tour Set," *Monterey Peninsula Herald*, August 25, 1965, 1.

"The supervisors were to visit," Edward W. Munson, "Summary of Information Provided by Officials at Anacortes," Monterey County Health Department memorandum, August 30, 1965, 1.

"There was a third refinery," Stan Cloud, "What Is A 'Modern' Refinery?," *Monterey Peninsula Herald*, August 28, 1965, 2.

"Gemini 5 splashed down," Ibid, 1.

"The organization of the trip fell to Henry," Ray March, "Refineries Stabilize Community Economy," *Salinas Californian*, August 28, 1965, 1.

"Greeted by a handpicked selection," "List of guests for the Anacortes luncheon at the Skyline Marina," Private papers of Warren Church, August 25, 1965.

"The chatter during the lunch," Stan Cloud, "No Comparison In Refinery Situations, Finds Hudson," *Monterey Peninsula Herald*, August 27, 1965, 6.

"Bechtel's experts emphasized that a modern refinery," Cloud, "What Is A 'Modern' Refinery?" *Herald*, 2.

"The days of the old robber barons," Ibid.

"March of The *Californian*," Ray March,

"Supervisors Learn Anacortes Likes Its Two Refineries," *Salinas Californian*, August 28, 1965, 1.

"The lack of agricultural damage," Stan Cloud, "Refinery Decision Tomorrow," *Monterey Peninsula Herald*, September 1, 1965, 2.

"aware that there was no air pollution," Munson, "Summary of Information Provided by Officials at Anacortes," Health Department memorandum, 1.

"that air pollution monitoring was 'not done routinely,'" Ibid.

"pointed out that the nearly continual," Cloud, "No Comparison In Refinery Situations, Finds Hudson," *Herald*, 6.

"Humble officials claimed that the Moss Landing refinery," Cloud, "What Is A 'Modern' Refinery?" *Herald*, 2.

"They give assurances that the amount," Ibid.

"I think we're doing everything that's reasonable," Ibid.

"Carmel resident L.J. Fletcher," "Anacortes – A Report On Smog," *Monterey Peninsula Herald*, August 27, 1965, 1-2.

"Wally Funk, former owner of the Anacortes," March, "Refineries Stabilize Community Economy," *Californian*, 2.

"During the tour Monterey County officials," Ibid.

"Cloud, in a story on his trip to Anacortes," Stan Cloud, "For Anacortes, Refineries Are Fine, State Residents," *Monterey Peninsula Herald*, August 30, 1965, 16.

"Cloud noted significant differences between Moss Landing," Ibid.

"Both March," March, "Supervisors Learn Anacortes Likes Its Two Refineries," *Californian*, 1.

"and Cloud," Cloud, "No Comparison In Refinery Situations, Finds Hudson," *Herald*, 6.

"Cloud stated that the only odor concerns," Cloud, "For Anacortes, Refineries Are

Fine, State Residents," *Monterey Peninsula Herald*, August 30, 1965, 16.

"Henry's goal in proposing the trip to Anacortes," Cloud, "No Comparison In Refinery Situations, Finds Hudson," *Herald*, 6.

"Hudson dismissed the idea that Anacortes," Ibid, 1.

"Henry pushed back against Hudson's position," "Supervisors Disagree On Comparison," *Salinas Californian*, August 30, 1965, 1.

"one of the Texaco officials admitted," Cloud, "No Comparison In Refinery Situations, Finds Hudson," *Herald*, 6.

"The *Watsonville Register-Pajaronian* looked at all," "Must everything depend on a count of noses?" *Watsonville Register-Pajaronian*, August 17, 1965, 20

19
WARREN CHURCH'S CONUNDRUM

"He made his mind up early," author's conversations with Warren Church.

"Church ran a few weeks-long write-in campaign," "The Vote," *Salinas Californian*, June 6, 1959, 1.

"The *Herald* called it," Earl Hofeldt, "Crabbe, Birch in Run-off for Tax Collector," *Monterey Peninsula Herald*, June 4, 1958, 1.

"Church was elected to the Monterey County Board of Education," Church conversations.

"Unlike his previous races, Deaver," "6 candidates seek north county supervisor's seat," *Watsonville Register-Pajaronian*, May 26, 1964, 9.

"a new interim zoning ordinance and building code," Church conversations.

"In the 1964 campaign, he touted," "6 candidates seek north county supervisor's seat," *Register-Pajaronian*, 9.

"It is not a coincidence," Deaver Contributors, Church papers.

"Allmond primarily garnered support," Ibid.

"Deaver had lost touch with many of his traditional," Church conversations.

"An important issue in the 1964 campaign was incorporation," "N. County Supervisor Aspirants Give Views On Incorporation Plan," *Salinas Californian*, undated article, between November 15, 1963 and February 24, 1964, no page identified.

"incorporation support did not stop at the borders," Ibid.

"The committee even drew up plans," "Castroville Lusts After Moss Landing's Industry," *the advocate*, April 1966, 3.

"Allmond was a member of the committee," "N. County Supervisor Aspirants Give Views On Incorporation Plan," *Californian*, no page identified.

"The other candidates either supported the incorporation," campaign summary, Church papers.

"The only candidate to openly oppose," "N. County Supervisor Aspirants Give Views On Incorporation Plan," *Californian*, no page identified.

"Church's platform also included creating," Eric Brazil, "Candidates for Supervisor Stage Big Political Show," *Salinas Californian*, May 28, 1964, 1.

"His goal was to kickstart the county," Church conversations.

"When Church officially filed for supervisor," "Nine Candidates Take Our Papers First Day," *Salinas Californian*, February 24, 1964, 3.

"Church's platform on protecting prime agricultural land," Warren Church Candidate for Supervisor: a county Democratic leader, Church papers.

"Church also made one other major campaign

promise," "Church Is Candidate For Board," *Salinas Californian*, undated, late 1963, 1.

"Commenting on his unofficial referendum plan," Ibid.

"The June 1964 primary," "Voting Precincts of Monterey County – by Supervisorial District," Church papers.

"Of the six candidates in that election," campaign summary, Church papers.

"Only Coffill expressed concerns," "North County Residents Express Varied Views on Proposed Humble Oil Refinery at Moss Landing," *Castroville Times and Moss Landing Harbor News*, August 31, 1965, 1.

"The November election pitted Deaver," Ray March, "Deaver Is Defeated By Church," *Salinas Californian*, November 4, 1964, 4.

"who conducted an extensive door-to-door," Election notes, Church papers.

"The *Californian* declared Church's," "Warren Church Upsets Deaver," *Salinas Californian*, November 4, 1964, 1.

"One of those exceptions happened in the days," "Refineries Smell Sweet," *Watsonville Register-Pajaronian*, February 17, 1965, 2.

"For Church in particular," Church conversations.

"Church asked the voters of his district," Random Survey – Humble Oil, private papers of Warren Church.

"it was now clear to him," Church conversations.

"The interim zoning ordinance that contributed," Ibid.

"Church would often mention," Ibid.

"there was also widespread support for tight controls," Ibid.

"Stanley Cloud, writing later in the year," Stan Cloud, "A Bettor's Guide to the Monterey County Board of Supervisors," *the advocate*, November 1965, 1.

"In his education on oil refining," Activities and Reasoning of Supervisor Warren Church in Regard to Humble Oil Application, Church papers.

"Church's request to delay came partly from his discomfort," Ibid.

"I did not want to rush into the Humble decision," Ibid.

"Crucial in Church's thinking style," Ibid.

"He even mentioned that there was a moral obligation," Humble Oil Application for Special Permit, September 2, 1965, Church papers.

Church also carefully noted that almost all," Activities and Reasoning of Supervisor Warren Church in Regard to Humble Oil Application, Church papers, 2.

"The new ones such as those at Anacortes," Ibid, 1.

"Years later, it was a position," authors' interview with Ruth Andresen, August 2, 2019.

"Another important factor in Church's decision-making," Activities and Reasoning of Supervisor Warren Church in Regard to Humble Oil Application, Church papers, 1.

"Gus Baumann of Citizens for Clean Air," Gus Bauman, "Outstanding," *Monterey Peninsula Herald*, September 6, 1965, 14.

"After the trip to Anacortes, Church firmed up," Church conversations.

"Church ventured on a solo fact-finding excursion," Ray March, "Supervisors Learn That Anacortes Likes Its Two Refineries," *Salinas Californian*, August 27, 1965, 2.

"conduct his own research with the community's inhabitants," Church conversations.

"his notes remark that both refineries at Anacortes were small," Anacortes notes, Church papers.

"Church also became aware during this trip," Stan Cloud, "Humble's Intent Still In Doubt," *Monterey Peninsula Herald*, March 31, 1965, 2.

20

THE OPPOSITION STRIKES BACK

"A gloomy and bitter *Monterey Peninsula Herald*," Allen Griffin, "Money Talks, So Hold Your Nose," *Monterey Peninsula Herald*, September 7, 1965, 1.

"The same supervisors who refused," Ibid.

"anger turned toward Supervisor Harold Henry" "Check Out Reports of Henry Recall Move," *Monterey Peninsula Herald*, September 4, 1964, 2.

"Mr. Henry's support has been waning anyway," Ibid.

"Ten days after the vote on the permit," "Air Control Plan Action Delayed," *Salinas Californian*, September 15, 1965, 1.

"Opposition to the air pollution control district," Stan Cloud, "Smog District Action Delayed," *Monterey Peninsula Herald*, September 15, 1965, 1.

"The ag community raised concerns," "Air Control Plan Slated For Hearing," *Salinas Californian*, September 13, 1965, 2.

"The farmers joined with PG&E," Cloud, "Smog District Action Delayed," *Herald*, 2.

"There is no urgency," "Air Control Plan Action Delayed," *Californian*, 1.

"Humble, on the other hand, expressed support," "Humble Oil Backs Plan For County," *Salinas Californian*, September 15, 1965, 1.

"At the Board of Supervisors meeting," Cloud, "Smog District Action Delayed," *Herald*, 2.

"There may be a little face-saving," Ibid.

"Michaud left frustrated," "Air Control Plan Action Delayed," *Californian*, 1.

"Although a few people, including Charles Kramer" Lillian Woodward, "New Resident for The Landing," *Monterey Peninsula Herald*, September 11, 1965, 10.

"Bill Burleigh, received the nod," "New City Attorney For Carmel," *Monterey Peninsula Herald*, May 12, 1965, 1.

"Burleigh, still a relative newcomer to the area," authors' interview with Bill Burleigh, July 25, 2019.

"I was the only one they didn't know," Ibid.

"Burleigh announced the circulation of petitions," "Referendum Is Sought On Humble Oil Permit," *Salinas Californian*, September 17, 1965, 1.

"The mayors of six Monterey County cities," "Mayor's Join Anti-Oil Campaign," *Monterey Peninsula Herald*, September 20, 1965, 1.

"This is the one (Humble controversy)," Ibid.

"Burleigh, a native of Virginia," "New City Attorney For Carmel," *Herald*, 1-3.

"I didn't get paid," Burleigh interview.

"two leaders of the Citizens for Clean Air," "Referendum Is Sought On Humble Oil Permit," *Salinas Californian*, September 17, 1965, 1.

"The petition drive caused the formation," "Oil Refinery Referendum," *Monterey Peninsula Herald*, September 21, 1965, 14.

"gathered a massive assortment of volunteers," "Humble Referendum Drive Into High Gear," *Monterey Peninsula Herald*, September 21, 1965, 1.

"women were an important part of the drive," authors' interview with Ruth Andresen, Aug. 2, 2019.

"To gain ballot status," "Humble Referendum Plans Are Opposed," *Salinas Californian*, September 21, 1965, 1-2.

"The matter should be decided by the people," "Referendum Is Sought On Humble Oil Permit," *Californian*, 2.

"In California, board of supervisors have considerable power," "County Structure & Powers," California State Association of Counties, https://www.counties.org/

general-information/county-structure-0, retrieved May 17, 2020.

"The basis for the referendum rested," "Humble Referendum Plans Are Opposed," *Salinas Californian*, September 21, 1965, 1.

"Even the anti-Humble *Santa Cruz Sentinel*," Alan Pugh, "Carmel Council To Seek Public Vote To Block Humble Oil Permit," *Santa Cruz Sentinel*, September 19, 1965, 9.

"As the *Monterey Peninsula Herald* called it," F.K. Arthur, "Thoughts on the Refinery, Jazz and an Alert Law," *Monterey Peninsula Herald*, September 21, 1965, 1.

"the legality of the referendum immediately faced criticism," "Humble Referendum Plans Are Opposed," *Californian*, 1.

"Tom Hudson responded with a 'No comment,'" Ibid, 2.

"Warren Church encountered refinery opponent," authors' interview with Ruth Andresen, Aug. 2, 2019.

"Burleigh announced that he had 6,300," "Anti-Smog Signatures Total 7,000," *Monterey Peninsula Herald*, September 23, 1965, 1.

"Burleigh brought a huge stack of petitions," "Supervisors Reject Anti-Refinery Petitions," *Monterey Peninsula Herald*, September 24, 1.

"Stoffers countered Burleigh," "Board Rejects Humble Vote," *Salinas Californian*, September 24, 1965, 1.

"In my opinion," said Stoffers," Ibid.

"Hudson moved for the supervisors," "Board Rejects Humble Vote," *Californian*, 1.

"If you feel the way you do," Ibid, 2.

"The supervisors voted down the motion 3-2," Ibid.

"The always process-respecting Church," Ibid.

"Burleigh, frustrated by the supervisors' rejection," "Supervisors Reject Anti-Refinery Petitions," *Herald*, 1.

21

MONTEREY COUNTY SETS A NEW STANDARD

"Humble officials estimated that the conditions," "Vote on refinery blocked by board," *Watsonville Register-Pajaronian*, September 25, 1965, 1.

"His notes and correspondence show engagement," private papers of Warren Church.

"A week later, DeMars added five more," "Humble Hearing Set Aug. 31," *Salinas Californian*, August 3, 1965, 1.

"most observers did not expect many changes," "Conditions For Humble Will Be Heard Friday," *Salinas Californian*, September 23, 1965, 4.

"Some, like the editors of the *Monterey Peninsula Herald*," Allen Griffin, "Money Talks So Hold Your Nose," *Monterey Peninsula Herald*, "September 7, 1965, 1.

"Others heard of Church's comments," "Humble Hearing Set Aug. 31," *Californian*, 1.

"The writers at the *Salinas Californian* predicted," "Conditions For Humble Will Be Heard Friday," *Salinas Californian*, September 23, 1965, 4.

"Debating their concerns over the possible conditions," "County to send 'observer' to refinery rules meeting," *Watsonville Register-Pajaronian*, September 22, 1965, 1.

"Also present for the setting of conditions," Stan Cloud, "Supervisors To Meet on Pollution," *Monterey Peninsula Herald*, September 23, 1965, 2.

"The 36 conditions," Ray March, "County Staff Men Study Controls on Refinery," *Salinas Californian*, August 21, 1965, 18.

"Stoffers, DeMars and Munson identified five," Letter from County Counsel to Warren Church, dated August 23, 1965, Church papers.

"After the supervisors dismissed the referendum petition," Stan Cloud, "Supervisors Reject Anti-Refinery Petitions," *Monterey Peninsula Herald*, September 24, 1965, 1.

"Earl Moser called for water cleanliness," "Board Rejects Humble Vote," *Salinas Californian*, September 24, 1965, 2.

"Dave Williams and Wayne Bowman spoke," "Conditions For Humble Will Be Heard Friday," *Salinas Californian*, September 23, 1965, 2.

"Andy Anderson wanted to keep," "Meeting Set On Oil Referendum," *Monterey Peninsula Herald*, September 27, 1965, 2.

"Tom Hudson tried repeatedly to delay," "'Big Three' Dominated Sessions," *Salinas Californian*, September 25, 1965, 1.

"it was Hudson who pushed back," "Meeting Set On Oil Referendum," *Herald*, 1965, 2.

"Hudson proposed some minor clarifications," "'Big Three' Dominated Sessions," *Californian*, 1.

"Both made efforts to clarify permit," *Herald*, 1965, 2.

"Atteridge scoffed at delays," Ray March, "Humble Gets Permit, 3-2," *Salinas Californian*, September 25, 1965, 1.

"Harold Henry seemed to disappear," Ibid, 2.

"Church came to the meeting," Activities and Reasoning of Supervisor Warren Church in Regard to Humble Oil Application, Church papers.

"The meeting would extend past midnight," "Meeting Set On Oil Referendum," *Herald*, 2.

"When the meeting began," Stan Cloud, "Board Issues Humble Permit," *Monterey Peninsula Herald*, September 25, 1965, 1.

"In contrast to past hearings," Ibid.

"Hudson tried to delay a vote," "Meeting Set On Oil Referendum," *Herald*, 2.

"urging that the board wrap things up," "'Big Three' Dominated Sessions," *Californian*, 1.

"Anderson, however, continued to resist," "Meeting Set On Oil Referendum," *Herald*, 2.

"At the forefront of agriculture's demands stood Jack Bias," March, "Humble Gets Permit, 3-2," *Californian*, 1.

"Dave Williams of Bruce Church Inc. broached," Ibid, 2.

"wrote in his notes that Humble," Humble notes, Church papers.

"During the supervisors' trip to Anacortes," Stan Cloud, "Humble's Intent Still In Doubt," *Monterey Peninsula Herald*, March 31, 1965, 2.

"R.A. Winslow, Humble's assistant general manager," March, "Humble Gets Permit, 3-2," *Californian*, 2.

"As the meeting wore on into the evening,' Ibid.

"Church, who had originally," Humble Conditions, Church papers.

"The other four conditions received support," Humble notes, Church papers.

"O'Connell included in his recommendations," Cloud, "Board Issues Humble Permit," *Herald*, 2.

"Church felt this gave Humble," Humble notes, Church papers.

"He requested that Stoffers include," "Humble Conditions," Church papers.

"Church's notes also included," Ibid.

"For Church, this was an essential," Humble notes, Church papers.

"nearly every vote made by the Board," "'Big Three' Dominated Sessions," *Californian*, 1-2.

"Observers reasoned that Hudson and Anderson," Cloud, "Board Issues Humble Permit," *Herald*, 1.

"a few original ones," "Curbs On Refinery Total 39," *Salinas Californian*, September 25, 1965, 1.

"Humble officials tried to put on a good face," "Vote on refinery blocked by board,"

Watsonville Register-Pajaronian, September 25, 1965, 1.

"At the Planning Commission meeting in July," "Humble To Appeal To County Board," *Salinas Californian*, July 29, 1965, 2.

"J. Prince Warner, Humble vice-president, "Proponents Too Tired To Cheer," *Monterey Peninsula Herald*, September 3, 1965, 5.

"One unidentified Humble official said," "Curbs On Refinery Total 39," *Californian*, 1.

"Another moaned about the county-imposed restrictions," Cloud, "Board Issues Humble Permit," *Herald*, 1.

"The *Californian* made note that these regulations," "Curbs On Refinery Total 39," *Californian*, 1.

"McGraw Hill," Letter received September 24, 1965, Monterey County Board of Supervisor archives.

"Oil and Gas Journal," Letter dated October 29, 1965, Supervisor archives.

"If this had been a boxing match" March, "Humble Gets Permit, 3-2," *Californian*, 2.

22

THE REFERENDUM GOES TO COURT

"Bill Burleigh announced that opponents," "Anti-Humble Group Meets," *Salinas Californian*, September 27, 1965, 1.

"Church said his group would fund Burleigh's," "Pledge Oil Fight To Fullest," *Monterey Peninsula Herald*, September 28, 1965, 1.

"the group sought $30,000," "Fund drive to fight refinery on," *Watsonville Register-Pajaronian*, October 14, 1965, 2.

'Church mentioned that a similar strategy," "Pledge Oil Fight To Fullest," *Herald*, 2.

"This is going to obtain," Ibid, 1.

"Burleigh followed with the announcement," "Letters Urged Against Refinery," *Monterey Peninsula Herald*, October 1, 1965, 4.

"Stirrings of a boycott of Humble products," Shirlie Stoddard, "Board Powers," *Monterey Peninsula Herald*, September 29, 1965, 14.

"Longtime opponent Gus Bauman," Gus Bauman, "A Moral Issue," *Monterey Peninsula Herald*, December 2, 1965, 22.

"On October 19, Burleigh filed," "Suit Asks Vote On Refinery," *Monterey Peninsula Herald*, October 19, 1965, 1.

"The county's position was that the granting," "Humble Opponents Seek Writ," *Salinas Californian*, October 19, 1965, 1.

"The power to be exercised is legislative," "Suit Asks Vote On Refinery," *Herald*, 2.

"Burleigh noted that the new air and water pollution," Ibid.

"The suit was presented to Judge Gordon Campbell," "Humble Opponents Seek Writ," *Californian*, 1.

"Campbell did issue an alternative writ of mandate," "Suit Asks Vote On Refinery," *Herald*, 1.

"Western Oil and Gas Association, a trade organization," "'Six Cities' Reacts To L.A. Smog Suit," *Monterey Peninsula Herald*, November 5, 1965, 4.

"This suit, by Western Oil and Gas," Ibid.

"Humble responded in Superior Court," "Humble Oil Files Complaint," *Monterey Peninsula Herald*, November 16, 1965, 1.

"it also argued that the area," Ibid, 2.

"Professor Church took advantage of Humble's complaint," Ibid.

"This action on the part of Humble Oil," Ibid.

"With the court hearing," "Judges Out On Hearing For Humble," *Salinas Californian*, November 22, 1965, 1.

"On the day of the court hearing," "Full Courtroom Hears Debate On Oil

Refinery," *Salinas Californian*, November 24, 1965, 1-2.

"Stoffers and Hamerly both proceeded to argue," Stan Cloud, "Hearing Opens On Plea For Oil Referendum," *Monterey Peninsula Herald*, November 24, 1965, 2.

"As he first began to present evidence," Ibid, 1.

"Burleigh then called Hudson to the stand," "Full Courtroom Hears Debate On Oil Refinery," *Californian*, 1-2.

"Burleigh continued to try to use Hudson's words," Cloud, "Hearing Opens On Plea For Oil Referendum," *Herald*, 2.

"Burleigh based his argument that interim zoning," Stan Cloud, "Refinery Issue Under Study," *Monterey Peninsula Herald*, November 25, 1965, 2.

"Burleigh read from a transcript from the board hearing," Cloud, "Hearing Opens On Plea For Oil Referendum," *Herald*, 2.

"Burleigh also noted that the Planning Commission is empowered," Cloud, "Refinery Issue Under Study," *Herald*, 2.

"Why did they take it away," Cloud, "Hearing Opens On Plea For Oil Referendum," *Herald*, 2.

"Stoffers countered that Burleigh was wrong," Cloud, "Refinery Issue Under Study," *Herald*, 2.

Burleigh challenged Stoffer's position," "Refinery arguments heard; decision 2 months away," *Watsonville Register-Pajaronian*, November 25, 1965, 2

"Burleigh also asked Don Compton," Cloud, "Hearing Opens On Plea For Oil Referendum," *Herald*, 2.

"Hamerly responded by calling Jack Gardner," "Full Courtroom Hears Debate On Oil Refinery," *Californian*, 2.

"As Burleigh ended his case," Cloud, "Hearing Opens On Plea For Oil Referendum," *Herald*, 2.

"I think it's only fair to tell you," Cloud, "Refinery Issue Under Study," *Herald*, 2

23
TOM HUDSON—HUMBLE'S BANE

"Andy Anderson, in the newly reconstituted fourth," Warren Church, Monterey County Supervisors 1852-2004, unpublished, 2004, 8.

"A court challenge earlier in the decade," "Robert Allen Griffin," California Press Foundation, https://cal-press.wildapricot.org/hall-of-fame_robert-allen-griffin, retrieved June 1, 2020.

"The other supervisor elected," Church, Supervisors, 4-10.

"Prior to the 1964 election," J. Morgan Kousser, "Tacking Stacking and Cracking: Race and Reapportionment in Monterey County, 1981-92," revised version, 26.

"The other supervisor elected in 1964," Church, Supervisors 5.

"Arthur Atteridge had only taken office in 1963," Ibid, 6.

"and Harold Henry in 1959," Ibid, 7.

"Often sporting a Stetson," Jack Fraser, "Monterey's Supervisor's a Young Man on the Go," *San Jose Mercury*, February 21, 1960, newspaper clipping from Monterey Public Library with no page number.

"even later in life while in his 50s," Margo Burke, "Years After His Death, Many Remember Fiery Tom Hudson," *Monterey Peninsula Herald*, October 21, 1985, 15.

"Hudson also possessed a pilot's license," email from Ray March, August 31, 2019.

"a peninsula resident once commented," Fraser, "Monterey's Supervisor's a Young Man on the Go," Mercury, newspaper clipping from Monterey Public Library with no page number.

"Hudson was either deeply admired," Burke, "Years After His Death, Many Remember Fiery Tom Hudson," *Monterey Peninsula Herald*, 15.

"He is one of those rare birds," Ibid.

"A Republican with strong conservation ties," Fraser, "Monterey's Supervisor's a Young Man on the Go," Mercury, newspaper clipping from Monterey Public Library with no page number.

"Hudson's family had long played," email from Tom Hudson, February 15, 2020.

"I hope my children," Fraser, "Monterey's Supervisor's a Young Man on the Go," Mercury, clipping from Monterey Public Library with no page number.

"Some called him a political scoundrel," email from Stanley Cloud, August 31, 1965.

"Behind the scenes he pleaded," author's conversations with Warren Church.

"he had a more personal reason," David Spradling, "Dreams of Cannery Row. After the Sardines, What?" Monterey Public Library, August 26, 2014, https://www.monterey.org/library/About-Us/Newsroom/dreams-of-cannery-row-after-the-sardines-what, retrieved April 10, 2020.

"described his interactions with the supervisors," email from Stanley Cloud, May 30, 2020.

"Cloud recalled a chance encounter," Stan Cloud, "The Making of a Demagogue: 1966," *the advocate*, August 1966, 6-7.

"when Hudson learned that Cloud wrote anonymously," Cloud email, August 31, 2019.

"two of the people Hudson targeted," Cloud, "The Making of a Demagogue: 1966," advocate, 7.

"Hudson's maternal grandfather, Alexander McMillan Allan," Jim Johnson, "Point Lobos Stone House Demolition, development plan rankle neighbors,

Monterey Herald, October 16, 2015, https://www.montereyherald.com/2015/10/16/point-lobos-stone-house-demolition-development-plans-rankle-neighbors/, retrieved May 26, 2020.

"Hudson's great-grandfather, also named Thomson Jay Hudson," "About New Thought Author Thomson Jay Hudson," New Thought Wisdom, https://www.newthoughtwisdom.com/thomas-jay-hudson.html, retrieved February 11, 2020.

"The book made the senior Hudson," "Thomson Jay Hudson, Hypnosis And The Power Of The Subconscious Mind, "self-hypnosis—the key, https://www.self-hypnosis-the-key.com/thomson-jay-hudson.html, retrieved May 26, 2020.

"His theories were an interesting mix of science," "Thomson Jay Hudson, Acclaimed Psychic Researcher," Cornerstone Books, http://thomsonjayhudson.wwwhubs.com/, retrieved May 26, 2020.

"Ironically, while in his 20s in Michigan," "About New Thought Author Thomson Jay Hudson," New Thought.

"Hudson's grandfather, Charles Bradford Hudson," Edan Milton Hughes, Artists in California 1786-1940, volume 2. Hughes Publishing Company, 1989. 271.

"as the world's finest illustrator of marine life," Jeffrey Morseburg, "Charles Bradford Hudson, Monterey Peninsula Landscapes, July 6, 2011, https://charlesbradfordhudson.wordpress.com/, retrieved February 11, 2020.

"Hudson's father, Lester Jay Hudson," "RADM Lester Jay Hudson," Find A Grave, https://www.findagrave.com/memorial/107787592/lester-jay-hudson, retrieved February 11, 2020.

"One of the most decorated," J.R. Potts, "U.S.S. San Diego (CL-53) CLAA-53), Military Factory, https://en.wikipedia.org/wiki/USS_San_Diego_(CL-53), retrieved February 11, 2020.

"Thomson Jay Hudson was born," Burke, "Years After His Death, Many Remember Fiery Tom Hudson," *Herald*, 15.

"faked a vision test," "'Young Man' Tom Hudson Finds Pace Hasn't Slowed Since 1957," *Monterey Peninsula Herald*, January 19, 1963, newspaper clipping from Monterey Public Library with no page number.

"Hudson had to tape his glasses," Burke, "Years After His Death, Many Remember Fiery Tom Hudson," *Herald*, 15.

"at the age of 32," "'Young Man' Tom Hudson Finds Pace Hasn't Slowed Since 1957," *Herald*, newspaper clipping from Monterey Public Library with no page number.

"At one point," Ibid.

"One of his passionate fights," "Two Found Dead in Crash Wreckage," *Monterey Peninsula Herald*, October 8, 1975, newspaper clipping from Monterey Public Library with no page number.

"(Hudson) had a lot of aggressiveness," Burke, "Years After His Death, Many Remember Fiery Tom Hudson," *Herald*, 15.

"He voted right before Hudson," "A Bettor's Guide to the Monterey County Board of Supervisors, *the advocate*, November, 1965, 1.

"His (Hudson's) usual method is to reveal the problem," Fraser, "Monterey's Supervisor's a Young Man on the Go," *Mercury*, newspaper clipping from Monterey Public Library with no page number.

"The opposing sides were still developing," "Humble To Abandon Refinery?" *Monterey Peninsula Herald*, April 13, 1965, 1.

"Yet Humble bristled publicly," "Humble Decision Deferred to May 31," *Salinas Californian*, March 31, 1965, 1.

"Humble Oil was in contact with the San Francisco Bay city of Benicia," authors' interview with Dr. Jim Lessenger, August 3, 2019.

"he opened a Citizens for Clean Air forum,"

"Experts on Pollution See Loss of Pure Air," *Monterey Peninsula Herald*, May 4, 1965, 2.

"he desperately tried to find an anti-Humble motion," Church conversations.

"they would routinely call out interference by local politicians," "Humble Eyes Alternate Location at Martinez," *Salinas Californian*, October 9, 1965, 1.

24
SHIFTING POLITICAL WINDS

"Supervisor Warren Church called for setting up," "Church Wants Smog Stations Built Now," *Monterey Peninsula Herald*, September 29, 1965, newspaper clipping from private papers of Warren Church, page unknown.

"I personally feel these stations," Ibid.

"Supervisor Tom Hudson immediately latched," Ibid.

"In about a month, Munson was back," "Humble Oil Monitoring Sites Picked," *Salinas Californian*, November 2, 1965, 1-2.

"Around this same time, Humble announced," "Humble Refinery Is Now on Design Basis, Gardner Says," *Salinas Californian*, November 20, 1965, 1.

"At the first board meeting in October," "Second Oil Vote Rejection," *Monterey Peninsula Herald*, October 5, 1965, 1.

"The people have spoken and have probably spoken," Ibid, 2.

"Church stated he would not object," Ibid.

"After Carmel City Attorney Bill Burleigh filed a writ of mandate in Superior Court," "Hudson Will Pursue Humble Vote Change," *Salinas Californian*, October 20, 1965, 1.

"This is the last opportunity that the board," Ibid.

"He tried again, for what be a fourth time,"

"Humble Oil Permit Is Signed," *Monterey Peninsula Herald*, October 26, 1965, 1.

"Professor Church said that a task force," "Area Anti-Humble Group Named; Function Not clear," *Salinas Californian*, October 27, 1965, 2.

"Word spread that other groups were forming," "Permit Granted Humble Refinery," *Watsonville Register-Pajaronian*, October 27, 1965, 2.

"When the Salinas Group was contacted," "Area Anti-Humble Group Named; Function Not clear," *Californian*, 2.

"Then, seemingly out of nowhere, came rumors," "Humble Oil Co. Deemphasizes Alternate Site, *Salinas Californian*, October 11, 1965, 1.

"Humble representative Jack Gardner appeared at a luncheon," "No Change in Humble Oil Plans, MCID Told," *Monterey Peninsula Herald*, October 23, 1965, 6.

"We're even more confident than ever," Ibid.

"By November, Gardner announced," "Humble Refinery Is Now on Design Basis, Gardner Says," *Californian*, November 20, 1965, 1.

"We would not build if we thought," Ibid.

"Air pollution had been a growing concern," Stan Cloud, "County Smog Violators Win Long Reprieve," *Monterey Peninsula Herald*, November 10, 1965, 1.

"Three major violators remained," Ibid.

"While all three were able to get variances," Ibid, 2.

"Multiple individuals stepped forward to complain," Ibid.

"Supervisor Church complained that if Kaiser," Ibid.

"Berman Steel said it was looking for a furnace," Ibid.

"The third violator was the county itself," Ibid.

"The *Herald* took particular displeasure," Franklin K. Arthur, "Sierra Club's Good

Advice: 'Think Twice,'" *Monterey Peninsula Herald*, March 10, 1965, 1.

"To the anti-Humble observers," Cloud, "County Smog Violators Win Long Reprieve," *Herald*, November 10, 1965, 2.

"While the county vacillated at enforcing," "Santa Cruz Favors Air Control," *Monterey Peninsula Herald*, November 16, 1965, 13.

"At the end of November," "County Takes Lead In Forming Air District," *Santa Cruz Sentinel*, November 30, 1965, 16.

"However, there was no guarantee," "Supervisor Henry Opposes Pollution Control District," *Monterey Peninsula Herald*, November 20, 1965, 26.

"The county's current air pollution control ordinance," Ibid.

"Yet as the air pollution control district appeared," Stan Cloud, "Farm Advisory Group Favors Smog District," *Monterey Peninsula Herald*, December 3, 1965, 3.

"The support of the ag committee for an air pollution control," Ibid.

"at the December 7, supervisors' meeting" Stan Cloud, "Hearing Set On Smog District," *Monterey Peninsula Herald*, December 6, 1965, 12.

"Prior to Monterey County's dealing with Humble," Arthur C. Stern, "History of Air Pollution Legislation in the United States," Journal of the Air Pollution Control Association, Taylor and Francis Group, March 12, 2012, https://www.tandfonline.com/doi/pdf/10.1080/00022470.1982.10465369, retrieved February 17, 2020.

"It was one of the reasons that Western Oil and Gas Association," "Six Cities Reacts to L.A. Smog Suit," *Monterey Peninsula Herald*, November 5, 1965, 4.

"Once again, a badly split Board of Supervisors," Stan Cloud, "Smog District Voted," *Monterey Peninsula Herald*, December 8, 1965, 1.

"The *Herald*'s editorial board embraced,"

"A Long Step -- More Clutter -- Smart Signing," *Monterey Peninsula Herald*, December 8, 1965, 1.

"The vote marked the first time that Church," Ibid, 8.

"If anything, the faltering vote on the Board of Supervisors," Ibid.

"Henry had already stated his opposition," "County Board Ok's Pollution Controls," *Salinas Californian*, December 8, 1965, 2.

"Anderson and Church both took strong positions," Cloud, "Smog District Voted," *Herald*, 8.

"Hudson, the indefatigable Humble opponent," Ibid.

"Included at the meeting was a Santa Cruz County delegation," "Burton Proposes Stop-Gap County Air Pollution Control," *Santa Cruz Sentinel*, December 10, 1965, 14.

"One of the topics of debate," Cloud, "Smog District Voted," *Herald*, 8.

"In the unusual position of playing down the middle," Ibid.

"A week later, the Board of Supervisors," "Moss Landing Zoning Extended for 1 Year," *Salinas Californian*, December 15, 1965, 1.

"In what the *Watsonville Register-Pajaronian*," "Zoning extended at Landing," *Watsonville Register-Pajaronian*, December 15, 1965, 2.

"Hudson and Anderson sought to exclude," "Moss Landing Zoning Extended for 1 Year," *Californian*, 1.

"When County Counsel William Stoffers informed Hudson," "Zoning extended at Landing," *Register-Pajaronian*, 2.

"Church said he did not support that position," "Moss Landing Zoning Extended for 1 Year," *Californian*, 1.

"Church preferred that the 50,000-barrel," Humble notes, Church papers.

"Hudson then turned away from the oil refinery exclusion." "Zoning extended at Landing," *Register-Pajaronian*, 2.

"Hudson did not abandon only Anderson," "Moss Landing Zoning Extended for 1 Year," *Californian*, 2.

"there was one more interesting development," "Anti-Humble Oil Forces Enlisting Tourists' Help," *Salinas Californian*, December 6, 1965, 4.

"Visitors who come here to enjoy," Ibid.

"Humble supporters such as Carol Leino," Carol Leino, "Smear Campaign Endangers Peninsula Tourist Trade," *Salinas Californian*, December 11, 1965, 6

25
HUMBLE WINS AGAIN

"In January, Vince Moore, executive director" "MCID Says 10 Refineries Would Be Bad for Monterey County," *Monterey Peninsula Herald*, January 22, 1966, 11.

"As the Crosby golf tournament," "Supervisor Deplores Pebble Beach Sewage," *Monterey Peninsula Herald*, February 2, 1966, 18.

"You could have Humble Oil," Ibid.

"Henry demanded that A.G. Michaud," Ibid.

"During this time, famed photographer," Ansel Adams, "We All Have a Stake," *Monterey Peninsula Herald*, February, 22, 1966, 14.

"the legal decision the Monterey Bay area," "Anti-refinery Petition Loses," *Monterey Peninsula Herald*, February 8, 1966, 1.

"The judge determined that the permit conditions," "Humble Issue Not Subject To Vote," *Salinas Californian*, 1965, 1.

"Harris then countered Burleigh's argument," "Anti-refinery Petition Loses," *Herald*, 1.

"Harris did leave a slight crack in the door," George Burkhardt, "Judge's ruling tips scales for refinery," *Watsonville Register-Pajaronian*, February 8, 1966, 2.

"The fight isn't over," "Anti-refinery Petition Loses," *Herald*, 1.

"I'm bitterly disappointed over this," "Anti-refinery Petition Loses," *Herald*, 1-2.

"Plaintiff William Howard Church promised," Ibid, 2.

"'Meanwhile,' said elated Humble executive," "Refinery Plans Are Still Alive," *Salinas Californian*, February 8, 1966, 1-2.

"the next day the Six Cities Fund," "Foes to keep up refinery battle," *Watsonville Register-Pajaronian*, February 9, 1966, 1.

"To the surprise of some," "New Legal Salvo Fired In Oil Fight," *Monterey Peninsula Herald*, February 18, 1966, 1.

"Burleigh contended that the interim ordinance," Ibid, 2.

"[V]ictory is in sight," Ibid, 1.

"The California State Parks Commission," "Humble opponent seeks support," *Watsonville Register-Pajaronian*, March 26, 1966, 2.

"The move surprised local officials," "State Park Commission Schedules Humble Oil Controversy Discussion," *Salinas Californian*, March 24, 1966, 7.

"When the parks commission met," Earl Hofeldt, "Anti-refinery Move Blocked By State Parks," *Monterey Peninsula Herald*, April 23, 1966, 2.

"Elsewhere, even the national and influential," Franklin K. Arthur, "Sierra Club's Good Advice: 'Think Twice,'" *Monterey Peninsula Herald*, March 10, 1966, 1.

"Questioned if the new lawsuit," "Monterey Peninsula Group Files Action To Block Humble," *Santa Cruz Sentinel*, February 18, 1966, 1.

"At least this has kept Humble," "Foes mount new legal assault on refinery," *Watsonville Register-Pajaronian*, March 18, 1966, 2.

"William Stoffers, Monterey County counsel," Ibid.

"Before the April 11 hearing," "County Group To Fight Smog," *Monterey Peninsula Herald*, March 9, 1966, 1.

"develop an organization with a long-term purpose," Ibid, 2.

"The April 11 hearing was short," "Refinery Arguments Heard," *Monterey Peninsula Herald*, April 11, 1966, 1.

"Burleigh staked his case," "Humble Tussle Before Harris," *Salinas Californian*, April 11, 1966, 1-2.

"I don't place much stock," Ibid, 2.

"Stoffers questioned if the Anti-Pollution Association," Ibid.

"Harris announced that he would have a ruling," Ibid.

"This time the ruling came," "Humble Oil Permit Still Stands," *Salinas Californian*, May 10, 1966, 1.

"However, Harris ruled against Stoffers' argument," Ibid, 2.

"Harris once again allowed Burleigh," Ibid 1-2.

"denying the defendants claim," "Anti-oil Petition Rejected," *Monterey Peninsula Herald*, May 10, 1966, 2.

"Years later, Burleigh said," authors' interview with Bill Burleigh, July 25, 2019

26
A HUMBLING EXPERIENCE

"During this time, Humble commissioned," "Poll on Humble in Progress," *Salinas Californian*, February 14, 1966, 1.

"the survey ran seven pages," "Humble Oil sampling opinion on industry," *Watsonville Register-Pajaronian*, February 16, 1966, 24.

"We're going full speed ahead," Ibid.

"In early March, Carmel City Councilmember," "Carmel In New Move On Humble,"

Monterey Peninsula Herald, March 10, 1966, 1.

"For some time, Tom Hudson," Stan Cloud, "'Card Club' Denied By Hudson," *Monterey Peninsula Herald*, April 1, 1966.

"On March 31, the *Salinas Californian*," "Humble Fan Club Planned By Hudson?" *Salinas Californian*, March 31, 1966, 1.

"The Sierra Club quickly squelched," "Sierra Club Won't Back Any Product," *Salinas Californian*, April 7, 1966, 1.

"The next day, the *Monterey Peninsula Herald*," Stan Cloud, "Card Club Denied By Hudson," *Monterey Peninsula Herald*, April 1, 1966, 1.

"Our directors do not share," "Battle Not Won, Says Church," *Monterey Peninsula Herald*, April 2, 1966, 1.

"At this same time, word leaked" "Supervisor Stays Silent On Humble," *Salinas Californian*, April 14, 1966, 4.

"often regarded as the most," Kenneth Reich, "Jesse Unruh, Key Political Figure in State, Dies at 64," Los Angeles Times, August 5, 1987, https://www.latimes.com/archives/la-xpm-1987-08-05-mn-809-story.html, retrieved February 24, 2020.

"President Johnson called him," President Johnson's Secretarial Staff, "President's Daily Diary entry 2/4/1968," DiscoverLBJ, https://discoverlbj.org/item/pdd-19680204, retrieved February 24, 2020.

"In January 1966, Hudson, a Republican," "Supervisor Stays Silent On Humble," *Californian*, 1 & 4.

"Around the time of the dinner, Hudson admitted," "Humble Fan Club Planned By Hudson?" *Salinas Californian*, March 31, 1966, 4.

"I don't think that warrants" "Supervisor Stays Silent On Humble," *Californian*, 4.

"Humble also had its own denial," Ibid.

"A few days before, Hudson, confident that Humble," "Supervisor Stays Silent On Humble," *Californian*, 1 & 4.

"including the *San Francisco Examiner*," "Monterey Oil Firm Eats Humble Words," *San Francisco Examiner*, March 31, 1966, 42.

"and *Los Angeles Times*," "Humble hints it might still build at Moss Landing," *Los Angeles Times*, March 31, 1966, part III, 9.

"Humble spokesperson DI Bolding announced," "Humble Oil Seeks New Site," *Monterey Peninsula Herald*, March 30,1966, 2.

"Bolding stated that Humble," "Humble Oil Options In East Bay," *Monterey Peninsula Herald*, April 5, 1966, 1-2.

"Economic changes affecting the industry," Ray March, "Humble May Abandon Area Refinery Plans," *Salinas Californian*, March 30, 1966, 1.

"If the economics are better somewhere else," "Humble Oil may pull out," *Watsonville Register-Pajaronian*, March 30, 1966, 1-2.

"The permits and the studies had at least cost," "Humble Says Refinery Plans Not Abandoned," *Santa Cruz Sentinel*, March 31, 1966, 1.

"tantalizing deepwater port was too rough," March, "Humble May Abandon Area Refinery Plans," *Californian*, 1.

"The *Watsonville Register-Pajaronian* snickered," "Did someone do a favor for Humble Oil?" *Watsonville Register-Pajaronian*, April 1, 1966, 18.

"The power company had been unloading oil tankers," Gary Griggs," Change at Moss Landing," *Santa Cruz Sentinel*, March 30, 2019, https://www.santacruzsentinel.com/2019/03/30/change-at-moss-landing-gary-griggs-our-ocean-backyard/, retrieved May 31, 2020.

"with a pipeline that extended 3,600 feet," U.S. Army Engineer District, San Francisco, Army Corps of Engineers, Summary of Alternative Systems for Delivery of Crude

Petroleum to the San Francisco Bay Area, June 1976, 6.

"and it used lots of fuel," "More smelly smog here than in Los Angeles," *Watsonville Register-Pajaronian*, August 13, 1968, 12.

"In 1976, the Army Corps of Engineers," Army Corps of Engineers, Summary of Alternative Systems, 23.

"Hudson stated that Jones saw," "Reaction Of Supervisors Varied," *Salinas Californian*, March 30, 1966, 2.

"Supervisor Andy Anderson suggested," Ibid.

Ibid, 2.

"Humble also followed up with a somewhat," Stan Cloud, "Humble's Intent Still In Doubt," *Monterey Peninsula Herald*, March 31, 1966, 1.

"My advice to refinery opponents," Cloud, "Humble's Intent Still In Doubt," *Herald*, 1.

"In an interview with the *Santa Cruz Sentinel*," "Humble Says Refinery Plans Not Abandoned," *Sentinel*, 1.

"Humble spokesperson Bolding admitted," Cloud, "Humble's Intent Still In Doubt," *Herald*, 2.

"Bolding took it a step further," "Humble sees refinery twice planned size," *Watsonville Register-Pajaronian*, April 14, 1966, 1.

"Elsewhere a new contender emerged," "Is Humble Abandoning Moss Landing Plans," *Monterey Peninsula Herald*, April 21, 1966, 1.

"However, the Sierra Club, which had already opposed," Ibid, 2.

"Bolding reacted immediately," Ibid, 1.

"Amongst the confusion and contradictions, Michael Haider," "Decision On Humble Denied," *Monterey Peninsula Herald*, April 18, 1966, 1.

"The studies Haider spoke," Ibid.

"At the end of March, in one of the articles" Cloud, "Humble's Intent Still In Doubt," *Herald*, 2.

"Fifty-four years later, Cloud could not recall," email from Stanley Cloud, February 15, 2020.

"The *Californian* hinted at a tougher time," March, "Humble May Abandon Area Refinery Plans," *Californian*, 2.

"The *Pajaronian*, in search of a response," "Reaction varied to refinery news," *Watsonville Register-Pajaronian*, March 31, 1966, 1.

"Church credited the ongoing opposition," Ibid.

"The Moss Landing Chamber of Commerce," "Chamber urges aid for Humble," *Watsonville Register-Pajaronian*, April 19, 1966.

"The Salinas City Council also got into the act," "Councilmen Reaffirm Humble Oil Support," *Salinas Californian*, April 12, 1966, 3.

"Monterey County Industrial Development reaffirmed," Reaction varied to refinery news," *Watsonville Register-Pajaronian*, March 31, 1966, 1.

"Monterey County Industrial Development," "A boost for Humble refinery," *Watsonville Register-Pajaronian*, April 30, 1966, 1.

"Cranston, who had already voiced his opposition," "Cranston damns refinery," *Watsonville Register-Pajaronian*, April 29, 1966, 2.

"Robert Finch, a Republican candidate for Lieutenant Governor," "Finch Opposes Oil Refinery In County," *Monterey Peninsula Herald*, May 9, 1966, 1

"Ronald Reagan, making his initial bid," "Reagan Stays Out Of Refinery Fight," *Monterey Peninsula Herald*, May 12, 1966, 1-2.

"Supervisor Henry, probably Humble's strongest voice," "Supervisor Harold Henry Dies Suddenly in King City," *Salinas Californian*, April 25, 1966, 1.

"Even the *Herald*, which butted heads," Ted Durien, "Monterey County Lost a Fighter," *Monterey Peninsula Herald*, April 26, 1966, 1.

27
HUMBLE'S PLAN B

"Almost from the beginning," "Humble To Abandon Refinery?" *Monterey Peninsula Herald*, April 13, 1965, 1.

"The *Monterey Peninsula Herald* announced that Humble," "Humble Scouts Martinez Site," *Monterey Peninsula Herald*, October 8, 1965, 1.

"more than 20 oil refineries and plants," "Refinery map from Citizens for Clean Air," private papers of Warren Church.

"The Oakland Tribune broke the Martinez story," "Humble Scouts Martinez Site," *Herald*, 1.

"We have 2,000 acres zoned," Ibid.

"Hughey said the only problem," Ibid.

"We reminded these people," Ibid.

"Jack Gardner of Humble's manufacturing division," "Humble Eyes Alternate Location At Martinez," *Salinas Californian*, October 9, 1965, 1.

"Nothing else is being given equal consideration," Ibid.

"The discussions between Contra Costa County," "Humble Oil Company De-emphasizes Alternate Site," *Salinas Californian*, October 11, 1965, 1.

"James Ritch, general manager of the Contra Costa Development Association," "Humble Scouts Martinez Site," *Herald*, 2.

"Ritch also contradicted Gardner," Ibid.

"Gardner admitted that a refinery in Martinez," "Humble Eyes Alternate Location At Martinez," *Californian*, 2.

"Humble opponents like William Howard Church," "Humble Oil Company De-emphasizes Alternate Site," *Californian*, 2.

"by late March of 1966, the Martinez site," "Humble Oil Has Options On 2 Sites," *Salinas Californian*, April 4, 1966, 1.

"Benicia was desperate to woo Humble," authors' interview with Reg Page and Dr. Jim Lessenger, Aug. 3, 2019.

"Benicia had a special problem," Ibid.

"The city, founded in 1849," "History," The City of Benicia, California, https://www.ci.benicia.ca.us/history, retrieved May 31, 2020.

"Over the next century," Robert B. Roberts, "Benicia Arsenal," The Posts at Benicia, June 23, 2017, http://www.militarymuseum.org/Benicia.html, May 31, 2020.

"Then came a fateful decision," Jim Lessenger, "How Benicia's Arsenal Became the Heart of the City's Tax Base," February 24, 2015, https://beniciaheraldonline.com/how-benicias-arsenal-became-the-heart-of-the-citys-tax-base/, May 31, 2020.

"Reg Page remembers that time," Page and Lessenger interview.

"Benicia historian Dr. Jim Lessenger noted," Ibid.

28
A TIGER TURNS TAIL

"At the beginning of May," "Farr Says Humble Pulling Out," *Salinas Californian*, May 3, 1966, 1.

"What Farr did not say," author's interview with Sam Farr, February 20, 2020.

"Humble spokesperson D I Bolding," "Farr Says Humble Pulling Out," *Californian*, 1.

"the Contra Costa Planning Commission granted," "Decision On Humble Delayed," *Monterey Peninsula Herald*, April 27, 1966, 1.

"George Swisher, project coordinator of Humble's manufacturing," "Rezoning For Humble Favored," *Monterey Peninsula Herald*, May 11, 1966, 1.

"The Contra Costa County Board of Supervisors finally granted," U.S. Environmental Protection Agency, Office of Water

Planning and Standards, Estuarine Pollution Control and Assessment. Proceedings of a Conference, Volume I, and II. U.S. Department of Commerce, March 1977, 598.

"Other opponents, including Tom Hudson," "Peninsula Assault On Humble," *Monterey Peninsula Herald*, May 16, 1965, 1.

"Hudson planned on gathering," "Foes of Humble in new stratagem," *Watsonville Register-Pajaronian*, May 7, 1966, 2.

"a development that the *Monterey Peninsula Herald*," Allen Griffin, "On Humble Oil, We Haven't Begun To Fight," *Monterey Peninsula Herald*, May 13, 1966, 1.

"Hudson's suitcase carried," "Peninsula Assault On Humble," *Herald*, 1.

"valued at over $3 million," "Owners of Jersey Standard in Monterey fight refinery," *Watsonville Register-Pajaronian*, May 17, 1966, 1.

"Hudson called the shares," "Peninsula Assault On Humble," *Herald*, 1.

"Hudson dismissed the failure," Ibid, 1-2.

"Some were cut up and some were whole," authors' interview with Ruth Andresen, Aug. 2, 2019.

"The modern credit card and modern credit card," Jason Steele, "The History of Credit Cards," Experian, March 15, 2018, https://www.experian.com/blogs/ask-experian/the-history-of-credit-cards/, retrieved February 29, 2020.

"One of those early protesters," "Peninsula Assault On Humble," *Herald*, 2.

"But on the morning of the Cleveland showdown," "Humble Retreats from County," *Monterey Peninsula Herald*, May 18, 1966, 1.

"The statement even declared," Ibid, 2.

"Standard Oil of New Jersey President J. K. Jamieson," Ibid, 1.

"In an interview with the *Salinas Californian*,"

"Humble Oil Quits Moss Landing Site," *Salinas Californian*, May 18, 1966, 1.

"Humble's attorney in Salinas, Paul Hamerly," "Mixed Reaction On Move," *Salinas Californian*, May 18, 1965, 2.

"A.G. Michaud credited the Humble issue," Ibid.

"This is a great tribute to men," "Humble Retreats from County," *Herald*, 2.

"It was a victory for the people," "Mixed Reaction On Move," *Californian*, 2.

"Naturally, I am pleased," "Anti-pollution Forces Still Man Bastions," *Monterey Peninsula Herald*, May 19, 1966, 2.

"[W]e feel the battle has been won," "Mixed Reaction On Move," *Californian*, 1.

"Humble's decision had been made," "Humble Oil Quits Moss Landing Site," *Californian*, 2.

"Their 44,000 shares of stock," Stan Cloud "Anti-refinery Plea In Ohio," *Monterey Peninsula Herald*, May 18, 1966, 1.

"Kramer pushed that the Moss Landing refinery," Ibid, 2.

"Salinas Mayor Sid Gadsby bemoaned," "Mixed Reaction On Move," *Californian*, 1-2.

"I think Monterey County is going to miss," Ibid, 1.

"One of the biggest boosters of Humble Oil," "County Industry Suffers Damaging Setback," *Salinas Californian*, May 19, 1965, 6.

"The *Pajaronian* sensed that Humble leaving," "Humble Oil picks up its refinery – it appears," *Watsonville Register-Pajaronian*, May 19, 1966, 18.

"*King City Rustler* publisher Harry Casey," "Anti-pollution Forces Still Man Bastions," *Herald*, 2.

"Burleigh considered that Humble's announcement," Ibid, 1.

"Benicia historian Dr. Jim Lessenger couldn't

recall" authors' interview with Reg Page and Dr. Jim Lessenger, Aug. 3, 2019.

29

THE AFTERMATH

"By the end of September," "Humble Oil gets permit in Benicia," *Watsonville Register-Pajaronian*, September 20, 1966, 1.

"announced that it would immediately," "Begins construction," *Watsonville Register-Pajaronian*, August 31, 1966, 2

"$135 million, 70,000-barrel-a-day," Sidney P. Allen, "How Humble Won the West," San Francisco Examiner, March 5, 1967, 8.

"promised to build an environmentally friendly oil refinery," Harold Gilliam, "Tragedy of the Commons – in Benicia," San Francisco Examiner, May 3, 1970, 27.

"The refinery was even designed to hide," Donna Beth Weilenman, "From military to industrial: Benicia's 'overnight' transition," Benicia *Herald*, September 8, 2014, https://beniciaheraldonline.com/from-military-to-industrial-benicias-overnight-transition/, March 2, 2020.

"Back in the spring of 1965," "Humble To Abandon Refinery," *Monterey Peninsula Herald*, April 13, 1965, 1.

"The Benicia refinery had a flare problem with burning gases," Gilliam, "Tragedy of the Commons – in Benicia," Examiner, 27.

"Air pollution tests claimed," Ibid.

"which was a fraction of what the Moss Landing PG&E plant," "More smelly smog here than in Los Angeles," *Watsonville Register-Pajaronian*, August 13, 1968, 12.

"Humble's refinery brought Benicia back to life," Gilliam, "Tragedy of the Commons – in Benicia," Examiner, 27.

"The legal battle that created environmental law," David Schuyler and Paul Gallay,

"The Battle for Storm King," Scientific American, August 30, 2018, https://blogs.scientificamerican.com/observations/the-battle-for-storm-king/, retrieved March 2, 2020.

"It would eventually drag," "The Scenic Hudson Decision," Marist Environmental History Project, Marist College, http://library.marist.edu/archives/mehp/scenicdecision.html, retrieved June 3, 2020.

"Burleigh continued to prepare his appeal," "Humble court ruling still under debate," *Watsonville Register-Pajaronian*, August 28, 1966, 7.

"Burleigh was continuing to appeal": *Watsonville Register-Pajaronian*, August 27, 1966

"concerns that independent sources," authors' interview with Ruth Andresen, August 2, 2019.

"Humble gave conflicting testimony," Stan Cloud, "Humble's Intent Still In Doubt," *Monterey Peninsula Herald*, March 31, 1966, 1.

"its officials still touted the sight," "Humble Retreats from County," *Monterey Peninsula Herald*, May 18, 1966, 1.

"As the *Watsonville Register-Pajaronian* once noted," "Did someone do a favor for Humble Oil?" *Watsonville Register-Pajaronian*, April 1, 1966, 18.

"Humble Says Refinery Plans Not Abandoned," *Santa Cruz Sentinel*, March 31, 1966, 1.

"The Army Corp of Engineers," U.S. Army Engineer District, San Francisco, Corps of Engineers, Draft Environmental Statement, Maintenance Dredging (FY 1974), Moss Landing Harbor, Moss Landing, California. March 1974. 8.

"Harold Zellerbach," "Anti-refinery Move Blocked By State Parks," *Monterey Peninsula Herald*, April 23, 1966, 2.

"James Ritch," "Humble Scouts Martinez Site," *Monterey Peninsula Herald*, October 11, 1965, 2.

"Paul Hamerly," "Mixed Reaction On Move," *Salinas Californian*, May 18, 1966, 2.

"Humble stated that complying," "Vote on refinery blocked by board," *Watsonville Register-Pajaronian*, September 25, 1965, 1.

"Humble's claim to have spent $10 million," Harold Gilliam, "Tragedy of the Commons – in Benicia," San Francisco Examiner, May 3, 1970, 28.

"Monterey County put a big monkey wrench," "Humble Gets Permit, 3-2," *Salinas Californian*, September 25, 1965, 2.

"Standard Oil of New Jersey Chairman Michael Haider," "Decision On Humble Denied," *Monterey Peninsula Herald*, April 18, 1966, 1.

"as Stanley Cloud of the *Monterey Peninsula Herald* reported," Stan Cloud, "Humble's Intent Still In Doubt," March 31, 1965, 2.

"the requirement for another permit," "Reaction Of Supervisors Varied," *Salinas Californian*, March 30, 1966, 2.

"I haven't any comment to make," Ibid, 1.

"It was Church who requested that the supervisors delay," "Humble Hearing Set Aug. 31," *Salinas Californian*, August 3, 1965, 1.

"Church attended the all-important Anacortes trip," Ray March, "Refineries Stabilize Community Economy," *Salinas Californian*, August 28, 1965, 1.

"Church actively pursued this restriction," "Humble notes," private papers of Warren Church.

"It was Church who days after the permit," "Church Wants Smog Stations Built Now," *Monterey Peninsula Herald*, September 29, 1965, newspaper clipping from files of Warren Church, page unknown.

"Church also broke with Atteridge and Henry," "County Board Ok's Pollution Controls," *Salinas Californian*, December 8, 1965, 1.

"there are also the comments that Church made," "Reaction varied to refinery news,"

Watsonville Register-Pajaronian," March 31, 1965, 1.

"The one argument against Church," author's conversations with Warren Church.

"Church recalled that he received," Ibid.

"There is one last piece to this puzzle," Church conversations.

"Both the Sierra Club," Environmental Protection Agency, "Estuarine Pollution Control and Assessment. Proceedings of a Conference volume I, and II." Washington, D.C., March 1977, 597.

30
EPILOGUE

"It is regrettable," Tom Wieder, "Pollution District Urged," *Monterey Peninsula Herald*, September 3, 1965, 5.

"Moser has a trail named after him," "Jack's Peak County Park," Monterey County Parks Department, https://www.co.monterey.ca.us/home/showdocument?id=24001, retrieved June 2, 2020.

"Kramer went onto serve," authors' interview with Ruth Andresen, August 2, 2019.

"Professor Church continued teaching," "William Howard Church of P.B., dies at age 80," Monterey County *Herald*, June 21, 1991, 4A

"Mits Nakishima, who pleaded to halt air pollution," "Plan for pollution authority," *Watsonville Register-Pajaronian*, August 23, 1966, 7.

"Credit for the creation of these districts," Alex Darocy, "Monterey Bay Unified Air Pollution Control District," localwiki, Santa Cruz, https://localwiki.org/santacruz/Monterey_Bay_Unified_Air_Pollution_Control_District, retrieved June 2, 2020."Dan Krishun, the planning commissioner," "90th Annual

Commencement Exercises, Salinas High School 1976 Graduation Program," Issuu, December 30, 2011, https://issuu.com/shardison/docs/salinashighgradprog1976, retrieved March 2, 2020.

"Burleigh was appointed a Superior Court Judge," Jeanne Cooper, "Big Sur marathon a hot ticket worldwide," SFGate, March 22, 2013, https://www.sfgate.com/travel/article/Big-Sur-marathon-a-hot-ticket-worldwide-4377488.php, retrieved June 3, 2020.

"Burleigh credited the appointment," authors' interview with William Burleigh, July 25, 2019.

"Burleigh would go on to found," Cooper, "Big Sur."

"Fred Farr, known as a pioneering conservationist," "Fred Farr," SFGate, June 12, 1997, https://www.sfgate.com/news/article/Fred-Farr-2822337.php, retrieved June 1, 2020.

"Farr also worked tirelessly behind the scenes," author's conversations with Sam Farr.

"By 1966 he was redistricted," "1966 State Senate," Join California, http://www.onevoter.org/wp-content/uploads/sites/4/2015/08/1966SD.jpg, retrieved June 7, 2020. "His family had staked that position," email from Tom Hudson, February 15, 2020.

"Hudson had long advocated," Margo Burke, "Years After His Death, Many Remember Fiery Tom Hudson," Monterey Peninsula Herald, October 21, 1985, 15.

"In 1957, the county created," email from Stan Cloud, March 21, 2020.

"Reporter Stanley Cloud of the Herald,"," Ibid.

"The plans Cloud refers to involved," Ibid.

"the Peninsula Area Master Plan came before," Stan Cloud, "Hudson at the Crossroads," the advocate, March, 1967, 5.

"The Salinas Californian ran an article," "Hudson Denies Conflict of Interest on Area Master Plan," Salinas Californian, February 21, 1966, 2.

"but the editors promptly told reporter Ray March," email from Ray March, February 18, 2020.

"The Monterey Peninsula Herald refused," Cloud email, March 21, 2020.

"At the time, Hudson was concerned," email from Tom Hudson, March 1, 2020.

"Hudson always denied that there even was a conflict," "Hudson Denies Conflict of Interest on Area Master Plan," Salinas Californian, February 12, 1966. 2.

"On February 21, 1967, Hudson abruptly resigned," "Hudson Quits Board In Surprise Move," Salinas Californian, February 21, 1967, 1.

""My God," said one," Cloud, "Hudson at the Crossroads," advocate, 3.

"At his last Board of Supervisors meeting," Cloud, "Hudson at the Crossroads," advocate, 5.

"Hudson may have finally grown weary," email from Tom Hudson, March 1, 2020.

"He considered higher office," "Supervisor Church won't run next year, may in '78," Salinas Californian, November 12, 1975, 9.

"Throughout the 1960s, he encountered," author's personal reflections.

"many did put Humble behind them eventually," Campaign Contributors 1972, private papers of Warren Church.

"By 1976, the county made its first steps," "Margo Burke, "Planned Growth Board Formation Is Proposed," Monterey Peninsula Herald, February 25, 1976, 12.

"took pride in efforts to preserve its rural nature," "Significant Accomplishments by Monterey County Supervisor Warren Church, 1965-77," Church papers.

"He pushed for the preservation of Elkhorn Slough," Mike Wallace, "Harbor Board,

Supervisor Clash," *Watsonville Register-Pajaronian*, May 11, 1973, 2.

"Church is also credited with lowering," "A Brief Review of the Board of Supervisors," Church papers.

"considered the "father" of the county parks," "Former Supervisor Church Honored at Special Event," North County News, May 13, 1977, 13.

"He resigned in September," "Supervisor Anderson Quits," *Salinas Californian*, September 19, 1967, 1.

"He had been wounded in the war," author's interview with James Anderson, June 2, 2020.

"speculated that he was uncomfortable," author's conversations with Warren Church.

"Anderson credited 'teamwork,'" "Andy Anderson Is First Mayor Named by the People," *Monterey Peninsula Herald*, May 28, 1964, A3.

"Church lamented," Church conversations.

"Atteridge engaged himself deeply," author's interview with Michael Atteridge, June 3, 2020.

"(The refinery) would have brought," Ken Peterson, "'65 Moss Landing Refinery Battle Determined Future of the County," *Monterey Peninsula Herald*, October 20, 1985, 4B.

"Atteridge remained on the board," "June 4, 1974 Monterey County Election Printout," personal papers of Warren Church.

"The *Salinas Californian* castigated Cailotto publicly," Ray March, "Humble Oil Permit Rejected," *Salinas Californian*, July 29, 1965, 1.

"Even worse, many of his customers," Peterson, "Refinery Battle," *Herald*, 4B.

"choose to die as one of the first people," Kathryn McKenzie, "A Good Day to Die," Voices of Monterey Bay," Voices of Monterey Bay, https://voicesofmontereybay.

org/2017/10/15/a-good-day-to-die/, retrieved June 7, 2020.

"Hudson died suddenly in a small airplane crash," "Two Found Dead In Crash Wreckage," *Monterey Peninsula Herald*, October 8, 1075, 1.

"In Monterey, at the corner of Polk and Hartnell," "Thomas J. Hudson – Monterey, CA," Waymarking, https://www.waymarking.com/waymarks/WMRK0K_Thomas_J_Hudson__Monterey_CA, retrieved June 7, 2020.

INDEX

INDEX 325

Enco 2, 37
Engle, Clair 249
Esso 2, 31, 34, 37, 54, 283, 284
Etienne, Myron "Doc" 74, 289
Evans, Keith 56, 81, 116, 295

F

Farr, Fred 9, 52, 67, 157, 199, 223,
234, 251, 253, 255, 272, 276, 286,
321
Farr, Sam x, xiii, 259, 317, 321
Faul, George 139, 141, 299
Firestone 7, 28, 50, 87, 128, 148, 155,
168, 217, 300

G

Gardner, Jack 6, 26, 77, 79, 119, 151,
203, 217, 244, 245, 290, 296, 300,
309, 312, 317
Gibson, Luther 249
Griffin, Allen 52, 64, 88, 90, 178,
204, 253, 288, 305, 306, 309, 318
Griswold, S. Smith 48
Grothe, Donald 85
Grower-Shipper Vegetable
Association 133, 192, 223

H

Haagen-Smit, A.J. 48
Haider, Michael 61, 198, 233, 239,
255, 263, 316, 320
Haltiner, George 48, 137
Hamerly, Paul 31, 41, 53, 66, 74, 104,
115, 149, 180, 185, 201, 242, 255,
262, 295, 300, 318, 320
Harris, Richard 201, 228, 234
Hayes, Rutherford B. 292
Hearne, Larry 231, 255

Henderson, Perry 56, 81, 116
Henry, Harold 4, 26, 67, 101, 131,
135, 158, 159, 165, 173, 179, 190,
204, 213, 215, 218, 228, 240, 242,
264, 266, 291, 301, 302, 305, 307,
309, 316
Hobbs, George 8, 280
Hotel Del Monte 94, 95
Hudson, Tom xi, 22, 26, 41, 67, 78,
101, 128, 148, 156, 160, 165, 167,
179, 184, 190, 204, 206, 209, 210,
213, 215, 228, 229, 234, 235, 244,
251, 252, 266, 273, 276, 281, 283,
285, 290, 301, 306, 307, 309, 310,
311, 315, 318, 321
Paul Hughey 245
Elgin Hurlbert 50

I

Individuals for Clean Industry 8, 132

J

Jones, Charles 140, 198, 228, 236, 238

K

Kaiser,Henry 70
Kaiser Refractories 27, 63, 70, 175,
180, 188, 218, 219, 267, 270, 288
Kirby, Joseph 74
Knight, Edwin 41, 52
Kramer Charles viii, xvii, 9, 47, 60,
62, 79, 88, 104, 113, 131, 139, 180,
212, 224, 242, 246, 268, 271, 281,
290, 305
Krishun, Dan 55, 272, 287, 321

L

Leighton, Philip 135

BIBLIOGRAPHY

Chernow, Ron. *Titan: The Life of John D. Rockefeller, Sr.* Random House, 2004.

Church, Warren. *The Overburdened Ark.* Self-published, 1967.

Beal, Chandra Moira and Beal, Richard A. *Santa Cruz Beach Boardwalk: The Early Years.* The Pacific Group, 2003.

Fisher, Anne B. *The Salinas: Upside Down River.* Farrar & Rinehart, 1945.

Hughes, Edan Milton. *Artists in California 1786-1940,* 2nd edition. Hughes Publishing Co., San Francisco, 1989.

Jacobs, Chip and Kelly, William J. *Smogtown: The Lung-Burning History of Pollution in Los Angeles.* Overlook, 2015.

Palumbi, Stephen R. and Sotka, Carolyn. *The Death and Life of Monterey Bay: A Story of Revival.* Island Press, 2011.

Steinbeck, John. *Cannery Row.* Viking Press, 1945.

ADDITIONAL READING

Fountain, Henry. *The Great Quake: How the Biggest Earthquake in North America Changed Our Understanding of the Planet.* Crown, 2017.

Hemp, Michael Kenneth. *Cannery Row: The History of John Steinbeck's Old Ocean View Avenue.* The History Company, 2019.

Lifset, Robert D. *Power on the Hudson: Storm King Mountain and the Emergence of Modern American Environmentalism.* University of Pittsburg Press, 2014.

Patterson, James T. *Eve of Destruction: How 1965 Transformed America.* Basic Books, 2012.

Santa Cruz Seaside Co. *The Santa Cruz Beach Boardwalk: A Century by the Sea.* Ten Speed Press, 2007.

Sharp, Robert P. and Glazner, Allen F. *Geology Underfoot in Southern California.* Mountain Press Publishing Co., 1993.

Weinberg, Steve. *Taking on the Trust: The Epic Battle of Ida Tarbell and John D. Rockefeller.* Norton, 2008